My Global Journeys in Search of the African Presence

My Global Journeys
in Search of
the African Presence

Runoko Rashidi

Black Classic Press
Baltimore

My Global Journeys in Search of the African Presence

Runoko Rashidi

My Global Journeys in Search of the African Presence
Copyright ©2017 Runoko Rashidi
Published 2017 by Black Classic Press

All Rights Reserved. No part of this publication may be reproduced in whole or in part, stored in a retrieval system or transmitted in any form or by any means, electronic, mechanical, photocopying, recording, or otherwise, without permission of the publisher. For information regarding permission, please send an email to: email@blackclassicbooks.com. You may also write to: Black Classic Press, P.O. Box 13414, Baltimore, MD 21203.

Print ISBN: 978-1-57478-121-2
eBook ISBN: 978-1-57478-150-2

Library of Congress Control Number: 2016959649

Printed in the United States of America by BCP Digital Printing,
an affiliate of Black Classic Press, Inc.

To review or purchase titles from Black Classic Press, visit:
www.blackclassicbooks.com.

You may also obtain a list of titles by writing to:
Black Classic Press
c/o List
P.O. Box 13414
Baltimore, MD 21203

CONTENTS

DEDICATION VII

ACKNOWLEGEMENTS IX

INTRODUCTION XI

PART I
AFRICA, MY AFRICA:
TRAVELS WITHIN THE MOTHERLAND 1

PART II
TRAVELS IN ASIA:
EAST, SOUTH, SOUTHEAST, AND SOUTHWEST 115

PART III
IN SEARCH OF THE AFRICAN PRESENCE IN EUROPE 163

PART IV
IN SEARCH OF THE AFRICAN PRESENCE
IN AUSTRALIA AND THE PACIFIC ISLANDS 245

PART V
IN SEARCH OF THE AFRICAN PRESENCE
IN THE CARIBBEAN ISLANDS AND IN CENTRAL,
SOUTH, AND NORTH AMERICA 299

Runoko Rashidi and Mother Tynetta Muhammad in Acapulco, Mexico.

Asa G. Hilliard and a descendant of Yaa Asantewaa in Ghana.

Runoko Rashidi with Dr. John Henrik Clarke.
Photo by Rolando Markland Sanchez.

Runoko Rashidi with Dr. Ivan Van Sertima.
Photo by Najah Naji.

DEDICATION

This book is dedicated to the spirits of those great pioneering Pan-Africanist scholars and visionaries who helped mold and shape me into who I am:

Drusilla Dunjee Houston

Joel Augustus Rogers

Chancellor James Williams

John Henrik Clarke

Asa Grant Hilliard III
(aka Nana Baffour Amankwatia II)

Ivan Van Sertima

Yosef ben-Jochannan

John G. Jackson

Runoko Rashidi with John G. Jackson.
Photo by James E. Brunson.

Runoko Rashidi and daughter Assata-Garvey in Egypt.
Photo by Anthony Gurley.

ACKNOWLEDGMENTS

Many, many people played important roles in the journeys I describe in this book. Many of them are mentioned in this text, but some simply have to be singled out right here. I hate to forget anybody important, but here we go.

They include, first and foremost, Zawadi Sagna, without whose existence I would not have seen so much of the world; Nias Harris, my good friend and brother in San Antonio, Texas, who was always there for me; my biological sisters Brenda and Carolyn, who have always been my angels; my dear mother Pearl Moore who, from the spiritual realm, watches over me constantly; Brother Inuni, who always had my back; Karast Unity Center for African Spirituality, for always providing me with a forum from which I could share the stories of my travels; my dear sister Hamara Holt, for opening doors for me in the Andean countries of Ecuador, Peru, and Bolivia; V. T. Rajshekar and a host of others who guided me through India; Gracelyn Smallwood, my dear sister in Aboriginal Australia; Yekengale, my brother in Jamaica; Ginger Tours, my support system in Egypt; the sisters of Marshe Breda, in the Netherlands; the d'Zert Club, instrumental in my travels to Spain, Morocco, and especially Egypt; Senghor Baye-El and Zama Cook, my Garveyite brothers; Citizens Uprooting Racism in Bermuda (CURB) and Nicole Stovell, for looking after me in Bermuda; Bankie F. Bankie, for helping facilitate my trips to Namibia; the Marcus Garvey Pan-African Institute, for invaluable help with my travels in Uganda; Sabelo Sibanda, for hosting me in Zimbabwe; Nzingha Barkley-Waite, Ligia Baldi, Arzinia, and Barbara Richardson, for being my family in Central America; Ishola Williams, for helping connect me with a broader world of African scholars in Africa; Hassan Samrounhi for opening the doors of Morocco to me; Rad Dockery and Winston Larose, for being my most consistent hosts in Canada; Drs. Rudi and Penda Guyan and the African Cultural Development Association, for my visits to Guyana; Mawiya Michaud, for hosting me in Haiti; and Mother Tynetta Muhammad, for reintroducing me to the Black people of Mexico and being all-around wonderful.

I am indebted as well to those African historians: J. A. Rogers, for paving the way; Jacob Carruthers, for giving me the instruction to "go and see the world" and "listen to what people say they are and not what I say that they are"; Asa Hilliard III, for being my friend and protector and always encouraging me; Yosef A. A. ben-Jochannan, for being my anchor in Egypt; John G. Jackson, Chancellor James Williams, and John Henrik Clarke, for providing the blueprint; and Ivan Van Sertima, for being my rock.

And a special thanks to my good brother, the highly respected publisher William Paul Coates, for encouraging me to compile this book. Last, for all those others whose names are not mentioned here, thank you for both the big and small things that you did that allowed me to make it through.

A marble head of an African in Hellenistic Turkey

INTRODUCTION

I am not quite sure how to categorize this book. It is a kind of travel book mixed with a kind of autobiography, mixed with a history and anthropology book. It is a first-hand look at the world—an adventure—from the perspective of a Pan-Africanist scholar, historian, and unabashed and unapologetic Race Man in love with his people.

This book is compiled upon the occasion and the extraordinary achievement of having visited one hundred countries, colonies, and overseas territories on every continent and virtually every major geographic region in the world, save Antarctica and the Arctic Circle. But it is not just a compilation of my notes on the places where I have been and the things that I have seen. It is an effort to make sense of it and extract lessons from it.

This is the story of many global travels, all in search of the African presence. It is about discoveries in museums and communities. It is about the highs and lows, the despair and exultation, the triumphs and the defeats along the way. It does not cover everything, but it covers a lot. It is an overview, a report, and observation on what I have seen of the Black world—our strengths, our weaknesses, the things that should serve to encourage us, and the things that reflect our low status in the world.

Although my international travels officially began in 1978 with a trip to Mexico City and Vera Cruz, Mexico, and continued sporadically through the 1980s and early 1990s, the really intense period of travel, in which I am still engaged, began in 1998 and 1999. Then, with my second divorce looming and with me living in a city and state where I had few friends and little family and never fit in, a fever to travel possessed me and took on a life of its own.

Looking back, I can see the milestones along the way. As a university freshman in 1972, through the intervention of Kwame Ture (Stokely Carmichael at that time), I read probably the most pivotal book of my life—The Destruction of Black Civilization by Chancellor James Williams. From that point on, I knew that I wanted to be an African historian.

By the early 1980s, I thought that I was well on my way. I got a job organizing "cultural awareness programs" at Compton Community College in southern California and began to work with Ivan Van Sertima. Ivan was one of our greatest scholars, and he kind of took me under his wing. The way I see it, I became his major protégé. I wrote more essays for him than anybody else, and we moved beyond the roles of student and teacher. We became, in time, friends, confidants, and colleagues—the culmination of which was the joint editorship of a major, groundbreaking anthology that went through three editions: African Presence in Early Asia.

For the second edition of African Presence in Early Asia, I, along with James E. Brunson, a great friend and my all-time-favorite research associate and collaborator, interviewed the historian John G. Jackson at his Southside Chicago apartment. I always loved and admired Professor Jackson. True, he was an embittered and hard-crusted old man by that time, but I loved him anyway. More than that, I admired his longevity in the field and greatly respected his intellect. In a word, I was in awe of him. During that interview, although the focus was on the African presence in Asia, we talked about a great many things, one of the most important of which was the major mentors in his life. Naturally, the name of the near-legendary, pioneering "anthrophotojournalist" Joel Augustus (J. A.) Rogers came up. Professor Jackson told us that when Rogers was a young boy in Jamaica that his Sunday school teacher had told him that "God had cursed the Black man and made him inferior, and Rogers wanted to prove that Black man was not inferior." He then informed us that Rogers had traveled to sixty nations.

Wow, I thought, how could anybody travel to sixty nations? I never forgot that. And I knew then or shortly thereafter that I wanted to surpass the master. The dream of traveling to more than sixty nations became my goal. Indeed, I thought that if I could somehow, during the course of my life, travel to sixty-five countries, not only would I, at least with regard to the number of countries visited, surpass Rogers, I would leave my own mark in history—that I would, in a sense, become immortal. The idea made me giddy.

In the ten-year period between 1999 and 2009, I visited more than ninety countries, colonies, and overseas territories, some of them multiple times. During one year alone, I visited twenty-seven countries. Once I started to travel I was afraid to stop, and I believe that mine could well be the most intense, concentrated, and comprehensive period of international travel in the life of an African historian, certainly in modern times.

My journeys encompass four pivotal points. In 1996, I got married for the second time; and in 1997, after having largely grown up in Los Angeles and lived there for twenty years, I moved to San Antonio, Texas. San Antonio is a friendly city, but I found it to be one of the most boring places I had ever been. Fortunately, the cost of living there is very cheap. So, putting those two factors together, it is easy to see that my situation fostered a great desire to see the world and not just read about it.

But, marriage is not always bliss, and the woman who promised to love me to "the end" decided in 1998 that the end was close enough, and she served me with divorce papers. I guess she just never understood me or my work. For example, when I was invited to keynote the World's Indigenous People's Conference in Toowomba, Australia, in 1998, my now ex-wife sweetly asked me: "I don't mean any harm, but why would the people in Australia pick you?"

The second turning point came in 1999 when the divorce was final. Then, I had even less reason not to travel. So, it was "Strap on your seatbelt, Runoko Rashidi!" And I never looked back!

Well, love is not to be denied, and that leads me to my third turning point. In January 2003, I traveled to France to present a lecture. There, I met this beautiful African woman. Sound familiar? She was my translator and it was love at first sight. So I started traveling to Europe—a lot. And here

Runoko Rashidi

comes turning-point number four: we had a baby! Yes, at the tender age of fifty, I, Runoko Rashidi, became a dad for the first and only time in my life.

Now I always had bad things to say about guys who fathered children and then disappeared. I promised myself that if it ever happened to me, I would play an important role in my child's life. And so I have. I have a beautiful daughter now and she lives in France, just outside of Paris. And Paris is a wonderful transit point for seeing the world, and see the world I have! Essentially, I went to as many places as I could in search of the African presence. I was determined to find as much primary documentation as possible regarding my people's ancient and current existence. I wanted to see the world and not just read about it. Indeed, during that time of intense travel, it is quite possible that I was with more different kinds of Black people in more settings than anyone else living. I visited multitudes of art institutions in search of African artifacts, scores of churches in search of Black icons, dozens of archaeological sites and ancient temples, and delivered lectures on the African presence in fifty-six countries and overseas territories.

So, this is my story. Almost all of the notes and letters here have dates affixed. Almost all of them were written during the time of the trip being detailed or shortly thereafter. I share here with you now my raw and unfettered feelings and emotions, as I felt them at the time, or my retrospect thoughts and reflections that came days and weeks after the journeys. I suspect, however, that some may challenge my scholarship in parts of this book, and to that, I say: I wrote it as I saw it, and I reported what I understood was being said to me. It was not my intention to write just a travelogue, nor did I write with only academics in mind. Through this work, I am sharing the world through my eyes, as I saw it. Nothing is made up; this is not fiction.

Others might say that this book is boastful. Well, I am not above saying that I am proud of my accomplishments and elated by the travel experiences that I have shared. But I would like to think that what I have done was not mere ego-tripping, that I was conscious during my writing that I was composing for posterity and for those who have never had, nor ever will have, the opportunities to see the world as I have.

Since there are some places that I visited but never, for one reason or another, wrote about, especially in the Americas, I have tried to compensate for it and to give this text a sense of completeness by including connecting sections. These added sections (written in France in April 2011) bind this work together and provide a glance back on those travels.

Runoko Rashidi
Paris, France

Runoko Rashidi

PART I

AFRICA, MY AFRICA:
TRAVELS WITHIN THE MOTHERLAND

The Coptic Christ in Cairo, Egypt

The first section of this book, not unnaturally, deals with Africa, and the first section of the first section—again not unnaturally—focuses on Egypt. This should not come as a surprise when you consider the role of Egypt in African and world history from ancient to modern times. Also, I have visited Egypt more than twenty times, more than any other country (with the possible exception of France, where my daughter resides) and over a longer period of time than any country discussed in this book.

The countries absent here in this section of letters and notes are Mali, Burkina Faso, Togo, and Zambia. When I was traveling in Mali and Burkina Faso, the Internet services in the hotels where I stayed were either non-existent, not user-friendly, or very expensive; nor did I feel compelled to write about my experiences there after the fact. I was only in these two countries a few days, and I never left their respective capitals of Bamako and Ouagadougou. Sadly, the museums there were unimpressive, I did not find the people I met terribly friendly, and the trips themselves were rather insignificant, except to say that I was there. Still, in hindsight, I wish that I had written about them anyway.

Mali is a huge country with a rich history and I do wish that I had seen more of it. But the city of Bamako, at the time of my stay there, was hot and dry, and I never took much of a liking to it. In Ouagadougou, Burkina Faso, I spoke, along with Molefi Asante, at a poorly organized conference. There, I met with Babu, the organizer of the annual, Los Angeles-based Pan-African Film Festival. I also met, for the first and only time, the African historian Joseph Ki-Zerbo. During his lecture at the conference, Ki-Zerbo made a simple but profound statement that really resonated with me. He said, "History is not finished." Later that night, Dr. Asante and I, along with many others, attended a dinner and reception at his home.

I more than made up for my limited experiences in Mali and Burkina Faso with visits to the Sahel in Niger. There, in the capital city of Niamey, I met members of the Hausa, Djerma, Wodabe, Peul, and Tuareg communities; stayed at an African-owned hotel; sailed on the Niger River with a descendant of the great African monarch Abubakari II; toured the university; gave a small presentation in the community; and viewed and handled several of the ancient Niger Manuscripts.

Togo is another African country that I visited but did not write about while I traveled there. Togo is a very small, poor, Francophone West African country. Although I passed through it on four occasions, I only spent one night there, in the capital city of Lome, and the Internet was down at the time. On my third trip to Togo, traveling with a group, I tried to give a lecture at the hotel where we were staying in Lome, but I was told that doing so was not advisable, given the turbulent politics of Togo at the time. In the absence of an essay or letter on or from Togo, I have tried to compensate by including letters from the neighboring country of Benin.

Also among the missing pages on Africa are my notes on Zambia. From Victoria Falls, Zimbabwe, where I was touring in June 2000, I crossed over the border into Zambia and spent a memorable day in and around the city of Livingstone. The highlight of the trip was viewing, from the Zambia side (I had already seen it from the Zimbabwe side), Mosi-oa-Tunya ("The Smoke that Thunders"), a magnificent series of waterfalls renamed Victoria Falls for the queen of England by the explorer David Livingstone in 1855. Of Mosi-oa-Tunya, Livingstone wrote in his journal: "…on sights as beautiful as this, angels in their flight must have gazed." It was simply spectacular, and I think that it is the greatest display of nature I have ever seen.

While in Zambia's neighbor, Malawi, I briefly crossed the border into Mozambique. I wrote about my earlier efforts to get to Mozambique in the note, "Mini-Bus to Mozambique." I had heard that Mozambique was a beautiful and vibrant country and I was honored to stand, if but briefly, on her soil. I will have to return one day and spend some quality time there.

Other places in Africa that I have visited are described and documented here, and several of the notes are fairly lengthy and comprehensive. So, there it is, and here we go! Fasten your seatbelts!

Dr. Leonard Jeffries, Jr., Dr. Asa Hilliard III and Runoko Rashidi at the wedding in Cape Coast of Anthony and Janice Littlejohn-Browder.
Photo courtesy of Anthony T. Browder.

Postcard of Akhenaten sent to Runoko Rashidi from Egypt by Ivan Van Sertima

Children in Juffure, Gambia

Runoko Rashidi

TO EGYPT AND BEYOND!

"When we speak of the Nile Valley, of course we are talking about 4,100 miles of civilization, or the beginning of the birth of what is today called civilization" (Yosef A. A. ben-Jochannan, New Dimensions in African History, 1991, 83).

First Things First:
A Tribute to Yosef A. A. Ben-Jochannan, Icon of African Historiography

Every person of African heritage should try to visit Egypt at least once during his or her lifetime. It is a pilgrimage to our sacred motherland—the cradle of civilization—and one is never the same afterwards. Although numerous study tours to Egypt are now available, undoubtedly the most celebrated are those of Dr. Yosef Alfredo Antonio ben-Jochannan, or "Dr. Ben," as he is affectionately known to many.

Dr. Ben's tours include the massive rock-hewn temples of King Ramses II and Queen Nefertari at Abu Simbel; the temple of the goddess Isis at Philae Island; the royal tombs of the Valley of the Kings; the west-bank mortuary temples of Makare Hatshepsut, Ramses II, and Ramses III at Luxor; the east-bank worship temples of Luxor and Karnak; the temple of the goddess Hathor at Dendera; the Sphinx and the massive pyramids on the Giza Plateau; the step pyramid designed by the multi-genius Imhotep at Sakkara; and the Egyptian Museum in Cairo.

Regarding these sites, the reader should know that Usemare Ramses II (popularly known as "Ramses the Great") ruled Egypt for more than six decades and emerged as one of the builders of history's most colossal monuments. Nefertari, his chief queen, helped him govern and was herself revered throughout Ancient Egypt. Isis was one of Egypt's greatest deities and, along with her husband Osiris and son Horus, formed one of antiquity's great triads.

Luxor is my favorite part of Egypt and the sites there are spectacular. The Valley of the Kings is the site where the bodies of some of Pharaonic Egypt's most significant rulers are entombed. Makare Hatshepsut was a great female monarch who governed for twenty years. Ramses III fought off two foreign invasions of Egypt and held the throne for thirty-one years. Across the Nile in Luxor, Karnak temple is the world's largest religious sanctuary. Luxor temple is also dazzling.

The enormous pyramids on the Giza plateau have been called "miracles in stone," while the step pyramid at Sakkara has the distinction of being the world's first large stone monument. The Egyptian Museum in Cairo is crammed full of the representations, physical remains, personal possessions, and writings of the pharaohs, queens, officials, and ordinary people of the ancient Nile Valley.

Dr. Ben's tours, like the man himself, stand out quite singularly. Born December 31, 1918 in Gondar, Ethiopia, he has devoted the better part of his life to the illumination of the indigenous origins of African civilizations. By profession, he is a lawyer, engineer, historian, and Egyptologist. Ben-Jochannan went to Egypt for the first time in 1939, and he moved to Harlem, New York in 1945. He was a student and colleague of George G. M. James, and he was exceptionally close to the late Dr. John Henrik Clarke. He knew Malcolm X personally. Since 1957, he has coordinated regular study tours and pilgrimages to the Nile Valley, directly exposing thousands of African people to the still-visible splendors of Ancient Egypt. Formerly an adjunct professor in Cornell University's Africana Studies Department, ben-Jochannan has also been a professor-at-large at Al Azar University in Cairo.

Dr. Ben continues to wield tremendous influence on African Studies, and he is indeed one of the most unrelenting twentieth-century advocates of the African origins of the Nile Valley civilizations and of Western religions. Though now advanced in years, he remains uncompromising in his views and has written extensively. By his own account, ben-Jochannan has prepared over seventy-five manuscripts for publication. He is the author of more than twenty books, including African Origins of the Major Western Religions in 1970; Africa: Mother of Western Civilization in 1971; Black Man of the Nile and His Family in 1972; A Chronology of the Bible: A Challenge to the Standard Version in 1973; and The African Called Rameses ("The Great") II, and the African Origin of Western Civilization in 1990. Several of his works have gone through a number of reprints and different editions. Although often controversial, all of them are well documented. As Leonard Jeffries has pointed out:

> "His extensive publications contain voluminous reference materials and sources to stimulate students and scholars to pursue more systematic and scientific research. He also includes very revealing photos, illustrations and charts that help the ordinary layman grasp the significance of the work." ("Tribute to Yosef ben-Jochannan," in Egypt Revisited, Ivan Van Sertima, ed., 1982, 4).

Indeed, Yosef Ben-Jochannan has probably done more to popularize African history than any living scholar. He has brought history to life for the masses of African people. This is perhaps his greatest legacy and gift.

Egypt is Inseparable From Africa

I must confess that I had been actively avoiding travel to the rest of Africa beyond Egypt, essentially taking that part of the continent for granted. I thought about sub-Saharan Africa all the time, however, and I knew that I would eventually get there. For me as an historian, Egypt has been exceptionally important because of her abundance of antiquities. Egypt is obviously not the only country in Africa with antiquities, but the ruins of Ancient Egypt have no parallel anywhere else in the world. Besides, the origins of Pharaonic Egyptian civilization have been such an intense battleground for so long that it became obvious some time ago that for me, as an historian, travel to Egypt was virtually essential.

I have since visited Egypt on five separate occasions. I have never been able to resist Egypt. I never wanted to, and I still don't. Egypt casts a kind of spell on you and compels you to return. Regarding Africa beyond Egypt, however, I knew that I would eventually see a great deal of it. I also knew that once I started going to that part of Africa, other travel destinations would dramatically diminish in importance.

Runoko Rashidi

I love Africa. More than any other part of the world, it is my home. As a result, I've tried to explore as many realms of the Global African Community as possible. And the Ancestors have really blessed me in this area, as I now travel international circuits fairly regularly. I take great pride in having been fortunate enough to have lectured on every continent in the world save Antarctica. Indeed, I have often been heard to say that "If I can find some Black people in Antarctica then I will go down there too, just to make things complete."

I love Africa, and all my presentations, which are mostly slide presentations with lots of stunning and stirring photographs, are about Africa's place in history and African populations scattered around the earth. In fact, Africa and African people are really all that I talk about. I am an African historian with a strong African-centered and Pan-African perspective, and I think that the major mission in my life, more than anything else, is to help make Africans proud of themselves.

Africans around the world must realize their attachment to Africa and its essential importance to us. Indeed, I am beginning to believe that there may be more Africans outside of Africa than there are in Africa itself. Along with countless others, I believe that Africa can never truly be free unless African people scattered around the globe play an active part in the freedom process. At the same time, African people outside of Africa can never be truly free until Africa itself is united, independent, and in control of its natural resources. We have a major stake in the future of Africa and, as African people, wherever we are, we must work together to ensure that future.

NIGHTS IN NAMIBIA[1]

"Of all our studies, history is best qualified to reward our research" (Malcolm X, Malcolm X Speaks, 1973, 7).

May 2000

On February 14, 2000, I received an official invitation from the Pan-Afrikan Centre of Namibia (PACON) to come to that nation in May to present a series of five lectures in commemoration of Africa Day 2000. The letter was signed by Ben Uugwanga, a PACON board member. I accepted the invitation joyfully and without hesitation.

I am so grateful to PACON for bringing me to sub-Saharan Africa, and to Namibia particularly. Namibia, a large and rather arid majority-Black country in southwestern Africa, has a population of less than two million people and is rich in minerals. It became independent in 1990, and has a progressive Black president.

I'd always hoped that I would be able to go to Namibia. Considering that the only part of Africa that I had visited previously was Egypt, and that PACON had promised to cover all my expenses, I was ecstatic. Indeed, I was so honored and became so excited about the invitation that I soon made up my mind that, if necessary, I would pay my own expenses to get there. It meant just that much

---

1 Dedicated to the Pan-Afrikan Centre of Namibia.

to me. My time had finally come to see more of Mother Africa—the birthplace of humanity and civilization.

My itinerary called for me to fly to Windhoek, the Namibian capital, via Frankfurt, Germany. PACON wanted me to journey to Namibia on Air Namibia, the national airline. It seemed appropriate.

Besides, I suppose that flying through Germany with an almost thirteen-hour layover in Frankfurt provided a practical kind of orientation for me. Germany had colonized Namibia and had brutalized and nearly exterminated large numbers of Namibian people. Even today, it plays a highly important role in Namibia's reality.

Overall, I found the masses of Black people in Namibia to be very poor and faced with a daily uphill struggle. The White people of Namibia, on the other hand, seemed to be very prosperous. This bothered me. Why should African people be poor and homeless in the land of the plenty? Windhoek itself is a very European-looking city and highly segregated.

Though initially I was reluctant to fly through Germany, it actually worked out okay. The Frankfurt international airport is a huge place. I was a little concerned by the fact that I was traveling by myself, spoke no German, and had only passed through Frankfurt once before. At is turned out, however, English was spoken widely, and the people were generally friendly. I was surprised at how many Africans worked in the airport. I was even able to walk outside a bit and do a little exploring of the adjoining area.

After almost two days of travel, I finally arrived in Windhoek early on the morning of May 23. . As soon as I got off the plane, collected my luggage, and finished going through customs, I went straight to work. I refused to allow jet lag and fatigue become factors. I was met by Bankie Forster Bankie, who was to be my almost-constant companion during the Namibian leg of my African journey.

Bankie turned out to be a very good brother. A strong and ardent Pan-Africanist and something of a career diplomat, he turned out to be business-like and very detail-oriented. He kept us on a tight and disciplined schedule. It would even be accurate to say that much of the success of the trip was due directly to Brother Bankie. I salute him.

We hit the ground running. Brother Bankie informed me that we were on our way to tape a television program and handed me a nice freshly pressed African shirt to change into. Although it did not bother me, I do not recall receiving an invitation to stop for breakfast or to check into the hotel for a nap. There was simply no time. I was brought to Africa to work! Well, as a soldier in the army of African victory I was up to the job.

The TV program went well and subsequently was broadcast all over Namibia. Indeed, at the risk of sounding vain, and with all due modesty, it was not unusual for me to turn on the TV set at seemingly any hour during my visit to Namibia and see images of myself lecturing and being interviewed. Actually, it was kind of nice! It got to a point that wherever I went it was common for people to see me and say, "I just saw you on TV!" All things considered, I got very good reviews.

Early on the afternoon of that first day, in a government-owned car and with our own private driver, Brother Bankie and I headed off to Walvis Bay in Namibia's Erongo region for a lecture in the Black township there. It was the first of three trips outside of Windhoek. After driving for several hours across what seemed like mostly uninhabited country, I was able to give the first of my presentations. Before my talk, I was introduced to the regional governor. At each presentation that I gave, each in a different regional capital, the governor of the respective region was on hand to welcome me and offer every possible assistance. The governors were present at each program from beginning to end, and all expressed great satisfaction with the results.

I quickly and happily realized that the brothers and sisters in Namibia were hungry for history and thirsty for greater knowledge of themselves. My Walvis Bay presentation, entitled "Unexpected Faces in Unexpected Places: The African Presence Globally," went well and was followed by a lively discussion period. Indeed, PACON insisted that significant time be left at the end of each presentation for dialogue with the audience.

Although we were in a Black township, quite a number of White people showed up, including several White teenaged students enrolled at the local schools. Strangely, there was not a single presentation that I gave in Namibia where at least one White person did not show up. Well, just because there were White people in the audience, I wasn't going to compromise my message or change my focus! The PACON representatives kept assuring me that they wanted me to take a straightforward approach and present an uncompromising delivery. They urged me to speak my mind and not hold back. Well, they got their wish!

It was obvious to me that the White people I encountered in Namibia were rather nervous, yet still arrogant. Although Africans effectively ran the country, White people dominated the economy and owned much of the land. With the reclaiming of African land taking place in Zimbabwe, there was great concern among the Whites in Namibia that the same phenomenon would spread beyond Zimbabwe to the rest of Africa.

The major ethnic groups in Namibia are the Ovambo, the largest group; followed by the Herero, Damara, Nama, Caprivian, and San groups. I was struck, however, by another category of people in Namibia. These people are called Coloreds, and they are the descendants of mixed, African-and-European unions, mostly of the Dutch and German colonization of southern Africa. Many of these unions were obviously not of a voluntary nature, and many of their offspring seem to be the product of generations of in-breeding. A lot of them look like albinos, with red hair and really pale skin.

During the pre-independence apartheid years, the Coloreds occupied an intermediary status between the masses of conquered Blacks and the descendants of White invaders. They were given a superior status to the Blacks in the region, and most have a definite air of being "better than" about themselves. In many ways I just feel sorry for them as they too are victims of White supremacy, whether they realize it or not. In both South Africa and Namibia, they had maintained, and still maintain, their own separate communities. They seem to take great pride in their status as collaborators to apartheid, and I generally found them to be more hostile than even the Whites themselves. But I try hard not to judge them as a whole. Some of them are warm and friendly. Africans have so many issues!

During the discussion after my Walvis Bay presentation, one Colored student asked me what I thought of the concept of "White Africans." I told her that I considered the notion absurd. She became highly indignant and pointed out that while I had just arrived in Africa that day, she and her White "foreparents" had been in Africa for four-hundred years and that she was an "African by birth." I responded by reminding her that her White foreparents had invaded Africa and stolen the land. I told her that both her culture and pedigree were European and that the Boers had not been invited to Africa. This unsettled both the Whites and the Coloreds in the audience. The Blacks, on the other hand, were delighted. I finished with a statement from Kwame Ture (who apparently picked it up from Malcolm X), who used to like to say that "just because a cat has babies in an oven, you don't call the babies 'biscuits.'" Place of birth by itself doesn't determine nationality, I explained.

On the long drive back from Walvis Bay, I was startled by how cold it was. Actually, I was absolutely shocked by how dramatically the temperatures in southern Namibia dropped at night. Riding back through the desert, in what seemed like the only car on the highway, I was also dazzled by the brightness and seeming closeness of the stars in the Namibian skies. It seemed that all I had to do was to reach out and touch one.

I have never seen anything like the skies of Namibia at night. Even the moon seemed brighter than I ever imagined. I will never forget those cold and star-lit nights. They were quite simply magical and awe-inspiring.

In Namibia, I gave five separate major presentations in five provinces over a period of five days. Following my Walvis Bay lecture on the 23rd, we headed southeast to Keetmanshoop near the South African border in the Karas region. Like the previous evening, we were joined by the regional governor, whom I thought bore a strong resemblance to Nelson Mandela. What made this presentation stand out was that it was heavily attended by Namas. These very interesting brothers and sisters, sometimes called Khoikhoi and pejoratively known as Hottentots, came up to me before and after my talk to introduce themselves. They also gave me considerable background on their history and present status in southern Africa. They told me that the Namas had suffered greatly at the hands of the Germans during the colonial period and had fought a heroic resistance. Their mere presence fascinated me, and I was tremendously honored by their attendance.

On the afternoon of May 25, I was in the Namibian capital of Windhoek, where the biggest Africa Day program in Namibian history was being held at the Safari Hotel. Africa Day celebrates the 1963 founding of the Organization of African Unity or OAU. The ruling party of Namibia, the South West African People's Organization (SWAPO), prided itself on its Pan-African principles, so my job that day was to explain that African people are found all over the world and that we Africans should not confine our emphasis to continental African unity alone but rather to the global unity of African people.

My presentation that day, the last in a very long program, was one of my best. On at least that one day, I succeeded in helping to make African people proud of themselves. I spoke before ambassadors, ministers, diplomats, students, and just plain folks and really lit up the auditorium. The response was so good that I became very emotional and sometimes spoke with a faltering voice. I also spoke considerably longer than I was scheduled to speak, but nobody interrupted me. The entire program, of which my presentation was a central part, was broadcast repeatedly across the nation.

I was not allowed much time to rest on my laurels. The next day, May 26, I had to get up much earlier, check out of the hotel, and embark upon my longest Namibian journey, heading northeast to Katima Mulilo in the Caprivi region. I was working hard but enjoying it, learning a great deal, trying to absorb everything, and savoring the experience.

From Windhoek to Katima Mulilo is a distance of more than five hundred kilometers. It was a long ride. The Caprivi region shares a common border with Angola and, during part of the journey, we had to ride in a military convoy. The convoy system of travel was deemed necessary because, at the time of my trip, the renegade army of UNITA (the National Union for the Total Independence of Angola), led by Jonas Savimbi, was launching violent incursions across the border into Namibian territory and slaughtering innocent civilians. The trip took so long that May 26 was the only day of my entire trip to Namibia that I did not lecture. It was a day devoted almost entirely to travel.

We arrived in Katima Mulilo at night and were fortunate to find a series of nice log cabins in which to spend the night. For once, I had a quiet, peaceful, and relatively early evening. I took the opportunity to peruse through two excellent books, written in French, on the life of Alexander Sergeivich Pushkin. They had been loaned to me by Brother Bankie. By that time, Bankie and I had really begun to bond and had developed a very good relationship. We didn't just respect each other—we believed in each other.

On Saturday, May 27, my last full day in Namibia, I lectured at Caprivi College in Katima Mulilo, just across the Zambezi River from Zambia. The governor of the Caprivi region was there. I spoke in the college gymnasium to a large group of mostly children, but the adults who attended grilled me with really serious questions during the discussion period. Some of their questions echoed those that came up repeatedly during my stay in Namibia, focusing mostly on the image of Africa in the western media, the role of African Americans in the African freedom process, the current status of Africans in America, my general impressions of Africa, and whether there would ever be an African American president. I tried to address every single question thoughtfully and honestly.

That evening, I gave my last and best presentation in Namibia in an African township in the city of Rundu in Kavango Province, which is separated from Angola by only a small river. Maybe because I knew that it was my last Namibian presentation, at least for this go-around, I was forceful yet relaxed. I had enjoyed my stay in Namibia and wanted to end it on a high note. I spoke to a fairly small audience in a rather small room that produced a special kind of intimacy. Not only was the regional governor in attendance, but the National Minister of Education, John Mutorwa, was there too. He had sent me a handwritten note welcoming me to Africa, which I felt was a real honor.

The Rundu program began with a series of performances by the Kambundu Cultural Group. They were excellent dancers and exceptionally graceful. A regally beautiful and enthusiastic African woman moderated the program. We had an excellent translator, and the slide projector worked perfectly. My slides seem to resonate with everyone in the audience, and the sense of communion I felt on that last evening of my Namibian journey was profound. That night everybody went home happy and inspired, full of hope for the African future, and proud of our shared African history and heritage.

My Global Journeys in Search of the African Presence

On that cold, magical, star-filled Namibian night, more than at any other time on that wonderful trip, I felt that the Ancestors were truly satisfied.

GREAT ZIMBABWE: AN AFRICAN JOURNEY[2]

The summer of 2000 will forever be for me a season to cherish and a time to remember. It was a glorious and spellbinding period. From May 22 through the last week in August, I traveled to ten countries, including Germany, Namibia, Zimbabwe, Zambia, the Netherlands, Australia, Trinidad, Guyana, Curacao (Netherlands Antilles), Barbados, and Costa Rica. I lectured in eight of these countries (nine, if you count Curacao) and learned a great deal in all of them.

Of all of my summer travels, only Australia, a country to which I led a tour group, surpassed Zimbabwe in terms of length of stay and depth of experiences. Indeed, my trip to Zimbabwe was a whirlwind of experiences, many of which I am only just now beginning to digest. Perhaps equally important, I achieved a tremendous amount of personal growth, inner development, and emotional maturity as a result of my rich travel experiences in Zimbabwe. Indeed, there were times when I felt that the Ancestors were giving me stern examinations in temperament, stamina, patience, tenacity, and humility regarding the applicability of my life's work. My thoughts on this, however, are revealed in later travel essays.)

June 2000

The word Zimbabwe is derived from the Shona language and means "houses of stone." Due significantly to the actions of Zimbabwe's president, Robert Mugabe, and the reclaiming of Zimbabwean land by its indigenous people, Zimbabwe has been catapulted prominently into the international news headlines. The economy is deteriorating, tourism is down, and a number of people, including several Whites, have been killed over the past few months. There has been great anxiety in many circles that the phenomenon of Africans reclaiming African land for African people will spread to the rest of Africa, but President Mugabe has gained heroic stature among African nationalists for advocating it.

After completing my Africa Day lecture series in Namibia, I caught an Air Namibia flight from Windhoek to Victoria Falls, Zimbabwe. The School of African Awareness (SAA) was the principal sponsor and coordinator of my trip to Zimbabwe. Its members organized my housing, transportation, lecture schedule, and overall itinerary.

The essential goal of the SAA, a nongovernmental and nonprofit organization launched in Bulawayo on Africa Day in 1997, is to "address issues pertaining to African cultural awareness and self-help and self-reliance." Its main focus is to "disseminate information to all those committed to the well being of Africa and its people." SAA's founder, Sabelo Sibanda, is an exceptionally articulate and extremely committed activist. Having lived and worked in African communities in both the

---

2 Dedicated to the School of African Awareness (SAA) in Zimbabwe.

United Kingdom and the United States, Sibanda has developed a keen sense of Pan-Africanism and is a strong proponent of the need for global African cooperation.

My journey to Zimbabwe took a little less than two hours. I quickly exited the plane and stood for the first time on Zimbabwean soil. It was wintertime in Zimbabwe, and the weather was dry and cool. The country was beautiful, the people seemed friendly, and I had the sense of great personal satisfaction that I had realized another dream of a lifetime.

Like Namibia, but even more so, I had wanted to go to Zimbabwe from way back. In fact, after Egypt, Zimbabwe was my favored African travel destination. The ruins of its stupendous stone cities, built by the Shona people of northeast Zimbabwe, had intrigued me for a long time. In addition to the historical, archaeological, and political aspects of the trip, and on a more personal note, my first name, Runoko—given to me as a university student a long time ago—is a Zimbabwean name.

Zimbabwe, in southeast Africa, is a country of more than eleven million people. More than 95 percent of its citizens are Black. Most of them, over seventy percent, are Shona, followed numerically by the Ndebele. Whites and Asians constitute less than five percent of the total population. English is the official language, followed by Shona and Sindebele. Most of the Whites are of English origin, with more than half of them coming to the country after 1945. There are probably fewer than 100,000 White people in Zimbabwe today. Known during the colonial period as Southern Rhodesia, the nation of Zimbabwe achieved its independence from White minority rule in 1980.

Geographically, Zimbabwe is bordered by South Africa to the south, Botswana to the west, Mozambique to the east, and Zambia to the north. The capital of Zimbabwe is Harare, in the northeast. It is a city of more than a million people. The second largest city is Bulawayo, with a population of about 700,000 people, mostly Ndebele. Most of my time in Zimbabwe was spent in and around Bulawayo.

My lectures in Zimbabwe began less than twenty-four hours after my arrival in the country. After securing my visa and a taxi and being driven for several hours from Victoria Falls to Bulawayo (where I ate a hot meal and caught a night's rest), I spoke the following day at the United College of Teachers. Interestingly enough, the college did not even have a history component, and the only reason the lecture materialized at all was through the tireless efforts of Mr. Sibanda.

I spoke first to a single class of prospective teachers. Both the students and the teacher were very receptive, and I gave a broad-ranging slide presentation that focused on the global African presence, ancient and modern. I repeated that presentation, with minor variations, with great success during the course of my stay in Zimbabwe. I tried to inspire the students with the history of African people and make them proud of themselves.

A key component of the success of each presentation was the period allotted to questions and answers that followed every talk. It was a real struggle though, for I was fighting what I perceived to be the strong belief that to embrace Africa was to embrace backwardness, while to embrace Europe was to embrace modernity. Almost all of the students wore western style clothes, consisting of shirts and ties for the men, and skirts and nylon stockings for the women. A good number of the women students wore their hair straightened. These were some of the not-so-pleasant realities of the trip.

I suppose that I, like others, have a kind of idealized vision of what Africa and Africans should be, and it is admittedly disappointing when the vision does not materialize. But I also met Africans in Zimbabwe who were unfortunately in the minority, and who, just like me, were struggling to realize that vision. Identifying and building with that minority made all of my hard work in that country worthwhile.

I set the tone for each of my presentations at the very beginning. I wore nice African shirts whenever possible, and I stated up front that I did not see myself as a visiting American scholar but rather as an African brother trying to share his knowledge while returning home in search of his family after a prolonged period of exile. This struck a highly responsive chord with my audiences throughout the course of my African travels and resulted in extremely close and familial bonds.

I gave four major lectures at the various teachers colleges in Zimbabwe, and two major talks in the African community, including a tribute to African women that I thought was one of my best. In addition to my talks, I toured the city of Bulawayo extensively, visiting both its poorest townships and its plushest neighborhoods.

With the various talks, private meetings, public discussions, and TV, radio, and newspaper interviews, every day was a busy one. I remained fully occupied throughout the course of the trip. Among the most important of the sessions in which I participated were the meetings of the Bulawayo Affirmative Action Committee and the Informal Traders Association. Through those sessions, I was able to gain some understanding about the local and national political scenes in Zimbabwe and to gather some insight into that nation's economic life. I was also fortunate enough to visit one of the White-owned farms that had been occupied by the Black veterans of Zimbabwe's independence struggle against colonial rule.

The veterans seemed resolute about holding on to the lands that they were occupying. Although they were sorely disappointed when I told them about the manner in which the western media was portraying their actions, their morale was high. It got even higher when I told them of the overwhelming moral support that they enjoyed from African Americans generally.

One of the great highlights of my Zimbabwe trip came on a day that I didn't lecture. That day, I was driven far from the confines of Bulawayo to an emotional ceremony held within the centrality of several villages. The ceremony was attended by the local elders and community residents, and augmented by dancers and drummers. I was received warmly and officially acknowledged as an African finally returned home. I was presented with a magnificent wooden staff and told that I had finally found my family. It was a wonderful episode and an experience I will never forget. I was so moved emotionally, that when asked to speak at the ceremony, I respectfully, but firmly, declined because I knew that I would have broken down and wept like a child.

Runoko Rashidi

IN THE MAGICAL LAND OF GHANA, WEST AFRICA[3]

I always knew that I would go to Ghana. As a youth growing into manhood, I was very much influenced by the speeches and writings of Osayefo Kwame Nkrumah. I read just about everything on and by Nkrumah that I could get my hands on, and I still regard him, along with Marcus Garvey and Malcolm X, as one of the greatest Africans of the twentieth century. So I knew that I would one day go to Ghana. I just did not know when.

Until recently, only two factors, albeit major ones, kept me away. The first was my personal belief that if I started to travel to sub-Saharan Africa on a regular basis (I had by then already made six trips to Egypt and enjoyed an extended lecture and research tour to Namibia, Zimbabwe, and Zambia), I might forget about the rest of the global African community and just confine all of my time and research to Africa itself.

The other factor was my fear of having to go into the European slave dungeons in Ghana. Visiting those torture chambers was an experience that I just did not care to undertake. So my plan was to wait until after my fiftieth birthday in August 2004, and then go for it. Apparently, the Ancestors decided differently, and away I went on the Asou Mankran ("Spirit of the River") Tour III at the age of forty-nine with one of my favorite scholars and teachers, Dr. Asa G. Hilliard III.

July 2003

We flew from New York's JFK Airport to Zurich, Switzerland, and from there to Accra, Ghana, via Lagos, Nigeria. I must confess that when we checked into the Novotel Hotel in Accra, I did not get the sense that I was even in Africa. Indeed, being in the hotel gave me the feeling that I could have just as easily been in Kingston, Jamaica; Manhattan, New York; or London, England. In truth, it was just hard for me to relate to my surroundings.

That first full day in Ghana, our group toured the Dr. W. E. B. Du Bois Center for Pan-African Studies. As I learned, the center was once the house where Dr. Du Bois spent the last years of his life working on the Encyclopedia Africana. Indeed, Dr. Du Bois was buried in that house. I was very impressed with the great doctor's personal library.

We next visited the Kwame Nkrumah Memorial, which houses Dr. Nkrumah's body and contains a small museum with excellent photos illuminating Osayefo's many achievements. This was followed by a general tour of the city, which took us to Black Star Square and James Town. James Town is an impoverished area of Accra where Dr. John Henrik Clarke once resided and where Kwame Nkrumah began his political career.

That evening, I gave a slide presentation-lecture at the Du Bois Center. This was a grand experience to begin with but it was particularly special in that I was hosted and introduced by Dr. Sekou Nkrumah, Kwame Nkrumah's youngest son and the director of the Du Bois Center. Brother Sekou

---

3   Dedicated to Dr. John Henrik Clarke (1915-1998).

and I hit it off from the very beginning, and before long, we were laughing and talking like we had known each other all our lives.

My presentation was a good one. I was very emotional, however, and got choked up a few times before I got my bearings. I showed a number of slides, including a photo of the Black Christ that I photographed in Egypt's Coptic Museum. I also showed several images of Africoid figurines from pre-Columbian America to emphasize that Africans were in America before the European intrusions of the fifteenth century. The audience really seemed to appreciate my message. I was able to engage the attendees in a lengthy question-and-answer period, which was particularly important to me because I wanted to get a good sense of the thoughts going through their minds. Afterwards, everyone was delighted when I presented the Center with a copy of John G. Jackson's Introduction to African Civilizations.

I consider this presentation to be one of the great honors of my life. I am particularly grateful to Brother John Ghansah and Dr. Maulana Hamid for making it happen.

We spent the next four nights in the Elmina/Cape Coast area. This is a hauntingly beautiful region marked by pristine beaches and dozens of large, decrepit dungeons where captive Africans were held and brutalized before being hoarded into the floating coffins that took them to the Americas. Strangely enough, it was here that I really fell in love with Ghana for the first time.

From the beginning of the trip, I was glad that I had come but I felt no sense of connectedness. Perhaps it was only after overcoming some of the dread that I felt before entering the Elmina dungeon that I could really enjoy finally being in Ghana. After that, I was able to relax a little bit more and appreciate more fully being in the land of my African Ancestors.

Of the more than forty dungeons (sometimes called castles) along the west coast of Africa, more than thirty of them are in Ghana. They are horrible places. What was it like to be inside one of them? I always feared that I would go into a dungeon and have a really bad emotional experience, but what I really felt in Elmina was anger and indignation. I could not take the tour that was being offered, so I broke away from my group to check out some of the individual cells and the large dungeon where the men had been kept. That was all I could stomach on that particular day.

By the time I got to the dungeon at Cape Coast, only a short distance from Elmina, I was a bit more prepared and I did take the tour. I went into the putrid men's dungeon and saw where my Ancestors had been packed away like sardines. I visited the women's dungeon also and saw where my female Ancestors had been held and raped by the White slave catchers. Believe me when I say that it did nothing to endear White people to me, and it is a good thing none of the White tourists wandering quietly around the dungeon's courtyard dared to even look at me. Otherwise, I fear the results certainly would have been perilous for them.

It was only after I walked through the infamous "door of no return" and back that I felt some of the burden lifted from my soul. I guess you could say that I am glad that I finally had that experience because I now know a little more about what my Ancestors endured in the greatest crime against humanity that the world has yet witnessed.

Runoko Rashidi

One of the happier, more precious highlights of the Elmina/Cape Coast visit was the traditional African marriage of Tony and Janice Browder. I first met Tony in the late 1980s, shortly after my first visit to India. He is a dynamic African brother, a great organizer, a genius at marketing, and a real scholar in his own right. Over the years, we have maintained a good and steady relationship, and so it was with tremendous satisfaction that I received an official invitation to their wedding. It was quite a ceremony. Among the other attendees were James Small, Leonard and Rosalind Jeffries, and Asa Hilliard. All of us were seated in the front row along with the traditional elders and chiefs. We enjoyed ourselves immensely, and we were all very happy about the new union. Janice seemed like a really good sister, and we all wished the new couple the very best that life has to offer.

It was also in Elmina/Cape Coast that most of the Panafest activities were being held that year. Panafest is a celebration for both continental and Diasporic Africans that was designed to bring us together in recognition of our common history, needs, and aspirations. A number of other African American tour groups were also attending the festival, including a large contingent from Philadelphia and a wonderful group led by Dr. Wade Nobles. Dr. Leonard Jeffries gave a rousing address to a Panafest audience that summed up my feelings for the entire trip when he pointed out that Ghana is probably our best chance for the salvation of Africa.

So my love affair with Ghana really began in the Elmina/Cape Coast area. I relished the wonderful Ghanaian cuisine and spent a lot of time at the beach. I even engaged in a libation ceremony at the seashore. There, I gave thanks to the Ancestors for allowing me to return to my African homeland and called on them to bless our trip.

From Elmina/Cape Coast, we headed north to the bustling metropolis of Kumasi--Ghana's second-largest city. Along the way, we stopped at Assin Manso, where the captured Africans were allowed to take a final bath before being marched into the coastal dungeons.

From our base in Kumasi, we journeyed to Mankranso, the adopted village of Nana Baffour Amankwatia II (aka Asa Hilliard), where we were well received and ordered to come back the following day for a grand durbar (procession) and a reception with the governor of the Kumasi region. This turned out to be a really big event. Based on Nana Baffour's introductions of me, I was informed that I was to be enstooled as an Ashanti chief in my own right. Somewhat to my dismay, however, I was also commanded to disrobe before the assembled crowd and put on the traditional dress and sandals befitting a man of that rank!

Can you believe it? There I was on my first trip to West Africa, and I am told that I would soon be a chief! It was a great honor and nothing to be taken lightly. After some discussion and a lot of deliberation with Nana Baffour, I pretty much decided then and there to accept direct responsibility for trying to uplift Africa.

Another of my wonderful experiences in the Kumasi region was visiting with the direct descendants of Queen Mother Yaa Asantewa of Ejisu, a great African woman who led an army of Africans to fight the British colonizers. The regal character and dignity of these sisters and brothers was written all over them. Our tour group relished this wonderful visit, and the people seem to have enjoyed us as well. We also visited the Ashanti royal palace of Prempeh II, where I was informed that, based on my physical appearance alone, I could easily have found my place in that region.

My Global Journeys in Search of the African Presence

In Kumasi, I took a full day away from the group and visited Bonwire, home of the world famous Kente cloth. From there I went to Lake Bosomtwe, a place that I did not even know existed. Lake Bosomtwe is, like most of Ghana, an enchantingly beautiful and serene place. I only regret that my time there was so limited.

The final leg of the tour took us to Akosombo in the Volta region. It probably was appropriate that we went there toward the end of the trip, for we may have never gotten much further. It was just that nice. The following morning, I had a leisurely breakfast from a balcony with a magnificent view of Lake Volta. The sheer beauty of the lake brought me to the verge of tears, and on that last day in Ghana, I began to dread returning to Europe and the United States.

On the return trips to Accra, the Novotel Hotel, and the airport, we stopped at the Akonedi Shrine at Larteh, described as one of the oldest traditional religious shrines in Ghana and further evidence that long before Islam and Christianity arrived in Africa, Africans had been practicing their own spiritual rituals, founded upon a belief in a supreme being, for thousands of years. It was a fitting way for us to end our tour in the magical land of Ghana.

Why do I call Ghana "magical"? Because it cast a spell on me, and I shall never be the same. I adore Ghana, and place my visit up there with my greatest trips to Egypt, India, and Australia. I will never be the same, and I can't wait to go back. While in Ghana, I realized as never before that the future of Africa hangs in the balance of Ghana's fate. Europe wants Africa, but we shall not give her up without a fight! Surely, Ghana will be a major battlefield.

For the success of my Ghanaian trip, I have to express my sincere appreciation to several people. These include Zawadi Sagna, Nias and Beverly Harris; Nana Ekow Butweiku I, John Ghansah, Dr. Maulana Hamid, Marie Bradley, James Small, Leonard Jeffries, Nana Baffour, and so many others. I owe each of you a debt that I can never fully repay. Medasi pa![4]

IN AFRICA'S HORN: MY FIRST VISIT TO ETHIOPIA[5]

"Ethiopia shall soon stretch out her hands unto God." (Psalms 68:31)

In March 2004, I was invited by the KJLH Radio Front Page tour group to travel with them to Ethiopia. In return for a few lectures and making myself available to the tour members, I would be given a complementary trip. Well, considering that I had wanted to travel to Ethiopia for a very long time, it seemed like a good idea to me, and I was exceptionally quick to endorse the idea.

The timing was perfect. For the past few years, I typically had taken a research trip/vacation in March, and here was a journey practically handed to me on a silver platter! The Ancestors had clearly blessed me once again.

---

4   "Thank you very much" in Twi, one of the languages of Ghana.
5   Dedicated to Baba Robert Donaldson.

Why was travel to Ethiopia so important to me? The answer is simple: because of its fabulous past. The term Ethiopia comes from the early Greeks and means "land of the burnt-faced people.' Indeed, in Antiquity, Ethiopia was seen as a vast land extending far beyond her current boundaries and stretching deep across both Africa and Asia. In the land now called Ethiopia are found the remains of the mighty kingdom of Axum, one of Africa's most prominent ancient civilizations. Also to be found in Ethiopia are the eleven rock-hewn churches at Lalibela (often dubbed "the eighth wonder of the world") and Gondar, with its royal enclosure and palaces and castles.

It was in Ethiopia in 1896 that the famous battle of Adwoa took place. At Adwoa on March 1, 1896, the Ethiopians, led by Emperor Menelik II, overwhelmed and routed the Italian army, which was a modern and highly mechanized European military force. Hence, the Battle of Adwoa is celebrated as one of Africa's shining hours. Additionally, Ethiopia has the distinction of having been exposed to the taint of European occupation for only a relatively short time, from 1935 to 1941. Also, Ethiopia houses the remains of Dinknesh—who, at an age of at least 3.2 million years old, is one of our earliest identifiable Ancestors.

So as an historian and a proud and conscious African man, I was absolutely thrilled at the possibility of visiting the ancient, noble, and tradition-steeped African nation of Ethiopia. I really wanted to lecture there, especially as I knew the trip would bring to forty the number of countries that I had visited in a five-year period and to thirty the number of countries in which I had lectured. Some time ago, I had set a goal for myself of lecturing in forty countries, and with the lecture series in Ethiopia, I would be three-quarters of the way home.

March 2004

As it happened, my trip to Ethiopia was one of the most emotionally demanding trips I have ever taken. Not surprisingly, I was tired to begin with. I had lectured in Europe and Canada in January of that year, and February, which is African Heritage Month in the United States, is always the busiest time of the year for me. And just weeks before taking off for Ethiopia, I had lectured at a number of venues in California, Washington, D.C., and Chicago.

Getting to Ethiopia was no joke, either. The tour group and I flew first from Los Angeles to Newark, New Jersey, and from there on Ethiopian Airlines to Rome, Italy. After an hour stop-over there, we flew another seven hours to Addis Ababa, Ethiopia's capital, founded in 1887 by Emperor Menelik II, conqueror of Adwoa. The name Addis Ababa in the Amharic language means "New Flower."

After what seemed like a very long journey, we arrived in Addis Ababa at night. After passing through customs and immigration, we departed the capital's beautiful new airport and were soon tucked away very comfortably in our quarters at the Hilton Hotel.

After a night of renewing bonds between the tour members and introducing ourselves to the hotel staff (until the bartender insisted, based on the lateness of the hour, that we bid each other adieu), we started our first full day in Ethiopia with a fine lecture on Ethiopian history and Pan-Africanism, given by a local scholar from Addis Ababa University. I also had the good fortune that morning of talking over the phone with the noted scholar Richard Pankhurst, author of over twenty books on Ethiopia and (of particular importance and excitement to me) a history of the Ethiopian presence in Asia, especially India. Afterwards, our group excitedly embarked on a tour of the city.

Ethiopia: A Rich History and a Great Poverty

I had been told by a number of people in advance of this trip that poverty was widespread in Ethiopia, but that first morning, traveling throughout the capital, I saw very little of it. It was only toward the end of that day, while sitting in front of a small gift shop, that it started to hit me. All at once, it seemed as if a whole collection of people, from very old to very young, were surrounding me with pleas for assistance. At first, I doled out some small sums of currency, but the pleas seemed never-ending. With a heavy heart, I forced myself back onto the tour bus and attempted to avoid eye contact with the numerous poor people clamoring around the bus.

That evening, I slept very fitfully. I could not help but remember those desperate faces, and I thought over and over again about all the money I had spent the night before at the bar in the hotel. That guilt stayed with me throughout the trip and haunts me even now.

Next morning, we flew to Lalibela, located in the mountainous region of Lasta. This city, I was later told, is Ethiopia's number-one tourist destination. Its fame is based on the several rock-hewn churches found there, which were carved in the thirteenth century and sometimes collectively referred to as the "eighth wonder of the world." Roha, as the town was known previously, was Ethiopia's capital for about two hundred years. It was renamed after King Lalibela, the most notable of the rulers of the powerful Zagwe Dynasty. Just after he was crowned, Lalibela began assembling world-class craftsmen and artisans to begin carving the churches. According to local legends, at least one of the churches was built by angels in a single day. King Lalibela gained such esteemed status that, after his death, he was elevated to sainthood by the Ethiopian Coptic Church.

That night at the Roha Hotel, I gave the first of my three lectures in Ethiopia. I was in top form. I confess that I was a little nervous to begin with, however. Lecturing on the history of Ethiopia was new territory to me, but I gave what I thought was a stirring talk on that African nation's history and cultural symbolism. I also talked about Greek and Roman views toward Ethiopia, about the spread of Ethiopia into ancient Asia, and about those African American scholars who wrote and spoke of Ethiopia with pride even during the dark days of the nineteenth century. I talked further of African American reactions to the 1935 Italian invasion of Ethiopia. I then invited our two Ethiopian tour guides to join in the conversation. Overall, the night was a rousing success and everyone celebrated my brilliance.

So far, so good, I thought of that evening. Beginning the next day, however, my experience in Ethiopia began to change, dramatically.

On the morning of our first full day in Lalibela, a good portion of the tour group was taken by motor coach to visit the Nakuta La'ab Cave Church. On the way to the church, after parking the bus a considerable distance from our ultimate destination, we passed through a small community inhabited, or so it seemed, by many scores of idle children. These children, raggedy and unkempt, began to follow us and stayed on our trail and at our sides throughout the tour. By that time, I had made up my mind to harden myself to their presence, but with only limited success. There were so many begging children swarming around us, it was virtually impossible to appreciate the church tour. This experience, for me, became characteristic of the entire rest of the trip.

Indeed, the allure of Ethiopia's antiquities soon began to fade into the recesses of my imagination as I became increasingly overwhelmed, not, as I had anticipated, by the country's past but more and more with the conditions of its present-day people . The reality of this really crystallized for me when I returned to the waiting tour bus after leaving the church and the village. A small crowd of people, from very young to very old, had gathered around the bus and were begging and pleading for money, ink pens, and plastic bottles. The tour members sat there for what seemed like a very long time, I suppose just hoping that the crowd would eventually dissipate and that the people outside the bus would all go away. But it never let up. In fact, it got worse.

So there we were. I guess that nobody, least of all the members of the KJLH tour group, wanted to witness such overwhelming poverty and need, especially among African people. The weather was hot and we were uneasy and rather uncomfortable, but here we found ourselves, literally surrounded by poor and ragged and pleading African people, children in particular, many of them with mucous running out of their nostrils and flies dotting their eyes. It was rough, sisters and brothers!

The pitiful scenario reached near rock-bottom for me when one of the brothers on the trip, a physician, told me that he had examined some of the children's eyes and had found a large dead fly underneath the eyelid of one young child. As you can imagine, it was very hard for me to enjoy the trip after that.

We were met with similar scenes at the famous Church of St. George, or Bet Giorgis, the most majestic of all Lalibela's churches. The church stands about sixty feet high and is excavated below ground level to reveal a sunken courtyard. It is truly a wonderful building, but for me the turning point of the trip already been reached. The joy and elation of being in Ethiopia had quickly become a downward journey into despair and impoverishment. The land itself seemed bleak and desolate, perhaps all the more so because it was the dry season. Just eking out the most basic existence in Ethiopia seemed to be a real chore for most of its citizens. It was not long before I began to question if Ethiopia, or at least the part to which I had traveled, was a place that God had forgotten. I wondered: Could the whole of Ethiopia outside of Addis Ababa be like this?

From Lalibela we flew to Gondar, one of Ethiopia's other major tourist attractions. Gondar is a more recent capital of Ethiopia than Lalibela, founded in 1635 by Emperor Fasilidas. It was Ethiopia's capital for 250 years.

I gave another good lecture in Gondar entitled "Classical African Civilizations." Unfortunately, it had been a very long day for me, and my fatigue must have been obvious. Much of my audience didn't seem to fully appreciate my efforts.

The next day, we went by bus from Gondar to the Simien Mountains National Park. Although the park was only sixty miles from Gondar, it took us all day, traveling over very poor roads, to get there and return. Again, despite the incredibly beautiful view offered by the Simien Mountains, the landscape was filled with more destitute Ethiopians. The only significant difference between the mountainous region and Lalibela was that it was very cold in the mountains and the children were not only ragged and dirty, they were also shivering from cold.

That just about did it for me. And as the members of the tour and I interacted with the Ethiopian sisters and brothers we encountered that day, we wondered what we could and should do. Should we give them our money? Should we give them our clothes? Should we just shut our eyes and try to ignore them? If we gave them money, we debated, would we be promoting a culture of dependency? How many lives would we prolong?

The problem seemed so enormous that I soon became terribly depressed. I began to question if we had not already lost Africa—or, at the very least, I wondered if the future of Africa and African people was even more precarious than I had been forewarned.

Triumph at Bahir Dar

Despite these early encounters, one of the highlights of the Ethiopian tour was a boat excursion on Lake Tana, located near the base of the Blue Nile River. About forty-five miles long, thirty-five miles wide, calm, and offering gorgeous views of the surrounding countryside, Lake Tana is Ethiopia's largest lake. Hundreds of years ago, religious groups sought refuge on the islands of Lake Tana and built a number of churches there. We were able to tour a fine example of one such church at Narga Selassie, along with its religious paintings, illuminated manuscripts, and multiple treasures.

Despite its poverty, Ethiopia remains an extremely beautiful country. The area around Lake Tana is particularly scenic. On our second day in that region, I lectured before twenty-five students and two faculty members of the History Department at Bahir Dar University, on the topic of the global African presence, with particular emphasis on early Ethiopia.

This third presentation was in some ways the most challenging of them all because I was actually talking, for the first time during this trip, directly to an Ethiopian audience. This presentation was arranged by our Ethiopian tour guides after they heard me lecture in Lalibela and reviewed my copy of the book, African Presence in Early Asia, which I had co-edited with Ivan Van Sertima. Both guides had graduated from the University at Bahir Dar and agreed that, even on short notice, I should give a talk at the school. It would, of course, be a feather in their cap, so naturally, although somewhat tired, I was both honored and elated to do my duty.

The lecture, titled "The Ethiopian Roots of Humanity and Civilization," provided a rough overview of the global African presence. I soon realized that the audience knew very little about the global history of African people. As a matter of fact, the head of the department himself told me that my thesis was "quite new and startling" to him. I think I was rather startling to him also!

Instead of standing at the front of the assembly at the podium, I sat right in the middle of the students themselves. When I had completed my lecture, the students seemed like they couldn't articulate any questions for me, so I reversed things and started to ask them questions. That was when the real action started! At the very start of my lecture, just to get them involved, I had told my audience about some of the negative general perceptions that far too many African Americans have of Africa. At the end, I asked them to share their perceptions of African Americans, and the whole place became energized.

There was no need for prodding, and the responses came forth as though they had been suppressed for a long time. The general consensus among them was that African Americans were a strong people who had survived slavery and were now up on their feet and prospering. Their major thrust, however, was that we African Americans generally were denying our African identity and had largely turned our backs on them. It was just heart-rending to hear them say that, and because they did, I had them turn to face the members of the tour group directly. Then we went back and forth about the ties that bind us, why African American s haven't done more to help, what we plan to do to help, and how the impact of slavery affects us all.

The discussion was both historic and pregnant with potential in terms of clearing the air and setting the basis for action. The students had never encountered African Americans before. We were the first such delegation to ever visit their university, and I felt so proud to be right there in the thick of this discussion.

The students also mentioned how much they wanted and needed books and computers, and how they would use the books and computers to liberate Africa, and how African-Americans were not at all rich and free. Afterward, I donated my copy of African Presence in Early Asia to the University, along with about twenty other books that some other concerned Africans and I had collected to present as gifts on this trip.

Bahir Dar University was essentially my last big moment in Ethiopia. After shaking hands with and embracing the history students and faculty and receiving the accolades of most of the tour members, our group got back on the bus. On the return ride to our hotel, we briefly visited the Blue Nile River. After that, I was pretty much out of it. I felt like I imagined a prize fighter must feel going into the late rounds of a bout, almost out on his feet and down on points, just trying to hold on.

An Enhanced Sense of Urgency

The following morning, we returned to Addis Ababa and the sanctuary of the Hilton Hotel. I barely made it to my room! I generally think of myself as a pretty tough guy, and I have been told that men shouldn't cry. But I suppose that there is a limit to everything and that afternoon, back in Addis Ababa, I came about as close as I can remember to crossing that line. I felt as if I was on the verge of some kind of emotional collapse. Embarrassed and shaken, I fought to pull myself together as I withdrew from the tour group and quietly bade my time until we left for the airport the following night.

Travel always evokes deep emotions of one kind or another for me, and I left Ethiopia with an enhanced sense of urgency, a deep foreboding, and a great concern. Indeed, I came away from Ethiopia grateful to the Africans who had invited me and really glad that I had gone there. But my initial elation had turned to deep despair when I realized, more than anytime I can remember, what a very long, hard way we Africans still have yet to go as a people. Right then, all the scholarly dialogue in which we engage and all the inspired discussions about spirituality that we embrace simply did not amount to much in my view, for I felt as if we were ignoring the harsh realities of life faced by so many of our people.

Sisters and brothers, my love for Africa remains as deep as ever, and my fighting spirit is unquenchable. But I definitely lost some of my romanticism about Mother Africa on this trip. My journey to Ethiopia reinforced for me, in a highly stunning manner, the realization that we have urgent work to do, and we must do it now. Otherwise, I am convinced that we stand a good chance of losing Africa altogether. I challenge anyone who says otherwise to go with an open mind to the regions that I visited in Ethiopia and to see and experience what I experienced. The time for fun and games is over. We must either get serious about Africa or say goodbye to it forever.

A NOTE FROM COTONOU, BENIN

October 17, 2004

It was another tough day in the Motherland for Brother Runoko. It is probably just me, but things rarely seem simple here, at least not on this trip. Anyway, I am writing to you, sisters and brothers, to try to keep the semblance of sanity that I think that I have remaining. And I know that I must sound like a big crybaby, but you are my lifeline right now. I am a seasoned traveler and have now visited fifty countries, but this is a major test, folks!

This morning, I got into a nasty argument with a Benin sister at the big and expensive hotel where I am staying. I was trying to exchange some money, and she treated me in a rude and off-hand manner. Now this sister was much younger than me, and I know that Africans in general respect their elders, so I went off on her! My anxieties have been building up for a couple of days now, and I was just not going to put up with her nonsense—not with all the money I have been spending in Benin and all the respect I have been sending out. So I talked to the manager, a really nice brother, who apologized profusely. He felt bad for me, and so did I.

As much as I love Africa, sometimes I think that brothers and sisters from the Diaspora, are seen too often only as wallets and purses, especially in French-speaking Africa. Anyway, I do not intend to ever allow myself to be disrespected anywhere, and that includes in Africa!

It was the same with my driver yesterday. This brother acted like I had a binding obligation to utilize his services. So I changed hotels and got another driver too! So now I am staying in a large and spacious, African-owned hotel located in a huge, park-like area. And the Atlantic Ocean is right behind me! It is like a dream!

My new driver took me to Abomey today, the heart of the Dahomey Empire. I toured the palace and museum, found out a lot about African women warriors—the so-called Amazons—and about King Behanzin, who fought the French invaders. I was deep in the interior of Benin, getting a full dose of Africa, and then the car broke down! I tell you, I was way past frustration, but I did not lose my temper. I didn't say a thing. What was there to say? And my driver was so humble and apologetic. I did not fault him. Fortunately, we were able to get back to Cotonou in one piece.

Runoko Rashidi

So here I am, trying to be brave and hang tough, but I am human too. Benin has been a real test for this African. Still, I love this place, despite everything that has happened, and I realize that I am trying hard to connect emotionally with the Mother from whom I was ripped so violently away those hundreds of years ago.

Am I making any sense at all? Perhaps my sanity is already gone. Perhaps it is just time for me to go. Wish that you all were here because I'm feeling a bit lonely and blue. I'm trying to decide whether to pull the plug on Benin early and head back to Ghana. I would just love to have a nice chat with someone. In the meantime, just consider this another note from a big crybaby who is trying hard to keep it together!

A Little Clarity About Benin, French-Speaking Africans, and Mother Love

I think I need to clarify some of my earlier comments about the people of Benin. First of all, I am glad that I went to Benin. The country has a rich history. I might even go again, but only under different circumstances.

I cannot say that I enjoyed myself very much in Benin. I went alone. I was not well prepared. I speak very little French, and I did not know anyone there. Plus, the contacts that friends and colleagues kindly suggested for me were either unavailable, unresponsive, unreachable, seemed to have bad intentions. So that is why I was so uptight. Still, I have no choice ultimately but to take most of the responsibility for my experience on my own shoulders. Nobody forced me to go to Benin. I went because I wanted to and because the opportunity was there. It simply did not work out as I would have liked.

To make matters worse, I had to make my own arrangements to get to Benin from Ghana by car via Togo and then back again. I learned a lot in the process, but I was nervous most of the time. And, as it turned out, the new car that I hired in Lome, Togo, to take me back to Accra broke down on the road, twice! When I finally did get back to Ghana, I let out a loud cry of joy!

So, unlike some, I do not regard French-speaking Africans as fundamentally different than English- or Arabic- or Portuguese- or Dutch- or Hindi- or Bengali- or Spanish-speaking Africans. We are all African people suffering from varying degrees of mental and physical colonization. Indeed, I have spent considerable time in France, and I have had no real problems there. Matter of fact, some of the French-speaking Africans who look after me when I come to Paris are among the most loving and African-centered sisters and brothers I have ever met. I would trust them with my life. So, I beg you, let us not be so harsh in our indictments of each other.

I love Africa, and I love African people, wherever we find ourselves. Yes, I do get frustrated sometimes. I am only human. I deliberately posted my whining note from Benin to show my human side. I am not ashamed of that. I am not trying to be "Mister Macho." I was trying to provoke some serious discussion. If that means I must become a lightning rod for criticism, I am more than prepared to accept that position. No problem!

I can't wait to go back to Africa, including French-speaking Africa. I want to visit the whole continent. Next year I hope to go to Eritrea, Kenya, Uganda, Tanzania, Cameroon, and maybe even

Nigeria. In 2006, I am looking to visit Senegambia, Mali, and Southern Africa. Here I come, Mother Africa, again and again! I love you, and I cannot get enough! . Frustration be damned!

And one more thing: I have made a commitment to build a library for the students at the Sunrise School in Accra, Ghana, and I need some help. Who wants to work with me on this?

Sisters and brothers, we talk and talk and talk until the cows come home about love for Africa and love for our people. Isn't it about time we did something about it? Talk is cheap! Family, I need your support and your help. Africa needs our support, our help, and our sacrifice. Now who wants to get on board and do some work?

If not us, then who? If not now, then when? Time to go to work!

DAYS AND NIGHTS IN TUNISIA

Like I always say: I love Africa. I love African people. And I especially love traveling around the world in search of the African presence. And so it was with keen anticipation and lofty ideals that I journeyed for the first time to Tunisia, North Africa, in 2006. Tunisia was country number sixty-one on my list of international travel destinations, which meant that I had surpassed the great Joel Augustus Rogers. I was in rarefied air.

Tunisia is a country about the size of the state of Washington in the United States. It lies nestled right between the much larger nations of Libya, on the east, and Algeria, on the west. On the north and northeast, Tunisia is bounded by the Mediterranean Sea. Its population is just over ten million people, most of them Arab. French and Arabic are the predominant languages.

I don't have the official statistics, but there is a small but highly visible population of African people in Tunisia, perhaps as small as one percent of the total population. I was told over and over again that most of the Africans in Tunisia live in the southern portion of the country, and this would seem to be the general rule for African people all over north and northwest Africa.

April 1, 2006

It was springtime, and I was due for another international trip. My beautiful and adorable little baby daughter was almost seven months old. She was happy and thriving, and I thought that I deserved a short research trip-vacation. From Paris, I flew direct to Tunis. The plane ticket was less than three hundred dollars, and the flight was less than three hours, but after arriving in Tunis, the capital of Tunisia, things got off to a bit of a rocky start.

It took me a good little while to get through customs and then, after I picked up my luggage, there was no one to meet me! So I changed some U.S. dollars into Tunisian dinars and finally found someone holding a sign on which my name was badly misspelled. After I identified myself, the man smiled and introduced me to my driver.

Runoko Rashidi

Now my experience with drivers in Africa is that they first shake hands with you and welcome you to their country. Then they take your bags and lead you to a waiting car. This guy didn't do any of that. He uttered something inaudible, turned and walked away with me following, bags in hand. No problem, I thought, maybe I am just catching him at a bad moment. Or maybe, I thought, that is just the way that they do things here. So I got into the car to be driven to the travel agency, where I hoped I would receive a warmer greeting.

But my official greeting at the travel agency was only tepid. The real wake-up call came when the agency's representative told me that she was going to charge me a whopping $240.00 per day for a car and an English-speaking driver! When I seemed perturbed about this, she pointed out that she had informed me of the transportation cost in an email that she had sent me before my trip. I told her that when I read the email I assumed that the rate was for all four of my days in Tunisia. I did not tell her that I thought the cost was outrageous, but I left her office with what we in the United States call "an attitude."

I did not like the hotel, either! So I had the driver take me to another, much nicer (albeit more expensive) hotel. There, I negotiated the room price directly with the duty manager, booked my own room, and found another car and driver that guaranteed substantial savings. Immediately, my sour disposition began to improve! I dismissed my original travel agent and headed out into Tunisia "on my own."

Indeed, I found a taxi driver who took me from my new hotel to the Bardo Museum for less than two U.S. dollars! The taxi driver even refused to take a tip!

The Bardo is the national museum of Tunisia. It was the logical place to start my Tunisian journey. It houses an excellent collection of mostly Roman mosaics. At the Bardo, I found a marble head of the African-born Roman Emperor Septimius Severus and two similar heads of his son and successor, Caracalla. I have a great interest in these two Africans, and my next book, should I ever finish it, will have a nice chapter on them.

But the most exciting artifact in the museum, for me, was the black limestone head of a woolly haired African woman from Carthage. I had never seen it in any book before, anywhere! So my first afternoon in Tunisia ended on a very good note.

That first night in Tunisia, I tossed and turned all over my mattress, as it had been very hot during the day and the air conditioning in the hotel had stopped working. But I had met a few other Black folks who were staying in the hotel, and that made me feel very upbeat. Also, I had enjoyed an excellent meal of grilled fish and vegetables that evening, watched an international news show on the television, and reread volume one of Langston Hughes' excellent autobiography, The Big Sea. Besides, the people in Tunisia seemed pretty friendly overall, and most moved at a relaxed pace. The big tourist season was still a couple of weeks ahead, and things in general—hotel meals and cars and English-speaking drivers aside—were fairly inexpensive.

In Kerkouane and Carthage

The following morning, after a light breakfast that I paid way too much for, I was driven to the tip of the Cape Bon Peninsula to visit the archaeological site of the ancient Punic (Phoenician) city of Kerkouane. It was a clear day, but a strong breeze was blowing. My English-speaking driver did not say much along the way, but he was not unpleasant and I consoled myself with how much money I was saving.

Kerkouane is located in a beautiful area on the coast of the Mediterranean Sea in the direction of Sicily. Although the city was destroyed more than two thousand years ago by the Romans, excavations have revealed much of its remains. . There was hardly anyone at the site when we arrived. In the nearby Kerkouane Museum, I found an exquisite depiction, done (I think) in terra cotta, of an African man riding what appeared to be an elephant. Like the piece in the Bardo Museum, this image depicted a Black African person. And, once again, I had never seen the artifact in any book before. Needless to say, just as I had done when I found the bust of the African woman in the Bardo Museum, I took a lot of photographs! Speaking of African women, I saw quite a few those days in Tunisia, and they were all beautiful and friendly. One Muslim sister, who was working at the entrance to the ruins of Carthage, told me that things used to really be bad for the Africans in Tunisia, but that conditions had improved recently. As an example, she pointed out that "beautiful Black boys" could now be seen in public with "beautiful White girls" on the streets of Tunisia. I just wish that she could have used a better example to denote progress!

After visiting Kerkouane, I was driven to Carthage, but not to the ancient African city-state of Carthage, or Khart-Haddas. Rather, I visited the Carthage located in one of the suburbs on the outskirts of Tunis. There I saw the remains of the Roman city that was built on top of the African settlement that the Romans destroyed after three titanic wars.

Carthage was founded in 814 B.C.E.[6] when a Phoenician fleet from the great metropolis of Tyre on the southern coast of Lebanon landed in what is now northern Tunisia. Phoenicia was the name given by the Greeks in the first millennium B.C.E. to the coastal provinces of modern Lebanon and northern Palestine, although occasionally the term was applied to the entire eastern Mediterranean seaboard from Syria to Palestine.

Phoenicia was not considered a nation in the strict sense of the word, but rather viewed as a chain of coastal cities, of which the most important were Sidon, Byblos, Tyre and Ras Shamra. To the Greeks, the term Phoenician, from the root phoenix, connoted the color red. It is likely that the name was derived from the physical appearance of the Phoenician people.

The Phoenicians were a coastal branch of the Canaanites who, according to Biblical traditions, were related to the Kushites (Ethiopians) and the Mizraimites (Egyptians), who were members of the Hamite (or Kamite) ethnic family. Spurred by increasing population pressures, the Phoenicians, who were becoming increasingly mixed racially, had developed a prowess on the seas by the middle of the

---

6   B.C.E. stands for Before the Common Era, and is used to designate the number of years before the approximate birth year of Yeshua/Jesus that an event occurred or takes place. Years designated B.C. (Before Christ) and B.C.E. have identical values.

second millennium B.C.E. and were in the process of establishing a network of colonies and trading posts that brought them prosperity and eternal fame. Together with the local people of North Africa, the Phoenicians founded the stupendous city-state of Carthage, or Khart-Haddas, which means "new town."

For hundreds of years, Carthage was the dominant nation in the western Mediterranean and a colossal naval power. At the height of its fame, the city boasted a population of 500,000 inhabitants. The leading family of Carthage was the Barca clan, one of which, Hamilcar Barca, founded the Spanish city of Barcelona. Of course, the most famous member of the Barca family was Hannibal Barca—perhaps the most distinguished general of ancient times.

Hannibal was the great hero of Carthage during the Second Punic War, which lasted from 218 B.C.E.to 202 B.C.E. Indeed, Hannibal came within an eyelash of defeating the Romans on the threshold of Rome itself. Perhaps his most outstanding moment came in 216 B.C.E. at the famous battle of Cannae, when the Carthaginian army, despite being vastly outnumbered, virtually annihilated a Roman force of 80,000 men.

Despite her early successes, at the end of the Third Punic War in 146 B.C.E., the Romans ravaged mighty Carthage and burnt her to the ground.

It is said that the city burnt for forty days. Only a small portion of the African city of Carthage remains. Its people were either massacred or sold into slavery. The Romans even plowed salt into the soil around Carthage so that nothing could ever grow there again.

It was not until the time of Julius Caesar, in 44 B.C.E., that Carthage was rebuilt, but this time as a Roman city. However, even now, and without difficulty, you can use your imagination and almost see those sleek ancient African sailing vessels sailing into port. You can hear ancient African people talking and trading with one another. You can hear great African generals giving orders to the soldiers and citizens, nobles, and commoners of Carthage to come to the defense of the city.

Sisters and brothers, I felt honored to stand on the site of ancient Carthage—a proud city that African people gave their lives to protect.

So that second day in Tunisia was a wonderful one for me. The night was pleasant and uneventful.

In Dougga

My third and last full day in Tunisia took me to the ancient Roman city of Dougga to see what the Africans of the Severan Dynasty had contributed to world history. Historians and archaeologists have commented that the region thrived under these African emperors, and I could hardly wait to see it for myself.

The ancient Roman city of Dougga is about 150 kilometers southwest of Tunis. Along the way, I was surprised by the beauty of the countryside and its scenery. The green rolling hills reminded me of California. The roads were good and, once out of Tunis, the traffic was light.

In just over ninety minutes, we arrived in Dougga. After paying the small admission fee to enter the site, I was approached by a short, elderly Arab man in a gray suit. Like many Tunisian men, he wore a red fez on his head, which I considered a sign of great distinction. He informed me that he was a guide and asked me if I desired his services. I knew by then that a good guide is as important as a good travel agent. His price was moderate, so away we went.

My guide was sixty-eight years old and his English was good. He had a good sense of humor and liked to talk. When I asked him how long he had been a guide, he told me with a big smile across his face that he was born in Dougga. He showed me all of the major and minor temples, including the temple of the goddess Tanit. Her temple he called "The House of Tanit." Tanit was the most significant of the female deities in ancient Tunisia, and her adoration survived despite the Romans. I had already seen signs of her importance amidst the ruins of Kerkouane.

Being an impatient man, however, it was not long before I asked my guide about the contributions of the Severan clan. Somewhat dismissively, he said that we would soon get to it. I assumed that he did not want to be pre-empted, and I could tell that he got a charge out of the fact that I was a man with some knowledge of history. I also gathered that not many African tourists came to Dougga because eventually, and again with a smile, my guide turned, and looking directly at me, exclaimed that Septimius Severus was the first African-born emperor of Rome—and "the one with the brown skin!"

This was my cue, I thought, and just as I had done with my earlier driver and the African Muslim sister at the gate to the Carthage ruins, I asked him, "Where are the Black people of Tunisia?" And again, just like the others, he said that they could be found "in the south." When I pressed him about numbers and exact locations, he mentioned a city or two there, but he could give no precise numbers as to the numbers of Blacks in Tunisia. But he insisted emphatically that "everybody in Tunisia is the same, and everybody is treated the same." He even told me that several governors in the southern portion of the nation were Black.

My guide later took me to visit the still-impressive arch honoring another member of the Severan Dynasty—Alexander Severus, the last representative of that clan. The old man actually turned out to be a very good tour guide. Even though he smoked a lot of cigarettes and had short legs, he managed to walk me right into the ground! I was huffing and puffing trying to keep up with him as he marched on with the agility and dexterity of a mountain goat, all the while telling me to "Take your time, take your time!"

One of the most interesting sites in Dougga was the reconstructed remains of an ancient mausoleum belonging to the family of the Numidian king Massinissa, a man who fought alongside the Carthaginians before abandoning them for the Romans. The mausoleum, which is located at the base of a hill, stands twenty-one meters high (taller than the Colossi of Memnon on the west bank of the Nile at Luxor) and is capped with a small pyramid. Close to it can be found the remains of the arch and gate of Septimius Severus, which were not in very good shape but are all that remains of a much larger structure. Still, I had it all to myself! There were no other tourists around. My guide informed me that the reconstruction of the gate and arch was scheduled to begin in 2007.

Several times during the tour, the old man pointed to what he said was the original road to Carthage. He even showed me the chariot tracks. At first, it did not make sense to me, but it finally dawned on my consciousness that the ancient engineers had actually constructed a paved road that led all the way from Dougga to Carthage, and the road went directly under the arch of Septimius Severus! I was really impressed!

As an added bonus, my guide suggested that I visit the ancient city of Leptis Magna in Libya, where Septimius Severus was born. The city was in remarkable shape, he claimed. So now, I have every intention of visiting Libya and paying further homage to the greatest of the African emperors of Rome.

On that note, my guide bade me farewell. I paid him his fee and even gave him a nice tip, which made him very happy. He wished me a safe journey back to France and the United States and encouraged me, with a big smile spread across his face, to bring some more Africans to Tunisia!

And that, sisters and brothers, that was my trip to Tunisia in northern Africa. I now have a much better sense of what the celebrated jazz artist Dizzy Gillespie might have had in mind when he composed the tune, "Night in Tunisia."

I had a good time on my all-too-short trip to Tunisia. I learned a whole lot, and I look forward to going back and visiting "the south" and parts of Libya as well. And don't you worry: even if you can't come with me, I will be sure to keep you posted so you won't miss a thing. Stay strong, and I will try to do the same. Life is good, sisters and brothers, and every day is a rich blessing.

My next international destinations: Morocco and Spain in search of the Moors!

MY RETURN TO SOUTHERN AFRICA

May 2006

I am now in Cape Town, South Africa, and I wanted to drop you a few lines. It is my first visit to South Africa. I think that coming here is essential to any understanding of Africa. Just like I know that I must travel to Nigeria next year. And so, here I am, and so South Africa makes sixty-two the number of countries I have visited in the past seven years.

I am pretty much on my own here. The folks handling my itinerary essentially dropped the ball. I guess that it just be's like that sometimes. We'll see how it turns out. They may pull something together at the last minute. I have ultimate faith in the power of our Ancestors.

I am here until early next week, and then I go to Namibia, where I have a very full schedule. After Namibia, I go to Botswana and Swaziland before returning to South Africa, but at that time to Johannesburg. Later this summer I will be visiting Kenya, Uganda, Morocco, Spain, Portugal, Egypt, Ghana, and the Malagasy Republic.

In Cape Town

It is wintertime in Cape Town. It is raining a lot, and I have found a beer and an Internet cafe that stays open twenty-four hours, so life cannot be all bad! Folks are pretty friendly, the sisters are so very beautiful, people are walking around, and it is a very interesting place.

Cape Town is an attractive city. I have a pretty nice hotel in a great location just beneath Table Mountain. There are a lot of African street vendors and many, many shops of all sorts.

I hear a lot about crime in the city, although it supposedly is not as bad as Durban and not nearly as bad as Johannesburg, from what I hear. And, of course, there is a great deal of talk here about race and race relations. I am told that (surprise!) the Whites are still running things! And I hear terrible things about right-wing White extremists. My driver from the airport last night told me that under apartheid in the area where I am staying, Blacks were not allowed to go out after dark.

One of the most interesting aspects about Cape Town is the racial divisions. Here, things are not just Black and White. You also have the Coloreds, those mixed-race offspring of Blacks and Whites. From what I gather, many of them do not see themselves as either Black or White, but as a race apart. For a brother from the U.S., who has grown up with the "one-drop rule," this is almost laughable. But people take it very seriously here. Personally, I find it rather tragic, but I still believe in a people's right to define themselves. What do you think?

Just walking through Cape Town is an experience, like in any African city. Just looking at the people! The African women look so good! But I love African people, so you should not be surprised to hear me say that. Today I found an excellent used bookstore and an even better information center, then I visited four museums and an art gallery.

The art gallery featured a display of San art. The San are the African people often referred to as "Bushmen." They are a fascinating group of folk. At the main museum in the area, the South African Museum, the highlight was a video of a San men's healing ceremony. It was a short black-and-white video (about fifteen minutes in length) of several San men apparently in some kind of trance. Never seen anything like it! Words really can't describe it. They walked round and round a camp fire. Women, young and old, were gathered around the fire. The music was awesome, and their movements were nothing short of incredible.

The second museum I visited today was the National Gallery. It was mostly full of paintings of dead White folks, with only a couple of exceptions. But what exceptions they were! The first was a special exhibit called "Picasso and Africa," and it featured numerous works by the Spanish artist, who, in his own words, paid tribute to Africa and his debt to Africa's culture in his work. I saw a similar exhibit in Barcelona three years ago.

The other outstanding feature of the National Gallery was a magnificent bust of the great African American actor Ira Aldridge. The bust was white except the face and beard, which were colored pitch black. I could have stared at it for hours. I understand that there is a similar piece in the foyer of the Schomburg Library in Harlem, New York. Aldridge is considered one of the greatest actors of all time. He toured Europe extensively, achieving critical acclaim in London in "Othello" and "The Merchant of Venice." He was named a German baron, created a sensation in Russia, performed before Alexander Dumas, père, at Versailles, and was buried with state honors in Poland in 1867. What a man he must have been!

The third Cape Town museum that I visited was the Slave Lodge and Cultural Museum. Yes, slavery existed in South Africa too! It was extremely brutal, and the museum is a kind of place of remembrance. This was a somber experience, but I was able to talk extensively with the museum director about a wide range of subjects, including slave resistance.

My last museum visit in Cape Town was the District 6 Museum. This museum is also a solemn place of remembrance, commemorating the forced removal of people of color in South Africa and their relocation to the various local townships. It proved a grim and depressing experience, but life is like that sometimes, and I am glad that I went there. It seems to me that life for the South African people under apartheid was much like the experiences of the Aboriginal Australians, except on a vastly larger scale.

So that was my Saturday in Cape Town. Sunday was just as interesting. First, I visited the African marketplace located right in front of my hotel. There, I saw some of the most beautiful African art, and I would like to have purchased everything! I also returned to the Distinct 6 Museum.

A Visit to the Townships

Later that day I took a short trip outside of Cape Town to visit three Black townships. The first was Langa, the oldest township in South Africa. Then I went to Khayelitsha, the second largest township in South Africa, smaller only than Soweto. I also visited Guguletu Township. There, I went to a shabeen (I think that I am spelling it correctly), or beer hall, where I drank some of the local brew, visited a traditional healer, and then went to the local Baptist church where the choir brought the house down. Life in these Black townships is not easy, but there is so much vitality inside them.

To end my day, I had a meeting and dinner with a local community and African National Congress activist, who gave me even more insights on Black Cape Town. To put it mildly, I had a weekend to remember!

A Meeting with Xhosa Elders

I knew I would be leaving Cape Town the next day for Windhoek, Namibia, and I decided to do something special before I left. So instead of a city tour or a visit to the waterfront or to the top of Table Mountain, I returned to Langa Township on a trip arranged by Sam's Cultural Tours, the only African-owned and -controlled tour company in Cape Town. A special meeting was arranged for me with two Xhosa elders. The Xhosa are the largest ethnic group in South Africa. Nelson Mandela is Xhosa.

Through an expert interpreter, I spent the better part of the afternoon talking and talking and talking with those two elders. One of the men was an advisor to the late king of the Xhosa, and our meeting took place in his residence, a small room in a former men's hostel. He was joined by his chief associate. Both were short men with dark complexions and white hair. I was in my element! I asked them just about everything I could think of, and they replied patiently and in depth. I really think that they enjoyed the conversation even more than I did.

The two told me many things. They told me that they believed that the Xhosa and all of the Black people of Southern African came from the Nile Valley many, many years ago! They told me that they did not see the White people of South Africa as Africans in any way. They told me that men and women were equal and that homosexuality, abortion, and divorce should be condemned in the strongest way. They told me that the Black people of America were Africans and should come home, and that they recognized and admired us so much. I was in paradise!

They also told me that they especially admired Venus and Serena Williams and were so proud of them. They told me that AIDS was a real problem in South Africa, especially among the young people. They told me that they were very hopeful for the future and had great expectations.

So that was my weekend in Cape Town that carried over into Monday. I wonder what tomorrow will bring?

Return to Namibia

I have now been in Windhoek, Namibia, in southern Africa, for four full days. After a great experience in Cape Town, I have had at least as wonderful an experience here in Namibia.

For those that may not know, Namibia is an exceptionally large country known during the apartheid era as South West Africa. It has a population of almost two million. This is my second visit here, having spent several days lecturing here in May 2000. This trip was coordinated by the eighteenth All-African Student's Conference and facilitated by my friend Bankie F. Bankie, the same brother who was so instrumental in the success of my first Namibia trip.

I have received a real education this time! Indeed, I hit the ground running. I arrived on South African Airways on Tuesday afternoon and started work immediately. Even before I checked into my hotel, I did a television interview with the national television network. It must have been a big hit because, since it aired, numerous people have been stopping me on the streets to shake my hand and welcome me to Namibia. I feel almost like a minor celebrity!

Following the television interview and my hotel check-in, I had a private meeting with the Deputy Minister of Education, a beautiful and dynamic African woman who is very much a Pan-Africanist and married to a Nigerian brother. She was relaxed and confident and insisted that we take photos together. Then we hurried off for the launch of Brother Bankie's powerful new book entitled Strengthening the Unity of Africa and its Diaspora, coauthored by K. J. Mochombu.

The book launch was a big success. I was seated right next to the Deputy Minister of Education and the Namibian Prime Minister, also a staunch Pan-Africanist, and treated with great respect. But my day was not over, as that evening I met with Bankie, student activist Naville Andre and Bernadus Swartbooi, Special Assistant to the Prime Minister.

Runoko Rashidi

Brother Swartbooi is Nama. The Nama have an unbroken history of tens of thousands of years and are scattered all over southern Africa, including South Africa, Namibia, and Botswana. They are some of Africa's greatest resistance fighters, having fought the Dutch and Germans for decades.

The next day, I had a private meeting with the Vice-Chancellor of the International University of Management and then spoke before a student audience of fifty or so mostly young people. The Vice-Chancellor himself introduced me, and I spent about an hour interacting with these future leaders of Africa, trying to instill in them a sense of duty and obligation to Africa. This was followed by a newspaper interview with the national paper and then a radio interview on the national radio station.

I later met with some members of a San organization called WIMSA (the Working Group of Indigenous Minorities in Southern Africa). WIMSA is a non-governmental network that coordinates and represents the interests of indigenous and highly marginalized San peoples throughout southern Africa. I was utterly enthralled by their story.

The following day began with a meeting with the Paramount Chief of the Herero nation, the honorable Chief K. Riruako. The Herero, like the Nama, were nearly wiped out by the Germans in the early twentieth century and are actively pressing their case for reparations. The Chief explained that he saw himself as a student of John Henrik Clarke, and we spent the first few minutes of our meeting swapping John Henrik Clarke stories. But as much as he loved Dr. Clarke, he said that his greatest influence was Marcus Mosiah Garvey! Garvey was "big" in Namibia, he claimed, and when I told him that my daughter's middle name was Garvey, we became friends for life!

Following the meeting with the chief, I did a big public lecture at the Polytechnic University of Namibia. Most of my lecture was not a lecture at all, however, but an intense discussion about African unity. I loved it, and so did the audience! I later had a wonderful meeting with Jean-Marie Ndimbira, a Rwandan economist.

My next day started with a meeting with a delegation of Nama activists at my hotel. Then I met with the greatest living Nama: the Reverend Hendrik Witbooi, the great-grandson of the greatest of all the Nama resistance leaders. Of all the people that I met in Namibia, he was both the most dignified and the most humble. He welcomed me into his house and treated me with tremendous courtesy and respect. We even took photos in front of a portrait of his great-grandfather, who died fighting the Germans in 1905.

I could go on and on and on, sisters and brothers, but enough for now. Just suffice to say that I am well and getting an education of a lifetime. I have been to three museums here and have met all kinds of folks, including Namas, San, Ovambo, Herero, Africans from various parts of Africa, Rastafarians, and more. So let me get out of this Internet cafe and head back to my hotel for yet another meeting.

On my way back to the hotel this afternoon, a brother stopped me, shook my hand, and shouted, "Save Africa!" That is the way it has been here!

Tomorrow I fly to Gaborone, Botswana.

Runoko Rashidi and Yosef ben-Jochannan in Harlem, New York

Runoko Rashidi

With the Batwa in Western Uganda

My Global Journeys in Search of the African Presence

Herumakhet (Great Sphinx)

Runoko Rashidi

The Pyramid Ship

My Global Journeys in Search of the African Presence

Makare Hatshepsut

Ramses II at Abu Simbel

Runoko Rashidi

A Nubian girl near Aswan, Egypt

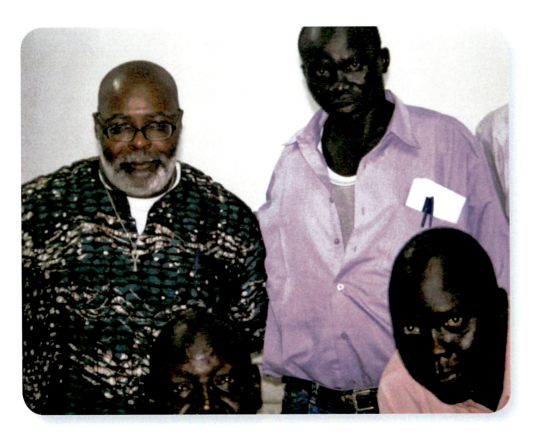

Runoko Rashidi in Juba, South Sudan

My Global Journeys in Search of the African Presence

An African bust from Carthage in the Bardo Museum in Tunis, Tunisia

Runoko Rashidi

BOTSWANA

> *"It should now be our intention to try to retrieve what we can of our past. We should write our own history books to prove that we did have a past, and that it was a past that was just as worth writing and learning about as any other. We must do this for the simple reason that a nation without a past is a lost nation, and a people without a past is a people without a soul"* (Seretse Khama, first president of Botswana, from a speech presented at the University of Botswana, Lesotho, and Swaziland, May 15, 1970; as quoted in the Botswana Daily News, May 19, 1970).

May 2006

Brother Runoko stays on the move these days! I am currently in Gaborone, Botswana, in southern Africa. This makes country number sixty-four for me. Gaborone is the capital of Botswana. I have only been here a couple of hours, arriving for once after dark. You should have seen the sunset as I flew out from Johannesburg! It all seems a bit like a dream!

Botswana is a large country, larger than the state of Texas, with a population of less than two million people. It is wealthy with diamonds, but the wealth does not seem to get to the masses, most of whom are Tswana. A lot of the country encompasses the Kalahari Desert. You have Namibia due west, Angola to the northwest, Zimbabwe to the northeast, and South Africa due south.

One of the things that you first notice in Gaborone is the relative absence of White people (which is a real good thing!) and of the folks that I saw so much of in Cape Town and Windhoek: the Coloreds.

I visited a Colored community in Namibia yesterday, in a town called Rehoboth, about eighty kilometers south of Windhoek, the capital of Namibia. During the end of the apartheid era, Rehoboth was the center of an active secessionist movement. It took the national army to suppress it. Anyway, I promised you a short note. Suffice it to say that Brother Runoko is on an adventure of a lifetime! I am having a learning experience that words cannot adequately express. Plus, I had some absolutely wonderful African food tonight, and tomorrow I am going to see Gaborone and its environs in the full light of day.

In Gabarone

This is my first full day in Botswana. I have a hotel room right in the center of Gaborone, a city of about 250,000 people. Today is Sunday, and the day is fairly quiet—everywhere, apparently, but the Internet cafe where I am writing this!

The hotel is quiet also. There seem to be only a handful of people here. I had some difficulty checking in, but after that, things have just gotten better and better. I had dinner in the hotel restaurant and happily let the waitresses laugh at my ignorance of the local languages. I laughed too, as I had never heard of most of the items on the menu and mispronounced practically everything.

The people are very friendly here, with one or two exceptions. One of the exceptions was a young sister whom I stopped and asked about the location of an Internet cafe. Apparently, she thought that I was asking her about something else and gave me a not-so-kind look before she turned and walked away! But for the most part, it is almost like being in a small country town in the southern part of the United States.

I have a nice room with good television reception. When I woke up, the Denzel Washington version of the movie, "The Manchurian Candidate," was on my TV screen. I had almost forgotten what a good actor he is!

Today I went, as you might expect, to the national museum, a bit of a ritual for me. The one in Gaborone was very good, and I got a lot of information on the colonial history of Botswana. I had a nice chat with a brother from northern Botswana, who was in charge of the museum. He gave me a lot of useful data about Botswana's history and culture.

After my museum visit, I went to Tsholofelo Park and the El Negro Cemetery. I had not heard of it until the brother from the museum alerted me to it. El Negro is the name given to remains of the San man (Bushman) kept on display in a Spanish museum until just a few years ago. He was originally from Botswana and somehow ended up in Europe more than 150 years ago. I guess you could say that he is the Botswana version of the much more famous Nama woman from South Africa: Sartjie Baartman, known as "the Hottentot Venus," whose remains were returned to South Africa upon the intervention of Nelson Mandela. El Negro now has a special place of honor in the center of the park. I took a number of photos of him.

I have been trying to walk a lot here, and as I walk, I carefully watch the world around me. This morning, I passed by a large church, relishing the beautiful sounds that came forth from it. A bunch of delightful children were playing near the church. I took photos of them as well, and they all wanted to know when they were going to get their copies!

The church was a very large and modern building and it seemed full. I suppose that the promises of prosperity and eternal salvation are as alluring here as anywhere else, just like in Ghana and South Africa, to name just a couple of countries. American televangelists are also very prominent here.

I notice quite a few Asians here, both South Asians from Pakistan and apparently India, as well—and East Asians too (I think Chinese). I ate lunch in a Pakistani restaurant and had a very pleasant chat with the owner about the shape to come of Asia and Africa, and I also managed to have a discussion with a prominent political activist here. So today was a pretty quiet day, but a good day nevertheless.

Last week, I got some flack via the Internet from a brother who seemed upset that I wasn't going to Zimbabwe on this trip to southern Africa. I had to remind him that I went to Zimbabwe in May and June 2000 at the invitation of my brother Sabelo Sibanda, one of our greatest Pan-Africanists. I stayed with Sabelo's parents, and everybody treated me royally. And thanks to Brother Sabelo, I was able to visit some of the farms reclaimed from the White settlers and even got to talk to some of the war veterans.

Runoko Rashidi

I have nothing but respect for the people of Zimbabwe and their efforts to reclaim Africa for the Africans—I want to go on record on that! Indeed, expect to get news from me in the very near future about the upcoming eighth Pan-African Congress due to be held in Harare, Zimbabwe, probably in October 2007.

Okay, Africans, enough for now. I don't want to wear you out, as you will be getting plenty of these notes from me as I travel around Africa and Europe (mostly Africa) for the next few months. Now I am going to do a little more walking and watching. The weather is bright and sunny in the daytime, with crystal blue skies. At night it gets a little cool. Tomorrow I am scheduled to visit a local village or two.

P.S.: Much appreciation to Asa Hilliard (Nana Baffour) for circulating these travel notes. With Asa on your side, how can anybody go wrong? Thanks, Nana!

FROM BOTSWANA TO THE KINGDOM OF LESOTHO

"Africa is the richest place with the poorest race/Oh my, oh my, what a disgrace!" (Jamaican songwriter/singer Peter Tosh, from the lyrics to "Not Gonna Give It Up," from the album, Mama Africa, 1983)

May 2006

When last you heard from me I was in Gaborone, Botswana, with one more day left on my schedule there. On that day, I went to the village of Mochudi, only about forty or fifty kilometers from Gaborone. I hired a local driver and car and spent almost half a day there. I found it to be a very interesting place with an interesting museum.

After Mochudi, I returned to the El Negro Cemetery in Gaborone. Remember what I told you about El Negro? Well, I got a bit more information about him. He actually died in southern Africa, and then his body was taken to Europe, where he was put on display. The body was sold round and round before he was finally returned to the Motherland just a few years ago. He is called El Negro because he was kept in a Spanish museum for a very long time.

Botswana is a beautiful place and rather like Namibia. It is sparsely populated, with wide-open spaces and a few mountains. Most of the people are polite and friendly, if a bit reserved.

I knew that it was time to leave when the hotel started to wear me down. Mind you now, this hotel was not cheap, but with the exception of the hotel manager and the waitresses in the hotel restaurant, the service was quite uneven and the basic amenities left something to be desired. The phone seemed to work when it wanted to, and it seemed like somebody always needed to check on something in my room.

The hotel was being refurbished, so there was also a constant pounding as the work was being done. And then the toilet seat broke apart! So it did not bother me that I quickly made up my mind to leave, but even that was not easy as the shuttle service was thirty minutes late getting to the airport! I would love to go back to Botswana, but to a different hotel and a different place!

In Lesotho

Now I am in the Kingdom of Lesotho (pronounced "Le-soo-too") Maseru is the capital, which is where I am now, sitting in an Internet cafe owned, I think, by Koreans. Lesotho is a rather small country about the size of Belgium in Europe. It is highly mountainous, and a lot of people come here to ski. Lesotho is encompassed by South Africa on all four sides. Most of its people are members of the Basotho ethnic group.

Lesotho makes country number sixty-five for me. That is a bit of a personal milestone, as my goal for the last several years has been to travel to sixty-five different countries. With my lecture in Johannesburg next week, I will be at lecture number thirty-five. I should hit number forty a little later this year. And the best part is that I am still only fifty-one years old and still have some gas in the tank! So who knows? I figure I can now travel to at least eighty countries. If the Ancestors continue to bless me, I might even hit one hundred!

I hope that Rogers and Langston Hughes and Chancellor Williams and John Henrik Clarke and all the other Great Ones are proud. I do believe that they watch over me and make it all possible.

I have to say that Lesotho is one of most unusual places that I have ever visited. First of all, it is very cold here, by far the coldest I have ever experienced in Africa. This morning, even at nine o'clock in the morning, there was a heavy fog, and steam issued forth with every breath.

The currency here is the maloti. In Botswana, it was the pula, which means "rain." In Namibia, it was the dollar; and in South Africa, it is the rand.

The people are extremely friendly but kind of—it is difficult to put into words—aggressive (?). They seem to love to talk and are very personable, kind of like being with family. I never felt anything quite like it. It started at the airport, continued at the hotel, the bar, the restaurant, on the streets, and everywhere. I have this full beard of almost all-white hair, and the people here call me "Brother" and "Uncle" and even "Daddy"! I just smile and chat a little with all I meet.

The down side of Lesotho is the tremendous poverty. It is almost overwhelming. And the specter of HIV/AIDS is everywhere. I've talked to people who have lost mothers and fathers and uncles and aunties and nieces and nephews and brothers and sisters and sons and daughters. In Botswana, the rate of infection is one in four persons. It was about the same in Namibia and only a bit less in South Africa, but on the rise. Here in Lesotho it is also about one in four. In my next destination, Swaziland, it is one in three.

Imagine that, sisters and brothers. One-third of all of the people in an entire country infected with the AIDS virus! It is really tough to take emotionally, and I confess to you that I, Runoko Rashidi, international traveler, who has seen so much is really on edge about it. Me, a grown man and something of a tough guy (or so I think!), I feel as if I could just break down and cry at any moment! I also feel like just reaching into my pocket and giving every last cent I have to those who are suffering here. But such is life in southern Africa.

Runoko Rashidi

I am staying in African-managed hotels, and my emotions must be showing because when I came back to my room yesterday afternoon someone had opened up a Bible to the book of Job and left it on my desk! The people here are really sweet! I guess I was supposed to get encouragement from reading about Job's trials and tribulations.

Today I go into the mountains. Hope I won't crack again, but I definitely feel it coming on. I felt the same way on my 2004 trip to northern Ethiopia. It just kills me to see all these wonderful African people afflicted with so many ills in the land of the plenty and the birthplace of humanity and civilization. What are we going to do?

Thanks so much for all the encouraging e-mails. I got some really nice ones from Vera and Wade Nobles. God keep me strong!

Evening Notes

When last you heard from me, early this morning, I was down and depressed and even teary-eyed. But right now, this moment, it is as though I have been transformed! I have fallen deeply in love with Lesotho! Despite the poverty, despite the AIDS, it is a wonderful place, and I just love it!

The people here are so warm and friendly, and today I was with two of the best. When I got to Maseru yesterday, I was in a grouchy mood. Naturally, my luggage did not arrive with me. This is getting to be almost routine for me now, but it still does not go down well. The shuttle driver said that he well understood my plight and that it happened all the time, so he proceeded to give me a running narrative of the past and present of Lesotho to console me as we drove from the airport to the city.

I was booked at a fairly expensive, resort-like hotel, and I asked the brother if there was something less costly and more centrally located. He took me to a place called Lancer's Inn. He told me that it was a popular spot, but he was not sure if a room was available. Fortunately, they found a place for me. It took a little while for them to organize my room, and while I was waiting, a Lesotho brother emerged from the hotel bar and told me that my twin brother was just inside! He beckoned me in and, sure enough, a pretty good duplicate of Runoko Rashidi was sitting at the bar having a brew!

I conversed with my twin for a good little while, and afterward the shuttle driver took me to exchange some money, saving me the hassle of standing in line at the bank. By that time, the driver had informed me that he also served a tour guide. When I asked him if he could arrange heritage/cultural tours for me while I was in Lesotho he told me that he was all booked up but he could suggest someone else. He referred me to Sematsatsa Tours. I called Sematsatsa and spoke to the boss, Masebina Claudia Kao, who assured me that she would have someone come by the hotel later that afternoon.

Later that day, I went out to check my e-mail. When I got back to the hotel, a young and very shy sister was waiting for me in the reception area. She told me that her name was Matsiu Diseko. We hit it off immediately, and she gave me some tour suggestions and prices. As we were talking, my luggage arrived at the hotel. Suddenly things were looking up!

The next morning, after eating my breakfast, which was served by some very nice Africans, and sending my e-mail to you, my tour of Lesotho began.

Lesotho is a beautiful country, and I got to see a lot of it today. The highlight was a climb up a steep mountain, on top of which is the grave of King Moshoeshoe the Great. This is an African who "stomped" on the Boers during the nineteenth century. It was wonderful just to learn about an African who beat on White folks and was never defeated. Indeed, he lived almost a hundred years.

But let me tell you, sisters and brothers, getting to Moshoeshoe's mountain gravesite was a real challenge! The site is located more than five kilometers up a steep and rocky incline and despite my best efforts I did not quite make it. But it was a lot of fun trying, and my guide, an elderly Basotho woman, and sister Matsiu and I laughed our heads off as we huffed and puffed up the hill. I probably could have made it, but I quite possibly would have ended up in a grave beside Moshoeshoe the Great! Too many beers and cigarettes and a somewhat wayward youth stood in the way. When I finally got back down to the bottom of the hill, we all laughed for a long, long time.

To be honest with you, the more I think about it, I really doubt that many people even make it to the top of Moshoeshoe's mountain. Maybe it was all just a big joke on me. If so, I took it in stride, gave my elderly guide a big tip, and took a lot of photos. And then we laughed some more.

I love the people here. I love to listen to them talk, and I love to listen them to laugh—and it is so easy to laugh right along with them. It's funny: this morning, I was ready to cry, but this afternoon I laughed more than I can remember! What a contrast! Africa can do that to you.

Tomorrow, I plan to take another cultural/heritage tour to see other parts of this country, but I'm not climbing any more mountains, at least not tomorrow!

Sisters and brothers, I love African people. I love to be around Africans, to look at Africans, to spend my money with Africans. Indeed, the reason I became a historian in the first place, those many years ago, was to help uplift African people. That is not to say that I hate other people, but charity starts at home, and I am an unapologetic Race Man.

Speaking of Race Men, in my earlier note from this morning, when I was mentioning some of the African scholars and writers I am attempting to emulate, I somehow managed to leave out one of the greatest of them all: Dr. Yosef A. A. ben-Jochannan. What a blunder! What could I have been thinking about? It was with Dr. Ben that I went with on my first trip to Africa in the early 1990s. So Dr. Ben, a thousand pardons. You are one of the best!

So that is it, African people. I am now on a natural high. How long it will last, I am not sure. But in the Kingdom of Lesotho, I am loving every minute of it!

Runoko Rashidi

A QUICK NOTE FROM SWAZILAND: THIS FEELS LIKE HOME!

June 2, 2006

Yesterday, my last day in Lesotho, I traveled to some other communities outside Maseru, but I did not climb or attempt to climb any mountains! Instead, I visited another museum and enjoyed myself tremendously. I also took what I think are going to be some excellent photos.

I arrived today, safe and sound, in the city of Manzini, Swaziland. It is the biggest city in the country. It is very warm here, with lots of haze. Of all the places that I have been, this one most reminds me of an African American inner-city community. If I didn't know better, I would think that I was in South-Side Chicago! The folks here look and act just like African Americans! I mean, the resemblance is uncanny, but most are Swazi or Zulu. Their official language is Swati, with English as a secondary language.

The more I travel in Africa, I find that I have acquired a bit more of the spirit of the adventurer, and it manifests itself in various ways. I don't worry quite as much about things that used to frustrate me to no end before. For example, if I can't book a hotel at my destination in advance, I simply find an African driver at the airport and go out to search for a place. I also try to be more "at one" with the people in the African cities and countries I visit. I have opened up a bit, and it helps big time.

Today, naturally, I went to the National Museum of Swaziland and also did a quick tour of Mbabane, the nation's capital. I saw the king's palace, went to the city of Lobamba, and drove through the Royal Valley of Ezulwini.

There are a lot of Africans here from Mozambique, which is where I intend to travel to tomorrow—specifically, to Maputo, the capital of Mozambique. I am not going to fly there or hire a driver. Instead, I am going by mini-bus. Mozambique was not originally on my schedule, but neither was Lesotho. Indeed, I have changed my schedule about five times now.

When I arrive in Mozambique tomorrow, I will be able to say with confidence that I have visited every country in southern Africa. And Johannesburg is looking good too; I'm scheduled to do my first lecture in South Africa there next week at an African-owned bookstore. I will post you the details directly, in case you can attend.

So, not much else to report today, folks. I am a little tired and have somehow managed to catch a slight head cold. I guess five countries in less than two weeks can wear just about anybody down.

At some point I am going to compile all of these southern African travel notes together into one large essay, and eventually all the essays from everywhere into a large volume. It should make for interesting reading, so you better reserve your copy now.

Be strong and stand firm, esteemed Africans. My next note should be coming to you from Maputo, Mozambique. Keep a positive thought for a brother!

MINI-BUS TO MOZAMBIQUE

"You are not an African because you are born in Africa. You are an African because Africa is born in you." (Dr. Marimba Ani)

June 3, 2006

Right now, I am supposed to be on a mini-bus to Mozambique, but it just did not work out. Maybe I will go tomorrow, but apparently today was simply not the day. Here is the story…

Yesterday was a rather quiet day. I got up early, paid my hotel bill at the Lancer's Inn in Maseru, Lesotho, and caught a shuttle to the airport for my flight to Johannesburg, South Africa, and then to Manzini, Swaziland. On the way to the airport, the shuttle stopped at another hotel. A young sister got on-board. When I heard her accent, I asked her where she was from and she told me Washington, D.C. She said she was working in Pretoria, South Africa, with some kind of AIDS-related program and had just completed an assignment in Lesotho.

As luck would have it, the sister and I were booked on the same flight, and we had an animated conversation about travel all the way to Johannesburg, where we parted ways. One of the things that she mentioned to me was that she had lived for a while in Java, Indonesia, not far from the epicenter of the recent earthquake. I don't know if you have seen the images of the people there on television, but they are clearly Africoid—just as Africoid, or so it would appear, as the people in East Timor, who are also going through turbulent times. I don't know how many of us in the States are talking about these two regions, but here in southern Africa they are two of the dominant news stories, along with news of the turmoil in Somalia.

I had an almost four-hour layover between flights in Johannesburg. The airport there is very attractive, nicer than Heathrow Airport in London and just as nice as Schipol Airport in Amsterdam. I was able to check my e-mail and read my Lonely Planet: Southern Africa travel book. Thumbing through it, I read that Swaziland shares a common border with Mozambique. It was then and there that I decided I would cross that border and go there.

The hotel where I had planned to stay in Manzini turned out to be something of a dump. It was isolated and forlorn-looking, so I asked my taxi driver to take me to a better one. So here I am, at a four-star hotel with a very friendly, all-African staff. I thought I owed myself a treat.

When I mentioned, at the front desk while I was checking in, that I wanted to go to Mozambique, this same friendly staff made it a high priority to help me arrange my trip. It all seemed set, and then it started to unravel.

I was told to get to the mini-bus station as early as possible, and before six o'clock this morning, I was on my way down there. The station was located in the parking lot right in front of a KFC. Yes, Kentucky Fried Chicken is big down here! In fact, I have seen KFC's in every African city I have been to so far. They have even gotten a dollar or two of my money.

Anyway, one of the friendly hotel staff members walked down to the station with me. I gave him a big tip and thought that he was going to wait with me until the bus came. Instead, he introduced me to the other two people, a sister and a brother, who were waiting there and went back to the hotel with my tip in his pocket.

Then it started to rain. I had not seen rain in southern Africa since my first couple of days in Cape Town about two weeks ago, and I was not prepared for it. To make matters worse, the sister and brother who were supposed to watch over me left without a word or a look back in my direction.

Okay, so I am a tough guy, I thought, and I am one with the people. But right then, there were no people for me to be one with, and I was standing in the dark in the rain—a stranger in a strange land, with luggage in my hand, in an empty parking lot in front of a Swaziland KFC.

Remember I wrote in a previous note that I had stopped worrying so much about my travel details? Yeah, right! I guess I stopped for about thirty minutes! It was 6:30 a.m., and no mini-bus had as yet arrived. It was getting light. A lot of people started to gather in the parking lot around me, and they brought all kind of things with them.

One person brought six chairs. Another had a car battery. Another had a large mattress for a large bed. Another had a big iron frame, presumably from a window. Another had a car-load of empty paper bags. Eventually, the whole parking lot was filled with people, all except the two people who were supposed to be looking out for me!

By 6:45 a.m., still no mini-bus. I started regretting more and more that I had given the brother from the hotel such a big tip!

A White guy from Australia arrived and immediately became the center of attention. But at least he spoke English. I asked him about the mini-bus situation and he told me that it ran on an irregular basis and that I should not worry about it. Nor should I worry, he said, about not having a visa or local currency or limited Portuguese or a hotel reservation or how crowded the mini-bus might be or where all of the assembled luggage and other odd items the folks in the parking lot had brought with them was going to go. So, naturally, I began to worry all the more.

By 7:00 a.m., still no mini-bus. The mini-bus company's representative, a Swazi man, finally came around and collected everyone's passports. He too told me not to worry. At least the rain had stopped by then. Another African brother came around with a lot of local currency to exchange, but he could not tell me the rate of exchange with U.S. dollars. He too said not to worry.

Finally, the mini-bus came, but it had a flat tire and was very low on gas. Again, I was told not to worry; the mini-bus would soon get another tire, get some gas, and be ready to go. By that time, however, it seemed as if the entire population of both Swaziland and Mozambique together was waiting in the KFC parking lot! Then it started to rain again.

At 7:45 a.m., something came over me and an inner voice whispered in my ear: "Runoko, collect your passport. Pick up your luggage. Go back to the hotel. Have a nice breakfast and relax. And don't worry."

The voice was very clear. And so, that is what I did, and that is where I am right now as I write this note to you. Tomorrow, I realize, is another day, and the mini-bus will be running again tomorrow. Maybe I will catch that one, maybe not. Today, I am just going to relax and listen to that inner voice. And try not to worry.

My Global Journeys in Search of the African Presence

P.S.: I have gotten quite a few responses to and a number of questions about my southern African travel notes. I even got a racist one from a European in Namibia who maintained that he was an African and I was not. (I responded with some pointed comments about his mother!) And then I thought, how childish it was to let that idiot annoy me enough to even take the time to respond. Some things are better left ignored.

In another e-mail, a sister from the States wanted to know more about what I called "the uncanny resemblance" between the Africans in Manzini and African Americans, especially those in South-Side Chicago. Well, this is what I meant: Manzini is crowded with people and cars, mini-malls and fast food places. African American music screams over the radios. As a matter of fact, the first song I heard when I got here was not traditional Swazi or Zulu music but Teddy Pendergrass' "I Don't Love You Anymore"!

I mean, the brothers and sisters over here even wear their hair and dress like Black folk in the U.S. They walk like we do and talk like we do and sound like we do. In many ways, they even act like we do! The cultural unity was stunning! If I had gotten out the taxi and walked on the sidewalk along with the Swazi sisters and brothers, I would have fit right in, and it would have felt as natural as breathing for me to be among them. Does that clarify it for you?

"CHILL TIME" IN SWAZILAND

June 5, 2006

I assume by now that you've read my "Mini-Bus to Mozambique" note, recounting my efforts to cross from Manzini to Maputo by mini-bus. The bottom line is: I never made to it to Mozambique. I tried, but I guess it was not meant to be. Even today, I tried to buy a plane ticket to Maputo but found that the cost was way too high. So for me, that's it, maybe next time!

So I just relaxed for an entire day. That doesn't happen to Brother Runoko very often. It seems I am always at work, even when resting. It did me a whole lot of good to chill out for a day. All I did was write a little, lounge around the hotel swimming pool, have a nice dinner, share laughs with the hotel staff, and watch movies and the French Open tennis tournament on TV. Indeed, the day was so pleasant that I have pretty much decided that on every significant trip I take from now on, I am going to set aside at least one day for leisure.

It helps to recharge the batteries, don't you agree?

A Visit to the World's Oldest Mine

After giving myself the day off due to the mini-bus fiasco, the next day I took a trip to the oldest mine in the world. It is called the Lion's Cavern, and it is located high in the mountains that straddle the northern border between Swaziland and South Africa. High up on Ngwenya Mountain, named for its resemblance to a basking crocodile (or so the tour brochures say), it is the site of the first mining excavation in the world, dating back to 43,000 years B.C.E., when the San (believed to be southern Africa's earliest inhabitants) began extracting ochre and hematite (forms of iron oxide) from the earth.

I believe I first read about the Lion's Cavern over twenty years ago in Carter G. Woodson's Negro History Bulletin. And I'm pretty sure I saw it mentioned again in one of Dr. Charles S. Finch's excellent works on African science and technology. So when I saw mention of it in one of the travel brochures I found in the hotel where I was staying in Manzini, I jumped at the chance to see it firsthand, even when the clerk at the hotel's front desk quoted me what I knew was a steep price to get there. I was ready to pay the money regardless.

But then I thought about Brother Luma, the young Swazi taxi driver who had picked me up at the airport and helped me find my hotel two days before. Luma was polite, well-mannered, and punctual, but rather quiet. In short, he was the ideal taxi driver. And his prices were excellent! Indeed, when I called him and asked him if he could drive me to the Lion's Cavern, he quoted me a price that was less than half of what the hotel wanted. I told him to come on, and the deal was sealed.

So bright and early Sunday morning, away Brother Luma and I went. To get to the mine, we had to drive through the Ezulwini Valley——-the Valley of Heaven—the historic center of Swazi royalty. It was both beautiful and peaceful.

Along the way, we passed the king's palace. In Swaziland, the monarchy is balanced between the king and the queen mother. Historically, women in Swaziland seem to have enjoyed a much higher status than their counterparts in Lesotho.

On we drove, through and past Lobamba, where the national museum and parliament are located. In the distance were the twin peaks known as Sheba's Breasts, named after Makeda, the legendary Queen of Ethiopia, with whom King Solomon fell madly in love. And then on to Mbabane, Swaziland's administrative capital, set high in the mountains and founded in 1903. The most interesting thing about Mbabane on Sunday was all of the sisters and brothers promenading on their way to church. Swaziland is largely a Christian country, and it was a sheer delight to see men, women, and children decked out in their Sunday finest on their way to fellowship and praise Jesus.

Up Mount Ngwenya we went. At the base of the mountain on the way to the mine, we picked up a young African geologist and guide. We were the only ones on the mountain that day, so we had it all to ourselves. The young brother took Luma and me on a personally guided tour. When I told him that I was an African historian from the United States, he seemed duly impressed and went on to tell us how important it was for those of us from the U.S. to come back to Africa to see what our Ancestors had done. He told us a particularly poignant story of an African American couple who insisted on being taken into the Lion's Cavern, where they broke down and cried with great emotion. I didn't cry, but I certainly had a day that I will never forget.

My experience on this southern African journey has been incredible, and I have nothing but good things to say. So far, I have been to five countries in fifteen days. My next destination should cap it off most appropriately. Next stop on the tour: Johannesburg, South Africa!

JOURNEY TO JO'BURG AND THE TOWNSHIPS OF SOUTH AFRICA

June 6, 2006

I am on the last stop of my southern African journey. This Saturday, I return to Paris for a few days before taking off for Kenya and Uganda. It will be my first visit to East/Central Africa, and it promises to be exceptionally exciting and extremely educational. Right now, though, I am deep into my second day in Johannesburg, South Africa.

I flew here from Swaziland on South African Airways (SAA) yesterday morning. It was my eighth flight on SAA since I arrived in Cape Town in May. SAA is a great airline. They serve good food and drinks, and the flight attendants are excellent. They are courteous and professional and mostly African. All the flights I have taken with them have been on time. If there is anything to complain about, it is that the luggage sometimes gets misplaced and arrives late. Other than that, it has been smooth sailing all the way.

Perhaps the best thing about SAA is how easy it is to make changes. I have now, during the course of this trip, changed my flight schedule on at least five occasions and have yet to pay a penalty. On a U.S. carrier, I would have had to take out a bank loan if I made that many changes.

Johannesburg is, for me, a strange place. If I did not know better, I would not even think that I was in Africa! A lot of that, I think, has to do with my surroundings. I am staying in one of the northern suburbs of Johannesburg, a place called Victory Park, in an elegant, African-owned and -operated bed-and-breakfast called the Ackee Guest House. I like to recycle African dollars, so here I am.

The Ackee is owned by Folami Harris, a sister from Jamaica. I think of her as an artist, but she is a woman of many dimensions, including public health worker. It is a beautiful place, a large structure set on the side of a hill, and filled with all kinds of African art, paintings, sculpture, photos, and so forth. I have the largest room in the house, the Shamfa Room, complete with my own shower, toilet, and television set.

My favorite part of the house is the study. That is where the computer is located and where the major library is housed. Looking over the shelves and shelves of books, I see volumes by Langston Hughes, Zora Neale Hurston, Toni Cade Bambara, John G. Jackson, and Chancellor Williams, just to name a few.

One problem, however, is that the Victory Park neighborhood is so far away from the things that I thought that I came to see. It was not my intention to stay here, but the hotels in Johannesburg are so darned expensive! And the city is really spread out. I had to travel more than thirty-five kilometers from the airport to get here.

But here I am. Johannesburg is in the South African province of Gauteng, in northeast South Africa. Gauteng, in Sotho, means Place of Gold. Geographically, it is the smallest province in South Africa, but it has the largest population. More than ten million people live here, more of half of whom reside in Johannesburg. The other large city in Gauteng Province is Pretoria, the capital of South Africa.

Runoko Rashidi

It gets very cold here. Once the sun goes down, you'd better have a coat and a sweater. A cap and perhaps even a scarf wouldn't hurt, either. And there is no really effective public transportation in Johannesburg, so those who can afford them either have their own cars or rely extensively on taxis.

Johannesburg, even now, is a highly racially divided city. In Victory Park, where I am staying, it is mostly White. I initially wanted to stay in the city center, but everybody warned me away from it. People told me that I would be crazy to stay there. When I told them that I grew up in the inner cities of the United States, they still warned me that I would be an easy target and that I'd best use my head for more than a hat and find a better location. The reason is that in South Africa, in addition to (naturally) a lot of discussion about race and class, the real focus of the discourse is on crime. And I'm not just talking about pick-pocketing and cell phone snatching. I am talking about really violent crime: rapes, armed robberies, carjackings, muggings, and murders.

Johannesburg is really unlike any major city that I have ever been in, and I am not sure how much I like it here. Last night, though, I met the major facilitator of my program here. Her name is Palesa Mazamisa. One of her great-grandfathers was the founder of the African National Congress (ANC), the political party that is currently running South Africa.

Palesa is a journalist, serious but soft-spoken, and just a real good sister. She came to pick me up at Ackee's with another sister, Rochelle Spadoni, and together, over Ethiopian food, they told me everything there was to know about South Africa in general and Johannesburg in particular. We talked about the ANC government, opposition parties, class struggle, violent crime, where to go and where not to go, violence against women (particularly the high incidence of rape), HIV/AIDS, the economy, White racism, the Boers, corruption, and the future of Africa. I got a real education.

Other than dinner last night and a nice discussion with Sister Folami early this evening, I have had a quiet experience in Johannesburg and have gotten a lot more rest than I wanted or anticipated. There is only one other guest here, and he keeps pretty much to himself. Sister Folami is working on a report, so that just leaves old Runoko to his own devices.

All of that should change very soon, though, as tomorrow promises to be a very full and action-packed day. Tomorrow night, I give my first lecture in South Africa. I hope to speak before a packed house, and I plan to be in fine form. I have a lot to share, and I look forward to a good community response. The lecture will be followed by an evening of jazz music.

Tomorrow morning, however, I pay my first visit to the world-famous community of Soweto.

Soweto and Beyond (June 9, 2006)

Soweto (an acronym for South West Township) became famous during the 1976 Soweto Uprising, when the South African Black Consciousness Movement was centered here. It may sound crazy to you, but I found Soweto to be a fascinating and friendly place. In the last two days, I have done two big lectures, one at an African-owned bookstore and the other at an African-owned restaurant. I had an evening of jazz and some very good and healthy food. I have also done two major radio interviews and visited two major museums: the Hector Peterson Memorial Museum and the Apartheid Museum.

The museums brought both tears and anger. At the Apartheid Museum, I cried for all of those Africans who suffered through that evil system. I saw replicas of the tiny jail cells in which the African freedom fighters were kept I saw the ropes that were used to hang them and the guns that were used to shoot them. I saw great photos of freedom fighters Steven Biko, Chris Hani, Walter Sisulu, Oliver Tambo, and Winnie and Nelson Mandela. I also saw images of the architects of apartheid—racist bastards like Jan Smuts, Hendrick Verwoerd, John Vorster, and P. W. Botha—and wished a plague on all their kind.

I drove by Bishop Desmond Tutu's and Winnie Mandela's houses. I went inside Nelson Mandela's old house, where the most interesting article, for me, was the championship belt that boxer Sugar Ray Leonard gave to Mr. Mandela, himself a former boxer.

I also traveled to the countryside to explore the Sterkfontein and Cradle of Humankind World Heritage cave sites. The Sterkfontein Cave is the home to some of the world's earliest proto-human fossils. One is called "Little Foot"; another is named "Mrs. Ples." Both are more than three million years old. Together, they reflect and reinforce Africa's role as the birthplace and cradle of humanity.

I don't believe I have ever been so far beneath the surface of the earth! The bottom of the Sterkfontein Cave has to be at least two hundred meters down. I had to crawl, crouch, and slide to get into some parts of it, and I emerged covered in red dust. The Cradle of Humankind is where the casts of fossilized early hominid remains and, in some cases, the actual fossils are kept on display.

My Soweto lectures were good ones. Both venues were standing-room-only. I didn't do slide presentations like I normally do. Instead, I just talked about all the research I have been doing these past thirty-plus years. I talked about the Nile Valley and about Africans in Arabia, Iraq, India, China, Southeast Asia, Australia, the Pacific, Europe, and the ancient Americas. I also talked about the trans-Atlantic slave trade.

My audiences were riveted, and there were extensive discussion periods afterward. I must have addressed fifty questions after both lectures, all of them interesting. Questions like: Did I think there would ever be an African American president? Is it better to use the word "Black" or "African"? Did I believe that only Black people could be Africans? How can African Americans help Africa? What does it mean to be successful? What did I think of the Hebrew Israelites? Why do I love Africa so much? And on and on and on. Believe me when I say that we had some lively exchanges!

The radio interviews were just as lively as the lectures and post-lecture discussions. They were for some of the big radio stations in South Africa that are listened to by Africans, Indians, and Whites. When the hosts asked me about my positions on global African unity, I responded and the phone lines lit up!

The first caller was a White man who complained about what a "racist" I was and how offended he was by my comments. He also said that he was an African, and that I was not. Boy, did I let him have it! First, I informed him that I was the African, not he. As I explained it, you can teach a parrot to speak but, in the end, it's still a bird. Likewise, I said, you can dress a monkey in a suit but, in the end, it's still an ape. I told him that his ancestors came to Africa uninvited, without passport or visa, stole the land, near-exterminated whole groups of people, and enslaved and colonized the rest. How, I asked him, could he be an African?

Runoko Rashidi

I continued: I told him that his pedigree was European, his history was European, his lineage was European, and his culture was European—so, logically, he must be a European! I guess you could say that I effectively silenced him because every other call that I received—on both programs, from Africans and Europeans alike—was extremely favorable about that exchange! Brothers and sisters, you would have been proud!

So now I'm tired and getting ready to leave South Africa. I think I'm ready to go, or maybe I just know that I am scheduled to go and have accepted the fact.

I did not do everything that I would have like to have done on this trip. I never made it to Mozambique, for example, and in retrospect, I should have scheduled a trip to Durban, South Africa's busy port city. I should also have visited Mapungubwe near the northern border between South Africa and Zimbabwe, where I just found evidence of what is, for me, a new African civilization.

No, I did not do everything I wanted to, but I did a great deal, even more than I thought that I would. I made a lot of new friends and contacts, and I am really glad that I made this trip. I also spent a lot of money! And the folks here are already making plans for me to come back later this year or next.

In other words, it was another trip of a lifetime for me, but now it's time to go. So tonight, just before midnight, I board a flight to Amsterdam and then to Paris. I get to spend four wonderful days with my family, get in a little administrative work, rest up, and get ready for Kenya and Uganda next week.

I would like to end this series of e-mails from southern Africa by thanking everyone, here and there, who helped make this trip such a success. Thanks for the contacts, for the encouragement, for spreading the word. I could not have done it without you!

NAIROBI, NAIROBI

June 16, 2006

I am now in the middle of my second day in Nairobi, Kenya. Nairobi is the capital of Kenya and the largest city between Cairo and Johannesburg. I do not know the official population statistics, but I suspect that Lagos, Nigeria, on the west coast of Africa, may be larger than Nairobi. I suppose that I will find out for sure next year because I have every intention of visiting Nigeria sometime in 2007.

Sisters and brothers, I love to write glowing reports about my travel experiences, particularly those to the African Motherland. But so far, this has been one of the most disappointing and frustrating trips I have ever experienced. And it started off on such a promising note.

It seems like a long time ago now, but two days ago, I flew from Paris to Amsterdam, and then from Amsterdam direct to Nairobi. The Amsterdam/Nairobi leg of the trip was on Kenya Airways. I had been hearing good things about this airline for a while before, and my flight with them confirmed all those good things.

First, the flight left on time. Then, the flight crew was very professional. I don't know about the pilots, but all the flight attendants that I saw were African. The seats were comfortable, the meals were good, everything was clean, and I had no complaints. (I can say the same thing for South African Airways and Ethiopia Airways.)

My plane landed at Jomo Kenyatta International Airport, the major airport in Nairobi and in all of Kenya, for that matter. I already had my visa, so going through passport control and customs was simple and easy. My luggage came immediately. I exchanged a little U.S. currency for Kenyan shillings, and that was that. I had arrived.

In the course of my international travels, I have found that perhaps the most important travel necessity—second, probably, to having enough funds to make the trip both possible and enjoyable—is having reliable contacts waiting for you on the ground. This can mean having either a good travel agent or other folks on the ready and waiting to show you the ins and outs of the particular part of the world in which you happen to find yourself. I had attended to these details beforehand, so I was not worried about Kenya.

However, I did not have a travel agent when I arrived in Nairobi. I didn't think I would need one. What I did have was a sister who had worked with our Ancestor, the late Afrikan-centered scholar, traveler, and activist Nana Ekow Butweiku I, on his "Nubian Agenda" program. She was supposed to be waiting for me at the airport, and indeed, she was. She even had a sign in her hands with my name on it. But it became apparent almost from the time that we met that her primary interest lay in what I had in my wallet and how much from it I was willing to spend.

According to the sister, anything and any destination was possible in Kenya—Mombasa, Mount Kenya, Mount Kilimanjaro, anywhere. It could all be arranged, she said. But when I told her that I would not need her services or the driver's all day every day, her mood changed dramatically. Apparently, she was expecting some kind of commission from the car company she had hired. I suppose she had led them to believe that she had hold of some foolish American with tons of money to spend.

Well, needless to say, I soon parted company with her. So much for my reliable contacts! I would rather be alone than to be played for a fool. Not that I thought my guide was a bad person, I just think she saw an opportunity in me and was prepared to cast aside her integrity to take advantage of it.

But that was just the first blow. Today, mighty Africans, I was supposed to present a big lecture at the University of Nairobi. I had been anticipating it for weeks, but the lecture did not take place. I went to the University yesterday afternoon to check everything out. The slide projector was being secured and the lecture hall had been reserved. I even met the young professor who was supposed to coordinate it all. I went to bed feeling confident and got a good night's rest.

I went to the university building where the lecture was to have been held ninety minutes ahead of schedule. I went to the lecture hall and met the professor. For a long time, nothing happened. The slide projector never arrived and nobody showed up. The professor stood around in the hall trying, I suppose, to look professorial, but he did nothing else.

Runoko Rashidi

Five minutes before the lecture was supposed to begin, one of the organizers came up to me to tell me that the program had been cancelled. To be honest, I don't think the program was ever even advertised! In effect, I had wasted a whole two days of my time and had nothing to show for it. And then, to make matters worse, I was told that some people came to the lecture hall after the program had been canceled!

I was hopping mad and, for the first time in a long, long time, I really considered striking someone—I was just that angry! But no matter how upset I got, all the professor did was give me a stupid look, which made me all the more angry!

So much of this note is being written out of frustration. Although I must confess that some good things have happened here and I have met some very nice people. For example, a very friendly and smiling young sister, an employee in a nearby Internet cafe, directed me to the Kenya Airways office when everybody else told me that they did not know where it was. Then, the sister in the Kenya Airways office was so pleasant, courteous, and professional that I was really moved. Then, a brother in the Kenya Airways office gave me some very positive suggestions about what to do and what not to do in Nairobi. Best of all, these sisters and brothers shared their time and services without expecting anything in return. They just knew that I was a stranger and a brother, and they offered me some genuine African hospitality. The sister in the Kenya Airways office even refused the tip that I offered her. Her smiling response was a simple, "No, I don't deserve a tip. I was just doing my job."

By far, the most exciting thing that has happened to me in Nairobi was the meeting I had yesterday with some of the top leaders of the Sudanese People's Liberation Movement. Apparently, many of them frequent the hotel where I am staying The Sudanese brothers gave me tremendous insight into the struggles going on in the southern part of the Sudan as well as in the Darfur region. They told me that they were fighting for an independent Southern Sudan, and that they expected to achieve their aim within the next five years. They also seemed to be tremendous Pan-Africanists, and I enjoyed our conversations immensely.

So life here in Nairobi has been trying and frustrating at times, but it has not been all bad. Indeed, I am glad that I am writing this note because it is allowing me to let off some steam. I mean, isn't it better to write an angry letter than to go around thinking about hitting someone? Besides, sometimes when you hit people, they hit you back. And then where would I be?

Anyway, tomorrow is another day, sisters and brothers, and I am confident that it is going to be a good one somehow. I just don't believe that things happen without reason. Could it be that the Ancestors are teaching me a lesson in patience and how to deal with a bit of adversity? Or maybe this trip was designed to be a lesson in humility? Could it be that my head is getting too big with all of the recent successes I have been enjoying, and I needed to be brought back down to earth? Perhaps it is a lesson in giving people second chances. Maybe it is an instruction—sometimes, even the best people do bad things and make commitments they can't keep. I'm not really sure, but time usually tells.

And besides, I am still in the Africa that I love. I have my health and self-respect. I am still standing firm and, after all is said and done, life does go on even when we suffer setbacks.

Tomorrow morning, I am supposed to visit a Masai village. That should be a great experience. And believe me when I say that after yesterday and this afternoon, I think I am well overdue for a great experience!

A Visit with the Masai and Kariba

At this moment, I am not far from the large and beautiful Lake Victoria. My guide has told me that a fantastic program of sites and experiences is in store for me over the course of the coming week, and I could not be much happier!

I was not sorry to leave Nairobi yesterday, and that saddens me because Kenya has such a rich history and is such a beautiful country. But I met up with some not-so-good people in Nairobi, and the city just did not "fit" me well. I wish that I'd had better and more reliable local contacts. Nevertheless, I am extremely glad to have visited, and several positive things came out of my trip there.

The first of these was my visit with the Masai, a very fascinating group of people. To see them, I secured the services of a Luo elder named Peter, who has been giving tours in Kenya since 1957. Peter is seventy-two years old, and he likes to tell jokes about European tourists. As we traveled by car from Nairobi to the Ngong Hills, a distance of about fifty kilometers, he told me about the Mau Mau rebellion and Kenyan resistance to British colonial rule.

The countryside was beautiful and green, and I saw a lot of cattle and goats. The trip seemed a lot longer than fifty kilometers, however, because some of the roads were bumpy and unpaved. But Peter displayed a lot of wisdom and a great sense of humor, so the trip was both educational and enjoyable. Plus, we stopped a couple of times for gas, beer, and coca cola.

The Masai are a proud and distinguished people. In person, they look just like the images I have seen in so many books and on countless television programs. The women are very beautiful, and the men seem like real warriors. I was able to talk to a few of them, and I took what I hope will turn out to be some fine photos.

The first group of Masai that I met consisted of four young women, who looked like they were in their late teens or early twenties. They were clothed in traditional Masai attire and were trudging up a hill along the dry, dusty road to fetch water. Peter stopped the car and chatted with them for a few minutes. They were very friendly, but all the while, they were looking at me and giggling just a little. Peter told me they wanted to know what tribe I was from. The second group that I interacted with was a group of about five or six Masai women and young children. They too expressed excitement and a bit of disbelief at my presence, and they simply would not believe that I was from America.

Peter and the Masai spoke in Swahili. Apparently, everybody in that region of Kenya speaks and understands it. I was left to rely on Peter's translations. Through him, I spoke briefly with a number of individual Masai.

The last group I spoke with was a group of four elderly Masai women. To me, they seemed almost regally attired in their traditional Masai garb. They were sitting proudly in front of a small grocery shop, and they looked so much like a scene from a picture post-card that and so I asked Peter to stop the car so I could take their photo. Wisely, Peter informed me that it just wasn't done like that. He told me that we first had to stop and joke a little with them, then ask them about taking the photo. We would also have to tell them what we were willing to pay so that they could then decide about the matter.

I just smiled and said okay. All the cash I had with me was five hundred Kenyan shillings, and I offered it gladly. The eldest Masai woman took word of my offer to the others. They agreed, and I took my photos. I just hope they are good ones!

On our way back to my hotel from the Ngong Hills, we passed through the African community of Kariba, on the outskirts of Nairobi. At first, Peter pointed Kariba out to me from a distance and indicated that he was reluctant to go there. I had to offer to pay him extra just to drive through the town, even then, he insisted that we lock all of the vehicle doors before we got there.

Like Johannesburg and a bunch of other places, Nairobi has a bad reputation with regard to violent crime. When visiting such areas, however, I try to use good common sense and not allow myself to be overwhelmed by the negative crime statistics and perceptions. I want to see my people, but, unfortunately, many of us are trapped in impoverished communities, where we find ourselves doing a lot of bad things just to survive.

Hundreds of thousands of African people, many of them very poor, live in Kariba. The community reminded me a lot of the townships of Langa in Capetown, Katatura in Windhoek, and Soweto in Johannesburg. Still, I am glad that I have visited Kariba and those other communities. Yes, there is tremendous poverty in each, but there is also within them a vitality and resilience that cannot be denied, and which I admire a great deal.

The next morning, Peter drove me to a large area of Kikuyu communities outside Nairobi. To get there, we traveled through heavily forested areas that he told me Whites dared not venture through during the height of the Mau Mau rebellion.

This evening, I finally got the chance to give a lecture. The attendance was small, but at last I had my say! Thanks to the intervention of Sister Pamela Morris, I also was able to meet this evening with a couple of sisters from Nairobi's African American community. They were so pleasant and enthusiastic that it really helped to make up for my disappointing experience at the University of Nairobi.

One of the sisters is doing some very important work in the field of education. I left her with a bunch of clothes and pens and pencils that Sister Zawadi and I collected to donate to a Nairobi AIDS orphanage. The other sister was formerly a student of Dr. Ivan Van Sertima's when he was at Rutgers University, and she is very familiar with my work. Both sisters were kind to me and very supportive, and they gave me a lot of information about the Kenyan scene.

So, all in all, Kenya was a good experience, and I would like one day to return to see much more of it. Thank you so much, Sister Pamela!

THE TRIUMPH OF PAN-AFRICANISM IN UGANDA

June 28, 2006

I am tired, sisters and brothers and, I think, justifiably so. I just finished spending nine days in Uganda. That is the longest I have been in any one place since I can remember. And every one of those nine days was eventful!

Here is the recap: On Saturday, I lectured at the Pan-African Center in Kampala. About fifty Africans showed up, and I presented my lecture and slides and fielded an extensive question-and-answer session. It all went very well. The discussion period was most animated.

Saturday evening, after the lecture and as I was on my way to a fabulous Ethiopian restaurant, I picked up a copy of The Monitor, Uganda's largest daily newspaper. It featured an interview and photo of me. While reading the interview, I tried what was for me a new food item. Yes, for the first time in my life I ate a handful of grasshoppers! They weren't bad!

Sunday featured a quiet afternoon and an informal dinner at which I was the guest of honor. Some very distinguished Africans showed up, mostly business people, but also the Ugandan ambassador to Malaysia. The food at that event was good too, but no grasshoppers this time!

On Monday afternoon, I was the guest speaker at Makerere University. This was big! A lot of distinguished Pan-Africanists came, including a daughter of Sekou Toure, the late president of Guinea, and a Uganda Supreme Court justice. Altogether, almost two-hundred people were in attendance, including students from the university as well as local public and private schools.

For once during my Africa travels, the sound system, slide projector, and Brother Runoko worked in near-perfect precision and coordination. Many in the audience told me afterward that it was an historic occasion. I am pretty sure you would have been pleased too, sisters and brothers!

That evening, I did a slide presentation at an orphanage that served mostly poor children whose parents had died of AIDS, located in one of the most impoverished slums in Kampala. It was a very moving experience. I tried to treat those children with the same, if not greater, level of respect and dignity that I accorded the audience at the university earlier in the day.

The next afternoon, I toured the Ugandan national museum for the second time. I also returned to the historic Kusubi Tombs, where the katakas (kings) of Buganda are honored, and revisited Lake Nyanza (colonial name: Lake Victoria). And I saw another man of the BaKongo group—another one of those fascinating and diminutive African populations commonly called Pygmies. I thought that these short-statured African people were the same as the other so-called Pygmies I was familiar with, but I was wrong. The "real" Pygmies are called Batwa, and they are even shorter than the Bakongo. I expect to visit with them when I return to Uganda next year.

Yes, I am coming back for more. Indeed, come next spring I expect to revisit Uganda and make my initial visits to Rwanda, Burundi, South Sudan, Tanzania, and the Democratic Republic of the Congo. The plans are already being made, and Uganda will be my base.

Runoko Rashidi

Over the past several months I have traveled virtually constantly, and have had a number of victories, including big lectures in Berlin, London, Paris, Salvador (in Bahia, Brazil), Johannesburg, Windhoek, and several venues in the United States, just to name a few. But I can honestly say that nowhere I have been have I found the spirit of Pan-Africanism more alive and vibrant than in Uganda. Perhaps not since my early travels to India and my encounters with the Dalits and Tribals have I felt such a surge of energy, enthusiasm, and African solidarity.[7] It was a rare, wonderful, spiritual, and revitalizing experience.

So now, I catch a plane and head back to Europe for two whole nights. Friday, I return to Morocco and then head to Spain in search of the Moors!

MORE EXPLORING IN THE MUSEUMS OF EGYPT

August 2, 2006

Things are looking pretty good here in this part of Africa, and I am feeling fine. I have been in Egypt since July 20 and have traveled from Aswan to Alexandria. I have not been ill for a single hour, nor have I been overwhelmed by the intense heat. It has been a very full trip for me. I have given six major presentations and a lot of small ones, seen dozens of colossal statues, visited five pyramids, toured two huge worship temples and several smaller ones, walked through three large mortuary temples, entered at least eight major tomb chambers, and wandered through at least six significant museums.

Those of you who know me realize that I am something of a museum fanatic. I love museums! Indeed, I believe that a big part of the reparations struggle has to include the reclamation of stolen African artifacts, wherever they may be. So that is what I want to concentrate on in today's e-mail: the museums of Egypt.

The Coptic Museum

The Coptic Museum is located in New Cairo and is not far from the Egyptian Museum. Not many African American tourists visit the Coptic Museum. Indeed, until my first visit in March 2001, I had not heard of it.

On that visit, I found a painting that I call "The Coptic Christ" or "Christ in Glory." I was struck by the painting and quickly identified it as the earliest known depiction of Jesus the Christ in the world. It features an image of Jesus emerging from his tomb after the Crucifixion. He has black skin and a large and prominent Afro hairstyle. He is surrounded by all of his disciples minus Judas, and they are likewise depicted with black skin and African hairstyles. Thomas ("Doubting Thomas") stands closest to Jesus and points to the wound in Jesus' side. It is a remarkable painting.

---

7   I discuss these experiences later in Part II of this book, entitled "Travels in Asia: East, South, Southeast, and Southwest."

I have spent much of the last five years trying to return to the museum. It was closed for at least three years after my 2001 visit, so I was more than pleased to find it open when I returned to Egypt a couple of weeks ago. Alas, however, the painting of Jesus and his disciples hanging there appears altered. Their images have been "whitened up"—their skin color is considerably lighter, their hair is straighter, and their noses seem longer!

The Egyptian Museum in Cairo

Simply put, the Egyptian Museum in Cairo is the largest repository of Egyptian art under one roof in the world. It is an old museum—hot, crowded, and the artifacts are poorly labeled. But it is just magnificent and has something for everybody. It has colossal statues, hundreds of papyri and canopic jars, tons of figurines modeling all aspects of Ancient Egyptian life, massive stone and wooden coffins, mummified human and animal remains, African wigs, and just about everything that you can think of. If you ever go to Egypt, don't miss this museum. In 2011, it is supposed to be relocated to a new site near the Giza Plateau.

The Luxor Museum

This is my favorite museum in my favorite city in Egypt. Not nearly as big as the Egyptian Museum in Cairo, it is well lit and the artifacts are nicely spaced. I have fallen in love with about six or seven pieces here, including a jet black image of the god Amen; wonderful pink granite busts of Senusret III and Amenhotep III; an incredible statue of Senusret I; a nice standing statue of Mentuhotep III and a exquisite seated statue of Amenhotep, son of Hapu.

The Nubian Museum in Aswan

This new museum is located in Aswan, the capital of Nubia. I met the manager and one of the curators during my visit there last week. The museum has a very good collection covering the history of Nubia from ancient to modern times. It includes marvelous stone heads of Twenty-Fifth Dynasty monarchs Shabaka and Taharka, and several stone statues of Egyptian governors of Nubia from the Middle Kingdom. It is a large museum in a very nice-looking building, and its staff is very friendly.

The Pyramid Ship Museum

This museum contains the pyramid ship of the Fourth Dynasty monarch Khufu. It is designed in the shape of a ship, and you have to slip on a pair of oversized slippers that cover your shoes before you begin your tour.

The Imhotep Museum at Sakkara

This is a brand new museum located in Sakkara near the Step Pyramid. I think it just opened a couple of weeks ago. Even some of the tour operators don't know about it yet, but I was able to visit it today for the very first time. Of course, the museum is named after the stupendous African multi-genius Imhotep. There is a small statue of him in the center of the museum and a bunch of other nice pieces too.

The real highlight of the Imhotep Museum for me was the limestone sphinx of Fifth Dynasty monarch Unas. Unas has historic significance in that his pyramid tomb chamber, more than forty-five-hundred years old, contains the world's first known religious literature. Unas also sent a diplomatic and trade mission to the land of Punt, probably modern-day Somalia. The Fifth Dynasty is one of my favorite periods in Egyptian history, so my visit to the Imhotep Museum left me in very high spirits.

So there you have it: a brief synopsis of my favorite museums in Egypt. My only regret is that the Greco-Roman Museum in Alexandria was not open when I went there on Sunday. Maybe I will catch it the next time. But I guess you could say that Egypt itself is one enormous open-air museum, and I have been trying to absorb as much of it as possible!

THE SLAVE DUNGEONS OF GHANA—PLACES OF MEMORY

August 9, 2006

I like Ghana. Actually, I love it! This is my third time here, and I can see myself returning on a regular basis. The people seem gentle, kind, and possessed of a quiet dignity. The country has a strong Pan-African spirit and the legacy of Kwame Nkrumah is still vibrant.

I am traveling with eighty sisters and brothers from the United States but, believe me, they are the most difficult, self-absorbed, individualistic, and obstinate group of people that I have ever traveled with! Many of them are in Africa for the first time, yet they act as though they don't want to take directions from anyone! They generally don't pay a great deal of attention and are frequently a real pain. Many seem obsessed with shopping and seem to do everything very slowly. They are a very diverse group, and apparently, each came to Africa with a different agenda.

Ghana makes ten the number of countries in Africa that I have visited so far this summer. Of those ten, in addition to Ghana, I enjoyed Lesotho and Uganda the most. I liked the physical beauty of Lesotho and the friendly and yet aggressive personality of its people. And then, I liked everything about Uganda! It is probably more accurate to say that I just loved Uganda and could easily find myself spending a great deal of time there.

But here I am now in Accra. The group and I spent Monday evening in Kumasi, the heart of the Asante region, where we toured a palace/museum and stayed in an African-owned hotel . It took a full day to get there from Accra. Along the way, we stopped in Bonwire, the center of Ghana's kente cloth weaving industry, where I bought a couple of really nice shirts. We had an excellent African lunch there.

The next morning, we headed to the Elmina/Cape Coast region, a beautiful area located near the ocean. There, we visited the infamous slave dungeons. These are horrible places, full of painful memories. Anyone who has ever been to one of these dungeons never forgets the experience. I have been to three: the Elmina and Cape Coast dungeons in Ghana and the Ouidah Dungeon in Benin. Actually, Ouidah was more fortress than dungeon but served the same function. And when you walk into the Elmina dungeon, the first thing that you notice is a large old white church right in the center of the edifice. What a contradiction!

During our visit, we went first to the women's dungeon, where, as I understood it, typically up to four hundred African women were held at a time. We saw the cannon balls to which those who refused to be raped were chained until they submitted. It is difficult to find words for the depravity and humiliation to which our Ancestors were subjected.

I left the tour group at that point and walked outside to wait for them. While waiting, a young White woman accompanied by an Asian man walked up to me and, smiling, asked me if I would take a picture of them in front of the castle. For a moment, I just looked at her, then I cursed her in some detail. I tried as hard as I could to be as rude and nasty to her as possible. She looked at me in shocked disbelief. I cursed her again before her boyfriend escorted her away.

Strange, I thought that venting like that on a White person would make me feel better, but it didn't. The whole episode, mixed with my chagrin over the tour group's demeanor and my upset over visiting the slave dungeon, was unsettling.

From the Elmina Dungeon, we went to the Cape Coast Dungeon, a place to me even more miserable. The tour group walked about for a time and passed through the door of no return, through which our Ancestors were taken before they were herded like cattle onto the floating coffins we call slave ships.

Then our group was ushered into one of the female dungeons, where a libation ceremony was held. During the ceremony, we each pledged to be more tolerant, and understanding, and loving of each other and to make our Ancestors proud of us. It was quite moving. Then we sang a song together and some of us cried.

I learned today that the remains of fifty-seven slave dungeons dot the coasts of Ghana. I would imagine that millions of Africans passed through those dungeons. Perhaps your own Ancestors were among them. Maybe mine, too. They are horrible places—places of memory, sisters and brothers.

Never forget, African people. Always remember.

UGANDA'S MOUNTAINS OF THE MOON

May 14, 2007

Today, I visited the Mountains of the Moon in southwestern Uganda. For me, it was a very emotional visit because, according to some accounts, this is the region from which the Ancient Egyptians came. After visiting the mountain range, I spent part of the afternoon with a community of Batwa, also known as the Bambuti or the Pygmies. This was my first time seeing these people, and it was both exciting and depressing.

The Batwa I visited lived within about fifteen miles of the eastern border of the Democratic Republic of the Congo in a heavy rain forest area, but similar groups of Africans live on both sides of the border. They were the shortest people I have ever seen! There were seventy-five of them, including women and children. I also met the king and queen, adding to the large number of royal personages I have met on this trip and of whom I have taken a lot of photos.

I talked with the Batwa for a long time and observed as they later performed some cultural rituals. The Batwa still practice many of their traditional beliefs, but their old ways are under attack since they have been relocated from their former homes in the rain forest to a squalid little settlement near the Uganda-Congo border. They now largely subsist by begging. That was the sad part of my visit.

The exciting part was that I got to see a lot of the beautiful country of Uganda and met a bunch of wonderful people. Plus, a couple of days ago I did a really big radio interview, and have now lectured very successfully at five universities in Uganda, with each lecture being better than the one before it. Altogether, I have probably addressed more than a thousand people here. Next year, I intend to accept a university lectureship in Uganda. All of my colleagues are inspired by that possibility, and so am I.

As I've said before, the spirit of Pan-Africanism is stronger in Uganda than anywhere I have ever been. And next May, I will be bringing a tour group here. I hope that you can be a part of it. It will be an experience you will never forget!

I have seen sunsets over Lake Nyanza and charted the stars under Mount Elgon. I have seen the source of the White Nile River and seen amazing lightning and rainbow shows. And they have these exquisite herds of cattle here, unlike any I have ever seen!

Thanks to the Ancestors for my hosts on this trip to Uganda: the members and staff of the Marcus Garvey Pan-Afrikan Institute. They are truly incredible sisters and brothers, and I am confident that Marcus Garvey himself would be proud.

Later this week, I am scheduled to travel to Rwanda. Next week, it's on to Southern Sudan and then to Dar es Salaam and Zanzibar in Tanzania.

RWANDA AND THE DEMOCRATIC REPUBLIC OF THE CONGO

May 18, 2007

I am now in Kigali, Rwanda, e-mailing away at a cyber cafe located right next door to the moderately priced, African-owned hotel where I am staying. I am happy to announce that all of the hotels in which I have stayed on this trip have been African-owned. Unfortunately, that may change next week when I go to Juba in South Sudan. It is my understanding that there is only one hotel in the entire city, and I don't know who owns it.

Anyway, today was another good day for me. My journey to Kigali began last night with a little nervousness on my part as I was not able to book a hotel before I arrived. Indeed, I found myself, for a short time at least, regretting that I had even bought the plane ticket that brought me here. Sometimes, you know, travel is not all that glamorous, but the short, fifty- minute flight from Entebbe, Uganda, to Kigali on Rwandair Express was pretty nice.

I was the first person off the plane. The airport staff people on the ground in Kigali were very pleasant. One brother even suggested a couple of hotels and gave me info about taxis and changing money and more. So that was comforting.

I did not need an entry visa for Rwanda and the beautiful African customs agent, who thumbed through my passport and noticed that I had not been to Rwanda before, wished me a pleasant stay in her country. That put a smile on my face! My luggage came right away, and I was able to get an English-speaking taxi driver, with whom I quickly became friends. I was pleasantly surprised by how widely English is spoken here.

Well, to make a long story short, I ended up staying in one of the most expensive hotels in Kigali! But a night of luxury and pampering from time to time is not necessarily a bad thing, and I rather enjoyed myself. This morning, however, I was determined to find a different location. And so, here I am.

Rwanda is probably the most breathtakingly beautiful country I have ever visited. It is hilly and full of mountains and lush green valleys. Some of the mountains here are volcanic. A lot of people, especially White folks, come here just for the scenic views and because this s where the gorillas are!

And today I saw a lot of that countryside. For a very reasonable fee, my taxi driver Peter, drove me from Kigali west to the city of Gisenyi on the banks of beautiful Lake Kivu, another one of East-Central Africa's great lakes. The drive was fantastic! Not only is the country beautiful, but the people are too.

Today was market day, so scores of them lined the roads all along the way. The women were dressed mostly in traditional African garb, and it was very common to see them balancing huge bags of vegetables on their heads or in their arms with their babies tied onto their backs. Vendors were selling all kinds of vegetables at the market—potatoes, onions, leafy greens, and more—so much it seemed as if this small country could feed the whole of Africa with only a little effort.

Rwanda is a land-locked country. It has a population of about eight million people, making it one of the most densely populated countries on the continent. It is surrounded by the Democratic Republic of the Congo, Tanzania, Burundi, and Uganda. (I don't have a map in front of me, so I hope I am not leaving anything out.)

One of the highlights of my day today was a journey across the Rwandan border into the city of Goma in the Democratic Republic of the Congo. The people on both sides of the border were very friendly, and it was not hard to get an entry visa. I confess that I did not venture very far, but I managed to walk about a mile until I found a nice hotel with a nice restaurant, where I enjoyed an excellent chicken lunch, which I washed down with the local Congolese beer. With all the Chicken

Tagine I had in Morocco, the Chicken Yassa I had in Senegal, and the grilled chicken I had in Uganda, it is rather astonishing that I have not yet started to cluck!

And the beer! I've had almost enough of it to float back to Paris!

Of course, the other big part of today was hearing the sad tale of the Rwandan "genocide" of the 1990s. According to my Tutsi driver, Peter, more than a million people, Tutsis and Hutus, were slaughtered over a period of just three months. And we should not forget the role of the Belgians and French in that tragedy. I am sure that I will uncover more information about this over the next couple of days.

So that is it for now, folks. Tomorrow, I may have another report for you. In the meantime, keep a positive thought for me because, with the exception of my taxi driver, I don't know a soul in the whole of Rwanda. But I'm hanging in there!

Anyway, there is an African restaurant with an excellent reputation right inside my hotel, and it is just about supper time right now. Guess what I am going to order? That's right: chicken! I just wish you were here with me to enjoy it.

Take care, sisters and brothers. Life is good, the Ancestors are great, and God is blessing me!

Postscript: More Notes on Rwanda (May 20, 2007)

Rwanda, probably even more than neighboring Uganda, is a breathtakingly beautiful place. Of all the places I have visited thus far, only Fiji and Bathurst Island north of Australia can compare. There may be other places, but those are the two locales that come immediately to mind.

Rwanda is also a rather strange place. Don't get me wrong, though—I don't mean "strange" in a negative way. It just seems that underneath all the smiles and laughter and pleasantries, there is a kind of melancholy lying just beneath the surface.

Since I wrote to you two days ago, I have been a rather busy man. First, I had to take care of some banking business because the ATM machines here don' take U.S.-based credit cards. The smaller hotels and business establishments don't accept them, and I was running low on cash. Then I went to the Kigali Memorial Center, located on the outskirts of Kigali in an area called Gisozi. Gisozi was the site chosen for the mass burial of the 250,000 people slaughtered in just over three months in Rwanda in 1994. The Center contains several mass graves and a kind of museum that details what happened there. According to the official accounts, armed Hutu militias went on a systematic rampage in the spring in 1994 that resulted in the murder, mutilation, rape, and torture of up to a million people (mostly Tutsis). What started in Kigali soon spread to all of Rwanda.

The Kigali Memorial Center's exhibits feature newspaper articles that tell what happened, video interviews with some of the survivors, skeletal remains, and photos of some of the victims, which included entire families and lots of children. I think I saw most of the displays, but I could not, or at least I did not want to, see all of them.

My reaction to those exhibits was neither anger nor even sadness. I walked through the memorial in a kind of stunned disbelief, wondering if these terrible events really happened in the way the "official" accounts say they did. I wondered, how could these seemingly peaceful and serene African people rape and shoot and hack and chop each other like that?

Today, I also went to the city of Butare, where I toured parts of both the national university and the national museum and talked to a number of people in an effort to make some sense of the Rwandan genocide. I confess, however, that I am still confused. On the one hand, I learned that until the Belgians came to Rwanda in the early 1920s, the Hutus and Tutsis lived in peace and harmony. The Hutus were largely farmers, and the Tutsis mostly cattle herders. They were not regarded then as ethnic groups but rather as socioeconomic classes.

Then the Belgians came and changed everything. They elevated the Tutsis above the Hutus and gave them virtually all of the social advantages in the educational and leadership spheres. They solidified the Tutsi positions as the native elites and ruled the Hutu majorities in Rwanda and Burundi through them. I guess that you could say that the Belgians played the strategy of divide-and-conquer to ruthless perfection.

When I asked the people I met if they were Hutus or Tutsis, I usually got a kind of sad and confused smile and seldom a direct answer. Sometimes they would say, "I am neither" or "I am both" or "I am just Rwandan." I suppose that this is part of the plan for national reconciliation.

Yes, sisters and brothers, Rwanda is a strange and beautiful place. And I remain more than a little confused and perplexed about it, but that is it for now, folks. You may hear from me tomorrow or the next day or the day after that—or you might not hear from me at all. I leave Rwanda for Uganda tomorrow night, and from there on to Juba in South Sudan the following afternoon.

I am told that the national press agencies will be waiting at the airport for me when I arrive in Juba, where I am to do a big press conference and lecture at the university there. I am not sure what to expect, so stay tuned. It could turn out to be a very big thing. When I find the time and a good cyber café, I will be sure to tell you all about it.

FROM SOUTH SUDAN TO THE SHORES OF LAKE VICTORIA

May 24, 2007

I am now in Juba, South Sudan. I arrived early yesterday morning. I was supposed to arrive the day before, but my flight from Uganda was delayed, and when we arrived over Juba we were told that it was too dark to land so we had to return to Entebbe!

So here I am. I have to say that Juba is the most impoverished urban area that I have seen anywhere in the world. It is really rough here. For most of the city, there is little clean water and hardly any paved roads. Indeed, Juba has the worst roads I have ever traveled. Electrical service is highly irregular. There is only one TV station and only a few Internet cafes, and most of the latter are no good. There are only a couple of hotels here, and they charge astronomical prices for extremely rudimentary rooms. The people are not very welcoming and most are suspicious of strangers.

Runoko Rashidi

What I am experiencing here in Juba is the result of a fifty-year racial war between northern (Arab/Islamic) Sudan and southern (Black African/Christian/traditional) Sudan. The Blacks in the south have fought the Arabs in the north to a standstill, and they are prepared and even expecting to fight again. They are determined to hold onto Africa for the Africans, and I cannot help but admire them for that despite the hardships imposed by the war. More than two million of them died during the fighting, but the survivors have maintained their culture. I am proud of them.

I do have some positive news to report, however. Yesterday afternoon, shortly after my arrival, I had a big press conference. The room was full of reporters, and I was given about two hours to get my message out. I talked about the importance of looking at history from an African perspective and the history and significance of Pan-Africanism. The response was absolutely excellent! You would have been extremely proud. A slightly edited version of the press conference was aired on South Sudan TV last night. I am supposed to get a copy of it shortly.

This morning, I met with a leading Pan-Africanist bishop and he gave me a comprehensive report on the war in South Sudan and Darfur. It seems the people in the south believe that the Arabs and "Arab wanabees" in the north are determined to exterminate all of the Blacks and seize their land. They are very clear and uncompromising about this. They sympathize with the Darfurians but recall that the Darfurians were used by the Arabs to fight their sisters and brothers. The bishop also explained that what is going on in Darfur is even worse than what was perpetrated in Southern Sudan, and he noted that a referendum to determine if the South Sudanese will form their own country will be held in 2011.

So I have a great deal to share with you, but right now I am hurrying to go give a big lecture at the University of Jubain a couple of hours. I am to speak on the subject of "The Global African Presence."

Anyway, this note is just to let you know that I am okay. I am learning a lot and sharing a lot, and the people here seem very excited by what I have to say. I hope to write more, either from Uganda or Tanzania over the next couple of days. In the meantime, keep a positive thought out for me and forgive the rush.

By the way, I suspect that this note might anger some of my Muslim sisters and brothers, but I am only reporting what the local leaders and ordinary folks are telling me and what I'm seeing with my own eyes.

May 25, 2007

Today I am back in Entebbe, Uganda. I had planned to leave for Tanzania tonight, but I guess the Ancestors had other plans for me.

Last night's program at the University of Juba was fabulous and historic. I spoke to an all-African audience of more than two hundred people, mostly students and mostly men. The lecture was very good, but the question-and-answer session was incredible. I tell you, those folks are ready for Pan-Africanism in a big way! The reaction I received in Southern Sudan was as promising as that I received in Uganda.

The Southern Sudanese Africans are real warriors in every way. They assured me that I was at home there, and we talked well into the night. You should have been there!

I have a whole lot to share with you and hope to write more during the course of the weekend. This is just to let you know that I am safe and sound and excited to be here on the shores of Lake Victoria, the largest lake in Africa, and not far from the equator. May the Ancestors be praised!

RETURN TO UGANDA

May 26, 2007

This is the first day (maybe) during this entire African trip that I have had virtually nothing to do! I don't have many days like this. And I am just about out of reading material, so now I find myself searching for other ways to spend my time. These are the times when I really wish that I had some good travel companions to hang out with! Plus, it seems that I don't know how to just "relax." So if you choose not to read this e-mail any further, I understand.

Anyway, I find myself today at the newest and brightest deluxe hotel in the whole of Entebbe, Uganda. Entebbe, by the way, is a companion city to Kampala, Uganda, and was, for a while, the capital of British-ruled Uganda. I have not explored it enough to say whether I like it better than Kampala or not, but, as with the rest of the Uganda, the people are extremely friendly, even by African standards.

All day yesterday, all I could think about was getting out of Juba, South Sudan. The infrastructure there is so poor that it was almost like being in a prison. The roads are awful! I think the officials in charge of roads and highways must have stolen all or most of the money allocated for improvements. There are no real restaurants or places to just hang out in Juba, and the hotel where I stayed, the Nile Comfort Inn, would be considered a dump just about anywhere else. Still, they charged me a whopping $180.00 per day, in advance, to stay there! However, most of the people who visit Juba stay in tents, so I guess that I was one of the fortunate ones.

About the only commendable thing I can say about my hotel in Juba was that it was located right on the banks of a branch of the Nile River I think this branch of the Nile is the White Nile. Yes, there are many branches to this mighty river. A few years ago I stayed by the Blue Nile in Ethiopia. Here in Uganda, a section of the river is called the Victoria Nile.

When I left Juba, I was rather relieved to get out of the place. Still, I could not help but admire the spirit of the people who live there. They are proud of themselves for beating the Arabs who encroached from the north. As one African elder told me with pride, "We have kept the rest of Africa free from Arabization!"

Speaking of which, I really pissed off a couple of my readers with my reports from Juba. They believe that I was not fair in my reporting from South Sudan and claim that I am biased against Islam. Well, I guess I will just have to live with it. I was only repeating what the people there told me. Young and old, they clearly see themselves as bulwarks against the Arabs and Islam. Who am I to argue with them?

So here I am, bored and idle at this fabulous hotel. This may sound crazy to you, but I truly believe that I am meant to be here. All day yesterday, I thought I would be in Dar es Salaam, Tanzania, last night, but the flight from Juba to Entebbe arrived late and a South African flight came in just before mine. So by the time I got through immigration and collected my luggage, it was too late to go any farther.

I thought that I would be able to find a cheap local motel and stay here in Uganda for a night or two. At the airport, I saw a sign for a shuttle bus for a nice hotel, but I got on the wrong bus. So when I got to this five-star place, I just decided that I wasn't going to go any farther. So, here I remain.

It is so beautiful and peaceful here. I think this is just the opportunity I need to sit for a minute, collect my thoughts, and organize my plans for the rest of my trip. For sure, by tomorrow night, God willing, I will be in Tanzania along the Indian Ocean. Just think of it, yesterday I was on the Nile, today I am on the shores of Lake Victoria, and tomorrow I expect to be on the banks of the Indian Ocean. It has indeed been quite a springtime in Africa for Brother Runoko! I even think that I will be able to take my long-awaited trip to Mozambique next week!

So enough for now. I am chilling out and counting my blessings. By the way, this is country number seventy-seven for me as I count on up to my goal of one hundred. And the way things are going for me now, I am going to surpass one hundred fairly soon and keep going from there.

TRAVELS IN TANZANIA AND MALAWI

May 30, 2007

I am here in the business center of the New Africa Hotel in downtown Dar es Salaam, Tanzania. The name Dar es Salaam means "haven of peace." For the most part, it has been a pretty peaceful place for me, but I went to bed last night feeling rather irritable and I woke up feeling pretty much the same way. So it is probably good for everybody concerned that I am moving on in a couple of hours. Indeed, my bags are already packed and just sitting outside the door. It is just a matter of checking out, paying my bill, and getting to the airport.

I think that the major reason I find myself on edge and rather annoyed here is because of Tanzania's large and prominent Indian community. They seem to have a real lock on the economy here. Generally, it seems that wherever there are dollars to be counted in Africa, you find Indians running things and doing the counting. I see them as arrogant and highly condescending toward the local Africans, even more so than the White folks. They are very exclusive and seem to have no interest in blending in and making a constructive contribution.

I have always championed the cause of Black people in India, but the Indians here in Africa, generally, are not Black and would probably be offended if they were so identified. Basically, I can't stand them! So I am ready to bid them a rapid farewell and hope that I don't run into any Indians in the next country or when I return to Tanzania next week, although it is probably unavoidable. In Uganda, thanks to Idi Amin Dada, the Indians are not so bad, but here in Tanzania and neighboring Kenya, they are insufferable.

Anyway, I am coming back to Tanzania in four days and will write more at that time, especially about my much-anticipated visit to Zanzibar. But here is a little a bit more about Tanzania for now.

I have been here for three nights, and the biggest thing that I have done, besides just observing the people, is visit the national museum. This is usually my first stop on every trip, and the national museum here is a good one. It was constructed in 1940, and it contains some very good reproductions of early hominid skeletal remains, although only one or two of the fossils may actually be authentic.

The second floor of the museum is where I lingered the longest. In that area, the more recent history of Tanzania is represented, including artifacts from the early Swahili states like Kilwa, which traded with China and India. Also on display is a black-and-white photograph of the infamous Fort Jesus, constructed by the Portuguese in Mombasa in 1593. The museum also displays a color portrait of Tippu Tib, the "African" who coordinated much of the slaving that took place in the area during the 1840s. African slavery was apparently a big thing in Tanzania, and Arabs, Europeans, and even Africans were very much involved.

The worst of the Europeans who came to Tanzania were probably the Germans. They were extremely brutal and, as in Namibia, they exterminated large numbers of Africans before they were ousted by the British in 1916. Of course, the Africans fiercely resisted European colonization and eventually achieved political independence in the early 1960s under the leadership of Mwalimu Julius Nyerere—one of modern Africa's greatest leaders.

Okay, sisters and brothers, I am out of here for now. And don't get me wrong, I like Tanzania and I seem to fit in rather well here. If only I could avoid these damn Indians!

Anyway, God willing, I will be in Malawi in a few hours. I hear it is a really beautiful country with wonderful African people. So look for a couple of nice reports from me.

June 1, 2007

I am tired, lonely, irritable, and running low on money, but other than that, I am just great! I am now in the city of Lilongwe, the capital of Malawi. I just arrived a couple of hours ago, and I seem to have gotten off to a rocky start. Actually, I think all this travel has started to wear on me.

I left the United States in mid-March after having spent five days in Barbados and St. Vincent in the Caribbean, and then ten days in Guam and Indonesia, followed by three weeks in France, fifteen days in Morocco, and six days in Senegal. After that, I spent another six days in France before spending fourteen days in Uganda, four days in Rwanda, an afternoon in the Congo, two days in South Sudan, three days in Tanzania, and now three days in Malawi. And before that, it was African History Month in the United States, and before that my surgery and the passing of my mother. So I am feeling kind of emotionally and physically whipped!

Runoko Rashidi

During this time of international travel, I have been to five continents, fifteen countries in numerous cities, thirty or so hotels, and a few private residences. I have flown on many, many planes and given quite a few lectures. My body is starting to wear down, and I am feeling it! Oh well, I have less than a week to go, and what a week it promises to be!

Tomorrow, I go to Lake Malawi. The next day, I drive back to Lilongwe. Then I fly to Blantyre, Malawi, and then back to Dar es Salaam. After that, I take the ferry to Zanzibar, followed by a day in Nairobi before returning to Entebbe for a night and a day. From Entebbe, I fly back to Paris via Amsterdam.

So I guess you could say that Brother Runoko is finally learning his limits. But it has been a tremendous experience, no doubt about it.

Let me tell you a little about Malawi. It is country number six that I have visited on this particular African journey. Originally, I thought that I would be traveling to Mozambique, but Malawi was a little closer and a little cheaper, and English is fairly widely spoken here. So here I am.

Malawi is a fairly small country surrounded by Mozambique, Zambia, and Tanzania that fits into the central, southern, and eastern part of the Motherland. It is a beautiful place full of nice people. It has been described as "the heart of Africa." Blantyre is in the southern part of the country. I liked it immediately, and the people seemed to like me, too. I checked into a very pleasant African-owned and -operated hotel here and had a great dinner. Afterward, I found a cheap Internet cafe. That night, I slept soundly.

It seems like a long time ago now, but yesterday I was driven north to the city of Zomba. It was a great trip on a beautiful, scenic route. We stopped at the national museum and then the national university. We then traveled up a high mountain, where I had lunch at a beautiful African-owned hotel that too was operated by an African staff, which makes a lot of difference for me.

On the way back to Lilongwe, I picked up a bowl of red berries and some sugar cane from some roadside vendors. There is so much agricultural produce here! Vendors sell maize, pumpkins, tomatoes, mangos, berries, sugar cane, and even roasted field mice. That's right—you can buy roasted mice by the side of the road! That was one snack I decided to decline!

June 3, 2007

When last you heard from me, I was fussing and griping from an Internet cafe in Lilongwe, Malawi. I was tired and near broke and ready to call it quits. Well, one day can certainly make a difference!

Yesterday morning, I left Lilongwe, a city that I did not much like, and journeyed by car to Lake Malawi. I don't know the exact name of the town where I stayed, but it was on the lake. It was a pleasant drive. Because we were so close to the Malawi-Mozambique border, with just a little coaxing I was able to talk my driver, a brother named Sydney, into crossing the border. That way, I was able to spend a little bit of time in Mozambique. That makes a cool eighty countries, twenty-five of them in Africa, that I've visited so far! Though I was there only briefly, I talked to quite a few people in Mozambique. I also added a big rock to my collection and have packed it up in my suitcase to bring home with me.

Following our excursion into Mozambique, we stopped at the Mau Mission. The mission did not impress me that much, but it had an excellent museum, where I was able to trace the history of Malawi. Just as I suspected, the first inhabitants of the region were the Batwa, the people that I met when I visited the Mountains of the Moon area in Uganda. The Batwa, I learned, were followed by the Chewa—a people with a strong matrilineal legacy, whose women were and remain very powerful among them. The museum contained lots of artifacts and information on the rites of passage ceremonies the Chewa conduct for their girls and boys and on their marriage, eldership, funeral, and burial customs. The Chewa were followed by the Ngoni, a very powerful warrior group from southern Africa. They in turn were followed by the Yao, who, according my guide, were very active slave traders.

My guide also showed me a room in the museum that was devoted to the advent of Christianity and Islam in Malawi. Much to my surprise, all of the depictions of Jesus were Black and Africoid! It was all very interesting.

We returned to Lake Malawi, arriving at the Sunbird Lodge late in the afternoon. The staff there was wonderful! The desk clerk booked me into a chalet right on the lake. Few places in my life have been so beautiful or tranquil! Delighted, I changed into a pair of shorts and waded out into the water. I just stood there, waist-deep, for a long, long time.

Lake Malawi is the third largest lake in Africa. You must come back here with me one day and spend some time here, but you have to get your own chalet, as I have left instructions that the one I stayed in, number nineteen, is mine alone!

After dinner, I went to sleep and woke up to the sound of the roaring waves. It was truly paradise. Today, I head back to Tanzania, where tomorrow I will visit Zanzibar on the Indian Ocean. What a way to wrap up a trip to East Africa!

IN EGYPT, OFF THE BEATEN PATH

In Search of the Rosetta Stone (July 20, 2007)

I am listening to an Aretha Franklin CD while relaxing in a nice hotel in Giza, Egypt. I guess you could call Giza a suburb or sister city of Cairo, the capital and largest city in Egypt. The hotel has a wonderful view of the Great Pyramid. The ancient African name of this miracle in stone means "Khufu on the Horizon." Khufu was the monarch in power when the Great Pyramid was constructed, almost five thousand years ago. Like much of what I have seen here on this trip to Africa, it is both magnificent and stupendous.

Today, I visited the hot, dusty, and very dirty town of Rosetta at the northwestern tip of the Egyptian Delta. I wish that I had a better description for the place, but I don't. Despite its appearance, however, Rosetta (the modern Egyptian name is Ar-Rashid) has great historical and geographical significance. Geographically, it is one of only two Egyptian cities (Damietta is the other) where the Nile River, which originates 6,680 kilometers from its source at Lake Victoria in the center of Africa, joins the Mediterranean Sea. Rosetta is situated sixty-five kilometers east of Alexandria. During the seventeenth and eighteenth centuries, Rosetta was Egypt's most vital port.

Rosetta's historic significance is that it marks the location where in 1799 the famous basalt slab now known as the Rosetta Stone was found. Currently on display at the British Museum in London, the Rosetta Stone marks the anniversary of the coronation of Ptolemy V by the priests of Memphis, Egypt, on March 27, 196 B.C.E. The decree is recorded in two African languages (Medu Netcher and Demotic) and in Greek.

A French soldier working in the Rosetta fortress during the time of Napoleon's invasion of Egypt stumbled upon the stone in 1799. The British stole it from the French shortly afterward. I guess that you could stay that, in the European order of things, at least: "To the victor, go the spoils."

It was through the Rosetta Stone that the French scholar Jean-François Champollion was able to come to some understanding of the writing of Ancient Egypt. Today I gazed upon and stood at the very spot where the Rosetta Stone was unearthed–a pretty historic moment, in and of itself—certainly in my life. I took some photos of the site and then took a boat ride, sailing on the Nile, the world's mightiest river, near where it empties into the sea. It was quite a day for Brother Runoko, and well worth the long drive from Cairo and Giza.

Tomorrow, I journey south to the city of El Minya. I've never been there before (then again, I had never been to Rosetta, either), but it is near a series of majestic ancient tombs that depict African men in martial arts postures, perhaps the first such scenes known to man. I hope to take some good photos.

Sisters and brothers, my tour operator told me today that I was the first African American that he was aware of to visit Rosetta. He also told me that he has never been to El-Minya before, so we both are making some giant steps here. I am feeling pretty blessed.

Desert Tombs, Palaces, and Pyramids (July 23, 2007)

I am confident that I am okay, but as of right now if anyone were to call me crazy I probably would not dispute them. I have spent the past three days climbing in and out of cliffside tombs, scouring isolated archaeological sites, and wandering in the deserts of Egypt—in temperatures exceeding one hundred degrees Fahrenheit!

To many, this may qualify me for the insane asylum. I have to admit that some people here have been looking at me as though I should be wearing a straightjacket. Allow me to recap my adventures for you. I will try not to be overly long and rambling:

Early Saturday morning, July 21, accompanied by a good driver named Brother Abdul (my travel agent's operations manager), and a constant police escort, I left the comfort of my deluxe hotel in Giza and headed south to the border of Upper Egypt and the city of Minya. For foreigners in Egypt, this is regarded as dangerous territory. It was not far from Minya, for example, in the city of Mallawi, to be exact, that Anwar Sadat's assassin was born. The entire region has a reputation as being a breeding ground for Muslim fundamentalists. But I chose Minya as my base for three days of exploration and discovery.

By mid-morning on Friday, we passed through Minya but did not stop there. Instead, we went straight to the tombs of Beni Hasan—a place that I've been wanting to visit for at least twenty-five years now—for this is where, as far as I know, one can find the first known depictions of martial arts on earth. Ivan Van Sertima and I published photos from one of the tombs in the first and second editions of our African Presence in Early Asia anthology. And there I was, finally, face to face with them!

Of the thirty-nine tombs of African noblemen at Beni Hasan, all of which date to about thirty-eight hundred years ago, only four are open to the public. With the help of some small bribes, however, I was able to enter six of them. A few extra dollars placed in the right hands goes a long way here!

I went first into the tomb of the nobleman Baqet, which features brilliantly painted scenes of Egyptian martial artists. I then visited the tomb of Kheti, which presented even better scenes than those in Baqet's tomb). This was followed by a visit to the tomb of Khnumhotep, which displays exquisite, green-colored hieroglyphs), and to the tomb of Amenemhet, the most magnificent of them all. I was spellbound, to the extent that I barely remember the rest of the morning at all!

The whole experience was just incredible, and getting up to the tombs, which are carved into the side of a cliff, was no joke. We had to climb a thousand steps to reach them! By the time we got to our destination, my legs were like rubber! I hardly recall the last two tombs that we entered, I was so exhausted. The intensely hot weather did not help either. I descended the steps, physically and emotionally drained. Thank God, I was able to get a few photos!

From Beni Hasan, we drove farther south into the desert. Among the highlights of that excursion were visits to the gigantic remains of two stone baboons, representing the deity Thoth, that once stood in front of a temple of the great Amenhotep III; and to a magnificent tomb of a fourth-century B.C.E. Egyptian high priest in which the colors even now remain as bright and vivid as they were centuries ago. What a day!

Our adventures on Saturday equaled that of the previous day. Driving even farther south, we visited the ancient city of Ahketaten, known now as Tell el-Amarna. Ahketaten was the marvelous capital of the pharaoh Akhenaten and his chief wife, Nefertiti. To get there, we had to drive through an untold number of back ways and villages, and then cross over by ferry to the west bank of the Nile. While there, I photographed the remains of Nefertiti's palace, complete with a swimming pool, and of the meager remains of what was once a great temple.

But the true highlight of the day was a journey into Akhenaten's tomb . Even the Discovery Channel could not have staged anything as dramatic. And like my trip to Beni Hasan the day before, there were no other tourists around. It was just us.

Akhenaten's tomb is simply enormous, and it contains several large, rock-cut chambers. The tomb was badly damaged fourteen years ago when it was inundated by a major flood. You can still see a lot of the damage done by the water. On the walls, however, remain several excellent depictions of Nefertiti and three of her daughters. It seemed to me that the shape of their bodies alone, more than anything else, demonstrated beyond any doubt that they were African women.

Nothing could really top what I saw that morning, but our visit to the cliffside tomb of the Egyptian high priest Meryre came close. I think I went into four or five tombs that morning, but Meryre's had possibly the most beautiful wall paintings that I have ever witnessed. They just took my breath way. And, for the first time during those three days, I saw a few other tourists—a small group of Dutch sightseers.

Later that day, we traveled to the town of Mallawi, home of Sadat's assassin, to tour the local museum there. I think all the local people in Mallawi must be keenly aware of their town's reputation because when word got around that someone from the United States was visiting, everybody in the museum went out of their way to welcome me and make me feel comfortable.

On Sunday morning, we began our journey back to Giza. We stopped for a prolonged visit at the Fayoum Oasis, an area with a definite anti-foreigner reputation. A police escort of eight men with machine guns accompanied my guide and me during our stay there. I have to confess that it was a bit unsettling, but their presence did not stop our explorations, and we bribed them to give us a little more flexibility in our movements.

We were the only tourists at the oasis, and we visited three pyramids while there. The first belonged to Senusret II of the Twelfth Dynasty. Unlike the pyramids at Giza, Senusret II's was made of mud brick, but it was still wonderful to look at. We next visited one of two pyramids constructed during the reign of Amenemhet III, my favorite monarch of all time. Amenemhet III's pyramid is also made of mud brick, and it too is splendid. In front of it are located the scanty remains of the structure the Greeks called the Great Labyrinth and described as the largest building in ancient times. I walked way down into the tomb chamber of this pyramid until I was stopped by a deep pool of water. The third pyramid was that of King Huni, built between the time of the architect Imhotep's Step Pyramid, designed for King Djoser in the Third Dynasty, and the massive pyramids on the Giza Plateau built during the Fourth Dynasty.

So, to make a long story short, I had three days that I will never, ever, forget. Your prayers must have worked. Instead of being intimidated by the dangers we faced, I became bolder and went about with no fear. I actually had fun and ventured out every night, something I rarely do during my travels.

Tomorrow, I will revisit the Egyptian Museum in Cairo. This time, I intend to take my time and spend the better part of the day there. Specifically, I am looking for a large fragment of the beard of the Great Sphinx and to see the newly discovered, mummified body of Queen Makare Hatshepsut.

God willing, I will post you the results of my search tomorrow. Right now, I think that I'm going to take a little walk. I have a lot of reflecting to do.

The Church of St. George in Lalibela, Ethiopia

Little girls in Asmara, Eritrea

Runoko Rashidi

The walls of Great Zimbabwe

A young boy in Tunis, Tunisia

The ruins of the slave market in Kebili, Tunisia

My Global Journeys in Search of the African Presence

With the Niger Manuscripts in Niamey, Niger

A memorial to enslaved Africans near Ouida in Benin

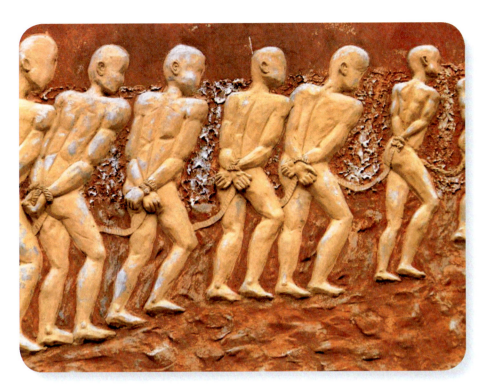

A detail of the memorial to enslaved Africans near Ouida, Benin

The entrance to the Enfants' Dungeon on Goree Island, Senegal

My Global Journeys in Search of the African Presence

A statue of Kwame Nkrumah in Accra, Ghana

School girls in Ghana

Young children in Togo

Gathering at the Osun Festival in Nigeria

A Black Berber woman in Morocco

In Windhoek, Namibia with a descendant of Henrik Witbooi

My Global Journeys in Search of the African Presence

The Renaissance Monument in Dakar, Senegal

Runoko Rashidi

More Museum Musings (July 24, 2007)

It is another hot day here in Egypt, but the pyramids are still standing. The city of Cairo has a population of about eighteen million and traffic jams that you have to experience to believe. A lot of people here drive like lunatics. It is amazing that dead bodies are not littering the streets!

Anyway, today I spent about three hours in the Egyptian Museum. I specify the amount of time because, in this hot weather, three hours is about at the limits of human endurance, the inside of the museum offered no reprieve from the heat. It was like a steam bath in there!

The Egyptian Museum was opened in 1858 by the French Egyptologist Auguste Mariette. It is old and dusty with little ventilation. Add to that discomfort the enormous crowds that visit the museum yearly, and you have a real tough situation on your hands. Notwithstanding, the museum's collection justifies all of the hassle and. It holds more than 120,000 artifacts from all phases of Egyptian history, mostly from the Pharaonic Age.

Folks who know me know how much I love museums. I have visited most of the major Egyptian collections around the world, including those in England, Scotland, Holland, Belgium, Denmark, France, Germany, Austria, the Czech Republic, Spain, Italy, and Russia. About the only major collection in Europe that has escaped me so far is the one in Athens, Greece, and that is not for lack of trying. Indeed, I have attempted to visit the Egyptian collection in the National Museum of Archeology in Athens twice. The first time, the museum was closed in preparation for the Olympic Games. The second time, the museum was open but the Egyptian section was not. But that visit was not so bad because I took the opportunity to visit the big archaeology museum on the island of Crete. I'd still like to see the one in Athens, though. And, of course, I've seen most of the major Egyptian collections in the United States and Canada. I have even visited the Egyptian collection in Adelaide in southern Australia.

But I tell you straight up, sisters and brothers, if you put all of the aforementioned collections together—and I am talking about a lot of artifacts—it would still not measure up to the masterpieces in the Egyptian Museum in Cairo. The Egyptian collection is just that impressive. Big words like "awesome," "overwhelming," and "breathtaking" all manage to fall short.

I've been to the Egyptian Museum fifteen or twenty times now, and still I never quite get enough. This time was no exception. I did, however, have one thing going for me today: I had all the time that I desired and no one to escort. I was on my own, although I confess that I was a little lonely. I wished that I had someone with me to whom I could point out things that I had not noticed before or things that I have, for the most part, generally walked right past, as well as most of my old favorites.

Here are some of the highlights of today's visit and a few words about some of the pieces you are guaranteed to see when you come to Egypt with me: When you walk into the museum, the first thing you notice is the gigantic statue of two of the great figures from Egyptian royal family number eighteen—King Amenhotep III and his beautiful wife and queen, Tiye (for what good is a king without a queen?), along with one of their daughters. This is one of my all-time favorites. The statues are sixty feet high, and the couple seems genuinely happy and proud to be together and very much in love.

In front of the statue of Amenhotep and Tiye is Narmer's Palette, a monument recording the unification of the two lands of Upper and Lower Egypt, and nearby is the glass-encased statue of King Djoser, the Third Dynasty monarch who enlisted the talents of the great Egyptian architect Imhotep. Not far away from these pieces are three statues of Menkaure, builder of the third large pyramid on the Giza Plateau, and two statues of two African goddesses. Not far from these are three large fragments of the beard of the Great Sphinx. The pieces are not marked, so most people walk right past them without even a glance. The last masterpiece on my list of pyramid-age artifacts is a tiny statue of King Khufu, the most powerful monarch of his time. This last piece was found in the city of Abydos in 1903 and shows the king wearing the red crown of Lower Egypt.

Further into the museum, you get to the artifacts of my favorite period in Egyptian history: the Middle Kingdom, the classical era of Egyptian writing and literature. The pieces that stand out the most to me are the black statue of a seated King Mentuhotep II and the black statues and sphinxes of King Amenemhet III. They are just magnificent!

Moving along, you get to the New Kingdom exhibits, where the masterpieces are simply too numerous to mention and include a series of sphinxes and statues of Queen Hatshepsut; the great lioness-headed goddess Sekhmet; and some exquisite depictions of King Amenhotep III, Queen Tiye, and King Akhenaten. And, of course, images and statues of Nineteenth Dynasty Pharaoh Ramses II dominate. You will also see a statue of the god Asar (Osiris), with the goddess Ast (Isis) fluttering above him in the form of a bird—a scene from perhaps the first known immaculate conception.

Some of the pieces in the museum are not labeled. Others are not placed in sequential order, like the magnificent statues of some of the Senusret kings; a black granite statue of Amenemhet III; and a beautiful, black, life-sized statue of a queen that I had never noticed before. The list just goes on and on.

Upstairs is the King Tut exhibit, along with a display showcasing the wigs used by the priests of late-period Egypt. These hairpieces, rarely seen in books, are made of thick, matted hair, braids, and locks—and are clearly Africoid in appearance. Countless papyri also are on display, many showing the god Asar as jet black in appearance.

Among the greatest of the Egyptian Museum's highlights are the displays housed in the mummy rooms. This is one of the most sensitive exhibits in the museum, one that elicits mixed feelings from the museum's African visitors, for it displays the mummified bodies of many of the great kings and queens of Egypt for all the world to see. A few of them appear so Africoid that no one with eyes could doubt their African identity. This is especially true for four of the queens of the Twenty-First Dynasty. They are just incredible.

The newest mummy on display is reputed to be that of Queen Makare Hatshepsut. Her mummy was actually found way back in 1903 and is just now being put on exhibit. Of course, the mummy itself is controversial and some do not believe that it is the great lady. I confess that I simply do not know, and I guess you will have to judge for yourself.

Runoko Rashidi

Yes, the Egyptian Museum in Cairo is phenomenal and arguably the world's greatest. Besides the negative or controversial factors I discussed earlier, the only other real downside to the museum is that taking photographs is no longer allowed. So, sisters and brothers, you will just have to come and see for yourself! I'm taking groups to Egypt in January 2008 and July 2008. I'd really like for you to take part.

Well, tomorrow will be a different experience for me as I return to the Egyptian Delta to visit some of the ancient sites. I promise to write you about it!

A Visit to the Pyramids (July 26, 2007)

Today I visited the two pyramid fields of Abu Sir and Dahshur. I went to Abu Sir last July for the second time. The first time, I believe, was in 1999 with my good friend Carl Franklin. I visited Dahshur in 2001 with another good friend, Brother Jamaal Goree. Both of the sites are spectacular. The Abu Sir pyramids, three of which are big ones, were built during the Fifth Dynasty and date from about 2200 B.C.E. Two of the Dahshur pyramids are considerably older, dating from about 2700 B.C.E., and belong to the mighty Fourth Dynasty King Sneferu, father of Khufu, the builder of the Great Pyramid. The other pyramid at Dahshur belonged to Twelfth Dynasty monarch Amenemhet III and is about thirty-six hundred years old. None of those pyramids was built by slaves.

Although the Abu Sir pyramid field is officially closed, I was informed that the guards at the site are amenable to bribes to allow entry. An official delegation was visiting when I arrived at the site this morning, but I was told to come back later this afternoon!

Of the two Dahshur pyramids belonging to Sneferu, one is called the Bent Pyramid because the top of it sags a little. One of its most interesting features is the large limestone casing blocks that still surround it. Sneferu's other Dahshur pyramid, known as the Red Pyramid, is the first true or classic pyramid and one of the two or three largest pyramids in Egypt.

The Dahshur pyramid belonging to Amememhet III is known as the Black Pyramid. Unlike Sneferu's, this pyramid is made of mud brick and is pretty much inaccessible because of the soft sand that surrounds it. I could only admire and photograph it from a distance.

On Monday, I returned to the Fayoum Oasis to visit the pyramids of the pharaohs Huni, Senusret II, and Amememhet III. Three weeks ago, when I took a tour group to nearby Sakkara to see Imhotep's Step Pyramid, we went inside the tomb chamber of King Teti's pyramid and viewed the splendid hieroglyphs on its walls. There are at least three other pyramids at Sakkara. The one that belonged to King Unas houses the world's first known religious literature. The other pyramids at Sakkara belonged to kings Userkaf and Pepi I. Sakkara is also the site of the unfinished pyramid of King Sekhemket.

After all that, you might figure that I am "pyramided out," and that I've had enough of these wondrous monuments, but that is hardly the case. Indeed, if I had my way, I would view them all! There are over ninety pyramids, some say as many as 118, in Egypt, and each one is unique. I have now visited, I think, twenty of them, and have been inside at least seven.

Although there are many theories about how the pyramids were built and what they were designed for, the general consensus is that they once housed the bodies of some of Ancient Egypt's greatest families. Indeed, Egypt's first Golden Age is chiefly recognized as the famous epoch of pyramid building, but, again, these edifices were not built by slaves. They were erected by free African people and remain even now a source of awe, wonder, and inspiration.

The pyramids—particularly the three built on Egypt's Giza Plateau over an eighty-year period during the reigns of the Fourth Dynasty kings Khufu, Khafre, and Menkaure—reflect the genius of African people and are arguably the world's most enduring expressions of architectural prowess. Khufu's pyramid, the Great Pyramid of Khufu, is the largest of the three. Known to the African people of Ancient Egypt as "Khufu on the Horizon," it has been called "the purest geometric form in human architecture," and was, by far, the greatest of the so-called "Seven Wonders of the Ancient World."

The Great Pyramid originally stood 481 feet high, or forty-eight stories. It has been calculated that the Italian cathedrals of Florence and Milan and St. Peter's cathedral in Rome as well as London's Westminster Abbey and St. Paul's Cathedral could fit inside it with room to spare. This massive structure is composed of 2.3 million granite blocks, each weighing an average of 2.5 tons and reaching a maximum of fifteen tons. The French emperor, Napoleon Bonaparte, estimated that with the amount of stone used to build the pyramid of Khufu, one could construct a wall measuring ten feet high and one foot wide around the entire country of France. The precision that went into the pyramid's construction is such that even now one would have to struggle to place even a thin razor blade between the stones. The entire structure was covered with fine white limestone, and it could be seen from hundreds of miles away.

The Arab invaders of post-Pharaonic Egypt were so struck by the pyramids that they coined an expression to describe them: "Men fear time, but time fears the pyramids." I agree. The pyramids were designed to last for all time, and they were designed to be perfect—and they are.

And right now, African family, I can see the top of the Great Pyramid, "Khufu on the Horizon," standing tall and majestic right outside of my hotel window! I only wish that you were here to see it with me.

Last Notes (August 8, 2007)

The highlight of yesterday's museum tour was my first-time viewing of one of the most controversial artifacts in the museum's entire collection: artifact number 6347, a 2,000-year-old wooden model, presumably of a bird. The question currently being posed about this item, however, relates to whether it is really a model of a bird or that of an ancient glider. According to at least one account, that of researcher and photographer Mohamed Shady:

> "There is evidence of Pharaonic fascination with flight dating back nearly 4,500 years....However, no flying instrument or even model plane had been found—until the discovery of artifact number 6347, a unique model of what some think may be an ancient Egyptian airplane."

Runoko Rashidi

The artifact in question was found in 1898 by a group of British archaeologists excavating an area near the Step Pyramid at Sakkara—that wondrous monument designed almost five thousand years ago by the great architect and multi-genius Imhotep for Pharaoh Djoser of the Third Dynasty. For more than seventy years, this small model was exhibited in the Egyptian Museum's bird collection. In 1969, during a visit to the museum, a distinguished astronaut commented that, it seemed to be a model "of an airplane more than of a bird."

If the artifact is indeed an ancient glider, it raises an important question: How did the African people of Kmt, or Ancient Egypt, make such a precise model, which displays knowledge of the rudiments of aviation engineering more than two thousand years before the Wright Brothers? The answer to this question, along with a great many others, may well be buried underneath the African sands, or perhaps even in the museum itself.

Officially, no one is allowed to take pictures of the model, but let's just say that I ended up with a few photos anyway!

EXPLORING MOROCCO'S AFRICAN HERITAGE

November 20, 2007

In 2006, I had my first taste of Morocco and instantly fell in love with the place, so much so that I've been to Morocco twice so far this year. During a brief visit in late April, I was able to experience springtime in Morocco. The people were friendly and the country beautiful. I vividly remember the blooming flowers, lush countryside, green rolling hills, sandy beaches, and high mountains.

I began my short stay in Casablanca and from there journeyed north to Rabat, where I visited the national archaeological museum. I later toured the city of Fes, where I spent a day in one of the most memorable medinas (non-European parts of a city) in Morocco.

In Volubilis, I saw the magnificent arch that stands in commemoration to one of Imperial Rome's African emperors and his mother. I also visited Moulay Idriss, a beautiful city perched on a mountainside and named after Morocco's most revered saint.

And who could forget the vibrant and high-energy city of Tangier? Let me tell you more…

Tangier and the Story of the Moors in Spain

Located on the coast of the Mediterranean Sea, Tangier is one of the most fascinating cities in Morocco. It is also the birthplace of one of history's most storied travelers and writers—Ibn Battuta, born in 1304—whose journeys took him from West Africa to India, China, and Southeast Asia. For me, Tangier was the launching site for my search for the African heritage of southern Spain, as Morocco is a wonderful base from which to visit many of the neighboring regions, including southern Europe and western Africa. I was searching for knowledge about the early Moors of southern Spain—the people who helped to reintroduce civilization to Europe after the long period known as the Dark Ages.

But just who were the Moors anyway? According to the Oxford English Dictionary, as early as the Middle Ages and as late as the seventeenth century, "The Moors were commonly supposed to be mostly black or very swarthy, and hence the word is often used for negro." Dr. Chancellor Williams described them as follows: "The original Moors, like the original Egyptians, were Black Africans." To the Christians of early Europe, there was no question regarding the African ethnicity of the Moors, and numerous sources support the view that, at the very least, a significant portion of the Moors were black-skinned people.

The epic thirteenth-century romance tale, Morien depicts the adventure of a heroic Moorish knight who was supposed to have lived during the days of King Arthur. Morien is described as "all black: his head, his body, and his hands were all black." In the French epic known as The Song of Roland, the Moors are described as "blacker than ink." William Shakespeare used the word Moor as a synonym for African. Arab writers further buttressed the African identity of the Moors, with one Arab chronicler describing the powerful Moorish Almoravid (Muslim) emperor Yusuf ben-Tachfin as "a brown man with wooly hair."

Early in the eighth century, Moorish soldiers crossed over from Morocco to the Iberian peninsula. The man chosen to lead them was General Tarik ibn Ziyad. In 711 A.D., the bold Tarik, in command of an army of 10,000 men, crossed the Iberian straits and disembarked near a rock promontory which, from that day since, has borne his name: Djabal Tarik ("Tarik's Mountain" or, as we know it today, Gibraltar. A fortress that Tarik constructed during his passage is still standing at that site.

In August 711, Tarik won a paramount victory over the opposing European army. On the eve of the battle, Tarik is alleged to have roused his troops with the following words: "My brethren, the enemy is before you, the sea is behind; whither would ye fly? Follow your general; I am resolved either to lose my life or to trample on the prostrate king of the Romans." Wasting no time to relish his victory, Tarik pushed on with his dashing and seemingly tireless Moorish cavalry to the Spanish city of Toledo. Within a month's time, they had effectively terminated European dominance of the Iberian peninsula.

Musa ibn Nusayr, Arab governor of North Africa, joined Tarik in Spain and helped him complete the conquest of Iberia with an army of 18,000 men. The two commanders met in Talavera, where they commanded their soldiers to subdue the northwest of Spain. With vigor and speed, they set about that mission and, within three months, they had swept the entire territory north of the Ebro River as far as the Pyrenees Mountains and annexed the turbulent Basque region of Spain.

In the aftermath of these brilliant struggles, thousands of Moors flooded into the Iberian peninsula. Indeed, so eager were they to come to Spain that some are said to have floated over on tree trunks. Tarik himself, at the conclusion of his illustrious military career, retired to the distant eastern part of the country, we are informed, to spread the teachings of Islam to the Europeans of his day.

Runoko Rashidi

Fascinating Marrakesh

The city of Marrakesh is located in the south central region of Morocco just below the High Atlas Mountains. It was founded almost a thousand years ago, in 1062 A.D., by the Moorish Almoravid leader Yusuf ben-Tachfin. Ben-Tachfin left an indelible mark on southern Spain, and his conquests extended deep into Senegal and Algeria. He must have been quite a man and, like Moulay Ismail of Meknes (whom I discuss below), he utilized a great many Africans in his armies. The descriptions that we have of him leave no doubt that he was Black African.

Indeed, the biggest highlight of my first trip to Marrakesh (in July 2006) was a visit to his tomb, which, perhaps like the man himself, was quietly splendid, yet simple and unassuming. I felt honored to visit his tomb. Situated on a crowded street in the midst of the bustling city of Marrakesh, the tombsite was empty at the time of my visit—except for the two tomb attendants (a mother and daughter), my personal guide, and me. I did not even see any mention of the tomb in any of the tour books, so I believed myself to have been really blessed to be there. It was the sort of experience that historians dream of!

But I have never been anywhere quite like Marrakesh. With its modern-day population of about one-and-a-half million people, it is one the imperial cities of Morocco and one of the most important cultural and artistic centers in the Islamic world. Red is the official color in Marrakesh. All of the buildings are sort of an ochre color. Like Fes, another imperial Moroccan city in the north, it is famous for its medina or non-Europeanized sectors. Built within ancient city walls, Marrakesh's medina is crowded, with people. The narrow streets, lanes, and alleys are filled with a little of everything–shops, stalls, vendors, barbershops, banks, butcher shops, pharmacies, bakeries, restaurants, cafes, vegetable stands, fruit stands, mosques, jewelry stores, candy stalls, leather goods, cyber cafes–just about anything conceivable. You'll find Black people and White people of many varieties, Berbers and Arabs, Moroccans and foreigners. Some of the people wear traditional North African dress, others wear western dress. You will hear many varieties of music, including the songs of the muezzins calling the faithful to prayer.

I can honestly tell you that of all of the places that I have been, I have never been anywhere quite like Morocco. I have never felt so much like I have stepped back into time; never, with the possible exception of India, felt so much like I was in another world.

A Trip to Zagora

From Marrakesh, ever in search of the global African heritage, I journeyed to Zagora, a town in the southeastern part of Morocco. Zagora is deeper into the Sahara Desert than Marrakesh and about sixty miles west of Algeria. I went there in search of African people and, as the expression goes, be careful for what you ask for because you just might get it. Well, I got it, alright!

To get to Zagora, my guide and I had to cross the breathtakingly beautiful High Atlas Mountains. Along the way, we passed through many Berber villages. We then drove through the Anti-Atlas Mountain range, which is just as beautiful as but very different from the High Atlas mountains.

As we continued east to Zagora, it seemed that the farther we drove, the more African the people became. These were the Black Berbers or, more specifically, the Almoravids. Everything was brown: the mountains, the buildings, the people. Their houses were rectangular-shaped with square towers and made of mud and straw.

It rained for most of the day, but the weather was very hot. We stopped several times for cactus fruit and mint tea. In the afternoon, we stopped for lunch and had Tagine, the national dish, made with lamb. Many of the people we met refused to believe that I was not Moroccan. One woman insisted that I was Nigerien (from Niger). Even when I showed her my U.S. passport, she would not believe me. The whole day was like something out of a dream. Of all the places I have been, few have been as fascinating as the Saharan region of Morocco, and especially Zagora.

Ouarzazate

From Zagora, after an overnight stay, we drove to the city of Ouarzazate (pronounced War-zazat) in south central Morocco. This city of about 40,000 people, many of them Black, is still in the Saharan region yet closer to Zagora than to Marrakesh. Indeed, the most beautiful African woman was cleaning my room as I checked into my hotel. I was tempted to ask her if I could take her picture, but several of the people I had asked to photograph in Morocco had previously turned me down flat, so that put a damper on that. You have to respect people's wishes. (To my good fortune, however, she reluctantly allowed me to take a quick couple of pictures of her the following day!)

Folks seemed friendly in Ouarzazate, and the town appeared to be a good fit for me. English seemed to be a little more widely spoken than in most other Moroccan cities I have visited so far. Of course, everybody spoke Arabic and French, and many spoke Berber.

In addition to the Black folk that I met in Ouarzazate, the structures called kasbahs—those administrative, fortress-like structures seen all over Morocco—were also very interesting to me. My first stop on my last day in Ouarzazate was at the eleventh-century kasbah of the famous Yusuf ben-Tachfin. It is a magnificent monument and, like much of Morocco, it has to be seen to be fully appreciated. Indeed, you may have already seen it, as it was used for the background of such movies as "Lawrence of Arabia," "Gladiator," and "Kingdom of Heaven." It was just a wonderful sight!

Saharan Morocco is an exceptional area, but it was not the only part of Morocco that stood out to me. So before I conclude, let me take you back to the north of Morocco for more on my never-ending search for signs of African heritage there...

To Volubilis

Volubilis is just a short drive from Fes. It is not really a city, in the modern sense, but a collection of ancient Roman ruins. Indeed, it marks one of Rome's farthest frontiers in northwest Africa and is well worth a visit.

Runoko Rashidi

In 211 C.E.,[8] the African-born Roman emperor, Septimius Severus, was succeeded by his son, Marcus Aurelius Antoninus, who ruled for six years. The son was born April 4,188 C.E., in Lyon, France, where his father had been serving as governor under the emperor Commodus. Originally, the child's name seems to have been Lucius Septimius Bassianus, a cognomen (or third name) commemorating the family of his Syrian mother, Julia Domna. When he was seven years old, however, his name was changed to Marcus Aurelius Antoninus. The boy was also given a nickname, originally a derisive one—"Caracalla"—by which he was and is widely known, but which was never used officially.

The year 212 C.E. saw a flurry of administrative reforms under the young Emperor Caracalla's leadership. Soldiers received increases in pay and in legal rights, but the most noteworthy change was the bestowal of Roman citizenship upon all free residents of the empire. In gratitude, a triumphal arch was erected in honor of Caracalla and his mother in Volubilis. (On my July 2006 trip to Morocco, I gave a brief lecture at the site of the Caracalla Arch to a touring group of d'Zert Club alumni.[9] That was a real feather in my cap!)

Caracalla's rule was followed by the short reign of another African: the Mauritanian-born soldier, Marcus Opellius Macrinus. Macrinus, born in 168 C.E., was the Roman Empire's Praetorian prefect (high-level administrator), the first Mauritanian and the first non-senator to become emperor. He took the name Severus to endow his reign with some of the stature and continuity of Septimius and Caracalla; however, he only served as emperor for fourteen months, between April 217 and June 218 C.E.

Last But Not Least: Meknes

Meknes, the third of Morocco's four imperial cities (the others are Rabat, Fes, and Marrakesh) is known as the birthplace of Moulay Ismail and has been referred to as the "Versailles of Morocco." Moulay Ismail came to power in 1672 and remained firmly in control for fifty-five years. The key to his reign was his military, the core of which was the near-legendary Black Guard. Early during his rule, Ismail brought sixteen-thousand "unmixed" African soldiers from the interior of the continent to Morocco and provided them with wives. They were loyal soldiers and, by the end of his reign, they had increased in their number by ten times. I was told that many of the Black people that I saw on the streets of Meknes were the direct descendants of Moulay Ismail's original Black Guard.

Of all the cities that I visited in northern Morocco, Meknes quickly became my favorite. I loved the architecture and enjoyed the wines I tasted there. But mostly I enjoyed just seeing so many Black people! And there you have it—interesting architecture, good wine, lots of Black people—that makes Meknes my kind of city!

---

8   C.E. stands for Common Era.
9   Boasting over 25,000 members, the *d'Zert Club* is an African American youth organization that specializes in the production of positive entertainment and cultural events for elementary, middle, and high school students. The club also sponsors cultural trips for adults and children to places of interest to African Americans. Those trips are designed to facilitate the study of the peoples, culture, and history of the descendants of enslaved African people dispersed throughout the Diaspora.

A JOURNEY TO NIGER

December 21, 2007

My trip to Niger probably would never have happened were it not for Professor Hassane Souley, a brilliant Nigerien scholar based in France. Indeed, one of the best things about living in France is that I am so close to Africa. I want to thank Brother Hassane formally here. I met him a few months ago, and the doors to my trip there just started to open after that…

Niger is a very large, land-locked country located in north central Africa. To the east it is bordered by Chad, to the northeast by Libya, to the northwest by Algeria, to the west by Mali, to the southwest by Burkina Faso and Benin, and to the south by Nigeria. Niger has a population of about ten million people, made up largely of Hausa, Djerma, Fulani, and Tuareg. It was colonized by France beginning in the nineteenth century and declared its independence in 1960, but French remains the official language.

Most of the petroleum in Niger comes from Nigeria and Libya, but Niger has a lot of uranium. Still, it is regarded as one of the poorest countries in the world. Unemployment averages about seventy percent, and I was told that there is only about one doctor for every 100,000 people. Hard to believe, isn't it? But that is what I was told.

Niger is also listed very low in terms of education, but one of the things I liked about it is that, unlike numerous other African nations, the people of Niger (Nigeriens) are taught history from the time of the great African empires and not beginning with the arrival of the European. A lot of Nigeriens know about the work of the great African historian Cheikh Anta Diop. Niger is also an overwhelmingly Muslim country. When I arrived at the airport in Niamey, I saw throngs of people, inside and out, waiting to go on the pilgrimage to Mecca.

I did not get far beyond Niamey myself. This capital city straddles the Niger River, which can be traversed by crossing the John F. Kennedy Bridge, built there a few decades ago by the United States. I found Niamey to be kind of dry and dusty, but the pace was much more relaxed than that of its neighboring capitals of Dakar, Senegal, and Cotonou, Benin. The roads were fair, and there were plenty of small, white taxis around.

Many of the Nigeriens I met voiced suspicions about the roles of the French and Libyans in stirring up strife in Niger by supporting the Tuareg rebellion in the northern part of the country. Neither France nor the French are well-liked by the masses of Nigeriens, who view the latter as brutal and ruthless colonizers who slaughtered, raped, and pillaged their country and gave back virtually nothing in return. I did not see a lot of foreign tourists in Niamey, but I suspect that most come to Niger to visit Agadiz, northwest of the capital. I hope to visit Agadiz in the not-too-distant future myself.

In the meantime, I can say that I enjoyed Niger a lot more than I did some of the other former-French colonies that I've visited in the region, including Mali, Benin, Togo, Senegal, and Burkina Faso. I found the pace of life relaxed, and the people very friendly. Of course, my principal companions in Niger had a lot to do with my success there. Three or four Nigerien brothers never

Runoko Rashidi

left my side whenever I went out. I could not have asked for more diligent companions, and I will be forever grateful to them. If I'd had companions like them looking out for me in the countries I just mentioned above, I'm sure I would have benefited a lot more from my travels there than I did. If there is one lesson that is more apparent to me now than ever before, it is that if you go somewhere that you've never been before and you don't speak the local language, don't know anybody, and have not done a lot of research—you are almost sure to have a less-than-wonderful time.

The food in Niamey was good; the beer, not very. Crime seemed to be rare. I was very impressed by the dignity of the people. The Wodabe and the Tuareg were the most interesting. To be honest, I was expecting to find a lot more Arabs in Niger, but almost everybody was dark-complexioned. And some of the women were just oh-so-beautiful! Just looking at one Fulani woman almost took my breath away. Even she had to laugh!

And, thank God, I did not see evidence of the skin bleaching that I found so common in Senegal. You do see a lot of it, though, in the music videos that bombard the TV screens in Niger, along with the deification of western clothes and jewelry, European standards of beauty, and sex, sex, sex! I found this very disturbing.

A Quick Look at the Niger Manuscripts

While I was in Niamey, visited the Institut des Recherches en Sciences Humains (IRSH), a research institute affiliated with Abdou Moumouni University, to view the acclaimed Niger Manuscripts firsthand. These documents comprise a massive collection of more than four thousand historic Islamic documents in six volumes, all of which were written by Africans. Collected from various parts of northwest Africa, the manuscripts address such subjects as history, religion, grammar, geography, astronomy, and sociology. Five hundred of them have been catalogued under the title, Catalog of Islamic Manuscripts, compiled by Dr. Hassane Mouleye and edited by Professor Ayman Fu'ad Sayyid. The Catalog was published in London in 2004 by the Al-Furqan Islamic Heritage Foundation.

The first two hundred manuscripts catalogued thus far focus on history. They include works by such illustrious authors as Mahmud Kati, Abderahman es-Sadi, Ahmed Baba, and Cheikh Baba. Some of the histories are about the great African patriot, Usman Dan Fodio. Some are as long as fourteen-hundred pages and are stored in tall metal file cabinets. Some are bound in leather. Most are in Arabic, but others are in Hausa and Tamashek and date to the fifteenth century.

At the Institut, I was actually allowed to hold a few of the documents in my hands, but I was afraid that I would damage them because the pages were so very fragile. The Niger Manuscripts are truly some of sacred Africa's great treasures. Sadly, the government of Niger seems little interested in preserving them. I am not aware of any government funding for the Institut, for either the staff or the preservation of the manuscripts themselves.

IN SAHARAN MOROCCO WITH THE BLACK BERBERS

April 12, 2008

I am in my element: I am in Africa, traveling with a small group of African Americans. Specifically, we are in the great city of Marrakesh, in the center of Morocco and the northern boundary of what I call Saharan Morocco. Marrakesh was founded almost a thousand years ago by Yusef ben-Tachfin. I guess that you could say that he is "the great man" in these parts. Yesterday, we visited his tomb, and I chatted with one of his descendants, who maintained the site.

Today, we are surrounded by the people commonly referred to as Berbers, and I must confess that they are among the most fascinating people I have ever encountered. Two days ago, outside the city of Ouarzarzate (probably my favorite city in Morocco), we climbed all the way to the top of the high hill where Yusuf ben-Tachfin constructed a fortress with a commanding view of all the adjoining region. I must have been inspired because I thought all of my climbing days were long since behind me. I even surprised myself! I climbed with an agility that would have made a mountain goat envious! Well, I might be exaggerating a little bit there, but I did make it to the top!

I was soon wondering, however: what's next, a quick climb to the top of the Great Pyramid of Giza? Indeed, over the last week, I have covered about two thousand miles on the ground. I also wondered: Why do I like this area of Saharan Morocco so much? I like it about as much as I like Uganda, Malawi, Rwanda, and Ghana-——places I have long regarded as among my favorite parts of our sacred African Motherland.

Today's tour began with a long drive through one of the Atlas Mountain ranges. We traveled all the way from the city of Fez into the Sahara, arriving in the city of Merzouga after stopping many times along the way. Merzouga is located in an area of massive sand dunes very close to the Algerian border. I would have loved to have crossed into Algeria, but our first important stop was the desert city of Erfoud. Erfoud is actually the jumping-off point for the desert and the center of the Moroccan fossil industry.

The local people of Erfoud have made a business of digging deep into the earth for this mostly black-colored fossil stone. They then polish it and sell it to tourists. I bought several pieces at good prices. It is really beautiful stuff! And the person who sold the stones to us was a coal-black brother of mixed Berber/Tuareg origins. He was both brilliant and friendly, and I felt an immediate bond of ethnic solidarity with him.

At Erfoud, we exchanged our van for a four-wheel-drive jeep. Our driver was a Tuareg, one of the nomads of the Sahara. He took us to a small town called Khamlia, a place that I had never heard of before. In Khamlia live the Gnawa, a Black African people originally from Senegal and Mali, who, as far as I could tell, originally came to Morocco hundreds of years ago as slave soldiers during the reign of the Moroccan sultan, Mulai Ismael. The Gnawa are relatively unmixed African people, very poor, and great singers and musicians. They are also very acrobatic, and they often both sing and dance while they play their instruments, which include large drums, guitars, and castanets. Their music has a very spiritual vibration to it. Indeed, I have never heard anything quite like it before.

Runoko Rashidi

We went into a large building where we found a group of about six Gnawa brothers dressed all in white, with red sashes around their waists, playing their music. The band was called the Groupe Des Bambaras, led by Hamad Mahjoubi.[10] When my small group of African-Americans walked in, their mouths dropped! It was an immediate bonding of brothers. We just smiled and waved, and they smiled and waved back. Feeling right at home, I took off my shoes, poured some mint tea, and started to clap to the rhythms.

It was an auspicious beginning. Of course, we left quite of bit of the local currency with them! We took a lot of photos, chatted, bought their CD's, and laughed with the local children before we went on our way into the desert.

From Khamlia, we drove to the dunes, where I reconnected with another coal-black Berber brother. He and his people were very, very friendly. The next morning at sunrise, we rode a string of camels across the dunes very near to Algeria and, once again, I took a lot of photos with my new digital camera. If I can figure out how it works, I will send you some pictures!

From Merzouga, during a sand storm that buried our tents, we journeyed back to Erfound. From there, we went through another Atlas Mountain range and through the Todra Gorge. We ended up in my favorite city in Morocco: Ouarzazate, a mostly Black Berber city, whose residents are descended from the original Moors. I have been to Ouarzazate four times now, I think. I will definitely be going again, probably before the end of the year.

One of the great things about Ouarzazate is its incredible, earth-colored kasbahs. They are all around. Indeed, the area is known as the "land of a thousand kasbahs." I have been to a bunch of them, and you need to come see them and meet me at the kasbah!

I guess that that is enough for now, African people. I may well come back to Saharan Morocco early next month. I am so excited, but that should tell you something about the research possibilities that I am uncovering. They have enormous potential.

Tomorrow morning, we drive west to the Atlantic Coast of Morocco. Our tour is winding down. I will write you when I can.

WHAT DO WE DO ABOUT AFRICA?: REFLECTIONS FROM ANOTHER TRIP TO GHANA

July 27, 2008

What are we to do about Mother Africa? This is a bit of a dilemma for me, some of which I find to be something of a moral issue. Perhaps the real question is: What are we to do for Africa?

Yesterday, with funds donated by several of you, I bought a brand new Hewlett-Packard desktop computer to the children of the Sunrise School, located in the Teshie district of Accra, Ghana.

---

10   You can see and hear Groupe Des Bambaras online on YouTube at http://www.youtube.com/watch?v=uYvv7Lj78mw.

Teshie is pretty much an economically depressed community, and the delivery of the computer made those of us who presented it—me and several members of my Ghana tour group—feel pretty good about ourselves. The computer cost about a thousand U.S. dollars. A number of people made contributions, including one of the tour members.

I don't take credit for this action; I was simply the ring leader of the project. I give thanks, however, to those who really made it possible through their generous and heartfelt donations, and to the Creator and the Ancestors who put the idea into our heads in the first place.

What can we do for Mother Africa? I don't mean to sound arrogant and self-righteous, but a few weeks ago, when I raised the idea of buying a computer for the school, I got some immediate contributions but mostly a lot of suggestions. The most popular of these were, number one, "Why don't you buy the computer in the United States and take it to Africa?" This was not a bad suggestion, as I had initially floated the idea of purchasing a laptop. But because it was for the school library, we soon decided that a desktop computer would be more appropriate and therefore the idea of carrying it to Africa did not seem very practical. Plus, I thought that the computer would be easier to maintain and monitor if we bought it locally.

The other prominent suggestion was, ""Why don't you just let the Africans purchase the computer for themselves?" This suggestion came not just from Africans in the Diaspora but Africans on the Continent, and it really got to the heart of the matter.

What are we to do for and about Africa? I have been to Africa somewhere between twenty-five and thirty times now and it seems to me as I travel around the Continent that there is a very real possibility that we (those Africans at home and abroad) are in real danger of losing our sacred Motherland. I see Chinese and Koreans and East Indians and Lebanese and Europeans investing and exploiting in Africa, while most of the Africans themselves seem to be in poverty, sometimes desperate poverty. So what are we to do about it? What, if anything, do we owe Africa? What does Africa owe her children in the Diaspora?

I have heard on more than one occasion that we Africans in the Diaspora don't owe Africa anything! After all, some (I think foolishly) assert, "Didn't those Africans sell our Ancestors into slavery?" I get so exasperated when I hear that. Others say, "There are plenty of rich Africans on the Continent. We Africans in the Diaspora shouldn't have to do anything. We have our own problems." Then I just get mad! I have also encountered a degree of resentment from some Africans on the Continent who are annoyed at the perception that Africa is a charity case and that we even have to have discussions about what to do about Africa.

So what do we do about Africa? What can we do? Do we sit back and limit ourselves to "intellectual" discussions about what African people did in Ancient Egypt and how much Robert Mugabe deserves our support? Or do we have to do more than that? There is no doubt in my mind that Ancient Egypt was great, but this generation of Africans has yet to build a pyramid!

You know, contrary to what some sisters and brothers have said, and this might seem extremely naïve, I have high praise for people like Angelina Jolie and Brad Pitt and George Clooney and other such White folks who attempt to speak to Africa's plight. And, of course, I love our own family members, like Danny Glover and Don Cheadle and Forest Whitaker and even Oprah and so many others, who are doing their best to raise consciousness and are active in the African liberation struggle.

So what are we to do about Mother Africa? I pray that maybe before this trip is over, I will be a little more clear on that matter.

A Return to the Slave Dungeons of Elmina and Cape Coast (July 31, 2008)

Today, my Ghana tour group visited the Elmina and Cape Coast dungeons. It was quite an experience, and more than a little bit controversial, even in terms of what to call these structures. Most people call them castles. I have been taught to refer to them as dungeons. These were the places where the captured Africans were held before they were put on the floating coffins called slave ships and taken across the Atlantic Ocean to the Western Hemisphere.

The controversy actually surfaced yesterday when we stopped on our journey from Kumasi to Cape Coast at a point near the Assin Manso Slave River, where captured Africans were allowed to take a last bath before the final march to the dungeons. Our guide told us that Africans were brought there from as far away as Chad, Mali, Niger, and Burkina Faso. They were shackled and chained together—men, women, and children—and marched barefoot to the coast. He told us more about the history of the site and the memorial center located near it, then he took us to the river itself.

I found his presentation a little disturbing because he kept referring to the captive Africans as "slaves." I later sent him a note, reminding him that the captives were not slaves—they were people. It seems that he and I may have had some difference of opinion as to the distinction between the two. I think he failed to realize that the captured African people, in the greatest crime humanity has seen, were systematically turned into commodities and merchandise.

I also took issue with the commercial aspect of the memorial on the site. Inscribed on one of its brick walls, for example, were displayed a number of names of individuals and organizations, written in black ink. We were told that we could have our names added to the list for a fee of one hundred dollars. Now I realize that money is needed to maintain the memorial, but in my view, the appeal for donations had the effect of lessening what I would have liked to have perceived as the sacred nature of the place.

And then there was the attitude of some of the local people toward tourists. It seemed to some of us that the locals were not terribly respectful. Some were having rather loud conversations while we were trying to listen to the guide. Others were talking on cell phones. Still others tended to laugh from time to time and, in general, seemed rather frivolous.

So we left the river more than a little unsettled, wondering if the local people had any real knowledge and appreciation of the horrors of the trans-Atlantic slave trade.

As I understand it, there are three main slave dungeons in Ghana: Christianbourg, Cape Coast, and Elmina. Elmina, built by the Portuguese in the fifteenth century, was the first of the two dungeons my group and I visited today. It is a large and imposing structure that once held hundreds of African men and African women at a time. At its center is the Portuguese (and later the Dutch) church. We saw where the captives were tortured and where the European governors of the dungeon selected the captive women they wanted to rape.

We then traveled to the Cape Coast dungeon. We saw where the Africans were branded with hot irons. A large group of African American tourists came in while we were there. Some of them were young people, and they were even more disrespectful than the local people we encountered at the river. We actually had to ask them to be quiet so we could hear our guides.

It was as if they had no clue about where they were. I doubt that Jewish visitors to the Nazi death camps in Poland ever laugh. Is African humanity any less important? It was all very depressing.

At Cape Coast, we went into both the huge men's dungeon and the women's dungeon. We walked through the infamous "Door of No Return" and then came back through the "Door of Return." But the return was not a joyful experience. Then we said a prayer. I don't remember the exact words, but it was something about healing and being one Africa.

So there you have it. That was my day in Ghana. I guess it is easy to pick up that I am not much in the mood to try to be eloquent right now. So far, I have been to the slave dungeons in Ghana, Benin, and Senegal. I have also toured similar dungeons in Oyster Cove, located in Tasmania on the Australian continent, where the last full-blooded Aboriginal Tasmanians were held before they died. It is a kind of concentration camp.

It is never pleasant to go to these places, and it is never easy. They are places of memory, and they are places of horror. But we must go to these places. We must continue to go. The souls of our Ancestors demand that we go!

IN SEARCH OF THE BLACK PRESENCE IN NORTH AFRICA

May 13, 2009

To be clear, when I reference North Africa I am talking about the countries in Africa that border to the north the Mediterranean Sea—that is, Morocco, Algeria, Tunisia, Libya, and Egypt. Unfortunately, with the exception of those studies focusing on Ancient Egypt, I am aware of only a very few African-centered studies on the Black presence in this part of the world. And this, I suggest, is consistent with the lack of African-centered documentation of the history of the Global African Community in general.

Regarding the documentation that does exist, however, we are indeed blessed with Chancellor Williams' Destruction of Black Civilization, J. C. DeGraft-Johnson's African Glory, and UNESCO's General History of Africa volumes. Other than that, there is little"—and little is not enough. I would even go as far as to say, without fear of rebuttal, that most of the history of African people, including North Africa, has yet to be written.

Young people who come to my lectures and visit my Global African Presence web site frequently ask me for advice on research topics. Well this is a superb one: the Black presence in North Africa, from the most ancient times until today. Sisters and brothers, from what I have gathered, it seems that the Black populations of North Africa, once dominant over the entire Continent, have been pushed to the southern parts of the nations in that region. And it is mostly there that the larger Black communities of North Africa can be found today. I know this is the case in Morocco, Tunisia, and Egypt. It appears to be the case in Libya and Algeria as well. This seems to be the result, first of all, of the drying up of the Saharan region and, secondly, of the massive invasions of North Africa, particularly by the Arabs.

I have visited Morocco ten times and have planned a special tour there later this year (or early next year) that will focus on the African presence in Saharan Morocco. Now that is a fascinating study! I enjoy Morocco and have collected some excellent photos and written a number of short notes about my travels there. Unlike some African countries, Morocco has a relatively well-developed infrastructure (very good roads, many quality hotels, outstanding telecommunications network, etc.), which makes it very easy to travel there. And it is very close to Europe. From Paris, I can be in Casablanca in three hours. I have taken the ferry from Tarifa, Spain, to Tangier, Morocco, in forty-five minutes and, as a U.S. citizen, I don't even need a visa. From New York, I can be in Morocco in nine hours.

Among the Africans of Morocco are the Gnawa, famous for their musicians. Morocco is also home to large numbers of Senegalese and Malians whose families have been in that nation since very early times. A good many more sisters and brothers from Senegal and Mali are recently arrived to Morocco and attempt to use it as a base for their efforts to cross over into Europe. For these recent immigrants, life in Morocco is very hard, but such is the case for Blacks throughout North Africa, large numbers of whom come to North Africa from many parts of the Continent because they see it as a transit point to the get to the "promised land" of Europe.

Still, the largest numbers of Black people in Morocco appear to be Saharan or Black Berbers, member of the Almoravid ethnic group. They are descendants of the same Africans who, as "Moors" under Yusuf ben-Tachfin, expanded their empire into Spain in the eleventh century.

Out of my many trips to Africa, I have been fortunate to have visited Egypt sixteen times, and I have two more group tours to Egypt planned for July and August 2009. The Black presence in Egypt today is comprised of Nubians, Sudanese, Eritreans, and, of course, Egyptians. Although Egypt is officially the United Arab Republic, the farther south you travel, the more Africoid the people become. This is most apparent as you move from Cairo toward Upper Egypt, beginning in Luxor and beyond.

In other words, African blood still courses through the veins of the modern Egyptian—like it or not. And Nubia itself, with Aswan as the capital, is essentially a Black province.

Tunisia is a country about the size of the state of Washington in the United States. It lies nestled right between the much larger nations of Libya on the east and Algeria on the west. On the north and northeast, it is bounded by the Mediterranean Sea. Tunisia's population is just over ten million people, most of them Arab. I don't have the official statistics, but there is also a small but highly visible population of African people in Tunisia, perhaps as small as one percent of the total population, primarily in the southern portion of the country. I believe that percentage is much larger. Tunisia was the location of ancient Carthage, and this by itself gives it an exalted status in Black

Studies.[11] I visited the country in 2006 and liked it. God willing, I will be returning to Tunisia in July of this year to visit the Black communities in its southern regions.

I also plan to return to Libya as soon as I can. Currently, the outlook for U.S. citizens to tour Libya seems murky. From what I can gather, however, Libya too has a sizable Black population. It was, of course, the birthplace of the great African emperor of Rome, Septimius Severus, who founded a dynasty at the height of Imperial Rome beginning in 193 C.E..

Since I now spend so much time in France, I have come across a great many Algerians there, although I cannot recall how many Black Algerians I have met. Notwithstanding, one of the world's most heroic stories is the tale of the African resistance, led by Dahia Al-Kahina, to the Arab invasions of North Africa at the end of the seventh century. .

About 690 C.E., al-Kahina, whose name in English means "priestess" or "prophetess," assumed personal command of the African forces in Algeria. Under her aggressive leadership, the Arabs were forced to retreat, but only briefly. The Arabs were relentless, and as the Africans' plight deteriorated, our brave and audacious sister al-Kahina ordered her troops to follow a "scorched-earth" policy, burning everything in their path. I have heard that the effects of this devastation can still be seen in the North African countryside.

In 701, however, after fierce resistance, the Africans were defeated, and Dahia al-Kahina took her own life. Before she died, she sent her sons to the Arab camp with instructions that they adopt Islam and find common cause with the Arabs. As grown men, they participated in the invasion of Europe and the subjugation of Spain and Portugal. With the death of Dahia al-Kahina, however, ended a magnificent and heroic endeavor to keep Africa for the Africans—those at home and abroad.

We have so much history here in North Africa, sisters and brothers. Is it not time that we make it known to the world? As I once heard a brother exclaim, "We have the greatest story that has barely been told." What are we waiting for?

Let us record and continue to expand the documentation of the African presence in North Africa. And let us do it from the very beginning of time, lest we and other people come to believe that our existence began with the suffering and degradation of enslavement.

"HAPPY BIRTHDAY TO ME!": A MEMORABLE CELEBRATION IN ASMARA, ERITREA

August 16, 2009

Today is my birthday, and it has been a special one. To begin, I take some measure of satisfaction in being in Africa. So far, I have celebrated my birthday in France, Australia, Egypt, various parts of the U.S. This year, however, I am in Asmara, Eritrea. Eritrea makes African country number twenty-seven out of fifty-four (including Southern Sudan) that I have visited. And when I give my lecture

---

11 See my subsequent note in this book, entitled "Days and Nights in Tunisia."

next week, I will be able to say that I have lectured in more than fifty countries. As you can imagine, I am pretty proud of that.

My birthday luncheon today was held at the home of an Eritrean family. Quite a few people came to wish me well, and my hosts served a full range of organic Eritrean cuisine. There were no preservatives or additives in anything"—you would have been proud of me—and it was all so delicious! They even held a traditional Eritrean coffee ceremony in my honor. It was all very special, and I was very humbled by it. And best of all, the people who attended shared stories of the history and culture of Eritrea with me all afternoon.

Well, it is only about 5:30 p.m. now, and I am back in my hotel room, alone, with lots to think about. The sun has a long way to go before it sets, but I have no plans to go out again. There are only a couple of channels on the television, and I don't feel like reading, at least not yet. So while the Internet is up and going pretty good, I thought that I'd send out a few more notes just so I could feel connected. The kind of travel that I do, combined with my personality and lifestyle, can make me feel a little lonely sometimes—even after an celebration-filled day like today. So here goes…

Eritrea is in the part of the world called the "Horn of Africa." Eritrea became independent in 1991 and has a population of about 4.5 million people. The capital, Asmara, located in the Eritrean highlands, has a population of about five hundred thousand and is the nation's largest city. Eritrea is bordered on the west by Ethiopia, on the northwest by Sudan, on the southeast by Somalia, and on the east by the Red Sea—the latter of which I may get to visit in a couple of days. The currency is the nafka, which exchanges for fifteen nafka to the U.S. dollar. The official languages are Tigrinya, Arabic, and English; however, English seems to be the primary language of education.

The dominant ethnic group here (I refuse to use the word "tribe") is the Tigrinya. Altogether, there are nine ethnic groups in the country, and they seem to get along remarkably well. Muslims and Christians (predominantly Protestants, Catholics, and Coptics) live side by side. If someone could discover the secret to this harmony, he or she might be able to teach the rest of Africa a valuable lesson. Indeed, the Eritrean people are very down-to-earth. National ministers often ride bicycles to work, and the president often walks about, even in the nation's big cities. I don't recall seeing any police during my visit, and I have heard no one talking loud. There is almost no litter, and I have yet to see any graffiti anywhere. During Eritrea's war of liberation from Ethiopia, women made up forty percent of the army. Now, however, their status seems to have eroded some. Of the nineteen cabinet ministers, only three are women.

So far, I have found Eritrea to be a haven of peace and tranquility. In the course of my travels in Africa, only Malawi, Uganda, and perhaps Ghana and southern Morocco compare with it regarding the quality of the people. I love all of Africa, but these places just have super special folks.

HAPPY DAYS AND NIGHTS IN NIGERIA

September 26, 2010

I have been to ninety-nine countries in the last dozen years. I think of myself as a world traveler and a great African scholar, yet several Nigerians I have met over the years have told me, "If you have not been to Nigeria, you have not been to Africa!" Well, I can now say without reservation that I have finally and officially been to Africa! I just visited Nigeria for the first time last month. And last week, I returned to visit that nation for a second time.

Nigeria has been called the "powerhouse" of Africa. Indeed, one out of every four Africans on the Continent live in Nigeria. I guess it was just a matter of time before I got there, but up to this point, I was not in a great hurry to visit. This year, however, marks the fiftieth anniversary of Nigeria's independence, and I believe the official ceremonies commemorating the event will take place shortly. So right now, there is a lot going on in Nigeria.

Nigeria does not seem to engage in tourism promotion in the United States, and to be honest, most of what I'd heard previously was that Nigeria is a crowded, congested, corrupt country. Indeed, one of the last bits of advice I received before I left the U.S. for my trip there was, "Runoko, make sure you don't get kidnapped!" That was not at all encouraging!

My visits to Nigeria in August and September were the results of official invitations. I was invited to make major presentations at three conferences. The first was at the Global Black Nationalities Conference, held in the city of Oshogbo. At least two thousand people attended this conference, and its sessions were carried live on Nigerian television and radio. I was the first keynote speaker. I sat between a king and a deputy governor. At first, the former Nigerian president, General Olusegun Obasanjo, sat next to the deputy governor; later, the governor of Oshun State took his place. King Sunny Ade performed right in front of me. I kept thinking: "What a great honor it is for me to be here!"

The fact that I was an African from the Diaspora was lost on no one, especially me. In hindsight, I think that the conference was largely for politicians and mostly an occasion for expressions of solidarity. Still, I was delighted to be there and a bit overwhelmed at the experience.

The second conference was held in Iloko-Ijesa, also in Oshun State. This one was titled "Slavery, the Slave Trade, and Their Consequences." I gave a plenary presentation. It was short but powerful—kind of like Runoko Rashidi himself! I focused on what slavery made us forget—namely, that our history as African people did not begin with invasion, slavery, deportation, and colonization. I also gave a very spirited visual overview of the Global African Presence. The whole talk went over very well. Unlike the Oshogbo conference, this conference was mostly for scholars and partially sponsored by UNESCO.

The third conference was in Abuja, the federal capital of Nigeria, and it was sponsored by the Center for Black and African Arts and Civilization (CBAAC) and Panafstrag, the Pan-African Strategic and Policy Research Group. That meeting focused on the topic, "Pan-Africanism and African Cooperation and Integration." My presentation focused largely on the Ancient African

Diaspora. Like the conference on slavery, the Abuja conference was a real scholarly affair, with speakers from many parts of the world. There, I met the great Nigerian scholar Chinweizu for the first time. We had lunch together.

All three conferences were excellent affairs. All were well organized, logistically superb, and well attended. But beyond the conferences, how was my stay in Nigeria? What were my impressions? Well, in short, I loved Nigeria! It surpassed all of my expectations.

I was impressed first with the graciousness of the people. Everybody was exceptionally nice to me. I had no problems. Nobody asked me for anything. I was not kidnapped. I was the not the victim of an Internet scam. Nobody asked me to carry drugs. All of the negative media portrayals of Nigeria were as nothing.

I felt honored to be in Nigeria. I was treated like a V.I.P. Everybody was polite. Nobody was rude. People went out of their way to be kind and thoughtful. I loved the food. I loved the music. I loved the scholarship. I loved the hospitality that was shown to me thoroughly, throughout, and without reservation.

Of course, I did not like everything. The traffic jams in Lagos were atrocious! And I was very disappointed with the national museum. But, beyond that, I have nothing bad to say.

So, for now at least, Nigeria is behind me. I hope to return one day, but I have no definite plans to do so right now, nor do I have any outstanding invitations. But believe me, I would return in a minute. All you would have to do is ask!

Now, you ask, why did I write this note? I felt that I had to. First, because it provided me with a brief opportunity to summarize my experience in the powerhouse of West Africa, perhaps the whole of Africa. Mostly, however, I also wanted to write to you as a defender of Nigeria. Since my visits, I will not let anybody talk bad about Nigeria or Nigerians in my presence. I simply won't stand for it! Though it is true that I did not do a national tour of Nigeria and I only saw portions of it, I liked a lot of what I saw. I was most impressed by the character of the people.

When I think about all the negative press concerning Nigeria, I compare it to the negative images and stereotypes about African Americans. And that reinforces the following thought for me: "Don't believe the hype!"

To repeat, I loved Nigeria! I would go back again in a heartbeat. It was friendly and hospitable. I learned a lot, and I did a bit of teaching also. It was a wonderful visit. Happy Anniversary, Nigeria!

MY SPECTACULAR TRIP TO SENEGAL

December 10, 2010

Today was one of my very best days! I am in Dakar, Senegal, attending the third World Black Arts Festival and Conference, or FESMAN. The first FESMAN was in 1966, and the next in 1977. For mc personally, the 2010 event was all one shining moment.

I began my day by viewing a photo exhibit entitled "Great Women and Men of the African Diaspora." The exhibit, based largely on my own photographs, was at the La Meridien Hotel. While I was there, the president of Senegal, Abdoulaye Wade (pronounced "Wah-day") himself, stopped in to view the exhibit.

When someone pointed me out as the major contributor, President Wade stopped everything to chat with me. Indeed, much to my surprise, he had a French- language edition copy of my book on the African presence in Asia in his hand. He made a big deal of me autographing it for him. He later, or so I was told, showed his signed copy to the president of Benin, who insisted on keeping the book himself!

Both Dr. Iba Der Thiam, the first vice-president of the Senegalese Assembly, and later President Wade referenced me in their introductory remarks to the conference. Both men talked about the importance of African history and culture. President Wade actually waved my book around as he was making his comments. This was the president of Senegal, you all! I was the first official speaker at the 2010 FESMAN and gave one of my best-received presentations ever. In the audience were such notable Pan-African scholars as Dr. Leonard Jeffries, Dr. Wade Nobles, Dr. Julius Garvey (son of the great Marcus Garvey), Dr. Dieudonne Gnammankou, Dr. Hassimi Maiga, Dr. Joyce E. King, Dr. Vera Nobles, and on and on and on—but I was the star!

My presentation was titled, "The Ancient African Diaspora and the African Presence in the Middle East." I organized 135 of my best photos to accompany my presentation and kept it moving at a lively pace. I began with images of historians J. A. Rogers, John Henrik Clarke, Chancellor Williams, Yosef ben-Jochannan, John G. Jackson, Ivan Van Sertima, and Asa Hilliard III/Nana Baffour. Then I took the audience on a journey around the world and painstakingly introduced them to the descendants of Africa in Asia, Europe, Australia, the Pacific, and ancient America. I ended with a photo of Malcolm X and J. A. Rogers.

As the basketball players say, I "left it all on the court." My presentation received universal acclaim. By the end of it, I was covered with perspiration and had to stagger slowly back to my chair on the podium. It was truly as though the Ancestors, for that moment in time, completely possessed me. I hope that I made them proud.

After my presentation, President Wade excused himself, as he had to go to the airport to greet another head of state. Before he left, however, he established through his presence and his comments that the history of African people was sacred and could not be denied. After he left, I was told to sit in the chair that he had vacated and assume his role as conference chairman and president. During the course of the day, the president of Benin, who was also at the conference, told me that everyone he spoke with about my book wanted a copy of it. At lunch, the Senegalese ambassador to the United States insisted that I sit with her.

And that, brothers and sisters, was my day! Pretty exciting stuff, huh? FESMAN continues until the end of December, but today was definitely Brother Runoko's shining moment!

Runoko Rashidi

December 23, 2010

I think it is safe to say that when many of us receive news from the mainstream media about Africa and Africans, all too often that news is negative or disheartening. Generally, such reports are about conflict. It might be about the crises in Darfur or Eastern Congo. It is just as likely to be about Somali "pirates" or Somali "terrorists" or about the chaos in the Ivory Coast.

Today, from Dakar, I'd like to write about something positive from Africa. Specifically, I want to write about FESMAN 2010, particularly its major intellectual components. To my knowledge, this third FESMAN is the most comprehensive gathering of artists and intellectuals in recent times. It is the brainchild and creation of Senegalese President Abdoulaye Wade and Dr. Iba Der Thiam. Dr. Thiam is one of Africa's great intellectuals and the First Vice-President of the Senegalese National Assembly.

This month's FESMAN events (the festival and conference runs from December 10 through 31) have featured many of Africa's and the African Diaspora's greatest artists, activists, intellectuals, and educators, including musicians such as Youssou N'dour, Angelique Kidgo, Wycliff Jean, and the Kora Jazz Trio; and scholars such as Julius Garvey, Leonard Jeffries, Theophile Obenga, Chiekh Mbacke Diop, Joyce E. King, Hassimi Maiga, Johnnetta Coles, Wade Nobles, Ron Daniels, Julio Tavares, Ruth Love, Chief Benny Wenda (of West Papua, New Guinea), Dieudonne Gnammankou, Djibril Diallo, Runoko Rashidi, and many, many more. And all of its activities have taken place in the shadow of newly erected African Renaissance Monument.[12]

I am here as a member of the U.S. delegation to FESMAN. We are a high-powered group that includes Black mayors and elected officials, artists, athletes, actors, scholars, intellectuals, educators, and activists. The U.S. delegation was coordinated by Dr. Djibril Diallo, a Senegalese national who has worked in America for many years, serving in several high-level posts at the United Nations. Dr. Diallo is both brilliant and hardworking. He combines these attributes with a calm demeanor and an uncommon ability to focus. He is one of the most impressive people I have met in a long time, and I pray that he will play an active role in Senegal's future.

FESMAN is actually several conferences or forums. The first one, of which I have the honor of serving as president and chairperson, focuses on the African Diaspora. Dr. Sheila Walker is my vice-president.

The fact that this forum is being held first is an indication of the importance of the Diaspora in the eyes of the festival organizers. It was not something that we took lightly. Indeed, we worked on the structure and makeup of the forum for months. Our coordinator was Dr. Ibrahima Seck, a professor at Cheikh Anta Diop University in Dakar. Nobody worked harder for the success of our forum

---

12   The African Renaissance Monument (Le Monument de la Renaissance Africaine) is a towering bronze statue located on top one of the twin hills outside of Dakar known as Collines des Mamelles. Built overlooking the Atlantic Ocean, it is the tallest statue in the world outside Asia and the former Soviet Union. The statue was designed by the Senegalese architect Pierre Goudiaby after an idea presented by president Abdoulaye Wade. Originally scheduled for completion in December 2009, the formal dedication of the monument took place on April 4, 2010, Senegal's "National Day," commemorating the fiftieth anniversary of that nation's independence from France.

than Dr. Seck. And, as immodest as it may sound, I believe the Diaspora forum was the best and most powerful of the entire festival. It was certainly the best attended. It was introduced by President Wade himself and, like all of the other forums, it was presided over by Dr. Thiam.

On a personal level, I enjoyed working with Dr. Thiam very much. He seemed firm but fair. He is hardworking, pleasant, and consistent, and also a very dignified man who commands the respect of all around him. It was both a pleasure and an honor to be in his company.

Dr. Thiam's and President Wade's introductory remarks about the conference were lengthy, as they both discussed the history and importance of Pan-Africanism. Both also referenced my work in their remarks. President Wade went so far to wave a copy of my book on Asia in his hands as he spoke to the assembled crowd.

After my introduction as the first keynote speaker, I responded by giving one of my best presentations ever. As president, chairperson, and first speaker, I was determined to frame the African Diaspora beyond the realm of slavery. I began, however, by dedicating my remarks to President Wade and acknowledged several of the notable scholars in the audience, including Dr. Julius Garvey, Dr. Diallo, and Dr. Seck. I included over a hundred of my very best photographs in my presentation, and those images were broadcast throughout the huge auditorium on two gigantic television monitors.

I spoke with great passion and conviction. I spoke of Africa as the birthplace of humanity and of African people as the Aboriginal people of the world. I must have done a very good job because I received accolades for my presentation throughout the duration of my stay in Senegal.

My presentation was followed by that of Dr. Sheila Walker, whose lecture was entitled, "A Map of the Americas." In my view, Dr. Walker's greatest contribution was that she focused on African communities in the Andean and Hispanic countries of South America—areas often neglected in most of our Pan-African studies and discussions. Following her, was Dieudonne Gnammankou, who discussed the lives of those great Africans in Russia: Ibrahim Hannibal and his descendant Alexandre S. Pushkin. Next was Chief Benny Wenda, who discussed the plight of Blacks in West Papua, New Guinea.

Our forum concluded the following day with presentations by Professor Solmaz Celik of Turkey, who spoke on the enslavement of Africans in Ottoman Turkey and gave a very moving personal account of the current conditions of Black people in his country. Solmaz was followed by Dr. Hassimi Maiga, the great Songhoi scholar, who focused on the African basis of rice production in the Americas. Maiga was followed by the great educator, Dr. Joyce E. King, who shared insights on practical ways to implement our ideas. Dr. King's presentation was indeed one of the highlights of the entire festival. She was succinct, powerful, scholarly, and passionate. In a word, the sister was awesome!

Perhaps the most emotional moment of the forum came during Chief Benny Wenda's presentation. It was Chief Wenda's first trip to Africa and his first time being around Continental Africans, but his presentation, and his visit, were huge successes. For the first time, he told the audience, he was able to talk about the horrors of the Indonesian occupation of his homeland with non-Melanesian Black people. His incredibly moving presentation rose to its highest heights when he presented President Wade with the feathered headdress of a West Papuan chief and he and the president embraced each other.

Runoko Rashidi

The second FESMAN conference shifted its focus to the Nile Valley. Among the major speakers at that forum were Dr. Theophile Obenga, the great linguist from Congo-Brazzaville; Cheikh Mbacke Diop, the son of Cheikh Anta Diop; Dr. Mario Beatty of Chicago State University; Anthony Browder, who was at the time conducting the only African American-led archaeological dig in Luxor, Egypt; Dr. Rosalind Jeffries, who focused on the art and imagery of Kmt, or Ancient Egypt; and Marie Louise-Maes, the widow of Cheikh Anta Diop. All of their presentations were brilliant.

Indeed, all of the FESMAN forums were well done. Each was accompanied by excellent photo exhibits. The most impressive photo exhibit, in my view, was the one organized by Cheikh Mbacke Diop for the "Africans in Science and Technology" forum chaired by Dr. Garvey. It was marvelous!

The two other forums at the festival focused on the topic, "African Resistance to Invasion, Enslavement, and Colonization"; and "Africa's Contribution to the Free World and Democracy." The resistance-focused forum featured great presentations by Dr. Wade Nobles and a number of women, including sisters from Haiti and Jamaica, on the role of African women throughout the history of African resistance movements. I was most impressed with the latter forum, especially and interestingly enough by a speaker from Khartoum, Sudan, who emphatically described the contributions of Marcus Mosiah Garvey to that forum's focus.

Another of the highlights of FESMAN for those of us in the U.S. delegation was our group's visit to the presidential palace. There, many of us presented remarks about the conference and we each received the honorary title of "Goodwill Ambassador to the United States of Africa" from President Wade himself. The ambassadorship ceremony marked my third interaction with President Wade, who consistently impresses me as one of Africa's great contemporary visionaries. He honored me as the first recipient of the goodwill certificate.

Also at the palace that evening were several Haitian students who were being hosted in Senegal due to the massive earthquake that struck Haiti in December 2009. Many of us agreed that the presence of these students in Senegal marked a significant gesture of Pan-Africanism in practice.

Riding back to the hotel in the bus that evening, I got my clearest view of the African Renaissance Monument. It is both large and impressive. Surely, it will outlive us all, I thought.

The U.S. delegation completed its mission in Senegal by participating in the last major forum of the conference, this one focusing on HIV/AIDS. Dr. Diallo was at his best, and excellent presentations were made by Vera Nobles and Rosalind Jeffries.

Sisters and brothers, the gathering in Senegal was both historic and awesome. In addition to the artists and scholars and activists and athletes who attended, several African heads of state either appeared or were scheduled to appear. Of course, President Wade was there, but the former president of Benin and the presidents of Liberia and Nigeria were there too, along with President Moammar Khadafy of Libya.

It is wonderful to experience the sense of having been a part of history—of being involved in something, the results of which are destined to outlive you. The participants at FESMAN 2010 represented much of the African world. Scores and scores of papers were presented and circulated. The photo exhibits for all of the forums were exquisite.

Do I have criticisms of my stay in Senegal? Of course I do: I would have liked to have stayed longer! I would have liked to have had more interactions with students, particularly university students. I would have liked to have heard more presentations from the other members of the U.S. delegation because we had some really powerful people in our midst. But you can't do everything, I guess. At least not at one time.

And what of the criticisms directed against the festival organizers and hosts, including President Wade? All I can say, and I think I can speak for the entire U.S. delegation, is that we were always shown the greatest courtesy, dignity, and respect while in Senegal. Our hosts and the Senegalese people generally made great efforts to ensure our comfort, safety, and security. We were well treated well housed, and well fed. To those who say that the festival, and the construction of the African Renaissance Monument, was a lavish waste of resources at a time when many Senegalese are struggling to have regular electricity, clean water, good schools, and full bellies—I say: there may be some truth to that. But I really cannot judge. Not being Senegalese, the subject is not one that I feel competent to address.

But I do know that the problems we confront as African people will not be solved today, and that FESMAN 2010—the third World Festival of Black Arts and Cultures—was a bold attempt to link the past and present of Africa and the Diasporas a foundation for the future. It is my hope that, among other things, the festival and the monument will promote tourism to Senegal and stimulate its economy beyond today and into tomorrow. I am looking at the positives. Pan-Africanism is alive and well!

Although FESMAN 2010 was certainly the biggest conference I have attended so far, I participated in a series of other large meetings as well this year. In April, for example, I traveled to Mexico with a delegation from the Nation of Islam. There, we participated in a historic gathering with African descendants in Costa Chica, Mexico. In August, I was the first keynote speaker at the first Global Black Nationalities Conference in Oshogbo, Nigeria. That same week, and again in September, I spoke at two more scholarly Pan-Africanist gatherings in Nigeria. All of these gatherings demonstrate the importance of the relationship among African people at home and abroad. All bear witness to the strength of the Pan-African ideal.

Family, I regard the Senegal festival as a great triumph. Rarely, if ever, has an assembly of such distinguished Africans taken place. For me personally, it was clearly one of the crowning achievements of my life. I have rarely received such recognition. Dr. Diallo actually referred to me as "one of the world's great intellectuals." That is fine praise indeed! Plus, I was accepted as an equal and a peer by some of the world's most outstanding scholars.

Sisters and brothers, I think African people are moving in the right direction, in spite of the obstacles and setbacks. Who would have thought, hundreds of years ago, that the descendants of those same Africans who were led through the Door of No Return would indeed one day return to plot and plan and lay the basis for the return of Mother Africa to her ancestral greatness? And yet, here we are!

How great is that?

Runoko Rashidi

PART II

TRAVELS IN ASIA:

EAST, SOUTH, SOUTHEAST, AND SOUTHWEST

A 14th century Japanese image of the Buddhist deity Fudo My'o

With a group of African-Turkish women in Southwest Turkey

This section includes my letters from and notes about my trips to Japan and China in East Asia; to Turkey, Syria, Lebanon, and Jordan in Southwest Asia; and to Thailand, Cambodia, Vietnam, Myanmar, Indonesia, Bali, and Guam in Southeast Asia.[1] Of my three trips to Turkey in 2004 and 2005, it is unfortunate that I only wrote travel notes during the first one since it was by far the most exciting of the three. I can still feel the thrill of visiting with the Black women of Tire and experiencing firsthand the beauty of the Black Madonna at Mary's House in Ephesus.

The big hole in this section on Asia, however, and one that I will attempt to fill in the coming pages, is India. My first two trips to India were sandwiched around my first trip to East Asia, specifically to Japan, in 1994. Though I have included a short overview, written not long after the completion of my 1999 group tour to that nation, I am surprised even now that I never wrote extensive travel notes during my 1987 and 1998 trips there. Surely, these were two of the most momentous journeys of my life, if not the most momentous. They certainly were life-changing experiences.

Indeed, when I got to India, I felt as if I had completely left behind all that I knew of the world…

---

1   An appropriately brief but adequate mention of my visit to North Cyprus is included in Part III of this book, entitled "In Search of the African Presence in Russia and Europe."

My Global Journeys in Search of the African Presence

IN INDIA FOR THE FIRST TIME

The purpose of my October 1987 trip to India was to inaugurate the first All-India Dalit Writers' Conference held in Hyderabad the capital and largest city of Andra Pradesh, one of India's twenty-eight states. The conference was an historic event. It was also my first encounter with the Dalits, or India's "untouchables" or members of the "outcaste" group.

During that trip, I also traveled to Bangalore, capital of the neighboring state of Karnataka, where I gave a presentation and visited an archaeological site. I presented another speech to a second Dalit audience while visiting the state of Tamil Nadu. In Maharashtra state, I toured the slums and red light district of Mumbai, known at that time as Bombay.

Of all the trips that I have taken, my 1987 trip to India was probably the singularly most important travel experience of life. In many ways, it defined me as a scholar and historian. Through this trip and its aftermath, I largely and almost singlehandedly introduced an entirely new dimension to the African-centered world—namely, that of the Dalits: the Black untouchables of India.

The word dalit is a word peculiar to India and means "crushed, broken, and oppressed." It is a synonym for the people officially known as scheduled castes in India and often called outcastes or untouchables. In my view, the Dalits are the most oppressed minority and the most socially ostracized people in the world. By sheer weight of numbers, however, there are more Dalits in India than the entire population of western Europe.

Eleven years after my first trip to India, I returned to visit the Dalits again. My 1998 trip was perhaps the most adventurous I have ever had. That time, I went alone (in 1987 I traveled to India with my friend, now deceased, Njeri Khan) and spent nineteen days in India, beginning in New Delhi (in the state of Delhi). From there, I traveled to the state of Bihar where, from my base in the capital city of Patna, I toured the most downtrodden slum communities I have ever seen. In Bihar, I visited members of India's tribal populations—the aboriginal occupants of the land—for the first time. I also met with more Dalits in their home villages, also for the first time. Additionally, I saw the remains of the ancient Buddhist university at Nalanda and stayed overnight at a guesthouse in Bodhgaya, where the Buddha is supposed to have received enlightenment).

From Bihar, I took a second-class train to Maharastra State to see the ancient Buddhist paintings in the Ajanta caves, where I got stranded. After that episode, I hired a car to travel to the city of Nagpur, also in Maharastra, in the very center of India. There, I gave a speech on African-Dalit unity, interacted with more tribals, and met with representatives of the Kerala Dalit Panthers, a people's movement and political party that advocates for the rights and welfare of Dalits. (Yes, they took their name and inspiration from the Black Panthers of the United States!)

From Nagpur, I flew to the southwestern Indian state of Kerala on a visit hosted by the Kerala Dalit Panthers. In Kerala, not only was I surrounded by Black people, but given the tropical climate of the area, I also felt like I was actually somewhere in the Caribbean. The Panthers were incredible hosts. They escorted me throughout much of Kerala, taking me to villages and shrines. In Trivandrum, the Panthers and I marched through the city streets, and I gave was a rousing speech at a late-night rally and forum.

Runoko Rashidi

From the city of Cochin in northern Kerala, I ventured into the rainforests of India, where I met more of the tribals—this time, the Adivasis or "people of the forest." Like the tribals I met in Bihar, the Kerala tribals were extremely small people but not as dark-skinned. Some even had platinum-blond hair. I had never seen any people like them, even in the anthropological texts I read before my visit, and this experience dramatically and forcefully reconfirmed for me the importance of international travel and first-hand primary research.

The Kerala forest dwellers told me that strangers rarely visited them and that, when they did have visitors, they usually chased them away with their machetes. I asured them that I had come in peace. And what phenomenal caretakers they turned out to be! They walked me through the dense foliage of what seemed like half a mountainside. They took me into their homes and fed me. I drank tea and honey with them, and politely asked them all the questions I could muster.

The highlight and crowning memory of this phenomenal visit came when I was politely confronted by one of the community elders. She had been following me all day, up and down the mountainside. She was a small and serene woman who projected great dignity. What I remember her telling me through the translators was roughly this: "I know that you are not from here and must be from somewhere far, far away. But I feel that you are a part of me, and I will never forget you." That really floored me! It was very hard to surpass the emotions I experienced that day.

Yes, my travels in India were true adventures, almost the stuff that legends are made of. I felt young and invincible, but strangely, I never wrote in detail about either of these trips. And even here I am only giving you some of the highlights. I can only surmise now—twenty-four years after my first trip to India and thirteen years after the second—that I was simply too overwhelmed by the experiences and the emotions that were unleashed to write about them.

To compensate for this omission, at least in part, I am including below the transcript of the speech that I gave in Trivandrum in April 1998 on the occasion of the anniversary of the birth of Dr. Bhimrao Ramji Ambedkar (April 14, 1891-December 6, 1956), one of the founding fathers of independent India and one of the first persons of untouchable origin to enter a college in India. Ambedkar, popularly known as Babasaheb, was an Indian jurist, political leader, philosopher, thinker, anthropologist, historian, orator, economist, scholar, editor, and revolutionary. A prolific writer, he was also the chairman of the Drafting Committee of the Indian Constitution. I dedicated my Trivandrum talk, which I dubbed a statement of solidarity with the Kerala Dalit Panthers and the Black people of India, to Brother Kwame Ture.

Jai Bhim![2]

I bring you greetings from the Black people of America. I have now been in India for the last two weeks. I have visited Bihar in the North. I have just returned from Nagpur in Central India. And

---

2   Jai Bhim is a greeting phrase used by the Buddhists of India, especially those who converted to Buddhism with or upon inspiration by Bhimrao Ambedkar. Though mostly used by Dalit converts to Buddhism, the term is not religious in origin or meaning. It literally means "victory to Bhim"—that is, to Ambedkar.

now I am at home with my Black brothers and sisters in Kerala. For the first time since I have been in India, I feel that I have finally come to be with my family.

I proudly salute the Kerala Dalit Panthers. I have been told that it is my job to inspire you, but instead I am the one who has been inspired by you.

Thousands of years ago, the first men and the first women on this planet came out of Africa and they were Black people. Not only were the first people Black, but the people to develop the earliest civilizations in the world were also Black people. It is very important that we talk about the achievements of the past so that we can begin to give our people a sense of pride and dignity.

In India, Black people built the earliest civilization. In Africa, Black people built the earliest civilization. And then the White man came. In India, you call them Aryans. In Africa, we call them Europeans. The Aryans came and the Europeans came, and they enslaved our people all over the world.

Slaves did not come from Africa. Africans were captured in Africa, enslaved, and taken all over the world. In Africa, Black men, women, and children were hunted like animals. The people were branded with hot irons and our women were raped. Shackles and chains were placed on our hands and our feet, and we were taken across the ocean to America.

But every step of the way, African people—my people, my ancestors, Black people—fought the White man. Even when they burned us alive, even when they castrated us, even when they hung us from trees, our people fought. And that is what I wish to talk to you about tonight: the resistance of Black people to oppression. I am here tonight to help establish a bond between the Black people of America and the Dalits, the Black Untouchables of India, that will never be broken.

Our greatest leader was a Black man named Marcus Garvey. Marcus Garvey to us is what Dr. Ambedkar has been to you. He is our greatest leader. Marcus Garvey organized six million African people. He organized a Black army and he taught Black people in America to be proud of themselves. But the most celebrated of all the Black organizations of America has been the Black Panther Party.

In 1966 in America, an organization called the Black Panther Party was formed, and it was formed to defend the rights of Black people by any means necessary. Some of the members of the Black Panther Party were sent to prison. Some of the members of the Black Panther Party were murdered. But their deeds and their accomplishments will never die. The Black Panther Party was formed over thirty years ago, but time has not diminished the glory of their deeds.

The Black Panther Party is important to us because it showed that Black men and Black women can stand up and fight for the rights of Black people. The Black Panther Party of America struck fear into the hearts of White people in America—into the hearts of the White oppressors of Black people in America. You must strike that same fear in the heart of the Brahminical forces of India.

Although Black people in America are downtrodden, we are standing up and we will never be defeated. We realize today, perhaps for the first time, both in India and in America, that nobody can save us but us. The Communist Party will not save us. The Brahmins and the Aryans will not save us. Mohandas Gandhi and the Hindus will not save us. The only ones who will save us are us.

Runoko Rashidi

Today in America, Black people are standing up. Three years ago in the United States, more than one million Black men took to the streets of the nation's capitol. One year ago, two million—two million—Black women took to the streets of America to protest against oppression. This year there is a call for three million Black youth to take to the streets of New York City in America and stand up for the interests of Black people.

I never imagined when I came to India that I would be marching in a demonstration with my brothers and sisters with their fists in the air saying, "Black is beautiful! Black is strong!" When I go back to America, the fact that I have been with you will inspire our people to greater efforts once I tell them that there is a Black consciousness movement on the rise in India.

I am here to tell you, as I stand here drenched with perspiration, that I love you and that we are one people. I am here to tell you that the Black Untouchables of India—the Dalit—and the Black people of America form one human family.

Don't stop! Don't turn back! Be proud of yourselves and realize what a united people can accomplish.

We pledge our undying loyalty and our undying support to the Kerala Dalit Panthers. We will never forget you. We will never forsake you.

Jai Bhim!

BLACK SHOGUN: UNCOVERING THE AFRICAN PRESENCE IN EARLY JAPAN[3]

> *"For a Samurai to be brave, he must have a bit of black blood" (Japanese Proverb, quoted in Cheikh Anta Diop, Nations Negres et Culture, 1954).*

In 1994, I was invited to Japan to lecture at two United States military bases. It was to be my initial trip to East Asia and my second travel experience in Asia since my first visit to India in 1987. Japan turned out to be an exceptionally important trip for me. My lectures there went very well, I gained a great deal of information, and I had the opportunity to interact with the Ainu—some of Japan's most ancient residents—for the first time. I also attended a really excellent exhibit on women in ancient Egypt while it was on tour in Tokyo.

Now I have always thought of Japan as a fascinating country and felt extremely fortunate to be able to travel there. But I felt like I knew quite a bit about the Black presence in early Japan before I even touched down on Japanese soil. Was I ever wrong!

Although historically the island nation of Japan, which occupies the extreme eastern extensions of Asia, is assumed by many to have been composed of an essentially homogeneous population and culture, the accumulated evidence (much of which has been quietly ignored) places the matter in a vastly different light. Far more research needs to be done on the subject, but it seems indisputable

---

[3] Dedicated to James E. Brunson III and Wayne B. Chandler.

that Black people played an important role in Japan from the most remote phases of antiquity into at least the ninth century. Meaningful indications of an African presence in ancient Japan have been unearthed from Japan's distant past.

To begin with, and as a significant example, one should consider a February 15, 1986, report carried by the Associated Press. That article chronicled the following findings:

> "The oldest Stone Age hut in Japan has been unearthed near Osaka....Archeologists date the hut to about 22,000 years ago and say it resembles the dugouts of African bushmen, according to Wa-zuo Hirose of Osaka Prefectural of Education's cultural division. 'Other homes, almost as old, have been found before, but this discovery is significant because the shape is cleaner, better preserved' and is similar to the Africans' dugouts."

Additionally, anthropologist Roland B. Dixon wrote in 1923 that "this earliest population of Japan [was] in the main a blend of Proto-Australoid and Proto-Negroid types, and thus similar in the ancient underlying stratum of the population, southward along the whole coast and throughout Indo-China, and beyond to India itself." According to Dixon, "In Japan, the ancient Negrito element may still be discerned by characteristics which are at the same time exterior and osteologic."

In his last major text, Civilization or Barbarism: An Authentic Anthropology (published posthumously in English in 1991), the brilliant Dr. Cheikh Anta Diop pointed out the following:

> "In the first edition of the Nations negres et culture (1954), I posited the hypothesis that the Yellow race must be the result of an interbreeding of Black and White in a cold climate, perhaps around the end of the Upper Paleolithic period. This idea is widely shared today by Japanese scholars and researchers. One Japanese scientist, Nobuo Takano, M.D., chief of dermatology at the Hammatsu Red Cross Hospital, has just developed this idea in Japanese that appeared in 1977, of which he was kind enough to give me a copy in 1979, when, passing through Dakar, he visited my laboratory with a group of Japanese scientists.
>
> Takano maintains, in substance, that the first human being was Black; then Blacks gave birth to Whites, and the interbreeding of these two gave rise to the Yellow race; these three stages are in fact the title of his book in Japanese, as he explained it to me."
>
> Regarding linguistics, former Senegalese president Leopold Sedar Senghor noted in 1987 that "the people who populate the island of Japan today are descendants of Blacks." "Let us not forget," Senghor continued, "that the first population of Japan was Black...and gave to Japan their first language."

Of all the Black people of early Japan, the most picturesque single figure was Sakanouye no Tamuramaro (758-811 C.E.), a warrior symbolized in Japanese history as a "paragon of military virtues," and a man who has captured the attention of some of the most distinguished scholars of twentieth-century America. Perhaps the first such scholar to make note of Tamuramaro was Alexander Francis Chamberlain (1865-1914). An anthropologist, Chamberlain was born in Kenninghall, Norfolk, England, and brought to America as a child. In April 1911, the Journal of Race Development published his essay entitled, "The Contribution of the Negro to Human Civilization." In his discussion of the African presence in early Asia in that article, Chamberlain stated the following in an exceptionally frank and matter-of-fact manner:

> *"And we can cross the whole of Asia and find the Negro again, for when, in far-off Japan, the ancestors of the modern Japanese were making their way northward against the Ainu, the aborigines of that country, the leader of their armies was Sakanouye Tamuramaro, a famous general and a Negro."*
> Dr. W. E. B. Du Bois, perhaps the greatest scholar in American history,

In his book, *The Negro* (first published in 1915), placed Sakanouye Tamuramaro within a list of some of the most distinguished Black rulers and warriors in Antiquity. In 1922, Carter G. Woodson and Charles Harris Wesley quoted Chamberlain on Tamuramaro verbatim in the chapter entitled "Africans in History with Others" in their book, *The Negro in Our History*. In the November 1940 issue of the Negro History Bulletin (founded by Dr. Woodson), artist and illustrator Lois Mailou Jones contributed a brief article entitled, "Sakanouye Tamura Maro." As Jones noted in that article:

> *"The probable number of Negroes who reached the shores of Asia may be estimated somewhat by the wide area over which they were found on that continent. Historians tell us that at one time Negroes were found in all of the countries of southern Asia bordering the Indian Ocean and along the east coast as far as Japan. There are many interesting stories told by those who reached that distant land which at that time they called 'Cipango.' One of the most prominent characters in Japanese history was a Negro warrior called Sakanouye Tamura Maro."*

Very similar themes were expressed in 1946 in a section entitled "In the Orient" in Beatrice J. Fleming and Marion J. Pryde's *Distinguished Negroes Abroad*. Fleming and Pryde's book also contained a short chapter dedicated to "The Negro General of Japan: Sakanouye Tamuramaro."

The great Joel Augustus (J. A.) Rogers probably did more to popularize African history than any scholar of the twentieth century, when he devoted several pages of the first volume of his 1940 book, Sex and Race, to the Black presence in early Japan. Rogers cited the studies of a number of accomplished scholars and anthropologists, and even went so far as to raise the question: "Were the first Japanese Negroes?" According to Rogers:

> *"There is a very evident Negro strain in a certain element of the Japanese population, particularly those in the south. [French anthropologist H.] Imbert says, 'The Negro element in Japan is recognizable by the Negroid aspect of certain inhabitants with dark and often blackish skin, frizzy or curly hair.... The Negritos are the oldest race of the Far East. It has been proved that they once lived in Eastern and Southern China as well as in Japan where the Negrito element is recognizable still in the population.'"*

At a program in Trivandrum, India

With an Adivasi man and his wife in the rain forest of Northern Kerala, India

At a reception in New Delhi, India

My Global Journeys in Search of the African Presence

Le Tigress — image of a Black man in Shang Dynasty China

A monumental face at the entrance to Angkor Thom, Cambodia

An entrance to Angkor Thom, Cambodia

A head of the Buddha from 10th century Vietnam

A head of a Buddha from early Thailand

A painting of Antara the Lion in the medina in Damascus, Syria

Runoko Rashidi

With a Munda man in Orissa, India

A Black Bedouin in Petra, Jordan

My Global Journeys in Search of the African Presence

Sister Antonia with the Black Madonna at Mary's House in Ephesus, Turkey

A mannequin of the Chief of the Black Eunuchs in Istanbul, Turkey

The mosque of Bilal in Damascus, Syria

Runoko Rashidi

Rogers too mentioned Tamuramaro briefly in the first volume of his book, World's Great Men of Color, published in 1946. Regrettably, however, he was forced to confess that he had "come across certain names in China and Japan such as Sakonouye Tamuramaro, the first shogun of Japan, but… did not follow them up."

Adwoa Asantewaa B. Munroe also referenced Tamuramaro in her 1981 publication, What We Should Know About African Religion, History, and Culture, when she wrote that he "was an African warrior…prominent during the rule of the Japanese Emperor Kwammu, who reigned from 782-806 A.D." Mark Hyman mentioned him as well in his 1981 booklet, Black Shogun of Japan. As Hyman stated: "The fact remains that Sakanouye Tamuramaro was an African. He was Japanese. He was a great fighting general. He was a Japanese Shogun."

The most comprehensive assessment to date of the Black presence in early Japan and the life of Sakanouye no Tamuramaro can be found in the work of art historian and my longtime friend and colleague Dr. James E. Brunson III. Brunson is the author of Black Jade: The African Presence in the Ancient East and Other Essays, published in 1985, and several other important texts. In a 1991 publication entitled The World of Sakanouye No Tamuramaro, he accurately noted that "to fully understand the world of Sakanouye Tamuramaro, we must focus on all aspects of the African presence in the Far East." According to Brunson, Tamuramaro is regarded as an outstanding military commander of the early Heian royal court. The Heian Period (794-1185 C.E.) derives its name from Heian-Kyo, which means "the Capital of Peace and Tranquility," and was the original name for Japan's early capital city: Kyoto. It was during the Heian Period that the term samurai was first used. According to Edmond Papinot's 1910 Historical and Geographical Dictionary of Japan, samurai "comes from the very word samuaru, or better saburau, which signifies: to be on one's guard, to guard; it applied especially to the soldiers who were on guard at the Imperial palace."

The samurai have been called the knights or warrior class of Medieval Japan, and the history of the samurai is very much the history of Japan itself. For hundreds of years, until the restoration of the Meiji emperor in 1868, the samurai were the flower of Japan. They are still idolized by many Japanese today. The samurai received pensions from their feudal lords, and had the privilege of wearing two swords. They intermarried in their own caste, and their privileges were conveyed to all their children, except that only the heir of a samurai could receive the pension benefits after his father's death.

Tamuramaro was, in the words of James Murdoch, who wrote a number of history volumes on the Japanese, "the originator of what was subsequently to develop into the renowned samurai class." According to Murdoch, Tamuramaro "provided in his own person a worthy model for the professional warrior on which to fashion himself and his character. In battle, [he was] a veritable war-god; in peace the gentlest of manly gentlemen, and the simplest and unassuming of men."

Throughout his career, Tamuramaro was rewarded for his services with high civil as well as military positions. In 797, he was named "barbarian-subduing generalissimo" (Sei-i Tai-Shogun) and, in 801-802, he again campaigned in northern Japan, establishing fortresses at Izawa and Shiwa and effectively subjugating the Ainu. In 810, he helped to suppress an attempt to restore the retired emperor Heizei to the throne. In 811, the year of his death, he was appointed great counselor (dainagon) and minister of war (hyobukyo).

As noted in the 1987 book, African Presence in Early Asia, which I edited with Ivan Van Sertima, Sakanouye no Tamuramaro,

> "...was buried in the village of Kurisu, near Kyoto and it is believed that it is his tomb which is known under the name of Shogun-zuka. Tamuramaro is the founder of the famous temple Kiyo-mizu-dera. He is the ancestor of the Tamura daimyo of Mutsu. Tamuramaro was not only the first to bear the title of Sei-i-tai-Shogun, but he was also the first of the warrior statesmen of Japan.... In later ages he was revered by military men as a model commander and as the first recipient of the title shogun—the highest rank to which a warrior could aspire."

IN SEARCH OF THE BLACK PRESENCE IN THAILAND

March 1999

I came to Thailand on this, my first trip here, fully aware that it is a country with an extremely ancient but little known Black population: the forest- dwelling people called Sekai, who sometimes are identified by the pejorative term Negritos. These Black folks live in southern Thailand in the region straddling the border with northern Malaysia. I realized early on that due to their location, which is a considerable distance from Bangkok, and my lack of advance preparation and limited time, the chances of my visiting the Sekai were not very good. Because I pretty much anticipated this, I didn't feel too defeated. Perhaps in the future I will get to see them. After all, I plan to return to Thailand again and again.

In addition to the Sekai, the Black presence in Thailand is apparent in the numerous images of the Buddha found there. I came to the conclusion a long time ago that only a very ignorant person or a bigot could look at those beautiful sculptures and not see Black people. The highlight, therefore, of my first trip to Thailand was the national museum, where some of the finest and most African-looking Buddhist images in the world are housed, particularly those going back to the cultural phase known as the Mon or Dvaravati cultural period, when an independent kingdom flourished in southern Thailand from the sixth to the eleventh century. The Mon people practiced Theravada Buddhism, and it seems that the present-day Thais adopted Buddhism from them. Indeed, more than ninety-five percent of the Thais today are Theravada Buddhists.

With regard to the physical appearance of many Southeast Asian images of the Buddha, as far back as 1883 the African American scholar George Washington Williams pointed out the following:

> "In the temples of Siam [Thailand] we find the idols fashioned like unto Negroes....Traces of this black race are still to be found along the Himalaya range from the Indus to Indo-China, and the Malay Peninsula, and in mixed form through the southern states to Ceylon."

Runoko Rashidi

Even before Williams, Godfrey Higgins, argued in 1833 that, "In the most ancient temples scattered throughout Asia, where his worship is yet continued, [the Buddha] is found black as jet, with the flat face, thick lips and curly hair of the Negro."

November 1999

The highlights of my second trip to Thailand were a slide presentation, entitled "African Contributions to the World," that I gave at a private residence and a side trip to the city of Ayutthaya. The slide presentation was a rather lively one, and the discussion lasted well into the early morning hours. It was encouraging to know that, all over the world, small groups of African people are discussing our history in a new light and with a new emphasis.

Compared to the frenetic pace of Bangkok, Ayutthaya was a quiet and soothing getaway. Ayutthaya is an island city on the Chao Phraya River that served as the royal Thai capital from 1350 to 1767. It is the most important historical park within easy striking distance of Bangkok, located about forty-eight miles north of that city. Prior to 1350, Ayutthaya was a Khmer outpost. Although sacked, looted, and razed by invaders from Myanmar in the eighteenth century, the surviving ruins of Ayutthaya stand as profound witnesses to what was once a magnificent city.

I have to say, though, that Black tourists are a rare sight in Ayutthaya. I didn't see a single one while I was there. Indeed, the Black community is extremely minute all over Thailand. Fortunately, however, my travels in Thailand were productive and rewarding, and Thailand is now firmly established in all my travel plans to Asia.

LOOKING AT INDIA THROUGH AFRICAN EYES

April 13, 1999

I just returned from leading a successful sixteen-day educational tour of India, entitled "Looking at India Through African Eyes." I designed the tour to explore the historical, cultural, social, and anthropological components of ancient and modern India from an African perspective. It was coordinated by Allen Travel Service, an African American travel service based in Washington, D.C., which handled all of the participants' travel needs.

The trip marked my third visit to India but my first tour there. The tour was of historic significance, being the first such trip planned and actually carried out. I was accompanied by numerous local people and sixteen African American brothers and sisters, all experienced travelers.

We visited many of India's significant temples, tombs, castles, palaces, museums, and assorted great monuments. Included among these were the Taj Mahal, reputedly built out of grief for an Ethiopian woman and described as "poetry in marble"; the Amber Fort and the Palace of the Winds; the national museum in New Delhi; the massive Konarak temple in Orissa; the Buddhist temple caves at Ajanta; and the magnificent, colossal rock-cut temples at Ellora. We also visited the major cities of Delhi, Agra, Jaipur, Patna, Calcutta, Bhubaneswar, Chennai, Trivandrum, Mumbai, Aurangabad, and the abandoned city of Fatehpur Sikri. In Patna, in Bihar, we stood on the banks of the Ganges River.

Overall, the people of India were kind and considerate toward us. The Black people of India, however, the Tribals or original inhabitants of the land, were wonderful to us and embraced us as family. Among the Black folk with whom we interacted were the Dom, Santals, Mundas, Dravidians, Dalits, and Adivasis. We visited them in their homes, offices, and villages; in rural communities and urban slums, and in both university and academic settings. During our travels, we encountered a mosaic of Christians, Hindus, Muslims, Buddhists, Parsis, Sikhs, and Animists, and found that some of them engaged in the religious practices of our ancient African foreparents.

The sense of oneness and community we felt with the Tribals seemed almost mystical and magical. Everywhere we went, we reestablished bonds of brotherhood, sisterhood, and familyhood. We were treated as guests of honor at numerous receptions, cultural programs, and educational forums, many of which were sponsored or initiated by the Dalit Voice: The Voice of the Persecuted Nationalities Denied Human Rights, a publication founded and edited by V. T. Rajshekar. But whereas the individual members of my group were treated like visiting dignitaries and ambassadors, I was treated like a prince. At times, it was overwhelming.

Indeed, the Ancestors seemed to be traveling with us. At a major reception in New Delhi, the keynote speaker, Union Health Minister Dalit Ezhilmalai, focused his remarks on the life of Malcolm X. At a program in Bhubaneswar, the moderator, Dr. Radhakant Nayak, who reminded us of John Henrik Clarke, closed the afternoon with a stirring recital of Claude McKay's glorious poem of resistance, "If We Must Die!" In Trivandrum, I was presented with three ceremonial ankhs, symbols of the Egyptian hieroglyphic character for life, made of coconut shell and adorned with red, black, and green beads. At an airport reception, we were greeted with shouts of "Free Mumia Abu-Jamal!"[4]

We were also hosted by a number of Black youth groups in India, whose members told us of their life stories and village origins as well as their hopes, dreams, and aspirations. We were entertained by scores of singers and drummers and dancers. We met with Black women's groups who performed skits portraying family life and who shared with us a vibrant new spirit of resistance to domestic violence and centuries-old oppression. We visited some of the most downtrodden communities on earth, witnessed the miseries of the Black Untouchables, and were guests on several university campuses.

In Chennai, we were hosted by Bishop Ezra Sargunam of the Evangelical Church of India, where I was the guest speaker with Dr. K. Ponmudy, a major Dravidian scholar, in a program addressing the Black and Dravidian movements. In Orissa, I saw and photographed some of the blackest human beings I have ever seen. In fact, it was my impression that, in India, the blackest people were the

---

4   Mumia Abu-Jamal is an African American who was convicted and sentenced to death for the December 1981 murder of a Philadelphia police officer. Before his arrest, he was a member of the Black Panther Party, an activist, part-time cab driver, journalist, radio personality, news commentator, and broadcaster. Since then and from death row, he has become a controversial cultural icon, and his case has become an international cause célèbre.

Runoko Rashidi

most highly esteemed and considered more worthy than those Indians who were not so dark! In another city, at an elaborate and heartfelt public ceremony, my group and I presented school supplies to the entire student body of an aspiring educational institution, followed by cash contributions for the continuation of their work.

My "Looking at India Through African Eyes" tour was a resounding success and an incredible high! Indeed, I came away from this trip convinced that African people around the world truly are on the rise and that a real revolution is taking place in the hearts, souls, and minds of Black people everywhere. It was a great triumph. For me personally, it was only the first in a series of tours to India and other sojourns with African people around the world.

Africans Unite!

IN THAILAND AND CAMBODIA

December 11, 1999

"For the complexion of men, they consider black the most beautiful. In all the kingdoms of the southern region, it is the same." (Early Chinese Chronicler)

Four days ago, I returned home to San Antonio, Texas, from a two-week-long educational tour of Thailand and Cambodia. Quite naturally, the reason for my trip was to search for African people in that part of the world. It was my second trip to Thailand this year and my first ever trip to Cambodia. Until quite recently, however, I never really thought that I would have a chance to go to Cambodia, so my trip there was something of a dream come true.

You know by now that I am particularly interested in African migrations. You also know that the first humanity emerged from Africa, and that streams of African people have continued to flow across the world from ancient to modern times. It is therefore very important for us to address three questions: Exactly where did those Africans go? What did they do when they got there? And what happened to them subsequently? My approach to these questions is, of course, Pan-African in its nature and African-centered in its character. Consider my efforts an earnest attempt to reunite a family of people separated far too long.

The Khmers of Angkor

The most prominent and enduring kingdom of early Southeas Asia was that of Angkor (ca. 800-1431 C.E.), which was located primarily in Cambodia. The builders of Angkor were an Africoid people known as the Khmers, a name that loudly recalls ancient Kmt or pharaonic Egypt. In remote antiquity, the Khmers established themselves throughout a vast area that encompassed portions of Myanmar (Burma), Thailand, Cambodia, Malaysia, Vietnam and Laos. Noted Harvard anthropologist Roland Burrage Dixon wrote that the Khmers were marked physically by their "distinctly short stature, dark skin, curly or even frizzy hair, broad noses and thick Negroid lips."

The Khmers were sophisticated agriculturalists who created a splendid irrigation system with some canals as long as forty miles. They were also aggressive merchants who engaged in extensive and ongoing commerce with India and China, as well as intrepid warriors who designed machines to hurl heavy arrows and sharp spears at their enemies, and who rode into battle atop ornately decorated elephants.

In the Khmer language, Angkor means "the city" or "the capital." In 889 C.E., King Yasovarman I constructed his capital on the current site of Angkor. Over the centuries, consecutive Hindu and Buddhist Khmer kings augmented the city with their own distinct contributions. Angkor eventually covered an expanse of seventy-seven square miles and was designed to be completely self-sufficient.

The Khmers were magnificent stone builders, and for more than six hundred years, successive Khmer dynasties commissioned the construction of stupendous temple islands, marvelous artificial lakes, and incomparable mountain temples, including Angkor Wat—the crown jewel of Angkor—estimated to contain as much stone as the Dynasty IV pyramid of King Khafre in Old Kingdom Kmt or Ancient Egypt.

On Khmer Society

The earliest kingdoms in Southeast Asia emerged by the third century C.E. The region attracted the attention of Indian explorers and merchants as a rich source of coral, forest, and mineral products, all of which were extremely valuable to them. To secure regular access to these products, small colonies of Indian merchants were gradually established at strategic points throughout the area. With them came their ideas about government and administration, literature and religion, architecture and engineering, and the introduction of new technologies. Through the impetus of these Indian colonies (including strong Dravidian elements) and the native genius of the indigenous Mon-Khmer people, both of whom were highly Africoid and numerically significant, came the first known Southeast Asian monarchies.

The women of Angkor occupied an exceptionally high position in Khmer society, with upper-class women spending much of their time in intellectual pursuits. Not only were the genealogies of Angkor generally matrilineal in character, they repeatedly reveal the names of the grandmothers, mothers, wives, sisters, daughters, and granddaughters of the king. According to Christopher Pym, an Angkor scholar:

> *"Women occupied a dominant place in Khmer life, but the influence of upper-class women was marked. Usurpers of the Khmer throne had to show their relationship to previous kings through intermarriage. In priestly families descent and inheritance followed the female line."*

Pym further noted that all Khmer women basically had "burnished brown skin" and that the "common people" of Angkor were also "very dark, sometimes nearly black-brown."

Scholars too were highly regarded in Khmer society. Each Angkor temple possessed two library buildings, and manuscripts were abundant. The reign of Jayavarman V (969-1001), in particular, reflects a period of great intellectual prowess. Of that period, Lawrence Palmer Briggs, one of the most important modern chroniclers of the history of early Southeast Asia, wrote the following:

> *"There is probably no reign in the history of the ancient Khmers in which more distinguished ministers, scholars, dignitaries are mentioned in the inscriptions. The exalted trust to Prana by the king, the praises of Indralakshmi in the inscriptions and her erection of an image of her mother, and the foundations of Jahnavi, show the high social and political positions held by the women of Cambodia at this time. Chinese writers praise the women of Cambodia for their knowledge of astrology and government, and say the women of the royal family sometimes held high political posts, including that of judge."*

The reign of King Jayavarman VII (1181-1219 C.E.) marks the height and the beginning of the decline of the kingdom of Angkor. The earlier kings of Angkor had been Hindus, but Jayavarman VII was a devout Buddhist, whose second wife, Indradevi, noted by contemporary sources as "intelligent my nature, scholarly, very pure, [and] devoted to her husband") became the chief lecturer at a Buddhist foundation. Jayavarman VII was a militarist and a colossal builder comparable in stature to king Usemare Ramses II ("Ramses the Great") of Pharaonic Egypt. Altogether he lived more than nine decades, also like Ramses II, and ruled with strength and wisdom.

In Sanskrit, the word varman means armor; jaya means victory; Jayavarman thus represented the "protector of victory." True to his name, when Jayavarman VII was past sixty, he embarked on a series of military campaigns that extended the Khmer empire to Malaysia in the south, the borders of Myanmar in the east, and Laos in the north. Indeed, he was so successful in his wars with Vietnam that during the last period of his reign, central Vietnam was essentially an Angkor province. After his death in 1219, Angkor began to decline. By the beginning of the fifteenth century, the entire kingdom, which had been the most powerful entity in Southeast Asia since the seventh century, was on the verge of collapse.

During the fifteenth century, the Khmers endeavored to repulse a steady series of Thai invasions. Although the early people of the country now known as Thailand reflect a pronounced Africoid phenotype, the people I refer to here as Thai (sometimes called Siamese) were originally a tribal people without writing or an organized state. The Thai invaders of Angkor were Sinicized or Mongoloid types generally believed to be ethnically related to modern Chinese. In any case, they, or at least a large group or groups of them, lived in the southern and southeastern portions of the country now known as China. Similar peoples, Sinicized Vietnamese, brought about the final destruction of the kingdom of Champa in 1471.

The Thai invasions of Angkor were life-or-death struggles for the Khmers. Their impact on the Khmer economy was absolutely disastrous. Able-bodied Khmer men and the last remnants of the Khmer intelligentsia were abducted as captives and carried away, and the intricate irrigation system of Angkor, which required constant innovation and vigilance, ceased to work effectively. Excavations have shown that the Thais actually blocked the canals at Angkor so that the complex and elaborate irrigation system eventually ruptured.

In 1431, after a seven-month siege, the Thais occupied and ravaged Angkor and removed many of its statues. By the end of 1432, the Khmers physically abandoned Angkor and moved their capital first to the province of Sre Santhor and later to Phnom Penh and Oudong. Angkor eventually was retaken from the Thais and even experienced a brief renaissance in the late sixteenth century, but soon afterwards slipped into deep obscurity. However, even as late as 1860, a young French scholar and scientist named Henri Mouhot recorded in his diary that Angkor was "grander than anything left to us by Greece or Rome." Upon his first visit to the site, Mouhot wrote the following:

> *"In the province still bearing the name of Ongcor [Angkor], there are...ruins of such grandeur, remains of structures which must have been raised at such an immense cost of labor, that at first view, one is filled with profound admiration and cannot but ask what has become of this powerful race, so civilized, so enlightened, the authors of these gigantic works."*

The Ruins of Angkor and Angkor Wat

During my second tour of Southeast Asia in November 1999, I was able to travel to Cambodia and visit most of the major monuments of ancient Angkor. The 124-square-mile archaeological district of Angkor consists of several hundred monuments built of laterite, brick, and sandstone. Despite their partially ruined state, most of these monuments are absolutely splendid to gaze upon. Indeed, the monuments of Angkor stand as silent witnesses to the undiminished brilliance of the Khmer people. Most are dominated by images of King Jayavarman VII, and nearly half of the area's monuments are credited to him. Many depict his efforts to reconstruct the battle-scarred and essentially war devastated Khmer capital that he captured after being proclaimed king in 1181. The most magnificent of them all, however, is the towering monument known as the Angkor Wat.

My first full day in Cambodia began with a morning tour of the regal temple of Angkor Wat, the most famous of Khmer stone structures. It is truly magnificent to view this grand monument, which took thirty-seven years to build. The millions of tons of sandstone used in the temple's construction were transported to the site by river raft from a quarry at Mount Kulen, twenty-five miles to the northeast. Angkor Wat rises in three successive stages up to five central towers that represent the peaks of Mount Meru, the cosmic or world mountain that, in Hindu mythology, lies at the center of the universe and is considered the celestial residence of the Hindu pantheon. The towers of Angkor Wat, the tallest of which rises about two hundred feet above the surrounding flatlands, are Cambodia's national symbol. The temple's outer walls represent the mountains at the edge of the world, while the moat surrounding the temple represents the oceans beyond.

The Angkor Wat temple dates from the twelfth-century reign of Suryavarman II (1113-1150 C.E.). This was a time when the Khmer dominion over Southeast Asia was at its very pinnacle, when an empire known as Kambuja stretched from the South China Sea to modern Thailand, as far north as the uplands of Laos and as far south as the Malay Peninsula. Khmer history maintains that King Suryavarman II built Angkor Wat as a funerary temple for himself, and dedicated it to the Hindu god Vishnu, whom the king represented on Earth and with whom he integrated on his death.

Runoko Rashidi

Angkor Wat is decorated throughout with intricate bas-reliefs depicting stories from two epic Hindu poems, the Mahabrarata and the Ramayana. The images portray marching armies, fantastic demons, and vivid and sensual depictions of the celestial female dancers known as apsaras, whom French architect and archaeologist Henri Parmentier described in 1923 as "grace personified" and "the highest expression of femininity ever conceived by the human mind." During the era of Khmer rule over Cambodia, a walk to the center of Angkor Wat was viewed as a metaphorical journey of the spirit to the center of the universe.

As magnificent as Angkor Wat is, it is only one of 215 monument sites in the immediate region of Angkor. Other famous sites include the Bayon, the sculptured stone mountain at the center of the six-square-mile walled city of Angkor Thom (about a mile northeast of Angkor Wat) and the capital of the Khmer empire from the late tenth through the early thirteenth century. It is written that to protect Angkor Thom, Jayavarman VII constructed a moated stone wall around the city, along with five monumental bridges. The city and its environs must have had a considerable population because it is more spacious than any of the walled cities of medieval Europe and could have easily contained the Rome of the Emperor Nero's day.

The Bayon is my favorite Angkor temple. Second in size only to Angkor Wat, the Bayon is an intricate, eight-hundred-year-old shrine celebrated for the gigantic stone images of its builder, Jayavarman VII. An inscription on the Bayon temple pertaining to Jayavarman VII pays tribute to his status and esteem, stating that the monarch "suffered from the sicknesses of his subjects more than from his own: for it is the public grief which makes the grief of kings and not their personal grief." In 1297, a Chinese merchant named Chou Ta-kuan described this monument as shining with gold. On the eastern side of the structure, Ta-kuan wrote, was "a golden bridge, on each side of which are two golden lions, while eight golden Buddhas are placed at the base of the stone chambers." But I think I especially like this monument because, from a distance, it seems a mere mass of stone, but as you approach the temple in its park-like setting, you are immediately struck by the hundreds of huge African-looking faces sculpted into its walls.

The monuments of Ta Prohm and Preah Khan, which are almost has large as Angkor Wat, were also erected by the prolific Jayavarman VII. They were designed by him as mausoleums for his mother and his father, respectively. The inscription of Ta Prohm reveals that there were 102 hospitals in the Khmer empire when Jayavarman VII reigned. The medical personnel in each hospital consisted of two doctors, two pharmacists, fourteen guardians, eight male nurses, six female nurses, six orderlies, two cooks, two clerks, and sixty general assistants. The Preah Khan temple—a genuine labyrinth of pavilions, halls, and chapels—immerses about a square mile of ponderously wooded land just north of the enclosed city of Angkor Thom. According to the dedicatory stele dating to 1191, the site sheltered 515 pietistic portraits, each of which were embellished with immense quantities of silk veils and golden jewelry set with diamonds, emeralds, and pearls.

From the very beginning of my trip to Cambodia, I felt extremely blessed to have the opportunity to visit Angkor. Throughout the trip, I considered myself a pioneer, a pilgrim, and an honored guest.

I came away from my trip to Southeast Asia with the belief that the temples and monuments of Cambodia are about as impressive, with the clear exceptions of Egypt and possibly India, as any that currently exist anywhere in the world. Enshrouded as they are by massive jungle growth, the monuments of Angkor are simply splendid to look upon. They also reflect the sustained creative genius of Black people throughout history.

ON THE GREAT WALL OF CHINA

> *"How do we explain such a large population of Blacks in Southern China, powerful enough to form a kingdom of their own?" (Chancellor Williams, The Destruction of Black Civilization)*
>
> *"Most of the population of modern China—one fifth of all the people living today—owes its genetic origins to Africa." (Chancellor Williams, quoted in the Los Angeles Times, September 29, 1998)*

March 10, 2004

How many of us have wanted to visit China? I certainly did, so when the opportunity availed itself in March 2001, there I went. I was already in Hawaii anyway, and I was excited about going farther.

Not only was China the center of a great ancient civilization, it is a land with a deep history of African contributions. And me being a man with a keen interest in the global African presence, especially in Asia, I felt that I simply had to go. So it was that, buoyed by the fact that the trip was being handled by an African travel agency. I love to recycle Black dollars!

And so I arrived, all alone, in Beijing on March 4, 2001. And sure enough, sisters and brothers, it was not long after landing in China that I found myself, that same day, standing on the Great Wall. It was another dream come true.

But beyond the excitement of being there, how was it really? Actually, I was not all that impressed. I suppose that I had already been spoiled by Egypt. Indeed, after having visited Egypt a few times since my first trip there in 1992, I had come to the conclusion, by the time I visited China, that everything else pales by comparison.   I had visited India's Taj Mahal, Fatehpur Sikri; and Pink City; mighty Angkor in Cambodia; Great Zimbabwe in southern Africa; Bagan in Myanmar (formerly Burma); the rock churches in Lalibela, Ethiopia; Cusco and Machu Picchu in Peru; and a whole lot more—but none of those sites, though impressive, really matched up to the pyramids, tombs, and temples of Egypt.

But at least I can say that I was there, that I stood on the Great Wall of China. Good for me!

Following my visit to the Great Wall, I journeyed to the Ming Tombs, which I found interesting but not really awe-inspiring. It was during my visit to the Ming Tombs, however, that something happened which, in many ways, set the tone for my entire China trip: people started to follow me! Seriously! People, both men and women but especially young women, actually started following me around!

After a while, I just stopped in my tracks and asked my tour guide what was going on. He told me that my followers thought that I must be some kind of celebrity, and they were simply admiring me.

Runoko Rashidi

Well, after that explanation, I quickly calmed down and went on about the important business of sightseeing. But people continued to follow me around wherever I went in China, and it soon got to the point where folks were stopping me to shake my hand and asking to take photographs with me.

Well, worse things had happened to me, so I pretty much took all the attention in stride. Unfortunately, a lot more curious activity was to follow on my Chinese odyssey, and not all of it was as pleasant.

And so I got through my first day in China. After a long plane trip there, I had checked into a fabulous hotel, climbed China's Great Wall, visited the Ming Tombs, and been mistaken for a celebrity–all in a day's work in the life of Runoko Rashidi! I was fast on my way to becoming "a legend in my own mind."

Next day, fresh and relaxed, I went to the Forbidden City. I remember a lot of things about that second day. First, it was cold and windy. Second, there was not a scrap of litter on the streets. Third, I realized that language issues were going to be a big barrier. Fourth, none of the women wore tight or revealing clothes. Fifth, and perhaps more than important than all of the rest, I had not seen any Black people yet, either in a depiction or as an actual person! There were none in the Forbidden City, none on the Great Wall, and none in the Ming Tombs. So much for Blacks in Chinese Antiquity!

It also dawned on me that I hadn't seen any Blacks in the hotel, in the restaurants, or in the streets or anywhere. What is going on here, I wondered? Trust me when I say that this brother was starting to feel a little lonely.

On Day Three, I visited the Temple of Heaven and the Lama Temple, and unlike the other sites, I was impressed with both those places. This was followed the next day with trips to the Reed Moat Bridge, the Summer Palace, and Tianamen Square. I went to different restaurants every day, and the food was great.

So far, pretty good, but still no Black folks! What could have happened to them, I wondered? Wasn't this the place where Chancellor Williams said that we were once powerful enough to build a kingdom of our own? And hadn't my brothers James Brunson and Wayne Chandler earlier documented the existence of Black people in China? Hadn't Clyde Ahmed Winters done some pioneering work on the subject, and Reverend James Marmaduke Boddy written about the African presence in ancient China way back in 1905? And what about that 1998 DNA study, which concluded that most of the people of modern China had African genetic origins?

Again, I asked myself, what was going on? I admit I was starting to feel confused and a little lost.

The next day, I took an excursion about seventy miles out of Beijing to visit the East Qing tombs. I figured that if I couldn't find Black people in Beijing itself that I might have better luck elsewhere. The East Qing tombs were splendid and well worth the journey, although I still had not found what I was looking for. However, the people I met that day–peasants of Manchu stock, I was told—weren't friendly at all. Indeed, for the first time on the trip I met folks who actually seemed cold and even a little hostile toward me, and I didn't like it one bit. Then, when I asked my tour guides to tell me what the local people were saying about me, they just shrugged and asked me not to worry about it. I liked that even less.

By the fifth day of my trip, I had seen about enough of Beijing and the surrounding areas and felt that it was more than time for me to go. And so away I went to the city of Xi'an. You know the city: the one renowned for the terra cotta soldiers. I didn't get to see the soldiers the day I arrived, but I did make a long-anticipated visit to the Shaanxi Provincial Museum of History, said to be China's best museum. But it too was a big disappointment—not a sister or brother, ancient or modern—in the place! Damn!

In Xi'an, I went to the Tang Dynasty Museum. The Tang Dynasty represents one of the great high points in Chinese history, but there was nothing that I could say that was distinctly Africoid in the Tang Museum. My tour guides even brought the museum director himself out to meet me. They explained that it was the officially the director's day off, but when he heard that I was coming to the museum, he showed up anyway.

The director told me that he was honored to meet me and that I was the first Black man to ever visit the place. When I asked him about African people in the history of China, he drew a complete blank, claiming that he knew nothing about such a possibility. Well, at least he was consistent!

Although each of my three tour guides professed great stores of knowledge regarding early China, I could jar nothing loose from them regarding an ancient African presence. On the other hand, they all knew about the anti-African riots that took place in China in the mid-1980s. I was beginning to wonder if all of this, I mean my whole China experience, was kind of a dream or something.

The following day, however, was my best in China! I went to the Banpo Neolithic Village and drove past the tomb of Emperor Qin Shi Huang, and finally got to the museum where the magnificent terra cotta soldiers and horses are housed. These statues represent another high point in Chinese history, and I was impressed by the fact that both the tomb, soldiers, and horses all belonged to the same man who began construction of the Great Wall. The closest comparison I could make to that was to the great pyramid builders of Ancient Egypt.

For lunch that day, I went to another great restaurant, followed by a visit to an authentic Chinese tea house. All of the waitresses paused in their attention to the needs of the other diners to peep at me. Even the chef came out of the kitchen to take a look. And, oh yes, I also saw a couple of African American tourists and what appeared to be an African diplomat—and one of them actually talked to me! Wow!

In the next two days, I saw the Xi'an city walls, a Han tomb complex, a drum tower, and another museum. I noticed a few other things too. For one, it seemed that the Chinese, in general, smoke like chimneys, but are otherwise highly disciplined. Also, there are lots of unemployed laborers in China, but the street vendors seem overly aggressive and are everywhere. And there is a great deal of industrial pollution in China. The skies always seem hazy. Lastly, the Chinese people as a whole seem very proud to be Chinese.

Well, sisters and brothers, that was my trip to China. I am glad that went, but disappointed that I found no documentation of the African presence. I spent quite a lot of money in my search, too. I suppose I should have been better prepared, but based on all the work I had put into the African Presence in Early Asia anthology, I really thought that it would have been a simple process to find the

Runoko Rashidi

African imprint everywhere. The reality turned out to be far from the case. Even the artifacts that I saw dating from the Shang Dynasty period did not seem Africoid. At least they didn't to me.

And so, rather downcast, I returned to Beijing for one more night before catching an early morning flight back to the United States. After settling into Beijing's Mandarin Hotel, where I had a beautiful suite, I went out in search of what I hoped would be a really special meal before I departed the People's Republic of China. But it did not turn out that way. As a matter of fact, I never did get to eat that evening.

The first two restaurants that I went to were located in the hotel. In the first one, I waited about thirty minutes for service; when it didn't materialize, I simply got up and walked out. In the second restaurant, I felt distinctly unwelcome. Since I don't believe in spending money where I don't feel comfortable, I soon left that place, too. Then I walked around the block thinking that I would have more success outside the hotel, but the result was just more of the same. At one restaurant, I was quickly ushered in with a smile and what appeared to be words of welcome. Then, all of a sudden, all of the waitresses started to giggle and laugh. You better believe I got the heck out of there!

Sisters and brothers, I was livid! I not only let the front desk at the Mandarin Hotel have it about what I considered the overall rude treatment I had received at the hands of the Chinese, but I had plenty of venom left for my tour guides the next morning, too. All they could do was tell me how sorry they were and rather lamely explain that the local people were just not used to seeing Black folks, so I just blasted them some more.

So I guess you could say that my trip to China was a kind of bittersweet affair. Still, I'm glad I went because there is nothing like seeing a place for yourself. And many of the monuments I saw in China were indeed impressive, but I left there thinking that I would never go back again. And I could not help but wonder, again and again, about what happened to all of the Black people in China.

IN SEARCH OF THE AFRICAN PRESENCE IN TURKEY

November 3, 2004

This morning, I took a Turkish Airlines flight from Istanbul to the industrial city of Kayseri in central Turkey. The flight was pleasant and on time. My driver met me promptly at the airport and escorted me to the town of Uchisar in the Cappadocia region. Perhaps you can find it on the map.

I am sitting now, in my room in a very pleasant lodge, thinking that I have finally hit my stride here. I am having a grand day. Indeed, I am having the kind of day travelers dream about. First of all, it is so peaceful and serene here. There are not many tourists around, since the region lacks the big-city intensity of Istanbul. And the volcanic rock formations in the area are out of this world! They look something like gigantic mushrooms. I can think of only one other way to describe them, but you would probably think that vulgar (just use your imaginations and you may figure it out!).

So far today I have consumed, for the first time on the trip, a lot of things Turkish. I am talking Turkish coffee, Turkish tea, Turkish beer, Turkish grape juice, Turkish fruit, Turkish bread, and so forth–and I am loving it! And for once, I do not really mind being alone.

The atmosphere here is so laid back that I've had a lot of time to pause for reflection. For example, today I went out exploring in several of the rock caves in the area that were dug out long ago by Christian hermits. These caves have got to be at least a thousand years old and probably more. All of the images adorning their walls are of White people, and I am talking about a White Jesus, a White Mary, White saints, and everyone and everything White. However, I have learned not to let that bother me anymore, and the reason for that is because I believe that my thinking is quietly evolving. I mean, I was taught as a Christian growing up that God created me in his own likeness. Therefore, my reasoning is that if I am Black, then God, in some manner, must also be Black. Marcus Garvey said the same thing. Isn't that logical?

My thinking now is just the opposite: I believe now that people actually tend to create God in their own image, rather than the other way around. And that seems to me even more logical.

Anyway, reflect on that one for a while. Tomorrow, I am to visit an underground city and some more villages in central Turkey, before heading to the city of Ankara, the Turkish capital. But I will deal with tomorrow a bit later. Right now, I just want to continue to savor the moment a little longer. As the great Ancestor Imhotep is supposed to have said, "Eat, drink and be merry. For tomorrow we may die."

Discovering Magic in Southwest Turkey (November 8, 2004)

Every now and then during the course of my travels, something approaching magical happens. Today, in Turkey, one of those moments occurred. You should know by now that when I travel, I am always in search of the African presence, and this trip is no exception. Well, thanks to a diligent search, some prayer, an excellent travel agent, and an outstanding guide, I am happy to say that I have finally discovered just such a presence in Turkey, and it is a long-established one.

Today I am in the city of Kusadasi, located in southwest Turkey near the Aegean Sea. I was driven here this morning through the Black Mountains from the city of Izmir. It was not easy to get here because Kusadasi is far off the beaten path. It was raining (which I considered a good sign), and my guide, assisted by a small Turkish boy whom we picked up in a nearby village to serve as a translator, stopped at a house to ask directions. When he knocked on the door, two African women, a mother and daughter of Sudanese ancestry, peeked out of the window to see who it was. They seemed utterly shocked but very pleasantly surprised to see me sitting in the car. It was like they could not believe what they were seeing!

They beckoned us inside. I removed my shoes and, with a big smile, entered their house, followed by my driver, guide, and young translator. I guessed that the older sister was about fifty-five years old and that her daughter was about twenty-five. They both seemed a little nervous, but courteous nonetheless. The older woman immediately indicated that she would return shortly, leaving us with the young sister, who entertained us with small talk, still obviously flabbergasted by my presence.

When I asked her if she had ever met an African American before, she reacted as if I had asked her if she had ever been to the moon: with an emphatic "No!"

Within a few moments, the older woman returned. She was followed soon after by three more, older African sisters. They all seemed overjoyed to see me. They told me that they had never met an African from America before, and they claimed that because I looked just like them, that I was their brother. They served me Turkish tea, and we spent the entire morning together, talking and laughing. The whole time, they never stopped beaming at me!

I have rarely felt such joy and contentment. My search had been rewarded! And this is what we talked about: After I introduced myself as an African historian from America looking for documentation of the African presence in Asia, the sisters informed me that they originally came to Turkey from Sudan but that their families had lived in the Kusadasi community for generations, as far back as they could recall. They claimed that African people were sprinkled here and there throughout the southwestern region. They were all Muslims, they said, and that each reported having had three children, all of whom had attended the small local school. The sisters maintained that they and their children were discriminated against constantly by the White Turks. who treated them differently because of their color and called them Zanj ("Black"). They and their families were also very poor, they explained, because the income they generated from their hard, agricultural labor lasted for only for about three months of the year. The women also told me that they felt very much abandoned in Turkey, especially since each of their husbands had died many years ago. Sudanese government representatives had come to visit them about two years earlier, they said, but none had ever followed up on their promises to stay in touch.

Before my group and I left, I asked the women if I could take their pictures. They were real happy about that and jumped at the chance. So I photographed each one individually and then all collectively. Then I had my picture taken with each of them and took some additional photos of them with my guides. I also gave one of the sisters one of my business cards, but she told me that she could not read, so I gave it to her daughter. The daughter, I found out, was married to a White Turk, who had been imprisoned for some reason or the other that I did not press her about.

Knowing that the women and their families were very poor, I asked them, respectfully, if I could offer them a bit of money to help them out. They said yes, so I gave each of the elderly women about twenty million Turkish lira and the younger woman ten million. It is not as much as it might sound, but it was a substantial gift nevertheless. On top of that, I gave the eldest sister fifty US dollars and told her to share it with the rest. By then, they were all crying. I got kind of emotional too, but I was glad that I had asked them to accept the money and that they had not asked for it themselves. That way it was my idea, and they could maintain their dignity.

The sisters then offered up a prayer for me, blessing me and my travels. I told them that the morning we had spent together was by itself worth my entire trip to Turkey. They really liked that. They asked me never to forget them and said that they would never forget me. And with that, I left.

Yes, every now and then on one of my trips, there are magic moments such as these. I guess you could even say that my meeting with the African sisters in Turkey made a bit of history. Anyway,

My Global Journeys in Search of the African Presence

I think I'd better end this little travel note now as the emotions of this afternoon are starting to overwhelm me once again. I trust that you understand.

November 10, 2004

I am now back in London and missing Turkey. I left Istanbul for Amsterdam and London late this afternoon. I felt a little sad about leaving. So many incredible things happened during the nine days that I was there. It was the stuff of multiple lectures!

I met a number of other Africans in Turkey besides the Sudanese sisters I wrote about earlier, including a Black Egyptian family whose relatives have lived in the region for at least two hundred years. I met three other African brothers there, although I did not get to talk to them for very long.

I also visited the city of Anatolia, formerly known as Ephesus, site of a large Roman outpost in the western part of Turkey. St. Paul was said to have preached in Ephesus, and St. John was buried there. During my stay, I viewed St. John's grave, visited an ancient library, and toured the temple of Isis, within which the African deity Bes figures very prominent.

But there was one other experience that I had in Anatolia, among so many others, that really stands out. You can make of it what you will.

On a Sunday morning while I was visiting there, I traveled to an ancient house reputed by both Christians and Muslims alike, to be the dwelling where the Virgin Mary lived after the crucifixion of Jesus. Pilgrims come from all over the world to this site to pray for miracles. Now, although I was raised a Christian, I really had no interest in seeing the place, but my driver and guide took me there anyway. Initially, I decided not to bother with bringing my camera, as I was trying to save film, but at the last minute I threw it into my travel pack, and off we went.

So this is what I saw and what happened: Outside of the house was a brown statue of Mary. It did not make her look African, but at least the color was right. A young Christian nun was sitting on a bench at the entrance to the house. We went inside and viewed a number of images of Mary, most of which did not impress me. But then I my eyes landed on a statue of Mary and the infant Jesus that depicted both of them as Black!

Although no talking is allowed inside the house, I had to ask somebody about that statue. I quietly asked my guide if he knew the statue's age. Despite my quiet protests against disturbing the nun, he immediately went to ask her about it. I reluctantly followed, just to see if she would say anything. She mentioned, politely but very quietly, the rule about no conversation in the house, but told us that if we were really interested we could step outside very briefly for a word or two.

When we got outside, she told us that she thought the statue came from either Egypt or Ethiopia and that it was about five hundred years old. She also said that she believed that the black color of the figures represented something profound. Well, I thought that was a pretty good response and was prepared to let the matter rest, but she continued to talk about the statue's symbolism, even though she claimed she had no time to do so. She just kept right on talking. Soon, other people starting to gather around us to listen in on our conversation.

Runoko Rashidi

Through my translator/guide, I told her that I had seen a few Black Madonnas in my time and gave her the details about those images. She seemed very impressed and asked me for more information. More people gathered around us. I told her about the Black Madonnas I had seen in Russia and Spain and Costa Rica and France. She then shared that although the Madonna and child statue in Mary's house had originally come from Egypt or Ethiopia, it had been brought to Ephesus directly from La Puy in France.

I could not believe it! I had been trying to see the La Puy Black Madonna for twenty years, and there it was, right in front of me! I immediately launched into a short lecture on the history of La Puy and the Black Madonna, complete with references! I told her that Joan of Arc used to pray before that very statue. The nun said, in amazement, "Really?" and I said, "Yes!" Then she said again, "Really?" to which I again said, more emphatically that time, "Yes!"

By then, a large crowd was surrounding us—Greeks, Turks, Italians, Spanish, French, Japanese. I continued, explaining that one of the Crusades had been launched from La Puy. The nun was so flushed with excitement that she ran inside and brought the Madonna statue out of the house and into the sunlight, placing it right there in front of everybody while I just continued to lecture!

Thirty minutes passed, and the crowd continued to grow! I got even bolder and asked the nun if I could photograph the statue, even though I knew that it was strictly forbidden. To my surprise, she responded without hesitation, "Yes!"

I took about eight pictures of the statue, including one of her holding it. She even let me touch it! I felt like I was dreaming!

Then she told me to wait a minute and that she had some information inside for me. And that woman ran off and left me with the statue! Can you believe it? I could have put it in my bag and walked off with this precious icon! Anyway, a few minutes later, she came back with a lot of literature about her order and implored me to share it with the African community! Just to humor her, I agreed. Then, this nun—this young White European woman—grabbed my right hand and held it tightly for about five minutes. She did not seem to want to let me go! I almost had to snatch my hand away! I think we both had an experience that we will never forget.

And that is what happened on my last day in Turkey. A true story, sisters and brothers—believe it or not!

A BLACK MAN IN JORDAN

March 22, 2005

After a long flight, I arrived in Amman, the capital of Jordan, last night. This is my first visit to a "purely" Arab country, as I consider Egypt more African than Arab. I flew here from Athens, Greece, on Royal Jordanian Airways with a layover in Larnaca, Cyprus and then on to Amman. Someone from the tour company met me at the airport. Getting my visa was no problem, and in a short time there I was in the lobby of my hotel with the head of the tour company, a Palestinian with Jordanian citizenship. Indeed, about half the population of Jordan is Palestinian, including many of the Black people here.

After a bit of partying (yes, Runoko does like to have a good time here and there and now and then!), I hit the sack. I woke up early this morning to clear skies and balmy weather.

I like it here. I find the Jordanian people to be friendly and hospitable, so much so that I am reconsidering my attitudes about Arabs in general. That is the thing about travel, and I am honest enough to make the admission: quite often, things are simply not what we envisioned them to be.

Today, I did a tour of the city, including the big and beautiful King Abdullah Mosque, the Citadel, and, of course, the archaeological museum. I did not find the museum impressive but, like all the museums I have visited of late, it contains a number of Egyptian artifacts. The Citadel also houses an ancient Roman temple built during the reign of Emperor Hadrian.

From Amman I journeyed to Jerash, known in Antiquity as the Roman city of Gerasa. Among the early Roman outposts, Gerasa was even larger than Ephesus in Turkey. I rather liked the place. While I was visiting the museum in the historic district, a bunch of energetic young and not-so-young Jordanian children, out on a field trip, stopped in for a tour. It was a pleasure to see them, but the site was so large I was still able to find a bit of solitude.

And then came the highlight of the day: a journey to the Dead Sea and my first meetings with Black folks in Jordan, the most important of which, by far, was Brother Raja Juma.

Let me see if I can tell Brother Raja's story quickly. He was the Assistant Food and Beverage Manager at the Movenpick Resort and Spa Dead Sea. (The hotel is a wonderful place, and I am sure that the next time I bring a group of us to Jordan and Turkey we will definitely stay there.) In his position, Brother Raja was the "boss" of 270 people. He introduced me to several of them, three of whom were African, including a couple of family members.

Brother Raja was about thirty-five years old when I met him, a very handsome brother, extremely confident and proud, who spoke very good English. He looked like he could have come straight from the Congo. He told me that his grandfather was born in South Africa and moved to Palestine. His father later moved to Jordan.

Raja told me about all the dignitaries he had met, including former US presidents Bill Clinton and George Bush, former Secretary of State Colin Powell (whom he described as a "really cool brother"), former French Prime Minister Jacques Chirac, and many more. He said he had worked personally for King Hussein and the current King Abdullah, and that he liked them both very much. He even showed me photos that he had taken with them. He also explained that a lot of African American military personnel came to Jordan from Iraq on vacation, and that the reason he spoke such good English was through watching TV and talking to people.

To hear Raja tell it, about seven thousand Black people of various origins lived in Jordan—some from the Sudan, and others, like Raja's family, from other parts of Africa. Some have been in Jordan for a very long time, he said. Just how long, however, he could not specify.

Brother Raja told me that a lot of the Palestinians in Israel, Palestine, and Jordan are Black, especially those in Haifa and Jericho. He also claimed that Black people were not discriminated against in Jordan and that throughout his travels in the Middle East, including Saudi Arabia and the Gulf States, he had found that situation to be very similar. In fact, he said that the only time he had ever faced racial discrimination was during his three trips to the United States!

All the while Brother Raja was telling me this, I had a stunned and rather incredulous look on my face, but he just laughed and continued. In Jordan, he said, Blacks occupied high positions, particularly in the military. He concluded the discussion by telling me that he identified himself first as a Black man, then as a Jordanian, then as an Arab, and then as a Muslim. And then he paid for my entire, and I must say expensive, lunch and beverages.

It was quite an afternoon, and I think that Brother Raja and I definitely bonded. I think of him now as a friend. We are definitely going to stay connected.

Well, those are some of today's highlights. Tomorrow, I leave Amman and head south to the ancient city of Petra with numerous stops along the way. What a life!

A NOTE FROM SOUTHERN JORDAN

March 23, 2005

Today, I am in Petra, Wadi Musa, Jordan. Yesterday, I visited the ancient city of Petra. I was almost beyond words! Perhaps if I were to call it marvelous, or wonderful, or remarkable, or overwhelming, I might be able to come close. But I have never seen anything like it or been anywhere like it ever before!

The city of Petra is a couple thousand years old. It was originally built by people called the Nabateans–I am not sure who they were–then the Romans came along and built some more. Petra is, I think, the biggest ancient city I have ever seen. Just getting to the entrance point from the ticket office is about an hour's walk. Then you have to walk through this gorge for about an hour before you get to the first building.

This first building is called the Treasury, but it is really an ancient tomb. I've never seen anything quite like it. The stone is a kind of rust color with a lot of other shades blended in. The city itself expands out for many kilometers. I don't remember the last time I walked so much!

In Petra, I met the people who are today called Bedouins. Very interesting folks, the Bedouins. Some of them are very dark. They reminded me of the Gypsies I have seen while traveling in Europe. I shared a glass of tea with a few of them, and they informed me that many of the Bedouin are Black. I told them that I hoped to meet some of those Black Bedouin when I returned later with a tour group.

One of the big highlights of my visit to Petra was an ancient building known as the Monastery, which actually was an ancient tomb that was eventually converted into a church. Again, I had never seen anything like it. But first, of course, I had to get there. It is located on the side of a mountain, and you have to climb about nine hundred steps to reach it.

As I was walking up the mountain, I met this young Black Bedouin teenager who offered to take me to the Monastery on a donkey for five Jordanian dinar (the local currency). Since I figured that this would be a good way to chat with this young brother, I agreed. I am not sure if I would have made it otherwise. Several times, however, I feared that both the donkey and I were going to fall off the path. And I am talking steep mountainside here! I am glad that I did it, though. It was worth it. And getting down was no joke, either!

Following my visit to the Monastery, I visited the local museum, where I bought a book on the history of Petra and found a depiction of the Ancient Egyptian god Bes and what was described as "the face of a Black man." And then there was the walk back to my hotel! This time I was glad to find a donkey to ride. I would have preferred a horse or a camel or a carriage, but I was fresh out of dinars.

All things considered, it was quite a day. I ate some Bedouin food in the city of Wadi Musa, a town near Petra. You better believe that I slept real well that night!

So now I am ready to fly away. I have seen a number of Black people, talked to a few, ate some interesting food, made some lasting contacts, and seen Petra. Indeed, I am feeling humbled and subdued right now, and thinking about my upcoming adventures in Vietnam and Cambodia.

March 25, 2005

I am now in Amsterdam—that is, in Holland, the Netherlands. I was driven to the airport from Wadi Mousa to Amman last night and got aboard a very crowded flight from there direct to Amsterdam this morning. The roads in Jordan, just like those in Turkey, are excellent, and getting to the airport was a breeze.

The people in Jordan are rather laid back and open, even though the position of women is limited. I noticed, for example, that in all the hotels and other businesses in Wadi Mousa, I did not see a single woman employee. There were no women at the front desk of the hotels, no women working in the restaurants, no women cleaning the hotel rooms, no women working in the bars, no women vendors along the streets of the city. And strangely enough, throughout my travels in Jordan, with one exception, I did not recall seeing more than one Black person at a time.

By that last comment I mean that I never saw a group of Black people, except when I was at the Movenpick Hotel talking with Brother Raja. He introduced me to two of the brothers on his staff, and we took photos together. But beyond that, I only saw one here and one there, and most of them were very dark, which I thought was rather odd as well. But I met a brother who was working in a restaurant in Kerak, who told me that a lot of the Black people in Jordan were "Sudani" or Sudanese. That would explain the dark skin tones.

Otherwise, I would see Black man standing alone on the street, and another one working on a construction site with no other Blacks in sight. Then I'd see a "sole" sister walking down the street with a shopping bag, or a lone brother talking on a cell phone. I did see this one really fine sister working in a booth at the airport early this morning, but she seemed too interested in talking to a group of White men to notice me.

Runoko Rashidi

Although I never got the sense that there was a Black community in Jordan, none of the sisters or brothers that I saw looked "oppressed," either. Does that make sense to you? They just looked like ordinary folks going about their business. And absolutely everybody that I talked to, Black or White, Christian or Muslim, Bedouin or city dweller, assured me that there was no difference between them, that they were all simply Jordanians. It was tempting to believe them, but I guess I've been in America too long to fall for that.

The stars in the desert were beautiful last night. The moon was full and bright, and I had no problems to worry about. Jordan was a good experience, and I am glad that I visited there. I definitely want to see more of the Middle East, including Syria, Lebanon, Yemen, and even Israel and Palestine when the time is right.

More and more—from the historic record and from my travels around the world—I am discovering firsthand that African people are a global people. We are scattered far and wide and have made fantastic contributions to the world. And, for my part, there is nowhere on earth that I am not willing to go to find and further document the Global African Presence.

VIETNAM

April 11, 2005

This beautiful morning finds me in Hoi An, Vietnam. Hoi An is a charming port city. This is my first visit to Vietnam and already I have been in the north and now the center of the country. I leave for the south today.

It has been an excellent trip. I brought a tour group with me, and all of them have found Vietnam to be a wonderful country. Some of the major highlights so far, besides the general beauty of the country and its people, have been the two museums we visited and our trip to the ancient city of My Son. My Son is the religious center for the Cham, a clearly Africoid people, who were responsible for the classical civilization of Vietnam. The two museums were the Hanoi History Museum in the north, and the Cham Museum in Danang in central Vietnam.

We visited the Hanoi History Museum on two consecutive days. It was simply a delight to see both the new pieces on display there as well as pieces that I had seen previously only in books. A major section of the second floor of the Hanoi History Museum is devoted to telling the story of the Cham, but the Cham Museum, which houses the largest collection of Cham art in the world, is incredible. It ranks in the same category with the great museums in Egypt and Europe.

In a few days we will go to Ho Chi Minh City (formerly Saigon), where we will visit what used to be the national museum. That should be exciting. There is no telling what we will find there!

April 15, 2005

My tour group and I arrived in Ho Chi Minh City this morning. You may know the city as Saigon. Compared to the other Vietnamese cities I have visited, this is one huge city. It's like a cross between Paris and Manhattan.

The "big thing" that I've planned for my group during our visit here is a visit to the Vietnam History Museum. Those of you who know me know that I am something of a museum fanatic. I never pass up an opportunity to visit a new museum in my quest to find and document the global history of African people.

Indeed, the primary focus of my visits to Vietnam has been that nation's "ethnic minorities" (that's the politically correct term for indigenous people here) and the Cham. It has not been an easy search in either case. The Viets, the Mongoloid people of this region, are as much in denial about the role of Black people in world history as White folks—perhaps even more. And the Cham were as Black or Africoid as any group of people that I have ever heard tell of. I'm telling you, when you see the images of themselves portrayed in their art, you would think that you were looking at people from the Congo!

As for the ethnic minorities of Vietnam, there are Africoid people among them too, but you will have a devil of a time documenting them. The Viets will consistently tell you that there are no Black people in Vietnam. You can show them the photos from my book, The African Presence in Early Asia, and the photos of Africoid images in their national museums, and they look you right in the eye and say things like "They are just dark. They are not really Black." Those who are really in denial might say, "It is simply a bad photo," or "The photograph just looks dark." Others might say, "Yes, they used to be Black, but they are not Black now," or "Yes, they are Black, but they are not Black like other Black people!"

Isn't it amazing that this same syndrome of denial exists even here when it comes to the presence of purely Africoid people all over the world? Even our guides started spewing that racial nonsense during our museum tour today. They seemed to be nice people, but they stepped on my last nerve with that!

It is clear to me, sisters and brothers, that both White supremacy and Yellow supremacy are linked and tied, hand and hand. It is so frustrating! It also illustrates the extent of the work that must be done to construct the history of our people in Southeast Asia. Well, so be it! Perhaps that is simply the mission that the Ancestors have given us.

So you can understand that it is an emotional day for me. I have found artifacts that I never knew existed, and I have found further evidence of the spread of African people to the far corners of the earth. God Almighty and African Ancestors be praised!

Runoko Rashidi

IN SYRIA

October 31, 2005

It has been a while since I last sent out a travel note. After stopping in London for a few days a couple of weeks ago, I returned to France to relax for a bit. And by "relaxing," I mean working on my new book and playing with my daughter. She is just over five weeks old now, and she is starting to smile a lot. She is a beautiful child! But I guess that all parents say that, don't they?

I spent the past weekend in Istanbul, Turkey, and arrived early this morning in Damascus, Syria. This is my first visit to Syria, country number fifty-nine of all those I have visited.

I must confess that I was more than a little nervous about coming to Syria, but I said I wanted to see the world, so here I am. And, to my surprise, I actually like this country! The people seem friendly, and I certainly haven't gotten the impression that it is the kind of police state depicted by the US news media.

My day began, naturally enough, at the National Museum of Syria, where I saw a number of important artifacts relating to the African presence here, including a number of pieces from ancient Kmt and other artifacts that reflect a strong Nile Valley influence. I also saw an exquisite vase dated to about eighteen hundred years ago, depicting an African nobleman during the time of Roman dominance in this part of the world.

I later visited the Ummayad Mosque, considered the fourth most important mosque in the world. I was really impressed by it. Next to the mosque, near the medina (or the older, "native" part of town), is the house of one of modern Syria's early heads of state. In the house are three excellent paintings of Antar, a dashing knight and poet—and a Black man—regarded by the Arabs as the "father of modern chivalry." I took a number of good photos of that.

But the highlight of my day had to be my visit to the tomb of Bilal, the African from Ethiopia who is regarded as the closest companion of the Prophet Muhammad and considered to be the third person to adopt the Islamic faith. Visiting Bilal's tomb was not on my itinerary, but I found a way to squeeze it in anyhow, and was I ever thrilled to actually see the tomb, which is covered in a green shroud. I took several photographs of it and of the magnificent mosque next to it that bears his name!

To my delight, I saw many Africans along the streets of Damascus. In fact, I was surprised at so many Black folks! When I asked folks I met about this, I was simply told, in a matter-of-fact manner, that the Blacks were "just Syrians."

From Damascus, I traveled to the city of Palmyra. I had to cross the Syrian Desert to get here, as Palmyra is about one hundred and fifty miles from Damascus and about the same distance from the Iraqi border. It is an ancient city and full of history. The dominant personality from ancient Palmyra is a woman named Zenobia, to which J. A. Rogers devoted an entire chapter in his book, *World's Great Men of Color*.

So that's about it for now, African family, but I suppose that's an understatement because there is so much more I could tell you. Someone asked me recently, "Brother Runoko, don't you ever get scared going to all these places, especially by yourself?" My answer was, "Of course, I do!" I get plenty nervous and, yes, sometimes I am afraid. And I definitely get lonely and wish that I had some other Africans to talk to and share my experiences with.

I am not so tough that I don't sometimes wonder if I'm not taking my quest to identify and document the African presence around the world too far. But sisters and brothers, life is mighty short, and I am trying my best to live it as fully as possible. At the end of the day, I don't want the words, "could have," "should have," and "would have" coming out of my mouth. Life is good, and I am learning so much from my travels. I don't have many regrets about my choices, nor do I believe I would change a whole lot of them.

I do have one regret about this trip to Syria, however, and that is that it was not long enough. So far, I have found the local people here to be an incredibly friendly. Absolutely nobody has given me a hard time, and I feel safer here than I do in most places in the good ole' USA. I mean I really do like it here.

Anyway, keep a positive thought out for a brother. Tomorrow, I will visit the ruins of Palmyra, and the following day I get back on the road to Damascus, with some nice stops along the way. My travel agents are trying to arrange for me to meet with some members of the South African community there.

LOOKING BACK AT LEBANON

July 27, 2006

I was just in Lebanon earlier this year, in January, before the recent so-called Israel-Hezbollah War, which broke out a few weeks ago. I flew in to Lebanon from Paris via Italy and spent five days there. I had been told before my trip that Lebanon was a very safe place to travel to, so I went there all alone in search of the African presence, ancient and modern. I found a lot of it too.

I had some really memorable times in Lebanon. I met and talked with many Africans there who were Christians and Muslims and even Druze. I found the Lebanese people overall to be extremely friendly and welcoming. I was invited into a number of homes to share good food and drink a lot of tea. It was a very satisfying trip, so much so that I pledged to return.

I toured Beirut; traveled to the Bekaa Valley; met with a noted local archaeologist; and visited all of the major ruins at Baalbek, Byblos, Tyre, and Sidon. I even traveled to south Beirut, where so much of the recent devastation has taken place. That's why I cannot help but feel angry and saddened when I see news reports of the Israelis bombing Lebanon to bits. What a shame! What a tragedy! The Lebanese were so upbeat when I was there. They told me about the trials and tribulations they endured during the 1982 Lebanese civil war and how happy they were that the economy was strong again. They assured me that everybody was getting along.

Runoko Rashidi

Anyway, I am glad that I went to Lebanon when I did because it will never be the same. It was a safe country to visit then, but it is certainly not safe anymore.

REFLECTIONS ON BALI, INDONESIA, AND GUAM

March 6, 2007

I just flew in from Bali to Central Java, Indonesia. It is the rainy season here. It's hot and steamy, just after five o'clock in the morning, and I cannot sleep. I suppose that my restlessness may be a carryover from yesterday. There was a huge earthquake (some reports say there were two quakes) on the Indonesian island of Sumatra, followed by a tremendous rain storm in Central Java. No one knows exactly how many people died as a result. Officials are still counting the dead and injured, and tens of thousands of people are afraid to go indoors for fear of more destruction.

Ironically enough, I was just thinking yesterday morning that I probably should have included Sumatra on my itinerary. Good thing that I didn't! Don't worry, though, Brother Runoko is fine and well!

I am staying in a very nice hotel in the city of Yogyakarta (population about 500,000), called the heart and soul of the big island of Java. Most of the people here are Muslims. Indeed, Indonesia has the largest concentration of Muslims in the world—more than two hundred million. So far, however, I have not felt uncomfortable among the people here, even though I have only seen one clearly phenotypically Black person: a fairly light-complexioned young sister in the airport in Denpasar, Bali. I think she may have been from West Papua, New Guinea, which Indonesia invaded more than three decades ago. I spoke to her but got little response.

Bali is just the opposite of Java in that virtually everyone there is Hindu. I found that island, though pretty, to be very touristy (even though tourism was down) and a little overrated. I stayed within a short distance of the beach, but I was not terribly impressed with what I saw.

Still, everybody in Bali was polite and friendly to me. I managed to visit a couple of temples and naturally I went to the Bali Museum. I also rested a lot, as I was still a bit tired from February's African History Month activities.

But the real reason that I am here in Indonesia is within a hour's drive from my hotel. And believe me when I say that it was a real effort to get here. I left last Friday morning on a flight from San Antonio to Houston, Texas. From Houston, I boarded a thirteen-and-a-half-hour flight to Narita, Japan. From Japan, I flew to Agana, Guam. It was my fourth trip to Guam, and I spent the night there. It was great just to break up the trip and get a good night's rest. Then, late the next evening I finally arrived in Yogyakarta, where I got my visa, exchanged some money, caught a shuttle, and checked into my hotel. What a process!

And now I am where I am supposed to be, and I just hope that it will be worth it. I should know in a relatively short time, as just a couple of hours from now I will be on my way by car to the temple complex of Borobudur—the largest such structure in all of Southeast Asia. I don't know anyone else who has visited the place, so I suppose I will be something of a pioneer. Anyway, I have a car, a driver, a guide, a camera, and plenty of film. It is now just a matter of getting out and going!

March 7, 2007

This morning, I went to the magnificent Buddhist temple in Borobudur, about an hour's drive northwest of Yogyakarta. The Borobudur temple is one of major reasons that I came to Indonesia in the first place. It is a large temple, built around a small hill, and it ranks with the greatest temples in Southeast Asia, including those in Angkor (Cambodia), which I've visited three times, and Bagan (Myanmar), where I've been twice.

I consider myself very fortunate to have seen these temples. As a matter of fact, I think that Southeast Asia has the greatest monuments in the world outside of Egypt, even though I have yet to travel to the Sudan, Libya, Yemen, Iraq, or Iran. I have laid eyes on a lot of monuments in a lot of places--including Egypt, Ethiopia, Zimbabwe, Tunisia, Morocco, Peru, Mexico, Central America, India, China, Japan, Jordan, Syria, Lebanon, Turkey and southern Europe—but Southeast Asia is hard to top. Like I said, so far only the monuments, temples, and tombs of ancient Egypt have impressed me more. And Egypt, as you know, is in a category all by itself.

The Borobudur temple was built by the rulers of the Buddhist Sailendra dynasty in Central Java about twelve hundred years ago. It is made up of volcanic stone, and from a distance it has the appearance of a large pyramid. It took about a hundred years to build and it was in use for only a hundred years afterward.

The temple is said to have been conceived as a Buddhist version of the cosmos, built in stone. Its lower levels feature intricately carved reliefs, while the upper levels represent nirvana. Almost five hundred statues of the Buddha stare down at you from the heights of the temple, and at the very top is a large ornamental stupa. The edifice stood abandoned for almost a thousand years until the English and Dutch began the colossal task of restoring it beginning in the nineteenth century.

It is the "low" tourist season here in Indonesia, so there were not a lot of people at Borobudur this morning. By taking my time, I managed to climb all the way to the top of the temple, to the part of it called the Sphere of Formlessness. Although I did a lot of huffing and puffing, it was actually not a bad climb. The heat and humidity is what made it seem tough. But the view from the top was magnificent. The temple is surrounded by lush green hills and volcanoes, the latter of which some of the local people call "fire mountains."

I also went to see two related temples on my travels today. The first is known as the Mendut temple, which features a ten-foot-high statue of the Buddha inside. The second is called Candi Pawon. It is a small temple with a pyramidal roof.

The only problem I had with my visits to these temples was the vendors I encountered there. They besiege you, coming and going. Indeed, I have never seen such aggressive vendors, especially those at Borobudur. You practically have to pry them off of you with a crowbar once they come after you. And they just don't take "no" for an answer. Ignoring them doesn't help much, either. Even though I bought two nice shirts from one of them, a number of the others who were selling a variety of things that I did not want followed me all the way from the temples to the car, trying to make a deal. My driver, guide, and I laughed all the way back to Yogyakarta at their persistence!

Tomorrow, I visit the Hindu temple complex at Prambanan village. I should then be able to say "mission accomplished" in Indonesia!

March 8, 2007

Today, thank God, there are no earthquakes or rain storms or plane crashes to report. But I confess that I am starting to get a little bored. I have done pretty much what I came here to do.

This morning, I visited the Prambanan temple complex just northeast of Yogyakarta. It is essentially Hindu in character and is the largest such temple complex in all of Indonesia. And it is indeed impressive. All of the more than two hundred temples in the Prambanan area were built between the eighth and tenth centuries, when the southern part of Java was ruled by the Buddhist Sailendra dynasty and the northern part ruled by the Hindu Sanjaya dynasty.

The biggest of the Prambanan temples is called Candi Shiva. Candi is the Javanese word for temple, and this particularly grand temple is dedicated to the great Hindu deity Shiva. Candi Shiva is most imposing and stands close to fifty meters high. Like the Borobudur temple, it is composed of dark volcanic stone and covered with intricate reliefs telling the story of the Hindu epic called the Ramayana.

The Prambanan temples are spread out over an area of several miles. This morning, I was only able to see a few, including the larger ones. I would have seen more, but I accidentally ripped my pants climbing inside the big temple. Actually, I wasn't supposed to be inside at all. The place is surrounded by a high wire fence that was installed to keep people out, but I just could not resist the temptation to go inside, so I bribed a couple of the local guards to look the other way, and inside I went! The other impediment, in addition to the ripped pants (just a nice old pair of blue jeans), was that the heat and humidity were so high that I found myself soaking wet with perspiration after just a short time.

Believe me, sisters and brothers, I will never come back to Indonesia this time of year again! I knew that the climatic conditions were going to be tough here before I left the United States, but I had some extra time on my hands and some frequent flier airline miles to expend, so I came anyway.

I guess I really don't have anything to complain about, though. After all, how many people do you know who've been to Central Java? And here I am now after a day of sightseeing and exploring, sitting in the courtyard of an expensive and classy hotel, sipping exotic cocktails, typing on my laptop computer, listening to a nice compact disc of some Aboriginal Australian sisters that I bought in Alice Springs (Australia) a few years ago, and basically ignoring all the White folks, Japanese tourists, and Indonesians who are not-so-secretively scoping me out and trying to figure out what planet I came from! I tell you, my life is not all that bad!

March 9, 2007

I still have two more nights here in Yogyakarta, plus another night in Bali, and yet another in Guam before I return to the USA. Before I go, however, I wanted to share with you some of the basic observations I've noted about Indonesia.

First of all, Indonesia is a big place with a large population of over two hundred million people. It consists of more than 13,000 individual islands. Geographically, it stretches over five thousand kilometers or 3,200 miles (a distance roughly from San Francisco to New York or from Moscow to Madrid). It is southwest of Malaysia, north of the Indian Ocean and Australia, and southeast of New Guinea and the Pacific Ocean.

Compared to Japan, Europe, and the United States, Indonesia could be described as a pretty poor country. The average monthly salary of the employees in the hotel where I have been staying at for the last three days is about one hundred US dollars. Jobs are pretty hard to find here. I am told that national unemployment hovers at around fifteen percent. Apparently, the poorest people live in the rural villages. So far here, in the bustling city of Yogyakarta, I have only encountered two beggars.

Theoretically at least, men and women have equal status here. The former president of Indonesia was a woman, and a couple of days ago I saw a female security officer. I have heard nothing of rape or domestic violence. Both women and men work in the hotel restaurant, the bar, the business center, and in the reception area, but men clean the rooms. The hotel itself is spotless.

In Indonesia, education is compulsory for both boys and girls until the age of fifteen. I don't know what the literacy rate is. Health care, not surprisingly, seems to depend upon how much money one has. Generally speaking, Indonesia seems like a relatively conservative country. Divorce is legal, but abortion is not. Drug trafficking is punishable by death.

There are more than three hundred ethnic groups here and a lot of different languages and dialects are spoken. English is pretty widely spoken, although a good portion of the time I can't understand a word of what the people around me are saying, and I often have difficulty making myself understood. But the people are invariably polite, and a friendly smile goes a long way.

I still have not seen but one Black person in my Indonesian travels, although I am told that a number of people from West Papua, New Guinea, come to Yogyakarta as students and are well received. The people who are not so well received or well liked, however, are the Chinese. Chinese own many of the businesses here and, according to my guide, they live separate and apart from the Indonesians.

Most Indonesians are Muslims, but most don't seem to take their religion very seriously. I've only seen a couple of mosques. There are a lot of Christians here and some Buddhists, and the island of Bali is mostly Hindu. Although it does not seem as rigid as India, a four-tiered Hindu caste system exists in Bali, with the Brahman caste being the highest and the Sudra caste the lowest. My guide in Bali was a Sudra.

Runoko Rashidi

Indonesia is also a crowded country, especially the densely populated big islands of Sumatra and Java, and particularly Java. Indeed, Java alone contains more than sixty percent of the total Indonesian population.

I read and was told more than once before I came here that there was a lot of anti-Americanism in Indonesia and that I probably should not visit here at all. That may be the case in the capital of Jakarta or maybe on the island of Lombok, but I have not seen evidence of it in Central Java and Bali, or at least I have not been impacted adversely by it. Of course, I haven't heard anything positive here about George Bush, either.

The national currency in Indonesia is the rupiah. Today's exchange rate is about nine thousand rupiah to one US dollar, so right now, with 900,000 rupiah in my pocket, I am almost a millionaire.

The most popular way of getting around here is on a motorcycle. I don't think I have ever seen so many motorcycles in one place before! At traffic lights, for a few coins, guys with guitars serenade bikers and drivers alike, hoping to make a few rupiah in the process.

Some aspects of US society, like the popular American fast food restaurants, are common here. I have seen at least one McDonald's restaurant and several KFCs. I've also seen a couple of Pizza Huts and one or two Dunkin Donuts. I confess that I broke down twice at the latter and bought a couple of glazed donuts. Hey, I got weak! What can I say? Just don't tell my doctor!

Like I said, Indonesia has a tropical climate, and it has been hot and humid from the time I stepped off the plane from Guam. They grow a lot of rice in Indonesia, and there are rice paddies and lush foliage galore, as well as lots of fruit trees. I've seen more than my share of cockroaches and a handful of lizards. I'm also told that cobras are pretty common here.

Speaking of rice, it is served with virtually every meal. I do like the food here, even though my guide informed me that rodents and even dog meat are frequently on the menu. It's actually about lunch-time now, and I think I am going to grab a book, go down to the hotel courtyard, and order some fresh juice and a good steak. Maybe later tonight I will go check out a cultural performance somewhere.

So, for Brother Runoko, for this day at least, life is in the slow lane. Tomorrow, I return to Bali where I intend to spend my time walking on the beach and maybe do a little shopping.

March 12, 2007

I left Indonesia for Guam late last night. I guess it was time to leave, though. My visit there was one of the most boring trips I have ever had. Thankfully, there are always more temples to wander through, more beaches to stroll upon, and much, much more to see on the next distant horizon.

So off I went. I am looking now at the wide Pacific Ocean from the vantage point of my hotel room in Agana, Guam. It is a postcard-beautiful view, tranquil and serene. I am reflecting on my wonderful good fortune regarding my continued good health and contemplating some of the places that I plan to visit over the next few months.

Guam, a very attractive place, is a small island in the North Pacific. Officially, it is part of Micronesia, but it has a close relationship with the United States. There are a couple of US military bases here and thus a substantial American presence, combined with a lot of Japanese tourists and a large number of migrants from the Philippines. I have been here at least four times now since Guam has been an important transit point for some of my recent travels.

The local people in Guam are a pretty friendly group called the Chamorros. I really think they try to be especially nice to African Americans—at least, that is the impression that they give me. I wouldn't necessarily call them Africoid, but they do have beautiful brown complexions–not terribly different from those of the Indonesians.

Indeed, my biggest problem (or rather, disappointment) in Indonesia–not to say that the Borobudur and Prambanan temples were not nice—but unlike the ancient art in Vietnam and Cambodia and even Thailand and Myanmar, the imagery, statues, and reliefs in Indonesia did not quite reflect what I consider a phenotypically Africoid character. They just did not look overtly African to me. Only one of the statues that I saw inside a highly darkened Prambanan temple, a piece dubbed "the slender virgin," looked like a Black woman. But I guess that's the way it goes sometimes, and maybe that's what makes the temples in Southeast Asia that much more special.

So that is it for now, sisters and brothers. My mission in Indonesia has been accomplished! I am glad that I came here, but I would have loved to have seen more Africoid-looking things and people on my Indonesian journey. For now, however, Indonesia is behind me.

MYANMAR ON MY MIND

May 28, 2008

Although it has started to fade from the public consciousness (so many disasters have happened around the world!), I can't help but give a lot of thought to what has been occurring in Myanmar in Southeast Asia. I'm referring to the massive cyclone that took place in that country earlier this month and its aftermath. More than 100,000 people have been reported dead there.

I was blessed to visit Myanmar twice, first in late August and early September 2001 on my own, and then in either November 2002 or 2003, as a group tour leader. On both visits, I was nervous the whole time. Myanmar is a very poor and fairly isolated nation with a military government that keeps a tight lid on political expression and social activism.

Myanmar is a relatively large country by Southeast Asian standards and was known under British rule as Burma. I thought that the place was absolutely fascinating, but few Africans go there. Indeed, it is one of those places where, just by walking down the street, a Black person tends to stop traffic.

Myanmar first began to figure prominently in my consciousness in 1999, when my travel fever was just starting to rise. I remember being on a plane returning from Thailand to the United States listening to this White guy sitting right behind me going on and on about a train ride that he taken in Myanmar—a country that I had previously thought of as mysterious and foreboding. He simply could not keep his mouth shut about it! It was not the first time that I had heard about the place, but listening to him talk about it in such a manner left a clear and distinct impression on me.

The big draw in Myanmar, for me, was its temples. In a place called Bagan in north central Myanmar, the remains of close to five thousand Buddhist temples are located in an area of only about twenty-five square miles. It is truly a temple field come true! I don't think that there is anything else quite like it in the world—not even in the Nile Valley in Africa!

I don't know who the builders were, but the temples were erected over a period of about two hundred-fifty years from around 1050 to 1300 C.E. They are spread out over grassy fields on or near the banks of the Irrawaddy River. And no two temples are the same.

The Irrawaddy in Myanmar is similar to the Nile in Egypt and the Niger in West Africa. It is the region's lifeline. One evening, I got on a boat and journeyed down the Irrawaddy just to watch the life of the country unfold around me. I saw farmers using the river to irrigate their fields, fishermen casting their nets in it, children swimming and frolicking on the riverbank, women bathing in the river water and also washing their clothes and cooking utensils in it. And everybody, of course, on- and off-shore, watching me watch them. All seemed friendly, however, and most smiled and waved at me. For me, life, at least for those few moments, rarely seemed so tranquil.

The Bagan region is so agrarian that once you get away from the river, it is best to rent a bicycle or a horse and buggy so that you can move easily from temple to temple. It was not so easy securing a room in the Bagan Hotel, located along the banks of the Irrawaddy, with an ancient temple right on the hotel grounds. But I was able to do so, and believe me, I thought I was in paradise!

The hotel itself is built in the likeness of an early Bagan temple. It offered virtually no TV or radio access, and I really had no one to talk to, so all I could do besides visit temples was read and dream about all the other places I was going to visit. Of course, that was before "9/11" (September 11, 2001), and places like Yemen and Pakistan and Iran and even Sri Lanka were high on my list of potential destinations. And after the World Trade Center and Pentagon attacks, which took place exactly two days after I returned to the US from Myanmar, the whole world was turned upside down. I wonder now if I will ever get to see those fabulous lands.

But who knows? After all, I did get to visit Indonesia last year, so perhaps the dream hasn't completely died.

One of the things that stood out about Myanmar to me was the chalky substance that most of the women and many men there spread on their faces. I was told that they used it to keep their skin from getting dark and that light skin was much desired among the people of Myanmar. This inclination may have been as much about class as race and ethnicity, however. For instance, I was also informed that if a woman was dark-skinned, that probably meant that she was a peasant. If one was light-skinned, then it probably meant that they did not work laboring in the fields.

After leaving Bagan, I spent most of my time in Yangon, which was then the capital city of Myanmar. Even there, the cityscape is dominated by a temple: the massive and splendid Shwedagon Paya. Of course, I visited the big archaeological and ethnographic museums in both Bagan and Yangon, but I experienced some very different reactions from the people I met in each setting.

In Bagan, for instance, I encountered a group of young Myanmarian men who seemed to be having a good time making fun of and laughing at my African features. In Yangon, I encountered a group of young schoolchildren in a museum and one of them, a little girl, seemed absolutely terrified of me. The look in the girl's eyes could not have reflected more fear than if she had seen the devil itself! She was simply horrified by my presence. I've never had a experience like that before or since, and it was something that I will never forget. I will say, however, that experiences like that have happened to me only in Asia and nowhere else.

Research into the African presence in Southeast Asia, including Myanmar, should be a special area onto itself. Though some would deny the very existence of Africans in that region of the world, during my 2002 group tour to Myanmar, our tour guide informed me that he knew of an entire community of African pearl divers who lived twenty miles south of Yangon. Years later, I wonder if they are still there—or if time and circumstance, particularly the massive cyclone of a few months ago, destroyed or displaced that African community? And how did they get there in the first place?

Other local guides I have worked with in Southeast Asia have also informed me of "unmixed" Black people in east central Cambodia. And Black people clearly inhabit southern Thailand and northern Malaysia. There is also fairly well-documented evidence of indigenous Black people in the Philippines and the Montagnard communities in Central Vietnam.

Southeast Asia is an archaeological treasure trove. I miss it, and I miss Myanmar in particular. Maybe next year, I'll make one last grand trip to Southeast Asia in search of the African presence. And maybe I will do it right this time by returning to the old sites in Thailand, Vietnam, Cambodia, and Myanmar and visiting new places like Laos, Malaysia, and even the Philippines.

Runoko Rashidi

PART III

IN SEARCH OF THE AFRICAN PRESENCE IN EUROPE

A statue of a Moor in 17th century Italy

An African face from the Etruscan world, circa 450 BCE

I have long believed that Europe has a great deal to offer me in my search for and the construction of the African presence—principally, excellent museums and plenty of African people in the flesh and the here and now. Indeed, there have been times when I have wandered the streets of London, Amsterdam, and Paris and wondered if I was actually in Europe at all and not in Africa or the Caribbean. Even in northern European countries like Denmark and Sweden and in East-Central European countries like the Czech Republic, Hungary, and Poland, one can usually find a smattering or more of African people.

My travel writings on Europe are fairly comprehensive, but the major missing areas in my notes and recollections are of Scotland and Wales. In Edinburgh, however, I visited a castle and two excellent museums. One museum featured a rare depiction of one of the great kings of Kmt, Nebhepetre Mentuthotep II, which I photographed for my collection. I also met a handful of Black people from Scotland while there and got a tremendous kick out of hearing sisters and brothers speak English with a thick Scottish brogue. Their accents seemed almost unreal!

Wales, on the other hand, was largely uneventful. I took a day trip from London to Cardiff only to find the museums in my destination city wholly unimpressive. The only thing that really stands out about Wales in my memory was the train ride there and back and the delicious lunch I had at an Indian restaurant in Cardiff.

The only other part of Europe that I have visited but not written extensively about is Vatican City—the Holy See. I always thought of the Vatican as part of Rome and commented just briefly about my visit there (see "Eternal Rome": Black Power in the Roman Empire"). But I did enjoy the fascinating museums in Vatican City and would love to visit them again. Also, while I was there, I found an interesting postcard with an image of St. Peter as a Black man.

Yes, there is always more to see, more to do, and more to investigate. In any event, I began my European explorations in Russia, so I'll start there.

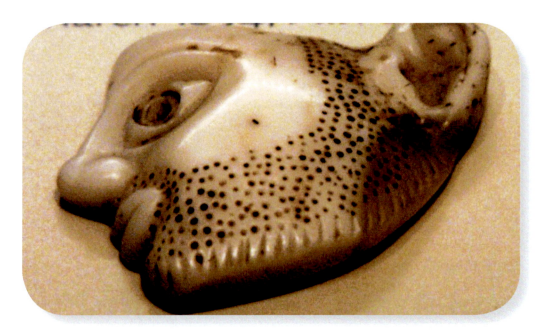

A shell inlay of an African man in ancient Crete

The ruins of Knossos on the island of Crete

Runoko Rashidi

Greek vases in the form of an
African head, Athens 450 BCE

Head of an African girl in ancient Corinth, Greece

Etruscan vases in the form of African heads

Ethiopian soldiers on Greek vases, 450 BCE

An Etruscan vase in the form of African and a Caucasian head

Runoko Rashidi

An Etruscan vase with the head of Hercules
on one side and an African on the other

A marble head of an African youth in ancient Rome

My Global Journeys in Search of the African Presence

An image of an African from ancient Capua, Italy

An African youth with a crocodile from ancient Rome

A Roman coin with African features, 215 BCE. Strongly believed to be Hannibal Barca.

A Roman vase with the features of an African youth, 250 BCE

Severus Septimius, founder of the Severan Dynasty of Rome in 193 CE

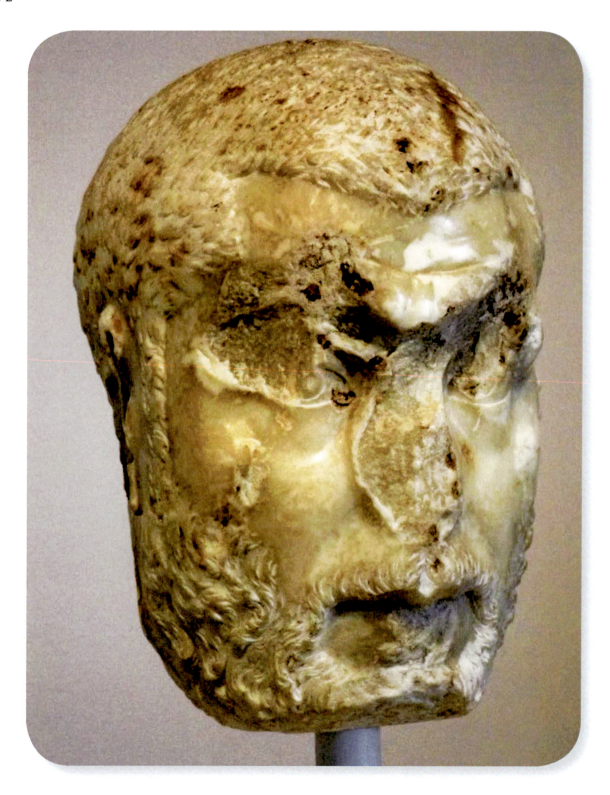

A marble head of the Moorish emperor of Rome, Macrinus

Runoko Rashidi

The Black Madonna at Halle, Belgium

The Black Madonna at Einsiedeln, Switzerland

A European coin depicting Christ, unknown date

My Global Journeys in Search of the African Presence

The Black Virgin of Paris

The Black Madonna in Prague, Czech Republic

The executioner from the Judgement of Solomon, at Chartres, France

Runoko Rashidi

Ethiopian Magi, Berlin

My Global Journeys in Search of the African Presence

176

The Ethiopian Magi, Lyons

Image of a prominent Black man in 16th century Holland

Runoko Rashidi

The remains of a Moorish castle in Sintra, Portugal

A golden head of a Moor in Bavaria

My Global Journeys in Search of the African Presence

UNCOVERING THE AFICAN PRESENCE IN RUSSIA: ALEXANDER PUSHKIN AND MORE[1]

"Pushkin was the Russian spring. Pushkin was the Russian morning. Pushkin was the Russian Adam" (A. V. Lunacharsky, quoted in John Oliver Killens, Great Black Russian: A Novel on the Life and Times of Alexander Pushkin, 1989).

June 9, 1999

I returned today from a nine-day study tour of Russia, most of which was spent in Moscow and St. Petersburg. It was my first visit to that country. The tour celebrated the 200th birthday of the brilliant Russian writer of African descent, Alexander Sergeievich Pushkin, and it included a two-day symposium on Pushkin at Moscow State University and visits to some of the major sites in Pushkin's brief life.

Alexander Pushkin, born in Moscow on May 26, 1799 (although several different birthdates have been offered for him), is widely regarded as the patriarch of Russian literature because he composed his major works in Russian during an era when most Russian writers composed in French. Among his most significant works translated into English are Eugene Onegin, The Ode to Liberty, The Captain's Daughter, and Boris Godunuf.

Pushkin was descended on his mother's side from Major General Ibrahim Petrovich Hannibal, reputed to be an African prince who became a favorite of Russian Czar Peter I (1682-1725). In an unfinished work, The Moor of Peter the Great, Pushkin paid great homage to his illustrious ancestor, repeatedly referring to him as "the Moor," "the Black," and "the African." By all accounts, Major General Hannibal was an extraordinary figure. Born in Cameroon, West Africa, he was captured as a child and taken to Europe, where he became a personal favorite of Russian Czar Peter I and rose to high rank during the reign of Peter's successors. As a young man, he assumed the name Hannibal to signal his affinity for one of the most outstanding figures in african antiquity.

Czar Nicholas I reputedly hated and feared Pushkin, yet he also called him "the most intelligent man in Russia." Allison Blakely, author of the 1987 volume, Russia and the Negro: Blacks in Russian History and Thought, maintained that "Pushkin was truly the counterpart to Shakespeare." Indeed, Russia's most distinguished writers have lavished effusive praise on Pushkin. Feodor Dostoevsky, for example, wrote that "no Russian writer was ever so intimately at one with the Russian people as Pushkin." According to Maxim Gorky, "Pushkin [was] the greatest master in the world. Pushkin, in our country, is the beginning of all beginnings. He most beautifully expressed the spirit of our people." Ivan Turgeniev's praise of Pushkin included the following: "Pushkin alone had to perform two tasks which took whole centuries and more to accomplish in other countries, namely to establish a language and to create a literature." Add to that the words of Nikolay Alexandrovich Dobrolyubuv, who wrote, "Pushkin is of immense important not only in the history of Russian literature, but also in the history of Russian enlightenment. He was the first to teach the Russian public to read."

---

1   Dedicated to Lily Golden (1934-2010) and John Oliver Killens (1916-1987).

Runoko Rashidi

Alexander Pushkin died prematurely on January 29, 1837, from wounds suffered defending his honor in a duel. Bronze statues of his likeness can be found throughout Moscow and St. Petersburg. Throughout Russia, cities, town squares, and museums are named after him, and his portraits are everywhere. He is much beloved and remains one of Russia's national heroes.

During the bicentennial tributes and celebrations of his life that took place in 1999, Pushkin was honored by hundreds of thousands of people. I personally gave two presentations on him and his historical significance while on my recent study tour. I also had the opportunity to visit the school that Pushkin attended and two of his residences. I found it quite interesting that on the desks upon which Pushkin wrote were figurines, apparently inkwells, depicting African men seemingly breaking the shackles of slavery.

The tour of Russia was a highly interesting experience. All the members of my tour group, most of whom were African American, appreciated the significance of the trip. We all felt that we were honoring Pushkin—in our eyes, a great African—with this pilgrimage. His presence seemed palpable to us all, almost tangible.

I took a great many photographs during the trip and asked a lot of questions. I learned a great deal and even tried to teach a bit. During the course of the two presentations I made in Russia, I felt that it was my mission to stress, first of all, that Pushkin was not an isolated entity in European history, and that other Africans before, during, and after him had made their mark in Europe and had left brilliant, even if sometimes little-known, legacies in that part of the world. Additionally, I was determined to demonstrate, to Africans and Russians alike, that Africans history around the world, including Europe, did not begin in bondage. My audiences' reactions and expressions seemed to indicate that I was successful on both counts. I felt as though I was honoring and championing not only Pushkin—our great Ancestor—but also African people everywhere.

Overall, I found Russia to be a fascinating place. Major cathedrals adorned with scores of dark-skinned icons abound. Likewise, Egyptian motifs are common. Plus, in St. Petersburg, a city built on the shores of the Baltic Sea and the Gulf of Finland, it remained light outside until 3:00 a.m. This provided more than enough daylight to engage in some excellent sightseeing. While there, I visited the famed Hermitage, reputed to be the world's largest museum. While in Moscow, I visited the Kremlin, Red Square, and Lenin's Tomb.

Like all journeys, however, my Russia trip was not without its share of headaches and problems. Russia is certainly not among the most pleasant places I have visited during the course of my global travels throughout the years. Most Russians speak very little English and gangs of racist skinheads roam the streets of its major cities at will. The cost of living is also high, and poverty is widely visible. Old women and children beggars are commonplace. (I must confess, however, that it did seem a little strange to see White people begging!)

But not for a minute do I regret having made my Russian tour. After all, Russia is the home of Ibrahim Hannibal and Alexander Pushkin. Still, when my Russian tour ended, I was more than ready to leave.

Sisters and brothers, I love Pushkin, but Russia is not the place for African people! I left there with the strong feeling that Russia is a White man's country, and in the words of Jamaican dub poet Mutabaruka: "It's not good to stay in a White man's country too long." How true, how true!

"Eternal Rome": Black Power In The Roman Empire

> *"At the time that the twelve African Christian martyrs died in A.D. 180, there were living two great African personages: Septimius Severus, who later became Emperor of Rome; and Tertullian, one of the greatest of Church leaders"* (J. C. DeGraft-Johnson, African Glory: The Story of Vanished Negro Civilizations, 1998/1954).

May 11, 2004

I flew into Rome on this, the first leg of my European journey, which I began in January 2003. And so it was that, after making the connecting flights from New York to London to Amsterdam to Rome's Leonardo DaVinci Airport, and after a late night check-in at the Royal Gambrinus Hotel in the Italian capital's city center, I was ready to begin my tour of "eternal" Rome—one of the world's most celebrated cities.

Actually, I had not even planned to visit Rome on this trip. I thought that I had secured a speaking engagement in Stockholm through some African brothers I know in Sweden, but when that fell through and with time in Europe on my hands, Rome became an attractive prospective destination. Much to my delight, I found that someone special would be looking out for me when I got there—none other than Samia Nkrumah: Kwame Nkrumah's youngest daughter!

During the course of the next several days, I really came to like Sister Samia, and not only because of her distinguished father. She had been described to me beforehand as a bright, young, and very energetic political journalist and as a person who could provide me with many important insights during my stay in Rome.

Indeed, Samia turned out to be both beautiful and charming, and a really good sister too. I enjoyed her company immensely. She even arranged for me to give a slide presentation at a local bookstore, so you know I liked that. As a result, not only did I visit Rome but I also lectured there! And, to top it all off, my lecture, which was translated to the Italian audience by Samia's husband, was followed by dinner, coffee, cocktails, and conversation that lasted well into the night.

Thanks so much, Sister Samia!

Alas, Samia was a sort of African oasis in a kind of Roman desert, as I saw only a scattering of other Africans during my visit, and they were mostly Somalis and Ethiopians. I also saw a handful of Algerians, Moroccans, and Tunisians, a few Senegalese, one brother from Ireland, and the occasional African American tourist.

Runoko Rashidi

The attraction that Rome had for me, and what made it such an exciting destination, was its vast store of antiquities, but there is really far too much to see in Rome than can be taken in during the course of only a week's time. Still, I did get to see a bunch of wonderful sites and monuments, including the Coliseum, Trajan's Column, the Baths of Caracalla, the City Walls, the Imperial Forum, the Circus Maximus, the Pantheon, the Pyramid of Caius Cestius, the obelisks of Thutmose III and Ramses II, and quite a few other places too. These were all impressive structures, and I was happy to see and photograph them firsthand, but I must say that, as a whole, they paled in comparison to the mighty ancient monuments of Egypt. I also visited the heavily scaffolded great obelisk of Axum, which was taken to Rome from Ethiopia by the Italians during the Italian occupation from 1935 to 1941. And, of course, I went to all of the major museums, including those in the Vatican, the Capitolini Museum, the Etruscan Museum, and two national museums: the Palazzo Massimo Alle Terme and the Museo Nazionale Romano.

The Vatican museums house a vast collection that includes a number of excellent Greek and Roman pieces and some exquisite pieces from ancient Egypt. Its Egyptian collections include a larger-than-life statue of Queen Tuya (wife of Seti I and mother of Ramses II) of the Nineteenth Dynasty, which was originally in Ramses II's mortuary temple (the Ramesseum) before it was taken from Egypt to Rome by the emperor Caligula. The Capitolini Museum, described as the "oldest public collection of ancient artworks in the world," also houses a set of ancient Egyptian artifacts and a superb image of Diana (Artemis) of Ephesus as a multi-breasted, Black fertility goddess. To give credit where it is due, however, I must say that the Romans worked wonders with marble. Probably the best and most stunning representations of their works in stone are housed in the Capitolini Museum.

The Etruscan Museum, whose halls I was able to wander toward the end of my stay in Rome, is likewise splendid. The Etruscans were the precursors of the Romans in Italy, and their culture reflects a considerably closer relationship with ancient Africa than that of their successors. Two or three Etruscan vases on display at the museum depicted obviously Africoid faces, and one of the more interesting of the Etruscan exhibits, dated 275 B.C.E., depicts what appears to be an African elephant. As in ancient Egyptian art, the Etruscan men are consistently portrayed as dark-complexioned, while the Etruscan women are portrayed as much lighter. Etruscan women seem to have enjoyed a freedom far greater than that of later Roman women, and women and men in general are portrayed frequently as happy and loving couples in Etruscan art. I was hard-pressed to find anything of the sort in Roman art.

An ancient African people, sometimes called Moors, are known to have had a significant presence and influence in early Rome. For example, Joel Augustus Rogers noted in his book, World's Great Men of Color, that the African-Roman writer and comic dramatist, Publius Terentius Afer (190-159 B.C.E.), rose to great prominence among the Roman elite. One of the most famous of Latin proverbs, "I am a man, and nothing human is alien to me," is attributed to him. Moorish soldiers were actively recruited for Roman military service and stationed in Britain, France, Switzerland, Austria, Hungary, Poland, and Romania. Many of these Africans rose to high rank in the Roman forces.

Lusius Quietus, for example, described as a "man of Moorish race and considered the ablest soldier in the Roman army," was one of Rome's greatest generals. The Roman emperor Trajan (98-117 C.E.) even named him as his successor. By the end of the second century of the Christian Era, more than one-third of all the members of the Roman Senate were born in Africa, and Africans were dominant in Rome's intellectual life.

Additionally, at least three popes of Rome were Africans. Saint Victor I became the first African bishop of Rome in 189 C.E. and reigned until 199 C.E. He was the first pope to write in Latin, and the first pope known to have had dealings with the imperial household. The late Roman scholar, Dr. Edward Vivian Scobie, described Saint Victor I as the "most forceful" of the second-century popes. According to Scobie:

> *"Although nothing is known of the circumstances of his death, [Saint Victor I] is venerated as a martyr, and his feast is kept on July the 28th. Today, in the history of the Roman Church, he is remembered, not only for his ruling that Easter should be celebrated on Sunday, but he has also been named in the canon of the Ambrosian Mass, and he is said by Saint Jerome to have been the first in Rome to celebrate the Holy Mysteries in Latin."*

Saint Miltiades, a Black priest from Africa, was elected the thirty-second pope of Rome after Saint Peter in 311 C.E.. Under Miltiades—after the issuance of an edict of tolerance signed by emperors Galerius, Licinius, and Constantine—the great persecution of the Christians came to an end, and they were allowed to practice their religion in peace. As a result, Saint Miltiades, who died in 314 C.E., is regarded as a Christian martyr.

The third of the African popes and the forty-ninth pope overall was Saint Gelasius I. Gelasius was born in Rome of African parents and governed from 492 to 496 C.E. He was described by a contemporary as "famous all over the world for his learning and holiness" and "more a servant than a sovereign." He died in 496 C.E. and, like Saint Victor I and Saint Miltiades, Saint Gelasius I was canonized. According to Dr. Scobie, however, "[Saint] Gelasius I was "great even among the Saints." As a saint, his feast day is held on November 21 each year.

The crowning highlight of my trip to Rome was my visit to the National Roman Museum, where all the information I had been reviewing for all these years was validated. There, on the last day of my trip, I found evidence of an African dynasty at the very height of imperial Rome. I had been in Rome for almost a week by the time I got to this museum, and while my trip had been, for the most part, a pleasant experience, I had not made the major and meaningful kinds of finds I had hoped I would. For one, I had not seen any really Africoid images of Hannibal Barca nor any Black Madonna statues or anything like that.

And then it happened. I was walking methodically through the galleries of the national museum when I gazed into Room XIII. There it was! With just a glance, I could tell that one bust, in particular, looked strikingly Africoid. I looked closer and read the caption on the bust. It read: "Alexander Severus." I was familiar with that name. Then I turned around and saw a marvelous bust of Septimius Severus. Beyond that, I saw busts and statues of Septimius' two sons, Geta and Caracalla—and they all looked Africoid too, some more so than others! I had stumbled (or was I divinely led?) into a room, previously unknown to me, filled with these images of African-looking Roman emperors!

Runoko Rashidi

The dynasty to which these likenesses belonged, known to historians as the Severan Dynasty, began with the accession to the throne of Septimius Severus in 193 C.E. Actually, Septimius shared the throne for two years with Pesennius Niger. I wondered if Pesennius Niger, another of Rome's outstanding military commanders, could himself have been an African—his name certainly suggests that possibility.

Septimius was born in Leptis Magna on the North African coast (modern-day Libya) in either 145 or 146 C.E., but he was not just born in Africa. At least one major painting of him, a wood panel of the man and his family, done around 200 C.E. (a color postcard of which I obtained from the Antiquities Museum in Berlin in 2003), shows him to be phenotypically Black—that is, somewhere between copper-colored and deep burnished brown in skin color. In my view, there is no doubt but that Septimius Severus, the last member of the Severan dynasty, was a Black man, but the face adorning the bust of Severus Alexander in the Roman museum was even more Africoid-looking than that of Septimius Severus, the dynasty's founder.

Young Septimius, coming from a family of Romanized Africans, received an education rooted in Roman literature and quickly learned to speak Latin. After completing his formal education, he adopted an official career and became a civil magistrate. Later, he became a military commander, and this took him to Rome, where he proved himself an able, popular, and conscious military leader. Around 199 C.E., six years after becoming emperor, Septimius journeyed to Egypt. (Can you imagine Emperor Septimius sailing on the Nile? Consider what he might have thought as he gazed at the pyramids and walked through the Karnak and Luxor temples.)

Around 203 C.E., Septimius had a mighty arch constructed in the Imperial Forum in Rome. This monument is considered one of Italy's most important triumphal arches. He is even said to have built a marble tomb for Hannibal Barca, early Rome's African nemesis. Indeed, given his African origins, Septimius has been referred to as "Hannibal's revenge."

After a distinguished career characterized by administration reorganization, exploits on the battlefield, and intensified persecution of Christians, Septimius died conducting yet another military campaign, this one in York in Britain, on February 4, 211 C.E. He was sixty-five years old and had been in poor health, suffering severely from gout for years. His reign lasted seventeen years, eight months, and three days. He was the last Roman emperor to die of natural causes for almost a hundred years.

Septimius Severus was succeeded in 211 C.E. by his sons Lucius Septimius Geta (211-212 C.E.) and Marcus Aurelius Antoninus, also known as Caracalla (211-217 C.E.). The two brothers are said to have plotted against one another constantly. Caracalla finally had Geta murdered in 212 C.E. It was under Caracalla that same year that Roman citizenship was granted to all freeborn inhabitants of the empire. Caracalla was also responsible for refurbishing roads and constructing a triumphal arch in Algeria, as well as a number of enormous public baths. Caracalla was murdered during a military coup in 217 C.E.

Geta and Caracalla were followed by the Mauritania-born Marcus Opellius Macrinus (217-218 C.E.), the Praetorian Prefect and the first non-senator to become emperor of Rome. Heliogabalus (218-222 C.E.), said to be either the son or nephew of Caracalla and a man of dubious character, followed Macrinus. Then came Severus Alexander (222-235 C.E.), who restored the Roman Coliseum to its ancient status, and with whose thirteen-year reign, the era of Severan domination of Rome came to an end.

The numerous busts, statues, and sculptures of the representatives of the Severan Dynasty strongly testify to their African identity. They are powerful images. Strangely, however, like many of the busts, statues, and sculptures of ancient Egypt rulers that I have seen or heard of, the noses on all of them are missing or have been otherwise defaced–save one of Septimius' son Caracalla.

I was, of course, elated and pretty much overwhelmed by the images of the Severan Dynasty that I saw firsthand in the Roman museums I visited. Actually, the whole trip was a high note, and as other horizons beckoned me, I began to think of my visit to Rome as a highly successful endeavor.

I feel good about having gone to Rome. I got a chance to see a part of the world that, until recently, I never had serious aspirations about visiting. I spent an exciting week exploring what was, for me, a brand new city. I had been given the opportunity to lecture there and my lectures had been well received in yet another country. Plus, I had been hosted and accompanied, for a few days at least, by the youngest daughter of one of our people's greatest leaders. To top it all off, I had confirmed that a small cadre of African men had ruled over and helped to guide the Roman Empire during the height of its imperial glory. Yes, indeed, this visit to Italy was a most successful trip!

Sketches Of Spain: Moors, Museums, And Madonnas

> *"Whatever makes a kingdom great, whatever tends to refinement and civilization, was found in Moorish Spain" (Stanley Lane-Poole and Arthur Gilman, Story of the Moors in Spain, 2010/1866).*

March 30, 2003

Well, sisters and brothers, I just returned to the United States from spending ten days in Spain. It was my first trip to that latter country, and while there I was able to visit the capital city of Madrid; the Andalusian cities of Sevilla, Cordoba, and Granada in the south; and the city of Barcelona and some of the surrounding areas in the eastern part of Spain.

But, of course, the real reason for this trip, from the very beginning, was to search for the African presence in Spain—specifically, to explore Moorish Spain. And so, equipped with a trusty travel guide and a CD of Miles Davis' 1960s classic, "Sketches of Spain," away I went!

The Moors of Spain

Although the Moors were not the first Africans to come to Spain, their presence was undeniably the most important. For those who may not know the history of the Moors in Spain, let me explain: The Moors were African people who traveled to Spain in large numbers beginning in the eighth century C.E. and who established a great civilization there.

Moorish soldiers led by General Tarik ibn Ziyad crossed over from Africa to the Iberian (Spanish) Peninsula in 711 C.E.. The bold Tarik, in command of an army of 10,000 men, crossed the narrow channel (or strait) that connects the Atlantic Ocean to the Mediterranean Sea and separates Spain from

Morocco. They disembarked near a rocky promontory, which, from that day since, has borne his name: Djabal Tarik—"Tarik's Mountain," or Gibraltar. Tarik subsequently won a paramount victory over the opposing Iberian army. On the eve of the battle, Tarik is alleged to have roused his troops with the following words:

> *"My brethren, the enemy is before you, the sea is behind; whither would ye fly? Follow your general; I am resolved either to lose my life or to trample on the prostrate king of the Romans."*

Wasting no time to relish his victory, Tarik pushed on with his dashing and seemingly tireless Moorish cavalry to the Spanish city of Toledo. Within a month's time, he had effectively terminated European dominance of the Iberian Peninsula. Musa ibn Nusayr, the Arab governor of North Africa, joined Tarik in Spain and helped complete the conquest of Iberia with an army of 18,000 men. The two commanders met in Talavera, where the Moors were given the task of subduing northwestern Spain. With vigor and speed, they set about their mission. Within three months, they had swept the entire territory north of the Ebro River as far as the Pyrenees Mountains and annexed the turbulent Basque country of northern Spain.

In the aftermath of these brilliant victories, thousands of Moors flooded into the Iberian Peninsula. So eager were they to come to Spain that some were said to have floated over on tree trunks! Tarik himself, at the conclusion of his illustrious military career, retired to the distant eastern regions of the country to spread the teachings of Islam.

It would not be inaccurate to say that the Moors helped reintroduce Europe to civilization, but let me tell you just a little bit more about who the Moors were. According to the Oxford English Dictionary, "The Moors were commonly supposed to be mostly black or very swarthy, and hence the word [Moor] is often used [as a substitute] for Negro." Dr. Chancellor Williams long maintained that the "original Moors, like the original Egyptians, were Black Africans." The Christians of early Europe had no question about the ethnicity of the Moors, and numerous sources support the view that the Moors were a black-skinned people.

The epic Spanish novel Morien recounts the adventures of a heroic Moorish knight who was supposed to have lived during the days of King Arthur. Morien is described in the novel as "all black: his head, his body, and his hands were all black." In the French epic known as the Song of Roland, the Moors are described as "blacker than ink." Even the renowned English dramatist Sir William Shakespeare used the word Moor as a synonym for "African." His contemporary, Christopher Marlowe, likewise used African and Moor interchangeably. Arab writers and chroniclers further buttress the identity of the Moors as a Black people, describing the powerful Moorish emperor Yusef ben-Tachfin as "a brown man with woolly hair."

So it was against this backdrop that I set out on my first trip to visit the Moors, Madonnas, and museums of Spain. My trip began and ended in Madrid, the Spanish capital. After a quiet day and a night in that large and sprawling city, I took an early morning flight south to Sevilla, the capital of Andalusia Province.

With a population of more than 700,000, Sevilla is one of the largest cities in Spain. At one time, it was also one of the chief centers of the Moors. My time in Sevilla, however, was uneventful, and I was more than a little disappointed with the museum there, which I found to be very mediocre.

From Sevilla, I journeyed east by train to Cordoba. It was a lovely and peaceful ride. I loved the architecture in Cordoba, particularly the great mosque there. According to Lane-Poole and Gilman's classic work, Story of the Moors in Spain, under Moorish dominance, "Cordoba enjoyed its period of maximum splendor, becoming famed as the most flourishing city and the cultural capital of the western world, with a magnificent university, fabulous libraries and sumptuous buildings."

The zenith of any trip to Andalusia, however, is the city of Granada and the impressive structure known as the Alhambra. The latter, a huge palace and fortress complex built in the 14th century by the Moorish rulers of Granada, is the greatest tourist attraction in Spain and one of the great architectural wonders of Europe. It is set under the backdrop of the Sierra Nevada Mountains and immortalized in the work of American writer Washington Irving (of Rip Van Winkle fame), who penned several books while living in Spain and later served as US ambassador to that nation. The Alhambra was the last Moorish stronghold in Spain and the battle for it was last great "statement" made by the Moors during their centuries of Spanish reign. When the Moorish troops defending the Alhambra surrendered to the forces of the European Spanish monarchs Ferdinand and Isabella in January 1492, the great shining light of the Moors in Europe was put out.

My only real disappointment about my visit to Andalusia and Moorish Spain was that I did not see more representations of the Moors themselves. I came away from my visit there thinking that if one did not know the actual history and ethnic make-up of the people in that region, one would probably never conclude that the Moors, who occupied Spain for hundreds of years beginning in 711, were actually African people.

After a few days in Granada and multiple visits to the Alhambra, I concluded my time in the south of Spain and journeyed northwest to the beautiful and charming city of Barcelona. Located on shores of the Mediterranean Sea, Barcelona was founded, presumably by the Carthaginians, in about 230 B.C.E. It was named for Hamilcar Barca, Hannibal the Great's illustrious father.

I enjoyed this part of my first trip to Spain more than any other. I spent most of my first day in Barcelona browsing the museums, including the city's archaeological and ethnographic museums. although the big attraction for most visitors to Barcelona is the Picasso Museum (which I toured as well), by far the highlight for me was the Pre-Columbian Museum. The latter holds some of the finest Olmec and Mixtec figurines I have ever laid my eyes on. One of images from this museum, a small figurine with the face of an unknown Olmec, is one of my most powerful and prized photos.

It was from Barcelona that I journeyed on a day trip to the monastery of Montserrat. According to the locals, "He is not well wed who has not taken his wife to Montserrat." The monastery there is almost a thousand years old and renowned for housing the La Moreneta: the Black Virgin of Montserrat and the patroness of the Catalonian region. The statue of La Moreneta, which depicts the Virgin Mother dressed in gold with the Christ Child sitting in her lap, is only about two feet high, but it sits high above the altar at the front of the monastery. In order to see it, I had to stand in a long line of hundreds of people, each of whom were trying to get as close to the miraculous icon as possible. It was truly inspiring to see the reverence accorded this small statue of a Black woman visited by so many.

A Note From Athens

May 25, 2004

I am now in Athens on my first trip to Greece, bringing to forty-two the number of countries that I have visited in just over five years. I am, of course, always in search of African people and things African around the globe, but I wound up here because my trip to South Africa unraveled and I thought that a visit to Greece might help fill the emotional void resulting from my failure to get there. I was scheduled to head to Europe anyway, so I simply added Greece to my itinerary, and here I am.

Everything is going pretty well so far. The Grecian people seem fairly friendly, and I have even seen, at a distance at least, a couple of Black folks. I must say, however, that my wanderlust seems to be ebbing a bit. Perhaps my travel fever is beginning to diminish, or maybe I am just feeling the need to start looking for a successor (or successors), but I have never felt like this before. Is it just the natural aging process, or am I having some morbid insights into my own mortality? Or am I simply feeling lonely or tired? Maybe all of the above, but whatever it is, I just don't have the usual excitement about travel that has possessed me for the last few years or so.

Maybe I'll get my edge back tomorrow. Perhaps a nice dinner of Greek food and drink will get me back on track. Something needs to get me heading in the right direction—and soon—because over the next month, I am scheduled to visit France, Holland, Austria, and Denmark in search of the African presence. I will also be lecturing in those countries and promoting my new French-language travel book.

I am disappointed, however, that the National Archaeological Museum, located here in Athens, is currently closed for restoration. That museum is considered one of the greatest n the world and contains the richest collection of artifacts from Greek antiquity worldwide. Oh well, I guess I'll just have to come back in the fall. Tomorrow I will begin my tour of Greek antiquities regardless, starting as I always do with the museums.

May 26, 2004

Today I am in Delphi in lower central Greece, about ninety miles north of Athens. I wish that more of my African sisters and brothers could be here with me. I see a slight smattering of Black faces on the streets of this modern city full of ancient ruins, but not very many. I asked my tour guide today, a little-bitty old lady who could have been three hundred years old by the looks of her, how many Black people live in Greece? To my surprise, her response was, "A lot! I don't know how many, but there are a lot!"

"A few years ago," she continued, "we didn't have any. Now there are a lot!" Well, wherever they are, I figured they must be keeping a low profile because they were hardly visible to me!

Today I visited the Temple of Apollo. It was a pleasant drive to get to a not-very-impressive temple. Like I've said several times earlier, Egypt kind of spoils you. Everything else shrinks to insignificance in comparison. But I did get to see some more of the Grecian countryside. Along the way, I saw the Corinthian Sea and the largest olive grove in Greece. I also had a delicious lunch of chicken and rice, washed down with a bottle (or so) of good white wine from the island of Crete.

Crete, by the way, is a large island situated right between Egypt and Greece. Not surprisingly, it was the seat of the region's first civilization. Even the Greeks admit it, that their first civilization came from the south—that is, from the direction of Africa. That fact is indisputable.

May 27, 2004

Today was probably my best day in Greece so far. I traveled about ninety-five miles southeast (I think) to the Mycenaean historical site. It was a beautiful ride. Along the way, the Corinthian Sea kept me company, as did the beautiful, mountainous landscape of the Grecian countryside with its scores of yellow wildflowers and bright red poppies.

We stopped briefly at the site of the ancient city of Corinth, which is one of places where, according to the Bible and the Book of Corinthians, the apostle Paul preached the gospels to the masses. But long before Paul, Corinth was the site of a temple honoring the Egyptian goddess Ast (or Isis). We also stopped to view the ruins of the early hospital and amphitheater at Epidaurus and the ancient site of Tiryns, which was part of the Myceanean Empire.

But just what is this place called Mycenae that I keep talking about, and why is it important? Mycenae was the first civilization in mainland Europe. I just found out today, however, that it had extremely close relations with Egypt. But why should I be surprised about that? Indeed, my readings of history tell me that the Myceaneans served as mercenary soldiers in the Egyptian army, and that they brought much of the religious ideas and technical prowess they learned in Africa back to Europe with them.

The Mycenaean historical site is the most impressive I have seen in all of Greece. It reminds me of Machu Pichu and the Inca ruins in the Andes Mountains more than anything else, and, for the first time on my Grecian trip, I am really impressed!

Tomorrow is my last full day here in Greece, and I intend to take full advantage of it. I will visit the ancient ruins in Athens, including the temple of Zeus and the Parthenon on the Acropolis. Then I will visit the temple of Poseidon. After that, I am, as they say, "outta Dodge"!

May 28, 2004

I will say this after visiting the Athenian museums: you can definitely see the Egyptian influence on early Greece, particularly in the art from the earliest phases of Greek history. The Benaki Museum and the National Museum of Clycladic Art, which I visited today, house a number of Grecian amulets depicting the Ancient Egyptian deities Sekhmet, Ast (Isis), and Bes.

Runoko Rashidi

I hope that I am not wearing you all out with all these notes, but it is about the only way I have to stay connected. Otherwise, I would be really, really isolated. I mean, nobody is making me do what I do, but it does get really lonely out here in the world! And since I have been here in Greece, I have not received one phone call from family or loved ones. I wonder what that means?

My travel writing also helps me to organize my thoughts and observations as I travel around the world. Who knows? One day, these notes might provide the basis for my autobiography!

But thanks, everyone, for putting up with me, and don't worry about me. I am losing neither my mind nor my soul. In fact, I just got some really good news. I just received an email from a sister in Vienna, Austria, who assures me that she is making contacts for my arrival there in a couple of weeks. It is indeed good to know that somebody has your back!

Nighttime Conversation In Vienna

"History is not finished" (Joseph Ki-Zerbo).

June 12, 2004

I left Austria yesterday morning a bit reluctantly. If I had been able to stay there for one more day, I would have seized the opportunity to visit Budapest, Hungary. Who knows when I will get that way again? Well, it is always hard to do everything.

Before I left Vienna, though, I was blessed to engage in an interesting but all-too-short late-night conversation with a small group of dynamic Africans who were part of a group called Pamoja: Movement of the Young African Diaspora in Austria. The sister who arranged that gathering, Araba E. Johnston-Arthur, provided me with the most information on the African presence in Austria. At age twenty-nine, Sister Araba was the "senior citizen" of the Pamoja organization, and she acted as its major spokesperson. She was joined by another beautiful and powerful twenty-six-year-old African woman who was raised in Germany but of Ghanaian origin, and by an articulate and energetic twenty-seven-year-old African man of strong views and Nigerian-Austrian parentage.

Although our discussion was somewhat short due to the lateness of the hour (plus, I had been sightseeing in the Czech Republic all day that day, and I was pretty tired!), it was a most interesting exchange. And I am so happy to say that in addition to seeing many of the finest art collections in Europe, I have also, on this trip, been able to have some very healthy interactions with representatives of yet another conscientious African organization. I have had similar meetings with sisters and brothers in Paris and Nantes in France and in Amsterdam and Rotterdam in the Netherlands.

Among the things I learned from my conversation with the Pamoja members was that, out of a total Austrian population of approximately eight million, there are about 20,000 Africans in Austria. About half of them are "Black Africans"; the rest are from Egypt. Many are refugees. There are also rapidly growing numbers of Turks and people from the former nation of Yugoslavia in Austria. Most of the Africans, however, are scattered over the twenty-three administrative districts in the city of Vienna (population 1.6 million), and while there does appear to be a sense of community among them, there is nothing that could be justifiably called an "African neighborhood" in Vienna.

The Pamoja members told me about rampant racism in Austria and the scarcity of African businesses and social institutions. They told me that many of the Whites in Austria apparently felt that they should be able to refer to African people as "niggers" without the Africans taking any offense to that. They told me about the limited opportunities for Africans to have successful careers in Austria and of the Vienna nightclubs to which they were refused entrance. They told me about the graffiti saying "Niggers out!" and "Niggers go home!" that is a common sight on walls and buildings throughout the city. And they told me about cases of anti-African police brutality that conjured up, for me, images of Rodney King and Ahmadou Diallo and Abner Louima in the United States.

One such case of extreme brutality involved a Mauritanian brother who was taken into police custody. According to Sister Araba and her colleagues, a number of police officers were videotaped actually standing on top of the man until he stopped breathing. Despite the videotape and the vicious nature of the incident, none of the cops were convicted of any crime. The case reminded me of similar stories of widespread anti-African police and civilian brutality in France—stories that were shared with me by Sister Zawadi Sagna of the Black Consciousness organization in Paris.

Does any of this sound familiar to you? Similar stories abound about anti-African violence perpetuated by police and skinheads and neo-Nazis in many parts of Europe, with some of the worst cases having been reported in Germany and Russia.

I repeat, does any of this sound familiar to you?

My newfound comrades from the Pamoja organization also told me the harrowing story of Angelo Soliman, an African who managed to become something of a court secretary in Austria about two hundred years ago.[2] Apparently, after Angelo Soliman died, despite his distinguished career, or perhaps because of it, his body, along with those of two other Africans, was actually stuffed like an animal and put on display. A bitter struggle ensued, led by Soliman's daughter, to gain possession of at least her father's skin. It was a struggle that she would not win: Soliman's body was housed in a museum in Vienna until that building was burnt down during the March 1848 revolution in that nation.

So much for the African presence in Austria!

In The Czech Republic

June 13, 2004

Well, I have had another interesting day in central Europe. Early this morning, I journeyed by car from Vienna, Austria, to Prague in the Czech Republic. The trip started out on a promising note, but went quickly downhill from there.

---

[2] A color photo of Soliman can be found in Henry Louis Gates' Africana Encyclopedia. The same photo appears on the cover of a German book, a copy of which was presented to me by a sister from the Bay Area of California.

After a very dull and uninteresting tour of Prague, I managed to get away from the little group that I was traveling with and go to the national museum. (I think this makes about forty-five the number of museums that I have visited now in Europe. Unfortunately, it was also one of the most boring!) To my dismay, virtually all of the display captions were in Czech—English is not widely spoken in Prague. Plus, I only saw one significant artifact from Egypt: a nice statue from a dynasty that I was not familiar with, and nothing at all from the rest of Africa.

I did run into a handful of Africans while visiting in Prague, however, and I even managed to talk to a few of them, particularly a brother from Senegal. As for the White folks there, I did not find them to be very friendly at all. And to top things off, the little Jewish lady that I was sitting next to on the tour bus seemed to talk non-stop! I could not wait to get out of there!

But the Ancestors must have had my back because, just when I was the most upset and telling myself, for about the tenth time, that I would never come back to Prague again–and also just as I was beginning to question my sanity, once again, for coming to Europe in the first place—something very strange happened that changed my mood entirely. Here's what happened: As I was crossing the border from Austria to the Czech Republic this morning, I was advised to change about twenty Euros (the currency of the European Union) into the Czech currency. After paying for the museum fee and a few liquid refreshments, I still had most of the Czech money in my pocket when it was time to leave. Just to get rid of it, I bought an English-language book with plenty of photographs about the city of Prague. I really did not want the book, but I wanted the local currency even less.

Anyway, the talkative Jewish lady I was sitting next to took a liking to the book and, probably just to shut her up, I sold it to her. I was glad to get rid of it and had not even glanced through it until, during a rare pause in her blathering before she put the book away, I decided to take a look at a few of the book's photos. Wouldn't you know it, one of the first pictures that I saw in it was a magnificent photo of a Black Madonna and child—one that I had never seen before!

Well, that changed everything and, quite naturally, I told the lady that I had changed my mind about selling the book and wanted to keep it after all. After putting up a small argument, she simply smiled and agreed to sell it back to me!

After seeing the photograph, my mindset changed altogether! All at once, the Czech countryside became beautiful. And when I finally got back to my hotel, who would I find working at the front desk but a beautiful, dark-skinned, Kenyan sister! My luck just seemed to be getting better and better! I mean, this sister was gorgeous! I felt good just looking at her! Back in my room, I looked through the book more closely and found yet another fascinating image: that of a Moorish brother, sculpted in the seventeenth century.

With that, I felt as if my mission—to uncover the African presence in central Europe—was, at least for the day, more than accomplished! I could sleep well and get up and out of Austria in the morning with a smile on my face. Life is not so bad after all!

In Denmark And Sweden

June 15, 2004

I am now in Copenhagen, Denmark, on my first visit to this part of Europe. The people here are much more pleasant than those in Austria, the Czech Republic, or France. Plus, it is raining and rather cool—just Brother Runoko's kind of weather! And I am staying in the city center, so virtually everything that I want to see is within easy walking distance. But believe me, I am getting my exercise. I am living my fantasies with this travel, and I feel ever so blessed. I am liking it!

I have only been in Copenhagen a few hours, and already I have visited the Ny Carlsberg Glyptotek Museum and the National Museum of Denmark. Both are very nice, especially the former. Both also have outstanding Egyptian collections and excellent gift shops that offer an abundance of good books and striking postcards. Their Roman collections are not bad, either.

The National Museum has a couple of nice pieces from the European Medieval/Renaissance period that depict an African as one of the Three Wise Men in paintings of the Adoration of the Magi. Apparently, it was the trend at that time, around 1500 C.E., to portray the youngest of the Three Wise Men as African. The two examples I saw today in Copenhagen are about the best that I have even seen. The museum also houses a very intriguing black statue of the Buddhist sage Bodhidharma and an excellent black marble bust of the great African Roman emperor Septimius Severus. The Ny Carlsberg Glyptotek Museum, on the other hand, has a wonderful bust of Septimius' eldest son and successor, Caracalla.

Anyway, I bought a whole bunch of postcards and took quite a few photos during my museum tours today. That being done, I have pretty much completed my business in Denmark. Right now, I am looking for something nice and healthy to eat for dinner while I try to gather the confidence to journey on my own by train to Sweden tomorrow. I have been in Europe for four weeks now, and I still have two more weeks to go. However, I expect to come out of this visit with lots of new knowledge and the basis of a new and excellent slide presentation, so stay tuned!

June 16, 2004

> *"I rescued hundreds of my people from slavery, and I could have rescued more if only they had known that they were slaves" (Harriet Tubman).*

Today finds me in Malmo, Sweden. I got a good night's sleep last night and, fairly early this morning, took the train from Copenhagen to here. It was a pretty simple process, but I must confess that I did have a bit of anxiety about taking the train alone from one strange city (strange for me, at least!) to another. But here I am, and I'm actually feeling pretty good about myself!

I am sitting now in an Internet cafe in Malmo, listening to a beautiful tune sung by Whitney Houston. Having just consumed a nice lunch of Indian food and with a bit of free time on my hands, I thought that I would update you on my doings. Sweden makes country number forty-seven for me, and as I race toward achieving my first-fifty countries mark, I suppose that I'm also racing against time as I turn fifty myself on August 16. My goal for now is a modest sixty-five countries, but the first fifty will be a hallmark, when I can say that I have visited about one-fourth of all the "recognized" nations in the world.

The train ride here was beautiful. Part of the ride was along the sea. Malmo is a large and attractive city with, like nearly everywhere I have been in Europe, a scattering of Africans here and there. The poet and world traveler Langston Hughes wrote in his autobiography, I Wonder As I Wander, that in all his travels he always found "at least one Negro everywhere." Apparently, Brother Langston was right on the money. (And I want to thank Brother Nnamdi for exposing me to that Ancestor's book, which has now become my major travel companion and something of a "travel bible" for me.) I too have found a least a few Africans everywhere I have been in the world. I must also confess, however, and with great disappointment, that I have not found any profound sense of solidarity among the Africans I have seen and met in my travels throughout Europe.

I have been in Europe about a month now and have visited France, Greece, the Netherlands, Austria, the Czech Republic, Denmark, and now Sweden. And while I am very interested in African people everywhere, I do not always get the impression that the Blacks in Europe are very interested in me. In a land with only a few Blacks, it seems only natural to me that when two Black people pass each other on the street, we should at least make eye contact and, if possible, speak. In Europe, however, my sisters and brothers all too often just pass me by as though I were invisible. Of course, there have been some notable exceptions. I have had some very fruitful interactions, for example, with Black people in France, the Netherlands, and Austria. But for the most part, that is not the case.

This disturbs me. Would they speak to me if we were both Ibo or Hausa or Wolof or Bambara? Is that what it is? I cannot help but wonder sometimes if our vision of Pan-Africanism is just that: a vision. I mean, is it all only a dream? Is it just a handful of idealistic people who envision the global solidarity of African people, or is that vision something that the masses of our people simply do not or cannot embrace? I suppose you could say that I, like Hughes, am wondering about that as I wander.

A few comments about Sweden before I go: McDonalds, Burger King, Pizza Hut, and Seven-Elevens are plentiful here. Seriously, if you did not know better, you would think that you were in Los Angeles. The cost of living is also very high in Sweden, and the weather is typically cloudy and cool. English is widely spoken, and the local people, like those in Denmark and Holland, seem a bit aloof but not unfriendly.

Lately, my closest friends and my family, biological and extended, have been urging me to come "home" for quite some time now. They tell me that they miss me and that I should come back to New York or San Antonio or Los Angeles, or wherever it is that I "live" when I'm not on the road. And though I miss them too, I have no urgent desire to return to the United States. Not once on this trip have I felt "homesick" for the US. I admit that I get a little lonely sometimes and am often frustrated in my travels, but could it be that, with all the travel I have been doing lately, I have finally come to the realization that the United States is no longer home for me?

I know that many of us Blacks from the States say that we are Africans, but do we really internalize our Africanness? That is another matter altogether. Am I at that stage in my life, I wonder? Is all my traveling contributing to my personal and internal growth and maturity as a Pan-African, or is there more to it than that? Like Brother Langston, I suppose I have a lot to think about as I wander, but I give thanks to our African Ancestors for blessing me with the opportunity to do so.

And I hope that you, my readers, enjoy my travel notes as much as I enjoy writing them. Writing about my travel experiences allows me to tie many of my thoughts together, and I hope that one day they will form the basis of a nice autobiography. The great J. A. Rogers, the historian to whom I am most often compared (and I am truly very flattered and honored by such comparisons), never wrote an autobiography. Thus, it has been left up to others to tell his story. I do not want that to be the case for me.

Oh well, I return to France in a couple of days. I have a lecture to present in Bordeaux this Saturday. Next week should find me touring more French museums (I have already visited sixteen up to this point) and checking out some more Black Madonna sites. There are a number of them in and around Paris, and you better believe Brother Runoko will find them and share the news with you!

A VISIT TO ANCIENT KNOSSOS AND THE ARCHOLOGICAL MUSEUMS IN CRETE

March 18, 2005

Today is my second day on the island of Crete, the largest and most populous of the Greek islands. I saw my first African today! I was beginning to think that I was the only one here. In fact, I was getting ready to compose a long, dramatic note to you to that effect, but just as I was contemplating that dire situation over a sumptuous Greek lunch, an African street vendor passed by me. We briefly mumbled pleasantries, and if I hadn't been so shocked to see him and if he did not have a handful of products to sell before the end of the day, I probably would have invited him to lunch! So today was a good day.

Today I also went to the archaeological site called Knossos, which is only about five miles from the city center. I took a taxi there and a bus back. (You know that I've really reached a comfort zone with a place when I start using its public transportation!) Anyway, Knossos is a heavily restored site and a heavily reconstructed one also. The work was begun there by the English archaeologist Sir Arthur Evans, with his own money, back in the 1920s or so. It is a lovely site consisting of an ancient palace with vivid frescoes and bright red pillars set amidst hills and trees. A gentle breeze was blowing during my visit, and most of the other visitors there were young schoolchildren.

I liked Knossos. It reminded me of Great Zimbabwe in southern Africa. I experienced the same kind of energy in both places.

The island of Crete, according to Cheikh Anta Diop and Martin Bernal, is the basis of the legends about the mythical lost continent of Atlantis.

Runoko Rashidi

(For more information, review Diop's Civilization or Barbarism and volume two of Bernal's Black Athena.[3]) According to mythology, the Greek god Zeus once looked down from the heavens to behold a beautiful Phoenician princess (an African woman?) named Europa—after whom, legend also has it, the continent of Europe was named. Zeus wanted her so much, they say, that one day, when Europa was at the seashore, he turned himself into a white bull and lay down in front of her. Europa was entranced by the bull and jumped on his back, at which point Zeus sped off with her to the island of Crete.

On Crete, Zeus raped Europa. (Does this sound like a familiar story?) From this union came three sons, one of whom was named Minos. Minos grew to become the island's ruler; indeed, the civilization of Crete—that of the Minoans—was named after him. The Minoans were a great maritime power in the second millennium B.C.E. They had many palatial cities, one of which was Knossos, an extremely important Minoan center, and they traded far and wide.

The Minoans had many connections to and relations with Kmt (Ancient Egypt). During the reign of the mighty Egyptian monarch Thutmose III in the late fifteenth century B.C.E., for example, Crete was an Egyptian vassal state. Some historians even believe that the impetus behind the rise of Minoan civilization was the arrival of African settlers from Libya and Lower Egypt, who moved to Crete when Upper and Lower Egypt were unified toward the end of the fourth millennium B.C.E.

So there are a lot of Egyptian connections in Crete. You didn't think that I would be spending all this money to come here on a humbug, did you? No, my visit to Knossos is something that I have wanted to do for a very long time.

Indeed, in my first book, Kushite Case Studies, which I self-published in 1983, I wrote a chapter on Crete and its ties to Ancient Egypt. I wrote about the migrations from Egypt to Crete at the end of the Egyptian pre-Dynastic era and about the intermittent and periodic Ancient Egyptian influences on Crete more than a thousand years later. I intend to develop in an entire book on the topic one day. And, since there's nothing quite like seeing something with your own eyes, I just had to come here.

After visiting the Knossos site, I went to the Heraklion Archaeological Museum. It too was well worth the visit, providing me with important additional data for my forthcoming book. One of the most intriguing things that was confirmed to me during my visit to this museum the prominence of the female in Minoan civilization. In ancient Crete, women enjoyed a status that was at least equal to, if not more important than, that of men. For instance, the goddess, and not the god, reigned supreme in Minoan culture. Now that does not sound like White folks to me!

Secondly, the museum houses a reproduction of a Minoan wall painting found in a northern Egyptian palace of the great Ahmose I, founder the illustrious Kamite (Ancient Egyptian) Dynasty XVIII. Even the color schemes used in this painting seem similar to those used in Egypt. For example, the women generally are painted a chalky color, while the men are depicted as reddish-brown in color. The museum also houses a depiction of a Black man from Knossos, dated around 1400 B.C.E., that is called The Captain of the Blacks. (I took a bunch of photos of that!)

---

3   My brother and research partner, Dr. James E. Brunson III, also did some very good work on the subject back in the 1980s. You can find it in Ivan Van Sertima's African Presence in Early Europe anthology.

Other key finds were another good Africoid depiction of Roman emperor Septimius Severus and two exquisite ancient drinking cups in the form of the heads of Nubian men.

So I had a very good day today, possibly my best day ever in Greece. And now I'm back in Irakleon, it's Friday night in the city, and the music is jumping! But that, I guess, may actually be my signal to return to my hotel room. I never was much of a partyer anyway, and I certainly don't plan to start here!

Tomorrow I will visit the archaeological sites of Festos and Gortyn. These two sites, though not as impressive as the Knossos site (even though Festos is larger), are located more than forty kilometers from Athens and will give me a chance to see another side of Greece. They are sure to give me an even greater appreciation of the Minoan civilization. I will post you from there if I can. If not, sisters and brothers, just look for me in the whirlwind!

TURIN, ITALY, AND THE MUSEO EGIZIO

June 24, 2005

It is late Saturday afternoon and I am in Turin, Italy, in the northern part of the country called the Piedmont area. I flew here direct from Paris. Turin is a fairly pleasant city, and I have seen a lot of Africans wandering the city center. So far, I have met a Kenyan, a Senegalese, and a Cape Verdean here. They were all very friendly and quite talkative.

Indeed, it is amazing how many African people I have encountered in Europe. I have now visited Europe on (I think) nineteen occasions and have traveled to numerous European countries, including individual trips to Russia, Sweden, Denmark, Germany, Switzerland, Turkey, Austria, the Czech Republic, Spain, Wales, Scotland, Belgium, twice each to Greece and Italy, five times to Holland, and six or seven trips each to England and France. And in every one of those places, I have found an African population, large or small. In a way, it is rather sad to see that so many sisters and brothers have left Africa, either as students or for what they perceive as a search for a better way of life.

I went to an excellent museum in the city yesterday and visited a boring one today. Yesterday, I went to the Museo Egizio (Egyptian Museum). Call me naïve, but except for my knowledge of the work of Giovanni Belzoni,[4] I did not know that the Italians took so much from Egypt. To my surprise, I learned yesterday that the Turin Egyptian Museum boasts the largest collection of artifacts outside of Cairo, including a number of pieces that I had never seen before, not even in books. All of the display captions are in Italian, but the artifacts themselves are magnificent!

I saw, for example, some especially good pieces from the nineteenth Ancient Egyptian dynasty. I also saw some particularly nice ones depicting the mighty monarch Ramses II, including the famous one that appears in Dr. Cheikh Anta Diop's book, *African Origins of Civilization: Myth or Reality*. I was so

---

4   Giovanni Battista Belzoni (born 1778 in Padua, Italy; died 1823 in Gwato, Benin), sometimes known as The Great Belzoni, was a circus strongman who later became a prolific explorer of Egyptian antiquities. He was the first to penetrate into the second pyramid of Giza, and was responsible for the removal of several notable pharaonic Egyptian artifacts and for their transport to Europe.

excited, I shot three rolls of film, bought a couple of books, and purchased quite a few postcards. And I am planning a return visit to this museum in a few days!

The boring museum that I visited today focused on Italian archaeology and anthropology. I didn't know it would be so uninteresting, but you never know what treasures may or may not await you until you go inside. As a saving grace, the museum did house a nice bust of Caracalla, son of Septimius Severus, Rome's greatest African emperor.

But the funny thing is that both the Museo Egizio and the boring museum were almost completely empty of visitors. There were like tombs! Maybe the only people who visit them are crazy people like me. Oh well, I can now pretty much boast that I have seen all of the major Egyptian collections in Europe, the United States, and perhaps the entire world!

June 26, 2005

Today is my third day in Turin, and I am about ready to get out of here. I have been to the Museo Egizio twice. I went there again earlier today. I went early because it is rather warm here and the museum, though it is indeed impressive, can get pretty hot and stuffy inside.

My visit to the Museo Egizio today focused on some of its more magnificent exhibits. Did you know, for example, that this museum houses an entire Nubian temple within its walls? The temple was removed, piece by piece, from the Valley of the Nile and rebuilt in Turin for this display. It was granted to Italy by the Egyptian government as payment to Italian archaeologists for their work in the Nile Valley during the construction of the Nasser Dam and the subsequent flooding of much of Nubia.

The museum also contains some notable relics from the early Dynastic to the Ptolemaic periods, especially the major statuary pieces featured on its main floor. These include four excellent statues of Ramses II, one of which is colossal, and another being the black statue of a seated Ramses II made famous by Cheikh Anta Diop. It also features two superb statues of Thutmose III and an excellent and very well preserved pink granite statue of Amenhotep II. The museum also houses an excellent black statue of Queen Tiye that I had never seen before and two large sphinxes of Amenhotep III. There are also two exquisite statues of Ptah, one black and the other made of a white material that I believe is gypsum.

Shall I continue? Additional wonders on display at the Egyptian Museum include twenty large statues of the lion-headed goddess Sekhmet and an excellent statue of King Tut and the god Amon. Then there are numerous excellent sarcophagi and a colossal bust of Queen Hatshepsut (I think) in the form of the goddess Asr or Osiris, along with an outstanding eighteenth dynasty statue of King Horemheb and his wife.

So that is how I spent this morning. I can give you a word of advice, however: If you are in Europe and want to see Africans, head to the city center, especially the markets and train terminals. African people seem to gravitate toward these areas. At least, I have found this to be the case in major European cities like Istanbul, Brussels, Amsterdam, Rotterdam, Leiden, Granada, and Athens. I saw a bunch of African people this morning as I was heading downtown to the Museo Egizio.

I have also seen plenty of Gypsies in Turin (and Paris too), only here they are called Roma. The Roma have a reputation for being thieves and rogues and generally making a nuisance of themselves. Nobody seems to like them much, and I am not fond of them, either. I first began to notice the Gypsy populations in Europe during a visit to Russia in 1999. Wherever I've encountered them, I get the distinct impression that they do not seem to think much of African people. Well, the feeling seems pretty much mutual!

And so, folks, another very positive travel experience is just about, as they say, "one for the books." Not sure if I will come back to Italy again, but both Rome and Turin have been beneficial for me. I return to Paris in a few days for a week of study. Early next month, for three days, I will be escorting a group of African American tourists around to what I consider some of the major African sites in Paris. Then I will resume another ten days of writing before heading back to the US. I won't be there long, though, as I will be spending the last two weeks in August moving around the island chain called Micronesia in the South Pacific.

All things considered, I guess I don't have much to complain about. God willing, in another two or three years, I will have visited seventy different countries. Last year alone, I went to twenty-one countries, and I expect to visit sixteen or so this year.

But lately I've been doing a lot of reflecting, and I have begun to envision myself maybe winding down my international travels over the next two or three years. Yes, sisters and brothers, I am beginning to think quite seriously about writing more and wandering less. Perhaps I'll think about doing some serious, sustained field research and spending more time with the folks that I see as my eventual successors. What do you think?

In the mean time, however, when are you guys going to start coming with me on some of these trips? That is what I want to know! We could start with my Zumbi tour to Brazil this November. There's still plenty of room, so please, get on board. You have just received a personal invitation to see the world with Runoko Rashidi.

What are you waiting for?

HANGIN' WITH THE D'ZERT CLUB IN PARIS

"One for all, and all for one" (Alexander Dumas, père, The Three Musketeers).

July 2005

Time is moving quickly. I have just recently returned to the United States from France. I was in Paris during the final week in May to deal with some personal matters, study French, and continue my search for the African presence in Europe. It was an excellent trip and an extremely successful one, and although I am a bit melancholy about returning to the States, I know that I will be back in France soon to do it all over again.

Runoko Rashidi

One of the great highlights of my recent visit to France was when Zawadi Sagna and I escorted the members of the d'Zert Club on a tour of Black Paris. The d'Zert Club, founded by Ali and Helen Salahuddin, is a longstanding Philadelphia-based organization that focuses largely on building the character, expanding the vision, and elevating the aspirations of African American youth.

Not surprisingly, my portion of the Black Paris tour began at the Louvre. The group had already been introduced to the general and African American aspects of Paris upon their arrival. They had also paid a quick visit to the Eiffel Tower, cruised the Seine, and learned all about the life of the fabulous Josephine Baker—the African American dancer, singer, and actress who, in the 1920s, 1930s, and 1940s, was the most successful American entertainer working in France. Now I truly do love Josephine Baker, but all along I envisioned something far more grandiose and much more ancient for the Black Paris tour, so it seemed to me that the Louvre was the best place to start.

The Palace du Louvre was erected as a fortress early in the thirteenth century and reconstructed during the middle of the sixteenth century for use as a royal residence. In 1793 it was turned into a national museum. In addition to its vast collection of European art dating from the past few hundred years, including Leonardo DaVinci's famous "Mona Lisa," it also contains a huge array of artifacts from early Greece, Italy, western Asia, and the Nile Valley. Indeed, it features a modern glass pyramid at its entrance, and the museum itself contains one of the largest Nile Valley collections in the world. The latter, according to my plan, was to be the focus of the d'Zert Club's visit.

As it turned out, the Egyptian collection in the Louvre alone is so large that I was only able to show my group a small fraction of it. And, for once, I discussed not only the history of ancient Egypt but also broadened my overview to include aspects of Egyptian culture and religion. I divided the group in two, and in the much-too-brief sessions provided both with large doses of information.

After a half-day at the Louvre, we had a wonderful lunch at a Togolese restaurant in Paris (we wanted to recycle African dollars whenever possible) and then returned, full and happy, to the hotel for my formal lecture. And, for the first time in my life, I gave what I hoped would be a fairly comprehensive lecture on the African presence in France from the earliest times to the present. At the risk of sounding immodest, my lecture was very, very good—at least (and I admit that I am decidedly biased), I thought it was! I discussed the history of African people as the first inhabitants of France and the transformation of those Africans into the White Europeans of today during the various glaciation periods in Europe. I also discussed the significance of the Black Madonnas and the Moors in France, along with a focus on the Black knights and the presence of other Africans among the early French nobility. Other topics included the presence of enslaved Africans in France; distinguished French men of African descent (especially the Chevalier de Saint Georges and the Dumas family); and notable African American and African Caribbean visitors to France such as boxer Jack Johnson, entertainer Josephine Baker, writer Langston Hughes, historian J. A. Rogers, the one and only Marcus Garvey, and novelist Richard Wright. I also told them about Cheikh Anta Diop and Frantz Fanon and their work in Paris. I wrapped up my lecture by talking about the various contemporary communities of African people in France.

Day two with the d'Zert Club started at the Place de la Concorde, where filmmaker and photographer Bob Lott captured the trip for posterity by taking a group picture. Afterwards, I pointed out to the group the presence of a 3,300-year-old pink granite obelisk of Ramses the Great, that outstanding African king of ancient Egypt's Nineteenth Dynasty, which stands directly in the center of the Place de la Concorde. While it is always good to see "things African" in Europe and elsewhere, I explained, this obelisk was especially good because Ramses was no ordinary person. Indeed, his name was synonymous with kingship for two centuries after his death.

I also shared with the group some important historical facts about the site where the Ramses obelisk, which was taken from Egypt in 1831, is located. I told them that this deeply incised and extremely well preserved artifact sits between the Arc de Triomphe (construction of which began in 1806, early in the reign of Emperor Napoleon) and the Parisian garden park called the Tuileries, where, over two centuries ago, stood the guillotine that lopped off the heads of the ill-fated French queen Marie Antoinette and her rivals Danton and Robespierre.

From the Place de la Concorde, we passed by Notre Dame Cathedral to visit the Cathedral of Our Lady of Paris. The latter is considered a masterpiece of Gothic architecture and is located in the very center of Paris. It was built directly over an ancient temple of the African goddess Isis. Inside the cathedral, however, try as we might, we could find nothing discernibly African, so we were forced to content ourselves with the building's historic location.

We later toured the Pantheon, one of my favorite buildings in all of Paris. Commissioned in 1750 and completed in 1789, it was converted two years later into a secular mausoleum for "the great men of the era of French history." My interest in the Pantheon began almost three years ago when I read that the African French writer par excellence Alexander Dumas, père, was being interred there. The Pantheon also contains a series of marvelous murals including an excellent depiction of what I believe are Ethiopian soldiers engaged in the battle for Jerusalem in the year 1099.

Alexander Dumas (1802-1870), who lived a near-legendary life, is one of three outstanding Africans to bear that name in nineteenth century France. The first is General Alexander Dumas (1762-1806), father of the great writer, who was born in Haiti and called "Alexander the Greatest" by the French. The son of the great writer is Alexander Dumas, fils (1824-1895), dubbed the "remaker of the modern French stage." The latter Dumas is also the author of the acclaimed novel Camille, who became president of the French Academy (the highest possible intellectual honor for a Frenchman) and the recipient of the Grand Cross of the Legion of Honor.

Alexander Dumas, pére, is the author of such immortal works as The Three Musketeers, The Count of Monte Cristo, The Man in the Iron Mask, The Black Corsican, and The Black Tulip. The superb Ibrahim Hannibal/Alexander Pushkin scholar from Benin, Dr. Dieudonne Gnammankou, recently shared a wonderful story about Dumas with me. He informed me that the fantastic African Shakespearean actor Ira Aldridge once gave a performance of Othello at the palace of Versailles with Dumas sitting in the front row. Aldridge's performance, it seemed, was of such a superlative nature that Dumas leapt upon the stage and embraced Aldridge in a enormous hug, shouting "I too am a Negro!"

Whenever I come to Paris, I feel as if Dumas' voice is calling out to me to pay him a visit. His sarcophagus lies just between those of his friend, the writer Victor Hugo, and the writer Emile Zola. On display just outside the crypt is a copy of the cover of Claude Ribbes' excellent book on Alexander Dumas' father, General Dumas, emblazoned with a reproduction of the elder Dumas looking both heroic and quite African.

Runoko Rashidi

On our visit to the crypt prior to the d'Zert Club's arrival, Sister Zawadi and I had noticed that Hugo's and Zola's stone coffins were adorned with flowers, while Dumas' coffin lacked any such floral adornments. We were determined to rectify that. We bought two bouquets of flowers from a nearby vendor and, with the members of the d'Zert Club right behind us, placed the flowers on Dumas' sarcophagus and engaged in a small but respectful and important ceremony at his tomb. We photographed and videotaped the whole affair. Afterward, with the Pantheon staff and a number of European tourists looking on with expressions that seemed to reflect both amazement and alarm, Zawadi and I gave a brief lecture on the three Dumas men.

We must have been feeling really inspired because just a few meters from Dumas' tomb, we noticed, for the first time, some additional inscriptions dedicated to other Africans. The other memorialized Africans included Louis Delgrès (1766-1802), who led the resistance against the re-establishment of slavery on the French island colony of Guadeloupe. And just near the Delgrès inscription is another dedicated to the famous African patriot and Haitian revolutionary, Toussaint L'Ouverture.

We were all quite moved by the ceremony and our discovery, very excited and very proud of ourselves. Everyone had a sense that we were making history, and they expressed hope that our great African Ancestors were pleased with our recognition of their storied existences.

After that, it was time to visit some bookstores, and the two that we selected were only a few blocks from the Pantheon. The first was Presence Africaine, founded in 1948, and the first African bookstore in France. I am sad to say, however, that we were treated rather coldly in that shop that day. The two White female employees looked at us with something approaching disdain and blew smoke from their cigarettes in our direction. After making a quick exit from there, we walked just a couple buildings away and Zawadi and I showed the group where Dr. Cheikh Anta Diop lived when he was writing his hallmark work, Negro Nations and Culture, in the early 1950s. Right there on the sidewalk in front of the building, I gave them a mini-lecture on the background to the life and works of this incredible African scholar and activist.

We then crossed the street to L'Harmattan Bookstore, a Canadian-owned store specializing in African books. Although not African-owned, both the African employees and White management staff seemed delighted to see us. To some extent, that made up for the rude treatment that we received in the African-owned Presence Africaine. That's rather ironic, don't you think?

The late afternoon highlight occurred in a quiet chapel in a serene setting in the Parisian suburb of Neuilly-sur-Seine, site of the largest image of the Black Virgin Mary I have laid my eyes on so far. At six feet high, the statue in Neuilly-sur-Seine is called the Black Virgin of Paris. It is made of marble (I believe) and depicts a standing, smiling Black woman holding the Christ child (whose closely cropped nappy hair is blond in color) and wielding a kind of wand or scepter capped by a fleur de lis—the symbol of the French monarchy. Atop her head sits a gold crown embedded with precious stones, and she is dressed in a gown of rich red, blue, and white. The statue, renowned throughout the world for its "miracle-working" powers, is believed to be about five hundred years old.

As I explained to the members of the d'Zert Club, the veneration shown to the French Black Virgin statue, and to other similar statues and images like it throughout the world, is attributed, in part, to their Blackness. The group seemed both captivated and pleased by the idea of a Black woman being depicted in a position of such overwhelming power and majesty. Indeed, an overwhelming aura of peace seemed to permeate the atmosphere at the Neuilly-sur-Seine site, and everyone seemed to pick up on it.

As if seeing one Black Madonna statue in France were not enough, the d'Zert Club's third and last day in Paris began with a visit to Chartres to see yet another. Chartres is an old and quiet little town about fifty miles southwest of Paris. The cathedral there is a large and magnificent edifice more than eight hundred years old.

At least two of the cathedral's marvelous, original, blue stained-glass windows depict Black Virgin figures in their centers. The cathedral also houses four statues of a Black Virgin Mary. One stands in a crypt underneath the main cathedral, but the most notable is called Our Lady of the Pillar. This statue, about a meter high, depicts a Black Mary standing on a pillar holding the infant Jesus. Mother and child are colored a very dark brown, and both are wearing white robes embroidered with gold. The Chartres statue is also highly venerated, especially among Catholics, and several of our tour members (including me) got down on both knees and whispered our prayers out of sheer respect. And, naturally, we took a lot of photos.

Sister Zawadi wrapped up the tour by pointing out to the group two images of African men amidst the grandeur of the Chartres cathedral. She explained that the most notable of these figures, which are carved onto two of the cathedral's prominent lintel blocks, is dated at almost seven hundred years old. It depicts an African soldier drawing his sword at the Judgment of Solomon. The other image shows a kneeling African man, perhaps a Moorish soldier, whose face is painted black. Both figures have tightly curled hair.

And with that, having completed my second visit to Chartres and shared my knowledge of the Black presence in France with the members of the d'Zert Club, we all said goodbye to Our Lady of the Pillar and returned to Paris. For my part, I relished the experience and reveled in all that I had seen there.

LONDON SUCCESS STORIES

October 18, 2005

I just spent a week in London, where I did twenty slide presentations, one lecture, and four radio interviews—and still found time to get my tourist visa to enter Brazil next month! I also visited three museums (the British Museum, the Victoria and Albert Museum, and the Museum of London near Moor Gate), Westminster Abbey Cathedral (to see the statues of the African martyrs that adorn the main entrance), and the obelisk of the mighty Eighteenth Dynasty Kamite monarch Thutmose III on the Thames River Embankment (which I visited twice). Whew!

I was also taken to an area called Black Friars, where I viewed a kind of metal sculpture, located next a large building, of a Black man dressed in medieval religious garb sitting upon a horse. My first visit to this sculpture was with three other brothers in the early evening in the middle of the week, and unfortunately, I did not bring my camera with me to photograph it. I came back a few days later to take some pictures but could not find the sculpture on my own, so I have nothing to show for my finding, but it certainly was interesting.

Most of the presentations I made in London were in the local public schools, primarily in Brixton. Brixton is in the London district of Lambeth, and it seems to be one of the city's heavily African areas. It has a very rich mix of Africans from the Caribbean (especially Jamaica) and from the Continent, quite a number of Asians, several different kinds of Europeans, and even some South Americans.

My programs were organized by one of the most distinguished residents of Brixton, Jah B, who turned out to be one of most hard-working brothers I have ever encountered. Jah B was a breath of fresh air in that he was not only a hard worker but also a perfectionist (just as I try to be) with a beautiful spirit and an air of great humility. We could use a million more Africans just like him! From the beginning, Jah B made it clear to me that I had not come to England to enjoy a holiday vacation. I was there to work, and work I did!

Here's how Jah B programmed my days and evenings. Each morning, I would meet him at a local subway station. (London locals refer to the subway as "the tube." I rode on the tube a lot.) From there, we would either walk or take a car to the school where I was scheduled to speak. We stopped first at the school's administration office, where someone was always expecting us (Jah B's groundwork was excellent!). Then we generally went straight away into a gymnasium to set up the slide projector and screen.

Then came the children, sometimes a couple of hundred of them or more. Their ages would range from about five to twelve years old. They would sit quietly on the floor and wait for me to begin. Sometimes, some of their parents would join them, and there was always a group of teachers.

Given my previous experience, and lots of it, especially that accumulated doing similar work in the Philadelphia public schools, I have learned that what works best for me in such settings is to engage the children immediately. In London, quite often I picked a bunch of them to help me operate the slide projector. They really liked that!

After selecting my slide-projector volunteers and giving a brief introduction, I started by asking them, "What kinds of things do you think about when you think of Africa and African people?" This was a good way to break the ice and involve them in the discussion from the very beginning, and I was able to be both firm and informal at the same time.

More often than not, I did not speak to the children from the stage but sat right down among them. I told them that they could call me "Dr. Rashidi" or "Sir" or either of my two new nicknames: "the Picture Man" or "the History Dude." They really got a kick out of that, but I made it clear to them that we were going to respect each other. I told them that to get respect, they must give respect, and that that would be our arrangement. I also made sure that they knew that I really cared about them, and that I was there to teach them something important. Not surprisingly, it all worked out remarkably well.

October is celebrated as Black History Month in Britain, so I had a kind of mandate to engage the children in some form of instruction. I told them that what they were calling "Black History" I called

"African History," and I asked them to agree not to limit their celebration and discussion of African History to only one month. They all agreed.

When I asked the children what they thought about when they thought about Africa, however, they generally mentioned wild animals and poverty. I got a few other answers also, but I almost always got those two, so I typically started my presentations by trying to destroy the modern mythology and common misperceptions of Africa held by many. I began with the basics: that Africa is not a country, but a continent; and that it possesses a great deal of natural resources and much diversity. In addition to the history of Africa and facts about its peoples and cultures, I talked to the children about Africa's natural beauty: her mountains and deserts and rainforests and rivers and waterfalls. I told them that Africans were the first people to wear clothes and shoes, to count and write, to farm, to build houses and cities and libraries, to play music, to bury their dead, to have calendars and clocks, to practice religion, and to have science and chart the stars in the heavens.

When I finished, it always got real quiet. That's when I knew that I had their full attention and that it was time for the Picture Man to go to work!

The first picture I showed was of an Ethiopian scientist holding the bones of Dinkinesh, the 3.5-million-year-old female Ancestor discovered in the Afar region of Ethiopia. I went from there to the Nile Valley, showing them pictures of Nubian and Egyptian kings and queens and children and monuments. I told them about the philosophical concepts, cultural patterns, and spiritual beliefs of the ancient people of the Nile Valley. I talked about Imhotep and pyramids and mummies. They ate it up!

Then I showed them images from other parts of Africa including Ethiopia, Nigeria, Ghana, and Zimbabwe. The children were actively absorbed in my presentation by then, but rather than wait until the end of my talk to let them ask questions and make comments, I engaged their inputs during the course of it. I insisted, however, that they not blurt out their questions and comments but first raise their hands to be recognized. I also told them that the only bad question was the one they didn't ask.

I told them about all of my travels and what I had seen and the people I had met and all of the interesting foods I had eaten. By that time, of course, they were having a ball. Then I took them around the world, showing them images—ancient and modern—reflecting the African presence in Asia, Australia, the Pacific Islands, Europe, and the Americas. The children beamed with delight when I showed them photos of the African presence in the countries of their birth.

In my London lectures, I practiced all the things I had learned during my rites of passage work with Philadelphia school kids. In the end, however, I think I had more fun than any of the children did! I must also confess that I was pretty impressed with the discipline and politeness of the majority of schoolchildren I encountered in England. In the US, many situations arise when I am tempted to throw an unruly kid out of a three-story school window. In London, the kids were essentially a pretty sweet bunch. I think they liked me too!

So, my London school presentations went well overall. Both Jah B and I were quite pleased with our accomplishments. We were certain that we had done a good job and offered congratulations all around to all who had been involved in the planning and who had participated. Even the White teachers would usually get up and rave about what a wonderful job I did. I think a lot of them were sincere in their comments too, but they usually looked pretty unsettled when I talked about ancient Egypt, and most seemed downright astounded when I showed the picture of the ancient Coptic Christ with black skin and woolly hair.

In addition to the London school presentations, I did four slide presentations in the city's community centers for children, their parents, and local residents. These presentations were even more powerful than the school presentations as they were attended mostly by African people and I did not feel as if I had to watch every word I said (like I had to in my school presentations). I could also be a little more unfiltered in my presentations, and I felt largely unfettered from the need to be "politically correct." For those occasions, I added some additional pictures and took more time with my explanations.

I also did two presentations just for "us"—that is, just us Africans. Those were especially good for me because I did not find myself, as I did in most of my presentations in both London and Berlin, speaking largely to ethnically mixed audiences. Now I don't have a real problem speaking in front of mixed audiences because I never change the essence of my message, no matter who the audience is. And that message is that Africa has a magnificent history and a lineage second to one, that we have the greatest story that has never been told, that we have a history before slavery and colonization, and that African people traveled all over the world without shackles and chains on their ankles and wrists. Telling that story to mixed audiences is a good exercise that only adds to my versatility, but at the end of the day, it's so good just to go home and speak to "family."

My last three British presentations took place over the weekend on Friday, Saturday, and Sunday nights. I spoke first in West Norwood on the Global African Presence, and the place was so packed, people had to be turned away! We had gotten some good radio publicity of the event and, combined with word of mouth, people really turned out. My Saturday night presentation was in a small African bookstore in Hackney. I spoke there on the Black presence in Australia, Tasmania, and the South Seas. The bookstore was small, and we filled it to capacity. Sunday's presentation was my last in London, at a venue in Stockwell, I believe. There, I dealt with the African presence in Asia and Europe. We had a good crowd, including a lot of Rastas. My presentation went splendidly and as well received as the others.

So this London trip was a really big success for me and one of my most gratifying travel experiences. I even managed to escort a small group through the British Museum on Saturday morning, and it was on that tour that I noticed a large fragment of the face or beard of Herumakhet (the Great Sphinx) on display. I was shocked! I had been to the British Museum several times before, and either they had just put it on display or I never noticed it, but that is quite a find. I took some photos and will do some more research on how this came to be.

Well, sisters and brothers, I had a great time in London, and I am looking forward to a return engagement so don't forget about me. I'll be back! Now I've got eleven days in Paris to enjoy my family, do some writing, and rest up a bit. I'm sure it won't be long before distant horizons are once again calling my name.

A QUICK STOP IN CYPRUS

October 28, 2006

This morning I woke up in Amman, Jordan. A car was waiting to take me to the airport, where I caught a pleasant flight of less than an hour to the city of Larnaca in the Republic of Cyprus, which is where I am now.

This is my first visit to Cyprus and I have yet to see a Black face, but I will continue to look. I came here mostly to visit the museums, only to find that today is a national holiday and the museums are not scheduled to reopen until Monday. I leave on Monday night, so I will try to stay positive and do as much as I can. Of course, I wish you all were here with me so that we could just chill for a while.

Cyprus makes sixty-eight the number of countries that I have visited in the last eight years. Not bad, eh? And my last lecture in Jordan makes forty-one the number of countries I've lectured in. Years ago, I set my sights on visiting sixty-five countries and lecturing in forty. I have now surpassed both goals, so now I am going to set my sights on visiting a hundred countries and lecturing in fifty. Plus, I figure that I have at least seven or eight more books left in me. If I can accomplish all that, along with all the other things that I am doing, I think I can go down in history as being on par with some of the immortals I admire so much.

It seems that since I hit the age of fifty, I have been thinking more and more about what my statement in life will be. I have also grown very comfortable with myself. I made up my mind a long time ago that I not only wanted to write history, but to make history too. So far, I think I'm moving in the right direction.

But enough of my musings! Another encouraging thing happened yesterday: I received an email from a Norwegian publishing house requesting permission to publish one of my essays on the African presence in Europe in a Norwegian textbook. They want to print several thousand copies and produce a CD as well. As you can imagine, I am very pleased about that as it makes me feel like I might be having an impact.

So here I am in Cyprus for a couple of days before taking the long journey back through Jordan, Turkey, and France to the USA. Cyprus is south of Turkey, southeast of Greece, and due west from Lebanon. I came here, as always, in search of the African presence and particularly to visit four museums, but I've already told you about the holiday snafu. What I'm finding, however, is that Cyprus has a character all to itself. The people here, who are mostly of Greek origin, are pretty friendly and English is widely spoken. It is pretty easy to get around too. Taxis are all over the place, but the island is small and compact enough so that you can even walk around and see lots of things on foot.

Tomorrow, I am going to try to go to North Cyprus, near the Turkish side. I have read that it is easy to cross the border. Then I think I'll just walk around some more, do a little sightseeing and perhaps go to the beach.

I decided to show some initiative today, so I got up and got organized, took care of some banking business, and then started my walk around the city of Larnaca. It is a small, compact city. I don't know the population numbers, but I figure twenty or thirty thousand people. I've seen a few Africans from the Continent here, usually walking by themselves along the streets. I also saw one African couple strolling along the beach. They all seemed pleasantly surprised when I greeted them.

The thing that stands out the most here to me, however, is the presence of large numbers of South Asians and Southeast Asians. I noticed it first on the flight from Amman yesterday. It seemed that more than half of the people on the plane were either from Sri Lanka (mostly Tamils) or Thailand, and almost all of them were young women. The reason that I knew their national identities is because I saw the covers of their passports; plus, I have been in Thailand enough to know the physical appearance of Thais and a few words of their language.

I asked a few people on the plane about this and came to the conclusion that most of the women were domestics—that is, maids and nannies. My taxi driver confirmed my hunch and told me that the older people in Cyprus tolerate the women a lot more than do young Cypriots. I also think that a bunch of them serve other purposes as well because most of them are young and rather pretty, and I have only seen a few Sri Lankan men and no Thai men. The cab driver told me that the women sometimes marry local men and are the victims of much sexual abuse.

October 29, 2006

Today I visited two museums, including the Cyprus Museum, and I was very disappointed with both. I did find a small bronze weight in the form of an African man's upper torso and head at the latter. I also found a glass case of pendants from Egypt, including several of god Bes; a couple of pendants displaying Ast (Isis); three or four eyes of Heru; a small statue of Asar (Osiris); a small bronze statue of a seated Imhotep posing as a scribe; four winged sphinxes that showed a strong Egyptian influence; and a fifteen-foot-high bronze nude statue of the African Roman emperor Septimius Severus; plus a few other pieces that I could not identify. And that was about it. The other museum had even less.

After the museums, I crossed over into North Cyprus on the Turkish side of the island. The Turks invaded Cyprus about forty years ago, and the Greek population is still seething about it. I got the impression that the Greeks and Turks hated each other. I had lunch and ice tea in the capital city of Lefkosia. Anyway, I can now say that I have visited a cool seventy nations!

When I get back to the US next week, I have to hit the ground running. I am to speak at a big conference in Beaumont, Texas, and then head to Philadelphia for a few days of mostly lecturing. After that, I will have to spend a day or two in the hospital undergoing some long overdue surgery and a week's recovery before dashing off to Los Angeles, where

I have a lecture weekend lined up and will be co-hosting a week-long radio show with one of Amiri Baraka's daughters. Her show is called "Front Page," and the station is owned by our own Stevie Wonder.

We are calling the program "AFRICA 101," and it is going to be very powerful. Our guest on day one will be Dr. Asa Hilliard III. That program will be followed by a day of listener call-ins and conversations, followed by a program featuring Dr. Toni Humber on the African presence in Mexico. The show after that will feature me speaking on the Global African Presence. Our last show will showcase Dr. David Horne, who will talk about why Africa is important to us and strategies for African liberation. It should be a tremendous week!

STUCK IN SHANNON (IRELAND)

June 13, 2007

Can you believe that I am in Shannon, Ireland? I was on a flight to Newark from Amsterdam when the pilot announced that the toilets were not working and we would have to return to Europe, specifically to the Shannon airport! I mean, I always wanted to visit Ireland, but not like this!

So I have been here, stuck, about four hours now, but it seems a lot longer! The funny thing is, the toilet maintenance problems happened on a US airline, not on Air Malawi or Rwandair Express or Kenya Airways (an excellent airlines), or Dairo Airlines or any of the often-maligned African airlines that I have recently flown on. So, way to go, Africa!

I've been wanting to come to Ireland for a long time. In fact, I think that I may have actually been here in another lifetime. For some reason, I have always been interested in Irish history from ancient to modern times. As I recall, the great Marcus Mosiah Garvey once sent a message of solidarity to the leaders of the Irish Republican movement. And, in the most ancient times, Ireland was said to be peopled by the Formorians, described as "African sea rovers," who fought for possession of that island.

Two good references on the African presence in early Ireland are The Story of the Irish Race by Seumas MacManus (published in 1926) and Ancient and Modern Britons by David MacRitchie, written in the 1880s. MacRitchie's work is a classic. I was able to review it in Ivan Van Sertima's African Presence in Early Europe. All three works should be in every library. Indeed, most of us have heard of the Black Irish but few have any idea who they are or were. I know I don't.

I'm thinking that it might not be a terrible thing if I ended up spending the night here. The people, at the airport at least, seem fairly friendly, and I feel like I can handle most anything. Time will tell, I guess, but I do think that I will get out of here later tonight.

Oh, and while I'm thinking about it, keep an eye out for Tony Martin's new work on Amy Ashwood Garvey. Brother Tony is one of our greatest scholars, and this work is long overdue. Stay strong, Africans!

Runoko Rashidi

A 13th century statue of Saint Maurice in Madgeburg, Germany

Saint Maurice and Saint Erasmus in Munich, Germany

My Global Journeys in Search of the African Presence

A portrait of Saint Maurice in 16th century Germany

The sword of Saint Maurice, Vienna, Austria

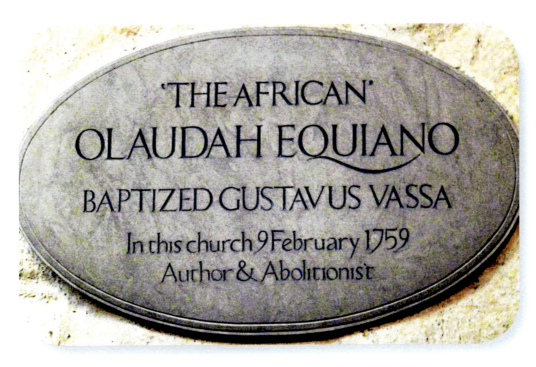

A plaque denoting the baptism of Olaudah Equiano
in St. Margaret's Church in London

A bust of Alexandre Sergeyevich Pushkin
in St. Petersburg, Russia

My Global Journeys in Search of the African Presence

A portrait of Queen Sophia Charlotte in
the Mint Museum, Charlotte, North Carolina

Runoko Rashidi

Standing with a painting of Pushkin in Moscow

Pushkin's library in St. Petersburg, Russia

My Global Journeys in Search of the African Presence

A sculpture of an African by Charles Cordier in the Orsay Museum, Paris

Runoko Rashidi

A sculpture of an African by Charles Cordier in the Orsay Museum, Paris

My Global Journeys in Search of the African Presence

PORTUGAL

May 3, 2008

All is well. I'm here in Lisbon. This is my first full day here, and a full one it has been. To begin, it took a long time to get here. I got on a plane Thursday morning and flew from Los Angeles to Houston. Then I went from Houston to Paris, and from Paris to Lisbon, with long layovers between each flight. And then, upon my arrival in Lisbon, I am sad to say, I found that my luggage had not arrived with me. (This is happening with so much greater frequency lately that it is becoming routine!)

Anyway, upon arriving in Lisbon, I learned that my bag was still in Paris. Thank God it was delivered to me early this morning. So, like I said, all is well.

Lisbon, the capital of Portugal, is a fairly attractive city of about six hundred thousand people. I am not sure about the numbers of Africans here, but there are more than I anticipated—although not nearly as many as in Paris and London, and probably less than in Amsterdam. There may be as many Africans here as in Brussels, but certainly more than in Rome, Madrid, or Berlin. I saw dozens of Africans in the course of my travels today, and there are even a couple of brothers working in the hotel.

Don't tell anybody, but I had lunch at a McDonald's this afternoon, and I found, to my delight, more Africans working there in one place than anywhere else so far! But I have not really talked to any of them, and so I have not heard their story. They also seem a bit reserved. Of course, I am pretty indifferent to the White folks here, like I am to White folks in most places. They do not seem terribly friendly, but they are not hostile, either. Indeed, some are almost pleasant.

Today was a museum day, and I went to four of them. As I am trying to save some money on this trip, I only took a couple of taxis. I did a lot of walking and used buses and trams instead. As a result, my legs got really sore. Plus, the layout of Lisbon is a lot like San Francisco, so I would just as soon not see any more hills for a very long time! And like San Francisco, Lisbon is built along the ocean. At one point, I stood a couple hundred meters from the spot where the pirate Vasco DaGama launched the voyages that so dramatically altered the course of world history.

The first museum that I went to, the one that I most anticipated visiting, was the Museu Calouste Gulbenkian, considered Portugal's finest. Calouste Gulbenkian was an Armenian who amassed a vast fortune in the oil business and decided to build a museum to house his likewise vast collection of art and artifacts. The highlight of his holdings was his Egyptian collection. It was not a big one, but it was a good one, the major treasures being a black basalt head of the great Twelfth Dynasty king Senusret III and a superb stone head of an unknown Nubian man. I found them to be excellent indeed! There were also two pieces depicting African images from the European Renaissance in the Gulbenkian Museum, one of the Adoration of the Magi and the other of an African at the baptism of Christ.

Museum number two was the Museum Nacional de Arqueologia (the National Archaeological Museum) in the Belem district. By contrast, that museum was a big disappointment. It is connected to the Mosteiro dos Jernonimos, a big Manueline monastery. If you have never heard of this monastery, don't worry about it. But if you have seen ads promoting Portuguese tourism, this is usually the one image they show. The monastery is a large, impressive building, but the museum did not thrill me, despite the small Egyptian collection it housed. Next to the archaeological museum was a small ethnological museum, which I also visited, but I found little of interest there, either.

It's still just so amazing to me that so many artifacts have been taken out of Egypt. It sometimes amazes me that there is anything left in Egypt at all! I suppose, however, that the biggest disappointment of this trip came from the fact that I could find nothing on the Moorish occupation of Portugal—and I mean nothing!

After my museum tour came my lunch at McDonald's. After that, I got lost on the tram and then walked for a couple of hours looking for museum number four: the new Museum of the Orient. Apparently, I was being punished because after that very long walk, I arrived at the museum to discover that it had not yet opened to the public—what a drag after I had searched high and low to find it! I even went into a police station for help with directions, but met with no success—I guess because I was soaking wet with perspiration (it was a rather warm day). Anyway, the Portuguese cops looked at me with great suspicion. And when I told them my story, they just laughed and pointed me toward what, in many ways, was the best museum find of them all, the last museum stop of my day: the Museu Nacional de Arte Antiga (the National Museum of Ancient Art), located in the Lapa district. But wouldn't you know it, it was the one museum in which I could not take photos!

The highlights of this museum were two large and impressive Nanban screens, on which were painted scenes depicting the early Portuguese presence in Japan during the sixteenth century. The first screen's painting included about thirty images of Africans working in the Portuguese navy. I did a little research on Nanban paintings almost thirty years ago, but until today I had never seen one in person. And although I could not photograph them, I was happy to find an excellent and not very expensive book on them in the museum gift shop. (If you are interested, the book is titled Biombos Namban by Maria Helena Mendes Pinto. It was published by the Museum Nacional de Arte Antiga in 1993).

So that was my morning and afternoon, sisters and brothers. Not a bad way to spend the day, huh? Tonight, I may go listen to some fado music, and tomorrow I am going to try to get out of Lisbon to continue my search for the Moors in Portugal.

May 8, 2008

Well, I am finishing up in Portugal and, God willing, I will return to France tomorrow night. I would have left sooner, but in coming here I bought a relatively cheap, non-refundable and non-changeable Paris/Lisbon plane ticket. It seemed like a good idea at the time, but those kinds of tickets are kind of dangerous because once you buy them, you are stuck with them. I did the same thing with my hotel reservations. So, stuck I have been. It has not been a bad trip, but it was very poorly planned.

Anyway, let me tell you what I have been up to for the past several days since I did my museum tour of Lisbon. The first day after that was a quiet one. I did little but stay in my hotel room and write. The hotel where I was staying was a bit isolated (but very expensive) and there was little to see or do around it, so that day I wrote the Preface to a new book by Mukasa Afrika on African education. I also deliberated about what I would do in the succeeding days, eventually making and remaking plans simply to stay in Lisbon.

The next day, I moved to a hotel in the Lisbon city center, and that made all the difference in the world. During the daytime, I explored the city and was pleasantly surprised at the size of its African population. I estimate that it is at least ten percent of the total population. The majority of the sisters and brothers come from Angola, Mozambique, Guinea Bissau, and Cape Verde, although the Cape Verdeans seem more assimilated to the Portuguese way of life than do those Africans from the other countries. The African population dynamic reminds me of Paris, where most of the Africans come from Guadeloupe and Martinique as well as directly from Africa itself.

Of course, the language barrier between me and the Africans I met in Portugal was a severe one, and I could only get bits and pieces of data from the sisters and brothers I encountered. For those of you who travel, I know you will agree with me that if you don't speak the local language and have no one on the ground to assist you, you can really miss out on a lot.

That night, I grew restless and decided to test Lisbon's nightlife. I got dressed, received some instructions from the concierge, and caught a taxi to the Barri Alto district for dinner, drinks, and the music called fado. There were a bunch of fado clubs in the area, but I was searching for one with live music.

I thought fado was kind of like the blues in the United States, but that turned out to be a major miscalculation on my part. When I finally found the club I was looking for, the singer turned out to be an old, rather plain, and matronly looking White woman. She looked like a domestic servant, and at first I thought she was cleaning up the place until she went up on stage and started singing and clapping, accompanied by two old White men playing guitars. I still don't know if I could tell you what fado is, but I can't say that I liked what I heard. I couldn't believe it. I asked some of the club's patrons if the woman was, in fact, singing fado, and they assured me that she was. I quietly finished my beer and left. My fado music experience may have been a big bust, but I ended the evening on a positive note with a nice meal in a Thai restaurant.

The next morning, I took a train to the small city of Sintra, the highlight of which is the Castelo dos Mouros, or what remains of an eighth-century Moorish castle. It was a nice experience. I climbed to the top of the castle, took lots of photos, bought some postcards, and gained an even greater appreciation of the contributions of the people called the Moors.

I have really tried to save a lot of money on this trip by relying less than I usually do on taxis and using mostly public transportation. The results have been most rewarding. Indeed, near the Rossio train station, I ran into an abundance of African people. I noticed that one sister had on a beautiful African dress, and when I innocently tried to tell her how beautiful she looked she reacted as though I had said something really dreadful, demeaning, and insulting–and her male companion did not look very pleased about what I said, either! Oh that big language gap! I don't know how they interpreted my comments, but I departed the scene very, very quickly and did not look back!

The last three days it seems as if I have been just catching buses and trains and going round and round and round with both eyes open. So on this, my last full day in Portugal, I am going to go somewhere other than McDonald's and have a nice, healthy lunch. Perhaps I will explore a bit more of the city. Right now, however, I am reading some nineteenth-century English fiction. I would love to get some nice African music CDs and sit down later today to write and read some more. I particularly want

Runoko Rashidi

to write about some of my experiences in Myanmar (Burma), where a deadly cyclone has had such catastrophic effect recently. And tomorrow, before I catch my flight to Paris, I hope to visit one more museum.

Overall, I would say that this trip has provided me with a wonderful, object, and costly lesson about what to do and not to do when planning travel. I made a lot of mistakes and miscalculations, but I guess it truly has been a case of live and learn. Anyway, the weather is pleasant and I have an incredible view from my hotel room, so life goes on.

And that is it for Brother Runoko in Portugal. I am alive and well. I am also really cheering on Barack Obama in his bid to become the first African president of the United States. African people, we are so blessed!

MUSEUM MUSINGS FROM BUDAPEST

August 6, 2008

I am in Budapest, Hungary. I got here last night after flying from Cairo to Paris and then from Paris to Budapest. It was a long day, with a long layover in Paris, and then a long flight delay after that. But here I am!

Hungary is a member of the European Union, but it still does business with its own currency, which is the Hungarian florint. The spoken language and script is Hungarian or Magyar. Budapest, a city of about two million, is the capital of Hungary, and, as far as European cities go, it is very beautiful. It reminds me of Paris and Vienna with a little bit of Amsterdam thrown in.

English is widely spoken here, and the people are not unfriendly. Black folks, however, are a rarity here. That is probably because Hungary is one of those few European nations without an African colonial legacy. So far, I have only seen about fifteen of us.

I was met last night by Marc Washington, an American-born African who teaches English in Budapest. He has been here since the early 1990s and seems to like the place. The other sisters and brothers here, to whom I have spoken only briefly, are mostly African immigrants and business people. I bumped into a sister from Accra, Ghana, while wandering around the hotel last night, and she made it very clear to me that she was there "doing business"—if you know what I mean! I wished her well, told her that I was not in Hungary to do her kind of business, and bade her a pleasant evening.

Some of the Black folk here seem genuinely glad to see you. Others, when you greet them, give you that kind-of "Do I know you?" look and keep on walking. One young brother, in particular, was with two young, blond White women. When I greeted him, he had absolutely nothing to say to me. Instead, he acted like he was in "Hungarian paradise" and simply ignored my presence.

So far, I have not encountered any overt racism, with one possible exception. I was on the metro this afternoon, and a little White Hungarian kid pointed at me and said something that he seemed to think was very funny. The lady next to him, I guess it was his mother, sternly rebuked him. I did not need a literal translation for me to gather that he was not being complimentary toward me! Good thing for all of us on the train that whatever he said was in Hungarian. Otherwise, I would have probably throttled the little brat! But children learn from adults, don't they?

I saw a lot today. I started early, got directions, and, instead of jumping into a taxi like I usually do, I took the metro to my first stop of the day: the Museum of Fine Arts. Actually, it was a pretty easy trip, and it was a good museum, with a better-than-anticipated Egyptian collection.

I saw several excellent pieces, but two artifacts in particular stood out. The first was an Eighteenth Dynasty sandstone image of a young African woman holding a standard of the Egyptian goddess Hathor. The other was a stone image of a Ramesside[5] king with dark brown skin and prominent happy-to-be-nappy hair. Those two pieces alone justified the trip for me.

I also found a nice marble head of African Roman emperor Severus Septimius and a painting of a White woman named Beersheba taking a bath assisted by an African woman servant. Another interesting painting was of the Spanish saint, Saint James, conquering the Moors. Last December, while I was in Sevilla, my tour guide affirmed for me that Saint James was Spain's most important figure and that the single best way to offend a White Spaniard was to disparage his likeness. In the painting, the Moor under the hooves of Saint James' horse is clearly Black.

Probably the most interesting single artifact that I observed in the museum today was a late fifteenth-century German painting of the martyrdom of Saint Bartholomew. In the painting, the saint is being seriously scourged by five clearly and distinctly African men. I mean, the brothers are really giving him a bad time! I took photos of everything and hope to share them with you some day.

I also found in the museum an excellent full-color postcard of a portrait of Duke Alessandro De Medici, a sixteenth-century Duke of Florence. In the portrait, his African heritage is very prominent. The actually painting, by Agnolo Bronzino, is permanently housed in the Uffizi Gallery in Florence, Italy. I bought several postcards of it and left the museum thinking that I had enjoyed a very, very good morning.

With the Fine Arts Museum behind me, I went in search of my next objective: the Asian art museums of Budapest. After a meandering walk, I found them. But what a disappointment—they were housed in only two small rooms, both of which I covered in less than ten minutes! I purchased a photo permit for both, but nothing in either museum inspired me to even take the camera out of my bag.

I got back on the subway and, after a short journey, found myself on banks of the Danube River. I had promised myself that I would have lunch on the Blue Danube one day, and this was my chance, so I found a rather expensive Hungarian restaurant and requested a menu. I settled for a chicken steak with vegetables and sour cream, a strong Hungarian beer, and some sparkling Hungarian mineral water. It was delicious!

Just across the river from the restaurant stood Castle Hill, a huge limestone block that dominates the twin cities of Buda and Pest. Castle Hill was my next destination—specifically, a place called Matthias Church—I just needed to figure out how to get up there. I had asked three or four people about this, and they each told me to take a train to the bridge, find a bus or walk across,

---

5 The term Ramesside refers to the eleven kings of ancient Egypt who took the name of Ramses.

Runoko Rashidi

and then climb up the hill on foot. Of course, I looked at all of them like I thought that they were insane and took a taxi instead! It seemed to me that only a lunatic would do as they had suggested, especially the part about climbing the hill!

I wanted to visit Matthias Church because my research had suggested that a statue of a Black Madonna could be found there. It was, but unfortunately, it is housed in the church museum, which was closed for renovation. I had to settle for a photo of the statue that I found in a book in the church bookstore. And after all that, I think the Castle Hill statue is actually only a copy of the Black Madonna statue found in Loreto, Italy. But at least I got a photo of it.

My last stop this afternoon was the National Gallery and, unfortunately, I did not find anything even remotely African in it. And that was basically my day.

So now I am back at my hotel. I am a little tired, and both my feet and my knees are sore from all that walking, but I am still feeling pretty pleased with myself. It is just five o'clock, I have a wonderful view of the Danube, and a beautiful room to read, write, and relax in. I'm guessing that tomorrow I will try to take a train or even a bus across Hungary's northern border to visit Bratislava, Slovakia, where, I understand, there is another museum with an Egyptian collection. I can almost hear it calling me. And if I make that trip, it will make country number ninety for me in my quest to visit one hundred nations in search of the African presence. So keep your fingers crossed for me. Perhaps I will have another interesting story or two for you in a few days!

A JOURNEY TO SLOVAKIA

August 8, 2008

I am in excellent spirits today. Yesterday, I took the train from Budapest to Slovakia, accompanied by Brother Marc Washington. We left about 9:30 in the morning, and in less than three hours we were in Bratislava, the Slovakian capital. You know, I have been saying for some time that one of the big keys to success in the type of international travel I do is to have reliable people on the ground to help facilitate things. Well, during my brief sojourn in Budapest, Brother Marc has really been there for me. Bless you, Marc, because it has been a real adventure, and I am not sure I would have had the courage and the tenacity to make this trip all by myself. Thank you ever so much!

With a population of about five million, Slovakia is Hungary's northern neighbor, but how many of you have even heard of it? You might be familiar with it under another name, for until 1992 it was part of what is now the Czech Republic, and together they formed the Central European nation of Czechoslovakia. Also known as the Slovak Republic, Slovakia is a land-locked country separated from Hungary by the Danube River. To the west is Austria. The Austrian city of Vienna, which I visited three or four years ago, is not very far away.

Bratislava is the country's social and economic center and also its largest city. A little over 400,000 souls live here. Unlike Budapest, English is hardly spoken in Bratislava, and so far I have seen only one Black person here, a young African woman who was coming out of the train station. I saw her from a distance, and I suspect that she is a tourist like me. She was with two White people, and I got the impression from her body language that she was much more oblivious than I was to being such a rarity.

Indeed, if there are many sisters and brothers in Slovakia, I feel sorry for them because they must lead a very lonely existence. And, I might add, the local folks are not terribly friendly. I have never been stared at so much in my life!

I can hardly wait to get out of here and, wouldn't you know it, the train for our return trip to Budapest is late! Still, despite my anxiety about being in such a minority situation, I am in a surprisingly good mood because today, sisters and brothers, I struck gold!

Now you may be asking, why did I go to Bratislava in the first place? The answer is obvious, especially for those of you who know me: to search for the African presence. Besides, Slovakia is fairly close to Budapest, but could it have been pure coincidence that on my first and only trip to Budapest, that in close-by Bratislava, just opening up to the public, was a major exhibit on ancient Egypt called "Thebes, City of Gods and Pharaohs"? This exhibit is the first that I am aware of that focuses solely on the great ancient city of Thebes—or, as the people of Kmt called it, Waset—and I only found out about it a few days ago!

The exhibit, as it turns out, was simply superb and featured antiquities that I was able to view for the first time. (The same exhibit was in Prague last year.) It included an exquisite stone fragment portraying one of my favorite monarchs of all time: the Eleventh Dynasty king Nebhepetre Mentuhotep II. To top it off, he was painted black as the night. It was magnificent!

Finding the exhibit, however, was a chore. After arriving in Bratislava, Brother Marc and I had to inquire repeatedly about the location of the archaeological museum where it was on display. Nobody in the train station seemed the least bit interested in helping us, and all our questions were waved off with the back of a hand.

Finally, we decided to take a taxi, but the driver took us to the wrong museum. Despite the temptation to give up and return to Budapest, after a lot of effort we finally found the right place. And we could not have been more satisfied. Even when we were told that we could not take photos, we were consoled by the availability of a large but fairly inexpensive catalog that contained images of all the artifacts prominently displayed. Naturally, I bought a copy.

To this day, I don't know what the alignment of the stars was and why such a magnificent storehouse of African art would be on display in such a relatively obscure place. But I was very, very pleased on the return train to Budapest.

The next day, since my flight did not leave Budapest until late afternoon, and since I got a late check-out time from my hotel, I decided to go out in search of a Black Madonna image and, if that worked out, to try to find the Hungarian National Museum. I ended up at the University Church, where, hanging over the altar, I saw a replica of the famous Black Madonna icon at the Jasna Gora Monastery in Poland. Later, instead of taking a taxi and despite the fact that it was becoming rather hot, I started to walk.

With some effort and some pretty good directions it did not take terribly long to find the National Museum. I was the first patron to enter that day. I paid the admission fee and then paid what I thought was an exorbitant fee to use my camera. During the early part of my visit, I found most of the displays to be largely a waste of time and I consoled myself with the thought that at least I had gotten to the museum. Better to know that there is nothing of real value someplace than to find out later that you missed a gem, especially considering that I will probably never return to Budapest again.

But I don't accept defeat very well. I mustered up all the determination I could find, and the African scholar-detective in me took over. In the end, it worked out most beautifully as I found much to treasure. Indeed, just when I thought that there was no point in scouring the rest of the museum, I came upon three pieces, one after the other, that justified all of my efforts and all of the expense.

First, there was a prehistoric figurine of a large-hipped woman from the most ancient period in Hungarian antiquity, made of stone and standing about ten inches high. I had seen many of these so-called "Venus" figurines, but this one was by far the best. I mean this sister—that is, her statue—had a behind on her that any Nama woman from Namibia or Khoi Khoi woman from South Africa would be envious of. I took a load of photos. And, to think, I had been just about ready to give up my search. My patience and tenacity had been rewarded.

Then, from the Roman phase of Hungarian history and the region called Transdanubia, the museum had on display a small bronze figurine of an African man with curly hair or locks playing the pan pipes. The figure was only about two inches high and was easy to miss, but there it was, visible to the discerning eye: evidence of an African presence in Hungary. Again, my persistence was rewarded.

Lastly, I found, on the top floor of the museum, my third treasure of the morning: a fifteenth-century parchment scroll featuring both Hungarian writing and two coal-black images of the heads of Moors. Both the Moors' foreheads had gold bands on them. I took several photos of each, completed my museum tour, and made my way back to the hotel with time to spare.

And that was my last morning in Budapest.

This past week has been an extra special, whirlwind one. I was in the Egyptian Museum in Cairo on Monday, flew to Hungary Tuesday, witnessed the Egyptian collection in Budapest Wednesday, and saw a major exhibit in Bratislava, Slovakia, today. And to top it off, I have been to ninety countries now!

Well, I guess that's enough for now. Today I head back to Paris, and from there I fly to Stockholm, Sweden, regarded by many as Europe's most beautiful capital. I hear it's rainy in Stockholm this time of year—my favorite weather. I expect to find another Egyptian collection in Sweden, plus I am scheduled to meet with members of Stockholm's African community. And then, God willing, I will journey from there to the Olmec and Mayan heartland of Mexico, where I will enjoy my 54th "earthday"! Who could ask for anything more? I guess you could say that I am really on a roll!

Right now, I better rush to get out of here, so pardon my haste. I have to hurry up and pack. Keep your fingers crossed for me!

A RETURN TO SWEDEN: DESTINATION STOCKHOLM

August 9, 2008

From time to time, I find myself in a situation where my resolve to travel is sorely tested. For example, I arrived in Sweden late last night and found myself immediately confronted by a series of challenges.

To begin, my flight arrived a little later than scheduled. I was supposed to arrive at 10:30 in the evening, which is not a really great time to arrive in a new city in a country that I have only visited once before (see my note on Denmark and Sweden in this book). Then, I learned that my luggage was not on the flight, something that has happened to me four or five times now since December. The first time, it took almost ten days for me to get my stuff back, with no apology from the airline and certainly no compensation.

Then, last night, by the time I filed a claim for lost luggage, the banks inside the airport were closed, which meant that I had no local currency. Although Sweden is a member of the European Union, neither euros nor dollars are any good here. Fortunately, I was able to find an ATM machine in the airport.

Then, I had to find a way to get to my hotel, but it was approaching the midnight hour and no shuttles were available. Plus, the airport is forty-five minutes from the Stockholm city center and taxis into town are really expensive. (By the way, when you hear people say that Europe is really expensive, you can take them at their word. It is all too true!) So, I ended up catching an airport bus to the city center with the belief that the bus would at least get me closer to my hotel, and if I had to take a taxi later, it would not cost as much. Nonetheless, it took me the better part of an hour to get into town. Fortunately, the bus driver was a really nice man from South Asia who spoke very good English, which was just grand since I speak no Swedish.

From the city center, I got a taxi to my hotel. I think the taxi driver was a White Arab. When he told me the price and the distance to my hotel, I was stunned. I might as well have paid the exorbitant taxi fee from the airport. My hotel, it turned out, was a long way from the city center; about twenty kilometers, in what appeared to be the middle of nowhere. None of this information, of course, was very reassuring. By the time I finally got to the hotel's reception desk, the reservation clerk told me that the price I would have to pay was considerably more than the amount on the receipt I had from the booking agency. Talk about adding salt to a wound!

My hotel was a very small one located in an isolated industrial park in the suburbs. And there I was, in the middle of nowhere, by myself, no Black people to be seen, and no other hotels, restaurants, cafes or businesses in the vicinity. The taxi driver, who swore he would wait for me as long as I promised to vote for Barack Obama, left as soon as he saw me go through the door.

To make matters worse, the hotel had no Internet connection. And it was about then that it dawned on me that I had not given my flight or hotel information to anyone close to me—not to any family members or to any close friends or associates. I had only given it to two local contacts in Sweden, and those were two brothers I had never even met! And their contact info was, of course, in an email, so with no Internet connection, I could not even get in touch with them. If something happened to me here, I worried, who would even know to tell my story or who to tell it to?

Anyway, once I got to my room, I lay down on the bed to try to figure what to do. I was full of anxiety and felt a strong sense of isolation. And, as you can imagine, I was not very happy.

August 10, 2008

When I woke up this morning, I found myself hoping that last night's experience had all been a bad dream. I am sad to say that it was not. Oh well, life, as they say, goes on, so I just got up and got on with my day. I recalled that yesterday morning in Budapest also started out on a discouraging note but soon changed to my advantage, and that helped fortify me for the day's challenges. So I got dressed while watching some of the Olympic Games on television, and turned immediately to the task of finding another hotel closer to the city center–and with an Internet connection!

I suppose the lesson to be learned from all this is that I can never afford to get complacent in my travels around the globe. In this case, I realized, I simply got lazy and took some things for granted. Well now I have to get my act together.

I am presently staying in a relatively nice and much better located hotel than the one that I stayed in last night. It too is located in a suburb of Stockholm, one called Kista (I believe). A steady rain is going, mixed with periods of sun. From my window, I see forests of trees in every direction. I have a great Internet connection and my luggage, left in Paris yesterday evening, should be here very soon. My spirits have risen as a result.

Stockholm is, to me, quite interesting. There seem to be quite a number of Asians here—East Asians, that is—as well as South Asians and White Arabs from Southwest Asia. There are also quite a few Africans here, especially those from the Horn of Africa. Apparently Sweden has had a long-standing relationship with that part of Africa, Ethiopia in particular, and Gambia has long been a "destination" for Swedish tourists.

So far, I have not been to any museums and churches. I will save that for tomorrow. But I just finished having a fascinating conversation with two serious brothers from the African community here, and, unlike in Hungary and Slovakia, where I focused mostly on the African presence in early times, I learned a lot from them about the status of Africans in Sweden in the here and now.

It was an interesting exchange. I asked most of the questions, and the two brothers did most of the talking. They told me that they were from Gambia. One of them has been in and out of Sweden for nearly twenty years, and I was very impressed with his clarity of thought. The other brother, I think he was the younger of the two (by a little), also had a lot to share.

My new acquaintances estimated that about forty thousand Africans live in Sweden, mostly those from the Horn of Africa, Central Africa, and West Africa, many of whom are economic refugees. The major population centers for Africans in Sweden, they claimed, are the cities of Stockholm, Goteborg, and Malmo. As in Paris, with the city center being so expensive, they said that the majority of the Africans in Stockholm are forced to live outside the city in the suburbs.

The brothers explained that Africans in Sweden often are the victims of institutional racism and White supremacy; that they face discrimination in the fields of employment, education, housing, and all the basic aspects of life; and that African women are even more marginalized than African men. When I asked them for details, they quite interestingly referred me to the work of Dr. Frances Cress Welsing.[6] They also repeatedly used the term apartheid to describe the conditions for Blacks in Sweden. They indicated, however, that a serious contingent of Africans in Sweden are very much drawn to the African-centered models advocated by such greats as Cheikh Anta Diop, Chancellor Williams, and W. E. B. Du Bois. And even though the Blacks in Sweden are not terribly cohesive and have such diverse origins, they felt that the ugly face of racism imposes a necessary solidarity. They also spoke passionately about the need to build a network of institutions for African development, and they were interested in a lot of my educational materials. Before we ended our conversation, we agreed that something like an African History Month to raise consciousness would help Africans in Sweden forge a closer connection to the Global African Community.

I have been watching television much of the day today, and the dominant news item is the war that has broken out between Russia and Georgia. I cannot help but think that if this is what White folks to do one another, what in the world will they do to you and me? Oh well, tomorrow, in addition to my museum quests, I have another meeting planned, this one a larger gathering, with members of the African community here.

August 12, 2008

It is approaching mid-morning here in Stockholm, and I am winding down my tour. Last night, it poured rain and more showers are predicted for today, so I am largely content to relax, read a little, and watch the Olympic Games on television, although it is a bit hard to follow when the coverage is in Swedish. Maybe I'll just go take a walk.

Yesterday was a full day for me. It started about nine in the morning with a trip to the city center. I was accompanied on my journey by Koro Sallah, one of the most prominent and activist members of Sweden's African community. We talked and talked and talked all the way to town. It was amazing how closely aligned our views were. The only major difference was my emphasis on history and his emphasis on the present. And in that sense, we actually complimented each other beautifully.

My first stop in Stockholm was the Museum of Mediterranean Antiquities. This is a relatively small museum and, after some general exploration, I was able to view two exquisite pieces representing the African presence in ancient Greece. One was a kind of vase or water sprout, and the other was a kind of ornamental drinking cup, both in the form of the heads of Black people (I think Black men). These artifacts are at least two thousand years old, marvelously detailed, and among the best representations of the type that I have seen. It is not uncommon, however, to find these kinds of artifacts in particularly good museums around the world. I have seen similar pieces in Boston, London, Paris, and Berlin.

---

6 Dr. Frances Cress Welsing is an African American psychiatrist practicing in Washington, D.C., who is noted for her "Cress Theory of Color Confrontation," which explores the practice of White supremacy.

The one exhibit that really stood out to me at the Museum of Mediterranean Antiquities was of a blue-and-white porcelain collection from the Topkapi Palace of Istanbul, Turkey. Part of the background to that exhibit was a scene depicting a group of distinguished dignitaries. One of them was as black as a lump of coal. I think he was from Central Asia, but it was hard to tell because the exhibit captions made little mention of him. And whereas I could take pictures in the Greek and Egyptian sections of the museum, I was told not to take photos in the part of the museum housing the Turkish exhibit. (I got off a few photos anyway before they stopped me, and they are excellent!)

Next on my list was the National Fine Arts Museum, where I was joined by another prominent member of Sweden's African community. During the course of the day, this brother, a noted artist from Namibia, told me many stories of his encounters with the former prime minister of Sweden, of his meetings with Malcolm X and John Oliver Killens, and of attending school with Angela Davis. I am sad to say, however, that the Fine Arts Museum was disappointing. I only saw two paintings depicting an African presence: one of a Black youth with a parrot and the other a beautiful painting of the Adoration of the Magi with two of the wise men portrayed as Africans. That was it.

After a lunch of Indian curry, it was time for more exploration of the Stockholm center city, and I was able to see, yet again, how beautiful and beguiling this city really is. Stockholm is built over a series of islands. Water and connecting bridges are everywhere, and there is an older section of town called Gamla Stan that is just enthralling. It was all simply gorgeous.

Then, it was back to business and a more than two hour-long meeting with another assemblage of Black men. No sisters were in attendance at that meeting, so regrettably I was not able to get the perspective of any African women about their experiences in Sweden. I wasn't able to get any in Hungary or Slovakia either, and that has been a big disappointment for me.

At the meeting, I was praised for coming to Sweden and asked to provide a summary of my work. I was happy to do so and engaged my audience in a series of mini-lectures followed by an extensive question-and-answer period. We had a fascinating discussion on the nature of African identity, and I was forced to realize that Africans, both on the African continent and in Europe, are probably as confused about this important issue as Africans everywhere else!

Finally, after dinner at a North African restaurant, it was time for the "crown jewel" of my journey through Stockholm: a visit to the studio residence of the noted African American artist, Harvey Tristan Cropper. Born in Harlem in 1931, this brother is the distinguished elder of the African community in Sweden. He was a gracious host and seemed genuinely glad to receive me. For a full hour, he regaled me with stories about Charlie Parker and Sonny Rollins and all the different artists, musicians, and intellectuals he has interacted with over the years. It seemed a fitting way to end my day, but I soon found out that it wasn't quite over yet.

On the train ride back to Kista, I was escorted by yet another distinguished African in Sweden, a noted filmmaker from Gambia, who showed me a series of newspaper clippings. The first was about a mixed-race, African-European child who had become a prominent neo-Nazi in Sweden. The second clipping was about the current conservative Swedish prime minister, and it revealed that he has an African American grandfather. The third clipping was one explaining that most of the shackles used to bind Africans during the enslavement period were manufactured in Sweden. I can't say which clipping shocked me the most, but they were not surprising.

So that's about it, sisters and brothers. I have been rewarded richly for my time and financial sacrifice in Sweden, but I do have a few regrets. First, I did not get any information on the Black Vikings. Second, I did not get to see the portrait of Adolph Badin, the great African of eighteenth-century Swedish court life. And third, I did not meet any members of Sweden's oppressed Sami community—those Arctic indigenous people inhabiting parts of far northern Sweden, Norway, Finland, the Kola Peninsula of Russia, and the border area between south and middle Sweden and Norway. But, all things considered, I had a great experience.

After having spent more than three weeks in Egypt, eight days in Ghana, and a week in Europe, I am ready to return to the US. My body is "feeling it," my wallet is definitely feeling it, and I am a little worn down. But it has been a productive experience overall, and I can easily see myself returning to Sweden and visiting other parts of Scandinavia in search of the African presence in the near future.

Other European countries that I want to visit in the future are Poland and Switzerland. I want to visit the major museums in Zurich and Warsaw and to go inside the churches with Black Madonnas near Lake Zurich and Krakow. I'd also like to return to Brussels, Belgium, and visit what is sometimes referred to as the "no-go zone" in East Germany. The latter is called that because of the large presence of skinheads and neo-Nazis there. It is said that African people and other people of color take their lives into their own hands when visiting there. There is, however, a church in the city of Magdeburg (about forty-five minutes by train from Berlin) in East Germany, where one can find a near-life-sized statue of Saint Maurice (also known as Saint Moritz, Morris, or Mauritius), the African leader of the legendary third-century, C.E., Roman Theban Legion and one of the favorite and most widely venerated saints of that group. I really want to see and photograph that statue, and I am ready to throw caution–and maybe even commonsense (?)—to the winds and go anyway, even if it means going alone!

Brussels, where I spent a day and a night in 2003, has a large population of Central Africans. Remember, the Congo was once the private property of the king of Belgium, so large groups of Congolese, Rwandans (and probably Burundians) make their homes in Brussels now. Yet Belgium has the reputation of being the most racist country in Western Europe. The museum that I visited there in 2003, however—the Royal Museum of History and Art—has an excellent Egyptian collection.

I can also easily see myself visiting Norway, Finland, the Baltic States, and returning to Denmark, although I don't give these nations the highest priority on my places-to-go list. But with Paris as my new base, everywhere in Europe—and, for that matter, Africa and Asia—is reachable. That means the sky is the limit!

I head back to Paris tomorrow and, from there, it's back to the USA for three nights before taking off for the Olmec and Mayan heartland of Mexico. And just wait till you hear about the trip to Aboriginal Australia and Melanesia that is being planned for me in October. Now that, my people, will truly be a story to tell.

Runoko Rashidi

DIE SCHWARZE MADONNA

March 16, 2009

I am in rarefied air. Today I realized a dream: I visited the chapel of Our Lady of the Hermits, in Einsiedeln, Switzerland—one of the most important Black Madonna sites in the world. I've always wanted to see it but never thought that I would. It was an incredible experience!

Our Lady of the Hermits ranks as one of the most venerated of all Madonnas. Located in a Benedictine abbey south of Lake Zurich, her titles include Die Schwarze Madonna ("The Black Madonna"), Madonna of the Dark Wood, and Our Dear Lady of Einsiedeln. She is represented in a beautiful statue, standing four feet tall, that includes a likeness of the Baby Jesus. The Black saint, St. Maurice, is one of the patrons of the church in which the Black Madonna is found. Ean Begg, author of the Cult of the Black Virgin (the definitive work on the subject), writes that Carl Jung, the psychiatrist and founder of modern analytical psychology, believed the Black Virgin of Einsiedeln to be a representation of the ancient African goddess Isis. In any event, that is what I saw and photographed this morning.

Indeed, I flew into Switzerland late last night from Amsterdam precisely so that I could get a few hours sleep and start out for Einsiedeln early this morning. Everything went according to plan, but I was taking no chances. Coming from Amsterdam, I was the only Black person on the plane. I got off in Zurich, went through customs, collected my luggage, hailed a taxi from the airport, checked into my hotel, got the train information I would need for the next day, called on the spirit of J. A. Rogers to guide me in my quest, and got a little rest.

Early this morning, I was up and at it. My wake-up call came before dawn, and shortly thereafter I found myself walking to the train station. I stood in line and bought my train ticket. Then I sat back as the train journeyed through the snow and mountains along the shores of Lake Zurich to the town of Einsiedeln. Once there, I left the station, walked up a steep hill—being careful to avoid slipping on the ice—and entered the large church of Die Schwarze Madonna. It was actually much easier than I thought that it would be (even when I had to change trains midway through the trip and all of the instructions were in German), so I was able to keep my nerves intact.

Yes, I admit that I often get really nervous on trips like these! But I can't afford to allow myself to get rattled, so I just focus on doing what I came to do. The results, more often than not, are more than worth the effort.

When I arrived at the church, a priest was saying mass. Mind you, it's a big church, but mass was said in and around the relatively small chapel housing the statue of the Black Madonna and Child. There were no Black people around anywhere. I had my camera with me and, fortunately, I did not notice the signs prohibiting photography until I had already taken half a dozen to ten photos, some of which are very good. But nobody, not the priest, the abbot, the nuns, or the congregants, made an effort to stop me from taking pictures. In fact, nobody said anything to me at all! Still, it was a house of worship so I tried to show some respect by not taking nearly as many photographs as I was tempted to. (I will add them to the fantastic photos I took yesterday in the National Museum of Antiquities in Leiden, the

Netherlands. I got some great shots there of the statues of King Mentuhotep II of the eleventh Kamite dynasty and Horemheb, the last great king of the Eighteenth Dynasty.)

The Einsiedeln Madonna statue is hundreds of years old and the object of adoration for millions of people. She is indeed the Black Lady, the Black Mother, the Black Virgin—and, in my view, a fitting incarnation of the goddess Isis. I could not help but behold her majesty and gaze upon her beauty, calm, and grace with awe.

I think I took more than a hundred superb photographs in and around the church and the local shops. I also purchased four or five small replicas of the Madonna and Child and a number of books that I hope to share with you over the days, weeks, months, and years to come.

The problem-free nature of this morning made me feel so confident that, on sheer faith and ambition, I bought a non-refundable and non-exchangeable train ticket for my travel the next day to Munich, Germany to visit the great Egyptian museum there. And who knows? I may even take a chance and try to go see the Black Madonna located in Bavaria near Munich.

But the primary focus of my trip to Munich tomorrow will be the Egyptian museum. Until this morning, it had never really crossed my mind to make such an effort to get to it, but tomorrow seems like such a wonderful opportunity. I may be a little nervous at first, but, bottom line, what is there to fear? I may never come this way again, and nothing beats a failure like a try. So off I go!

March 17, 2009

Today, I went to the city of Munich in the German state of Bavaria. I took the train—a long, four-hour-and-thirty-minute trip each way to and from Zurich, Switzerland. Once again, I got up before dawn, walked to the train station, and got on board. And once again, I did not return from my sightseeing journey until after nine o'clock at night.

Munich has a long history and played an especially important role during the Nazi era in Germany. Indeed, it was in Munich in the early 1920s that Adolph Hitler engaged in the Beer Hall Putsch (or failed coup) that put him and the Nazis on the political map. And it is just outside Munich that the famous Nazi concentration camp called Dachau was located. That is where I went this morning: to the city of Munich.

One of the first things I noticed upon arriving in Munich was a couple of Black people. One of them was a taxi driver. He was very friendly. Somehow I got the impression that he was from Cameroon, an African country to which I feel very closely connected and one that I intend to visit some day. It is no accident that I saw that brother at the train station. Like I've said before, if you want a to find Africans in Europe, a good place to start is usually around a train station. I don't know why, but they seem to gravitate there.

I traveled to Munich to visit the museums, and one museum in particular was my focus today: the Staaliche Sammlung Agyptisher Kunst Munchen, or the Egyptian Museum in Munich. I have known for a long time that the Germans did a lot of stealing from Africa, and Egypt especially, and .most of the prize pieces are in the Egyptian Museum in Berlin. But I knew that Munich had some good stuff too, a conclusion that was reinforced for me last week when I rediscovered a book on Egyptian art that I had left in Paris way back in 2004. Looking through the book, I noticed several outstanding works of ancient Egyptian art housed in the Munich museum.

So yesterday, while walking through the train station after my visit to Einsiedeln, I thought to inquire if train service was available from Zurich to Munich. It turned out that not only was such train service available, the price was not bad and I wouldn't even have to change trains. After a little effort once I got there, I found the Egyptian Museum.

The museum is housed in a former palace and consists of three large rooms and two or three small rooms. It does not have a big Egyptian collection, but several of the pieces are very rare. There was even a special exhibit on display, titled "Last Exit Munich: Egyptian Masterpieces from Berlin." The exhibit had just opened a few days before, so my timing could not have been better! The most prominent piece on display was the famous, and very Africoid-looking, wooden head of Queen Tiye, which is permanently housed in Berlin. The only bad thing about the exhibit was that, because it was a special exhibit, no photography was allowed. Fortunately, copies of most of the best artifacts were available for purchase in the museum gift shop in the form of books and postcards. And, of course, I bought a bunch!

So, my visit to the Egyptian Museum in Munich was a success. But unlike in Zurich, I soon found out that English was not nearly as widely spoken in Munich, and the Black Madonna site outside Munich that I wanted to visit was too far away. So was the Dachau concentration camp. So I walked to a taxi stand and caught a cab to return to the train station.

I had seen a Starbucks in the train station, and I figured that it was as good a place as any to wait the four hours for my train back to Zurich. I wasn't going to take a chance on exploring the city on my own because Germany has a strong neo-Nazi movement and I did not want to put myself in harm's way needlessly. After all, with my visit to the Egyptian Museum, I had essentially accomplished the purpose of my visit.

As it turned out, however, my taxi driver, a White German, was not only friendly but pretty fluent in English. So, while driving to the train station, I asked him if he knew of any other museum in the city with Greek, Roman, Etruscan, or other antiquities. And wouldn't you know it, he told me that we were just then within three or four blocks from two such museums! I figured that it must have been my destiny to visit those other two museums and, without hesitation, I told him to stop so that I could visit both of them. And what a good thing I did!

In the first museum, I found and photographed a great bust of Alexander Severus, the last representative of the Africoid Severan dynasty of Imperial Rome. Images of him are hard to find, and that museum had one of the best that I have seen. Of course—you guessed it—the nose on the bust was broken off at the base!

Afterwards, I walked across the street to the other museum and found five more African pieces from ancient Greece. I photographed all of them. I even found a book called Strong Women about the role of women in ancient Greece that even included an image of an Ethiopian woman! Now imagine if I had just gone on to the train station direct from the Egyptian Museum—I would have missed all of these African treasures from ancient Greece and Rome.

So altogether I had a very, very good day. I even saw a Muslim brother at the train station and greeted him with a great big "Assalamu Alaikum"! He gave me a warm smile and responded in kind.

Every day has been a good one for me lately. I spent much of last week with my daughter, visited the Louvre in Paris, and gave a good presentation in Bondy in a northern suburb of Paris. Friday, I flew to Amsterdam by way of Prague in the Czech Republic and had dinner with friends in a wonderful African-Surinamese restaurant. Saturday, I did a big radio interview and a bigger presentation in Amsterdam. Sunday, I visited the national antiquities museum in the Netherlands and flew to Zurich. Yesterday, I saw the Schwarze Madonna, and today I went to Munich. Tomorrow, I plan to visit five more big museums in Zurich. I am blessed! And I am collecting so many books and postcards that I don't know if I can fit them all in my luggage!

March 18, 2009

Today, all day, was another museum day for me, this time in Zurich. Quite frankly, I was getting a little tired of trains and, to be honest with you, I am also a little tired of museums now too! But museums are what I do, and today I did them well. My goal today was to visit five of the Zurich museums that I deemed most important. It turns out that I only got to three of them. The second two were a little disappointing, and the third one was especially so, but the first one made it all worthwhile. The first museum that I visited today was the Rietberg Museum. I first heard of it a little more than two years ago during a visit to a Cham exhibit in Paris. The Cham are an Africoid people who lived in Central Vietnam more than a thousand years ago.[7] Outside of Paris, the Rietberg had the best collection of Cham art that I have ever seen. It was the most distant from my hotel. It was too far to walk to and too much of a hassle to take the tram, and so I caught a taxi.

The taxi, however, because of road construction, could only take me so far. So I got out and walked the rest of the way. I had to walk around a corner and then up a fairly steep hill on a gravel road. I was getting really more than a little annoyed that I had to go through such trouble to get to the place, then, when I got there, I could not find the entrance! The museum encompasses two large, ornate houses and a modern annex. The museum's gift shop doubled as the entrance. The whole thing seemed really odd.

The young and pleasant East Asian woman working in the gift shop was one of the friendliest people that I've met here. So I rummaged through the shop, bought my rather expensive ticket, checked my bag, and found out to my relief that it was OK to taking pictures of the permanent exhibits. (Some museums don't let you take pictures at all, you know, but you never know for sure until you get there.)

Actually, I've learned that you can't take anything for granted when visiting museums. Sometimes, after great effort, you will find (to your disgust) that the museums are closed for renovations. Or more often, only the sections that you most want to see are closed. Other times, the specific artifact that you most want to see is on special loan to another museum. All of these unfortunate things have happened me on several occasions.

---

7   I discuss the Cham and their history, art, and culture in my 2005 travel notes on Vietnam in Part II of this book.

Think about how angry and hostile you would be after having flown great distances over land and sea, doing all of your research, checking dozens of web sites, and reviewing scores of travel books, only to arrive at the museum's front gate and find it closed! I can tell you firsthand that it makes you want to do something bad to somebody! But what can you do? I could write a book about it. But I've learned never to take museums for granted.

But back to the Rietberg. The Rietberg Museum has no elevators, so I had to take a long flight of stairs down to the lower level to view some nice African art, starting with several pieces from Nigeria. I took a few photos and slowly moved on.

Then I saw something that really got me excited: it was an eight-hundred-year-old wooden statue of Fudo Myoo from Japan. Fudo Myoo is one of the five "wisdom kings" in Japanese mythology. He is the patron of the Samurai, and he is always portrayed as a Black man with nappy hair!

The best two images of Fudo Myoo that I have seen are in New York. The University of Pennsylvania Archaeology Museum in Philadelphia also has a good one. The one at the Rietberg, however, was also excellent. I took a bunch of photos of it. I also got a wonderful photo of a Buddha from Japan that was on display there. The African features on that statue seemed to jump right out at me!

Still, I saw no signs of Cham sculpture. There were plenty of Japanese pieces and some nice pieces from China, some ancient art from India, and a few good pieces from Indonesia. I started to get a little nervous and apprehensive. (And, I have been told, I am not good to be around when I get like that!)

Where was the Cham art? I walked round and round the museum but could not find it. I began to fear the worst. I went into the other building, but found nothing there either. I looked and looked. Then, there it was! In one room, upstairs and across from the new annex, I found what I was looking for: two magnificent statues made of sandstone and dating from the ninth century and an excellent bust—both of Cham origin!

I don't know if I would have been any happier if I had won the national lottery! And, my goodness, did I take a lot of photos! Mission accomplished! Very little mattered after that. Just to make sure that I had covered all of my bases, I bought an expensive book from the museum gift shop detailing the background information on the sculptures, complete with photos.

I left the museum happy, walked down the hill, then strolled a few blocks more before boarding a tram. I rode the tram until I found a taxi stand and from there I caught a cab to the archaeology museum, my second planned stop. Finding no real treasures there, I headed to the Swiss National Museum. It wasn't very fulfilling, either. But the visit to the Rietberg made my day a good one.

So I am ready to get out of Zurich and Switzerland now. If I could fly out today, I would be content. I don't really much like Zurich. It is super expensive, and I don't find the people here very friendly. I just didn't seem to fit in here either, so I probably will not be coming back. Still, it was a good trip, and I am glad that I came. Next stop: Paris, by way of Amsterdam and Prague!

THE AFRICAN PRESENCE IN FRANCE

March 26, 2009

Last night I gave a lecture (the local people called it a "conference") in a northern suburb of Paris called Bondy. Bondy is a heavily African and Arab community. The program was sponsored by a French Congolese organization. I liked the members of the group, they seemed to like me, and we both indicated every intention of continuing the relationship. The association will serve me well as, through them, I should gain additional opportunities to have good interactions with the sisters and brothers in France.

Last night's presentation was on the African presence in early America. In all my years of coming to France, this is only the second time that I have spoken on that subject. It is not well known here. I believe that the great Ivan Van Sertima's classic work, They Came Before Columbus: The African Presence in Ancient America, was published briefly in French but, to my knowledge, that is about it. Besides, my views on the African presence in early America are not nearly the same as Ivan's.

In my presentations on the topic, I show a lot of photos and describe Black folks as the first people to populate the Americas. Then I look at the African presence in classical American civilizations, especially that of the Olmec, and then the Maya and increasingly the Moche of ancient Peru. Then I look at the Africans who were brought to the Americas against their will as a result of enslavement. At that point, I focus on the resistance to enslavement mounted by the Africans in the Americas. And then I look at African populations in the Americas today and especially those in places where we typically don't think African people live. I show some of the excellent photos I have taken during my visits to Honduras, Ecuador, Peru, Bolivia, and Brazil, and they usually have quite an impact on my audiences. (It's a pity that I don't have many good photos from my travels to Guyana, Venezuela, Costa Rica, and Panama!)

Last night, I even talked about great Black leaders of the Americas such as Marcus Garvey, Malcolm X, Martin Luther King, Jr., and Kwame Ture. It was a good presentation. The program had pretty good attendance too. It was put together on short notice and took place during the middle of the work week here. Nevertheless, close to thirty people crowded together in a fairly small room in a local community center. My presentation was in the African French community and for the African French community—something that I rather liked.

Interestingly, there were only two women in attendance, and they may have been the most enthusiastic two people in the room. Both of them, a sister from Haiti and a sister from Tunisia, acted as my translators.

I have learned through experience the importance of discussion periods at the conclusion of my lectures. It can really add a great deal to a gathering. For example, during last night's discussion, the focus of the audience discussion was on African identity. I'm not quite sure just how that topic came up, but I think it was me who raised the issue to the audience. The responses, however, were fascinating!

I have learned through experience that it perhaps is not best to try and force one's views on other people. So I generally try to initiate and stimulate the discussion in a certain direction, and then guide it along without appearing to dominate it. Last night, I began by asking the members of my audience

Runoko Rashidi

if they saw themselves as French or African. I asked that all respondents first give their names and their countries of origin before speaking. That way, I learned that several people from Congo and several others from Martinique and Guadeloupe (overseas French territories in the Caribbean) were in attendance. At least two people were from Haiti. Tunisia, Comoros, and Senegal were all represented as well. Representatives from other countries were also in the house, but not everybody, I am sad to say, got the chance to speak. We simply ran out of time.

I started off by asking the attendees to be perfectly honest. Then I asked them to raise their hands if they were Africans first. I followed by asking them to raise their hands if they saw themselves as French first. Quite a number of people participated, and the vast majority raised their hands and said that they were Africans first. One sister said that she was phenotypically African but culturally French! Some of the Congolese explained that even today in the Congo—a country in the heart of Africa—many people, as Black as they can be, see themselves as French or Belgian and not African! I must confess that this response came as a real shock to me.

The emphasis in the discussion then began to shift, and more and more people began to say that they were both African and French. Then one brother, who had not said a word up to that point, claimed that he was neither African or French and that his only identity was as a man from Guadeloupe! Another brother, from Comoros (an island off the east coast of Africa in the Indian Ocean) told me in private conversation that, even though he was a Black man, he saw himself as French because Africans inhabited France long ago. The Tunisian sister told me that saw herself as African, pure and simple. And, of course, I added my own little insight from some of the experiences I have had with Black folks around the world. For instance, I shared what I thought was the Aboriginal Australian point of view and a little of the South Pacific Islander point of view, and also what I have gathered from Black Berbers and African people in the Arab world.

For the most part, the members of my audience last night were cordial, polite, patient, and articulate. They seemed to be sincerely interested in sharing and learning and weren't concerned with trying to win an argument or debate. I felt as if we actually listened to each other! Some of our discussions were even funny. I only wish now that I had had the time to have a similarly pronounced discussion with the sisters and brothers I met during my recent stay in the Netherlands. I had bits and pieces of the identity discussion with Africans in Amsterdam, but I would have liked to have taken it much higher. That is not a criticism of the sisters and brothers in the Netherlands, of course. It is simply an observation in hindsight. I will have to do better when I return.

Sisters and brothers, I have found that the question of identity—that is, who we are and why—is of great importance to African people, wherever we are, and I am sure that the ideas of such thinkers as Kwame Ture, John Henrik Clarke, and Asa Hilliard have had a big influence on me. What about you? How important do you see the question of national and cultural identity? For me, it is a discussion that I hope to engage in more and more and more because I realize, for myself at least, that in my lectures and discussions, it is not enough to teach. One must also learn!

A BRIEF NOTE FROM POLAND

May 1, 2010

I am writing to you today from Krakow, Poland. It has been a couple of weeks since I traveled to Mexico to be among the sisters and brothers in the Mexican province of Costa Chica. Our people there suffer from very low self-esteem, so I gave them a great presentation on the Global African Presence. From there, I returned to the US for a pleasant week "back in the States" before traveling on to Germany and now Poland. In a few days, I travel back to Paris to be with my beautiful, darling daughter. I have not seen her in months, and I can hardly wait for her to jump into her Daddy's arms!

I tell you, it is lonely over here in Poland! I have seen only three Black people in three days! But I have also found and photographed the Black Madonna of Poland—the highlight of my visit. The Black Madonna of Poland, found at the Jasna Gora Monastery in Czestochowa, is regarded as the "Queen of Poland" and is one of the most important icons of the Catholic faith. It is also one of the leading "superstars" in the cult of Mary worshippers. And tomorrow, I journey by train to Warsaw, the capital of Poland, to visit the National Museum there.

If I find anything good, you will be among the first to know! Thanks so much for "being there" for me, wherever I have gone. May you be blessed without limit and fly gracefully on the wings of Maat![8]

AN INTERVIEW IN CRETEIL

May 12, 2010

It is a fairly quiet evening here in Creiteil, a southeastern suburb of Paris, and I am listening to the new CD by Salif Keita, the national singer of Mali.

Today, I had an interview with three young men representing a newly developed African youth organization. Their ages were seventeen, nineteen, and twenty. They were from Haiti, Congo Kinshasa, and Senegal, respectively. One of the great things about life here is that there is such a rich array of the African heritage. Black people from all of the former French colonies are all concentrated in and around Paris.

The young men had heard that I was coming to France and had pestered me for days about an interview. Finally, I relented. At first, when we sat down for the interview I could not help but chuckle. They looked like babies—teenagers, anyway. They could have been my children! But their intentions were solid, and their attitudes very serious. I told them that I admired them, but kept smiling all the while.

---

[8] Maat represents the ancient Egyptian concept of truth, balance, order, law, morality, and justice. The Egyptians personified Maat as the goddess who regulated the stars, seasons, and actions of both mortals and deities. They also believed that Maat set the order of the universe at the moment of creation.

They asked me all about myself, who I was, and what my mission was in France. They asked me how I got started as an African historian and what I hoped to accomplish. They asked me about my vision for Africa and the role of Africans in the Diaspora. They wanted to know who the big influences in my life were and what I thought about research on Kmt (Ancient Egypt). I answered all their questions as best I could, but because of my limited French, I spoke slowly and deliberately in English.

It was clear that the young men had done their homework, so I began to take them a little more seriously. They asked me about the Dalits of India and my work on the African presence in Asia. They asked me about my views on religion and spirituality. They wanted to know what I thought about the current generation of African youth. And the whole time we were talking, they were taking notes and videotaping. I treated them to coffee and orange juice and they seemed to be having a wonderful time. And so it went.

My conversation with the three young men reminded me of myself in my early days, when I would pester John Henrik Clarke and Dr. Ben and Jan Carew and Ivan Van Sertima and John G. Jackson—asking question after question. I recalled how gracious and encouraging those extraordinary scholars had been with me, and I realized yet again that youth must be served. It gave me great satisfaction to know, upon seeing their bright faces and listening to their questions, that we Africans have a sunny future after all. I felt confident that yet another generation was gearing up for the ongoing quest for African liberation.

As I write this, I am still smiling, sisters and brothers—not with derision, but with the inner joy that comes when one is secure about the passing of the torch.

A MEETING WITH A SAINT: REFLECTIONS ON A BRIEF VISIT TO GERMANY

March 31, 2011

I am in Berlin, the capital of Germany. I arrived last night on the first leg of a three-country trip through Western Europe. Today, I accomplished something that I did not believe I would ever do: I went into the heart of East Germany, right into the thick of neo-Nazi and skinhead land. I went to Magdeburg, Germany, to find and photograph the long-ago patron saint of the Holy Roman Germanic Empire–Saint Maurice, or, as the Germans know him, Saint Mauritius.

I have studied this man for the better part of thirty years and never seen an actual image of him. Everything previously had just been in books. But I had also been warned, by both White people and Black people, to avoid the Magdeburg area. Black men, they told me, have been beaten to death and chased through the streets of that city for no reason other than their ethnicity. Yet, something about going there, however, just nagged at me, again and again. Imagine having something that you have wanted to see and experience for decades being denied to you because it is located in a "no-go" zone for people of color!

Well, today, everything clicked for me. I had pretty much given up on Magdeburg, at least on this visit to Germany (my fifth), but on my way to the Egyptian Museum in Berlin this morning, I struck up a casual conversation with my Turkish taxi driver. He assured me that it was indeed dangerous for Africans and Asians to go to East Germany, and he seemed terribly frightened about the prospect himself, so I took his warning to heart. Still, we worked out a price (yes, it was expensive!) and we hit the road for Magdeburg immediately. Within two hours, we were there.

Well, we found the church, I took my photos, we got back on the road, and I am now back in Berlin to tell the story! But from Berlin to Magdeburg and back, I did not see not one single Black person! Not one! I wonder why? But we made it, and I am feeling a great sense of accomplishment. So that is my story for today, sisters and brothers.

I also had a wonderful time in the museums of Berlin, but that is another story for another time. Now it's on to Italy!

April 1, 2011

Right now, I am halfway to my next European destination: Florence, Italy. I left Berlin early this morning and am sitting in a Paris airport waiting for my flight. I tried to get an earlier flight, but the change would have cost me a small fortune. So here I wait.

I am going to Florence for the first time to see, as they say, "what I can see." Specifically, I'm looking for the paintings of Alessandro De'Medici, the reigning Duke of Florence in the sixteenth century—and a Black man. I also hope to find paintings of the Black magus (the singular form of magi) who came to pay homage to the Christ child in the manger in Bethlehem. It was common during the European Renaissance to portray Balthazar—the youngest of the three kings—as an African, specifically, as an Ethiopian. So keep your fingers crossed for me!

Since I have some time on my hands, I thought that I would share a few more details about the statue of Saint Maurice that I saw in the notorious Magdeburg area. One of the most significant things about this statue is that, unlike the numerous Black Madonna statues scattered around Europe, the facial features are purely Black African. I mean, we are talking about a real brother here! The statue is three to four feet high and stands near of the back of the Magdeburger Dom, which is German for the Cathedral of Magdeburg. The statue was erected around 1250 C.E. by the German king Otto I, and the church is at least that old.

Sadly, I was so nervous about being there—in Magdeburg, that is—that I did not take the best photos of either the statue or the cathedral. In hindsight, I should have spent more time exploring the church, but I was really anxious to get out of there and back to Berlin! I think you understand!

Upon returning to Berlin, I paid a visit to the Altes Museum. There, I found another real treasure: a tondo painting, on wood, of the Black Roman emperor Septimius Severus. Now I have seen numerous busts and statues of Septimius before, but this was the first image I had seen of him painted in brown flesh tones. I got some great photos of it. I also photographed two or three small images of Blacks from ancient Greece that were in the museum.

Runoko Rashidi

To cap off my last day in Berlin, I went to the newly renovated and relocated Egyptian Museum there. I would put this collection just behind that of the Louvre in Paris and maybe ahead of the British Museum's. Of course, the collections in Egypt itself are beyond compare, but the Berlin Egyptian collection is magnificent. I saw many pieces that I had only seen previously in books, such as the small wooden head of Queen Tiye and the famous bust reputed to be Nefertiti.

Altogether I took about two hundred really good photographs. I stayed at the museum until just before it closed and just before my camera battery went dead—and also just before my feet seemed about ready to fall off from all that walking! I didn't have enough time or energy left to visit the Pergamon Museum, Berlin's other big museum attraction. But I have been to the Pergamon twice before, so not stopping there a third time was not such a terrible loss.

If I have the same kind of success in Italy as I had in Germany, I will be a happy man, indeed. By the way, today (April 1) is the birthday of the great African historian John G. Jackson. He was born in 1907.

FLORENCE, ITALY

April 3, 2011

I have been in Florence, Italy, for two days now. I arrived late Friday afternoon from Berlin via Paris. Florence is a congested city of about 500,000 people. Unlike Berlin, it is very common to see Black people on the streets of the city center in Florence. Funny thing is, I see them—I think most of the Africans here are from Senegal—and I know a number of them see me. But none of them seems the least bit interested in making a bond with a brother! I actually introduced myself to African man I saw on the streets, and he told me that he was in fact from Senegal, but that was about all.

As for Florence, it just does not seem to be my kind of city. First, I haven't liked either of the hotels I have stayed in. They claim to be four-star hotels, and believe me, they are expensive—yet the first one, near the airport, did not even have a restaurant, its elevator only worked on certain floors, the telephone service in my room did not work well, and the air conditioner did not work at all. On top of that, my electrical adapters did not fit any of the hotel's outlets and the Internet stopped working after a couple of hours. It never did work in my room. And the second hotel I stayed in, the one in the city center, did not having working Internet either! So, as you can imagine, I have been very frustrated in Florence. I absolutely hate to feel so isolated!

I came to Florence, naturally, in search of the African presence. Principally, I wanted to the visit the Uffizi Gallery here. That was my first stop yesterday morning. When I got there, there was a large crowd waiting already and anxious to get in. Rather than wait in a long line, I bought a reserved ticket, and then I went away for an hour or so before I was allowed entry.

I was largely interested in seeing two things at the Uffizi. First, I wanted to find some images of Alessandro De Medici—the Black Duke of Florence, whom I have mentioned earlier (see "A Meeting

With a Saint: Reflections on a Brief Visit to Germany."). Second, I wanted to find images of the Black magus. I figured anything beyond that would be a bonus.

Well, I did indeed find a painting of Duke Alessandro, one done about 1600. I also found two or three paintings of the Black magus—the most notable of which was done by the German artist Albrecht Durer—and a couple of paintings depicting Blacks as servants. So the Uffizi was okay, but less that I had hoped.

I must confess that although I don't much care for Florence and didn't have the most exciting or rewarding time at the Uffizi, I was upset before I got here. For several days before my trip, I had been waging near-mortal combat with some of the Black Barack Obama haters that seem to be proliferating on the Internet. I myself am a huge Barack Obama fan, and I tend to have little regard for Black folks who seem so determined to attack him.

But that's another story for another day—or perhaps another book(!) Right now, I am looking forward to departing Florence. It may be the cradle city of the Italian Renaissance, but it is not the city for me!

TRAVELS IN THE LOW COUNTRIES OF EUROPE: THE NETHERLANDS, BELGIUM, AND LUXEMBOURG[9]

The Netherlands: A Missed Flight and Marshe Breda (April 13, 2011)

I have visited the Low Countries of Europe on multiple occasions, including several visits to the Netherlands (perhaps my most enjoyable country in Europe), three times to Belgium (mostly Brussels), and once to Luxembourg City. I like a lot of things about the Netherlands (or should I say "Holland"?), probably because all of my journeys there have been confined to the southern part of the country, the part that most people think of as Holland. I like the cool, damp weather there, and I have a fondness for the area's architecture. The cuisine is nice and varied too, and the country has a couple of good museums. There is also a fairly sizable African population in the larger cities of the Netherlands, like Amsterdam, Rotterdam, Leiden, and The Hague. Most of the Africans there come from places like Surinam and Curacao. English is also widely spoken and understood, and the public transportation is excellent. Amsterdam itself is a major transportation hub for Europe and the world.

The people in the Netherlands seem generally nice and friendly. And unless you knew better, you would never think that the ancestors of the nice White folks in Holland were the same ones who introduced apartheid to South Africa and who, for centuries, played such a cruel and pivotal role in the Trans-Atlantic Slave Trade.

Anyway, I like the Netherlands. I've lectured there on at least half a dozen occasions, done several radio interviews, and I think a couple of TV shows. I also like the liberal atmosphere—and the beer!

---

9   Dedicated to the queens of Marshe Breda: Sister Danitzah and Sister Sirelda.

Plus, the Netherlands is not a bad place to get stuck in, which has happened to me on a couple of occasions.

My most momentous layover in the Netherlands occurred in June 2010 when, much to my satisfaction, I was invited to speak at an education conference in Tripoli, Libya. I had been wanting to visit Libya for a long time and had been blessed with an all-expenses-paid trip to attend a conference. However, since Libya has long had such poor relations with the United States (the country of my birth), getting a visa proved tricky. At first, I tried to get a visa from Canada, but that didn't work. Finally, the conference organizers, seeing my plight, made arrangements for me to pick up my visa upon arrival in Tripoli. I confess that I was a bit skeptical, but the conference organizers told me that everything would be fine and sent me a bunch of travel documents in Arabic.

Well, what did I have to lose? So I flew from Detroit to Boston. When I presented my travel documents at the check-in counter in Detroit, there didn't seem to be any problem. As I boarded the flight from Boston to Amsterdam, everything seemed to be alright too. I even enjoyed my layover in Amsterdam. But when I attempted to board my flight from Amsterdam to Tripoli, that's when the trouble began.

I was told that I needed a visa affixed to my passport. I showed all of the travel documents the conference organizers had sent me to the airport personnel. They seemed unimpressed. Long story short, they would not let me board my flight to Tripoli.

I was so upset! I talked to one airport official after another. I called Libya. I had them call Libya. I emailed the conference organizers. Finally, I realized that there was nothing more that I could do, at least not that day. But I am not quick to give up. For comfort's sake, I checked into an expensive hotel for the night until I could figure out what to do. Someone at the airport had suggested that I contact the Libyan Embassy in The Hague. Surely, I was told, they could issue me a visa in short order. I figured that it was worth a try, but that try would have to wait until the next day.

The next day I went to the Libyan Embassy, as instructed. The personnel there were very friendly, but not very helpful. They told me that they would be happy to issue me a visa, but that it would be waiting for me in Tripoli. When I told them that I could not get to Tripoli without a visa from The Hague, their only response was a polite, understated, and subdued, "Well, that could be a problem."

Long story short, my prospects for getting to Libya did not look good. I was becoming distraught, so what did I do? I sent out a Facebook message! I fashion myself to be the "Pharaoh of Facebook." Lots of times I use it simply to vent, but I also use it to keep people informed about what is happening with me and where I am—and it helps a lot. It also helps me immeasurably to know that I can connect with others that way and to think that somebody cares whether or not I am safe and sound or if I have disappeared into the bowels of the earth somewhere.

Well, the gods must have heard my pleas because two angels responded via Facebook. Their names were Danitzah Jacobs and Sirelda Jackson, and they are the founders of an African woman's business organization in southern Holland called Marshe Breda.

Marshe, in Dutch, means market or marketplace. Breda is the city where the two women live. Mind you, these are two Black women, very Afrocentric in their worldview, who refuse to be victims. They have started a series of businesses designed to empower people like themselves. First, they started with a restaurant, then a catering service, but when they learned that I was stuck in the Netherlands, they decided to be my guardian angels!

They emailed me and told me that they would be driving to Amsterdam (just two hours away) immediately to pick me up. They also told me not to move and not to worry--they were going to take care of me! When I asked them what all this caring was going to cost me, they said, "It is going to cost you nothing. We only want to pick your brain. We will feed you, drive you around, and give you a place to stay with a nice TV and a good Internet connection." And that was that. They would accept no argument. I have rarely met people so sincere, so genuine, so selfless. Those two sisters won my heart, and they were there when I really needed them to be. They even arranged, on very short notice, for me to give a presentation in Breda.

So, as it turned out, I really enjoyed my first stay in the Netherlands. Of course, I really missed not being able to go to Libya, but under the circumstances, it was definitely a case of lemons turning into lemonade. God bless Marshe Breda!

Belgium

Most of my travels in Belgium have been confined to the capital city of Brussels. I have been there on four occasions, usually, but not always, in transit from one place to another. In July 2010, on my second trip to Brussels, however, I had a chance to get around some and visited the Church of Saint Catherine, where I saw another statue of a Black Madonna and Child on display, and, of course, to visit the museums.

Brussels was one of the major colonial capitals. Indeed, at one time, many decades ago, the center of Africa—now the Democratic Republic of the Congo—was the private property of the Belgian king, King Leopold II. The atrocities committed by the Belgians in the Congo were monstrous. Even the famous American author Mark Twain wrote about it. The Brussels of today is the capital of the European Union, and it has a pretty significant African population, mostly Blacks from Central Africa, along with several world-class museums. These two aspects—Africans and museums—should make it obvious to you what an irresistible lure Brussels has for me.

The greatest of Brussels' museums, for me, is the Royal Museum of History and Art. It has a very good Ancient Egyptian collection and also a very good collection of Classical American and Greek and Roman antiquities. Over time, the museum's camera policies have softened such that photography (without flash) is now permitted. As a result, you can bet that I have a number of excellent photos from this museum.

Three other museums in Brussels also stand out. The first is the National History Museum. It houses the Ishango Bone from Central Africa—one of the world's first known counting instruments. The Ishango Bone alone makes a visit to that museum very satisfying. Then, there is the Fine Arts Museum, which holds, to me, a single great piece: the wonderful painting by the Flemish (Dutch) artist Peter Paul Rubens, entitled "Studies of the Head of a Black Man." Third, and this may surprise you, I found the Royal Military Museum in Brussels to be of interest. During one of my visits there, it was hosting an exhibit on the Africans who had served in the Belgian army. This was a real revelation for me as I had never heard of such a thing.

Luxembourg

I visited Luxembourg for the first and only time in August 2010. I was based in Brussels at the time (my third trip there), and I had just finished leading a tour group to Egypt. Besides wanting to visit unchartered territory, I had one very compelling reason for visiting Luxembourg: I wanted to see the Black Madonna and Child statue in the Church of Saint John in Luxembourg City. It is reputed to be one of the most beautiful such statues in the world, but I almost missed my opportunity to see it.

This is what happened. One day, I had some free time on my hands, so I decided to go see the Luxembourg Black Madonna. But the Kenyan brother who was supposed to drive me from Brussels to Luxembourg City that day decided at the last minute that he had more important things to do. Not to be deterred, I decided to take the train. Now the trip from Brussels to Luxembourg City was a direct one, and Luxembourg City was the last stop, so it was virtually impossible to get lost or turned around. So away I went.

Getting to Luxembourg City was not a problem. Getting into the church to see the statue was. When I got there, the church was closed, and even though it and the statue are touted as major tourist attractions, nobody in the neighborhood surrounding the church knew anything about its hours. Most suggested (rather nonchalantly, I might add) that I simply come back another time, possibly another day—as if I had all the time in the world. I was terribly frustrated and disappointed, but I was not about to let the opportunity to see this beautiful statue pass me without a fight.

I know you must be asking, why these Black Madonna statues are so important to me? The reason is simple: these statues are the "superstars" of the cult of Mary. They are legendary. And unlike most other things Black in the European mind, their Blackness is seen as a virtue, not a curse. It makes them even more valuable and revered. And because they are Black, they are believed to be able to perform all kinds of miracles. About five hundred Black Madonna statues are scattered all across Europe, and I have seen about eight of them, including several of the most important. I love them.

So I instructed my taxi driver, whom I had asked to wait for me while I visited the church, to take me on a little tour of the area, drop me off at the local museum, and then bring me back to the church. That took about an hour. When we returned, however, the church was still closed. Man, was I disappointed! But I decided to wait a little while longer and told the taxi driver to hold on. Finally, I found a sympathetic soul in a nearby building and asked her to call the caretaker of the church to find out what was going on. She did, and a woman answered the phone. The woman spoke English and informed me that the caretaker was on holiday. She seemed very irritated by the call, however, and told me that she could open the doors of the church herself but that she was in the process of running some errands. Helping me out just did not seem to be a priority for her. I told her that I was an historian who had come all the way from America just to see the statue. She seemed unimpressed and told me to come back another time. . When I pressed her for a specify time to return, she hung up on me.

I was crushed. It seemed like a golden opportunity to see yet another Black Madonna was passing me by. I thanked the lady who intervened on my behalf and made my way back to the taxi and from there to the train station.

When I got to the station, I found out that my train would not be leaving for another hour, so I went to a nearby café for lunch and a beer. While reflecting on my situation, I plucked up my courage and decided that I did not come all that way for nothing. Brother Runoko is nothing if not a warrior, right? I decided to give it one last try. So I hailed another taxi and went right back to the church.

And guess what? It was open! I rushed inside, and there, in all its glory, was the Black Madonna of Luxembourg!

I took plenty of pictures, said a silent prayer, and thanked the Ancestors. Then I got back into my waiting taxi, rode back to the train station, and returned to Belgium both relieved and satisfied. And that was my first and only visit to the tiny country of Luxembourg in western Europe.

Runoko Rashidi

PART IV

IN SEARCH OF THE AFRICAN PRESENCE IN AUSTRALIA AND THE PACIFIC ISLANDS

A detail of a statue of Kamehemeh the Great in Hilo, Hawaii

There are few places in the world that I don't want to visit, particularly since I see myself, in the mold of the great Joel Augustus Rogers and John Henrik Clarke, as something of a "global detective" in search of African people everywhere. Those of us who consider ourselves Pan-Africanists talk quite a lot about uniting the African family of humankind. Traditionally, however, this dream has revolved only around the Africans in Africa itself, together with the Africans in the Western Hemisphere and Europe. I would like to think that a large part of my unique contribution to the vision of Pan-Africanism has been to help expand that vision to include the Black people of Australia and the Pacific Islands, and indeed, everywhere else in the world.

It should be clear to all of us by now that in order to truly unite the African family, we must first know exactly where that family is and then aggressively seek it out and reconnect with it. We absolutely must trace the routes of those Africans who long ago left home, find out precisely where they went, what they have done, and what they are doing now to clearly ascertain what their consciousness of Africa is or has been. This is a part of our sacred mission: to make African people whole again.

My interest in the Black people of Aboriginal Australia began when I was a young college student in the early 1970s. I always say "Aboriginal Australia," not just "Australia," because the Blackfellas, as the Aboriginal people of Australia tend to call themselves, are always the primary motivation for my travels there, and they are the original owners of the "land down under."

I have since visited that continent on six occasions from November 1998 to October 2008, but while I was in college, I chanced to read an article in the Los Angeles Times about the brutal treatment meted out to Australia's aboriginal people by the English convicts, administrators, soldiers, and missionaries who landed in Sydney's Botany Bay beginning in 1788. The article told of scores of Aboriginal people being tossed to their deaths from high cliffs and of rewards being offered for the scalps of Black men, women, and children. All this and more I was later to confirm for myself, but I learned then that during the nineteenth century it was not uncommon for Whites to shoot Aboriginal people for use as dog food. Indeed, during certain periods of martial law in Australia, it was not a crime to murder a Black man.

Other horrendous reports I read then told of entire families of Black people being rounded up by Whites and of the men of those families being handcuffed and then castrated, right in front of their screaming family members. The men's heads were then cut off and strung around the necks of their widows, who were then brutally gang-raped, right before their children's eyes. Following those bestial acts of brutality, the children were buried in the earth up to their heads, at which point White men kicked and clubbed the children's heads off while forcing the mothers to watch.

Still other accounts told of Aboriginal people being given blankets infected with the smallpox virus and of Aboriginal women and children being infected with venereal diseases through sexual contact with White men. The Aboriginals' waterholes were poisoned. It was only in 1967 that Aboriginal people in Australia were even considered human!

Today, the Aboriginals constitute 1.6 percent of the total population of Australia. Not surprisingly, however, Black men make up seventy percent of the prison population, while Black women make up fifty percent. The life expectancy for an Aboriginal man is forty-five years, and the infant mortality rate for Aboriginal children is among the highest in the world.

Despite these dismal statistics and grim history, of all the international trips that I have ever taken, my first visit to Aboriginal Australia is one of the hardest to top. It was truly a unique experience. Indeed, there were times on that trip that I momentarily thought I was in another world. I felt continually as if the Ancestors were with me, guiding and protecting me, keeping me safe and strong while I was there. I prayed regularly and passionately and had few worries along the way.

If I had to characterize the Aboriginal Australians in one sentence, I would simply say that they are "different." The Blackfellas I met, rather than being the primitive people they often are portrayed to be, turned out to be, to me, the most complex and spiritually profound brothers and sisters I have ever encountered or read about. During my first trip down under, for example, I learned how closely connected the Aboriginal Australians are to the land.

The indigenous Australians consistently refer to the earth as "Mother" and regard her as sacred. They have a harmonious relationship with Nature and take from it only what they need to survive. They see themselves as custodians of the land rather than as users or consumers of it. Speakers at all the public meetings I attended always began their comments with the words, "I want to thank the traditional owners of the land for allowing me to be here." Once, on my second trip to Aboriginal Australia, a colleague and travel companion asked why, if the Aboriginal people have been in Australia as long as the tens of thousands of years that they claim they have, no evidence of ancient buildings or cities has as yet been uncovered there. With unswerving confidence and consistency, the Aboriginals responded: "The earth is our mother. Why would we build a city on top of our mother?"

The Aboriginal Australians are the most spiritual people I have ever met, but they are also the most inclined to dismiss their African roots. With few exceptions, Aboriginal Australians see themselves as having sprung indigenously from the soil of Australia, not as having migrated there from anywhere else. Paleontological, archaeological, and DNA studies confirming that humanity began in Africa do not seem to impress them. Those studies even seem to upset some Aboriginal Australians, including the Aboriginal mayor of Palm Island, in the Australian province of Queensland, whom I met on my second trip. When I asked him how he would feel if I suggested that his ancestors came from Africa, he replied: "I would be offended by such a suggestion. We are taught, each generation, that we have always been here, that we have always been in Australia."

Despite such conflicting stances, there is no doubt in my mind that Aboriginal Australians are my people—my "peeps," as the young people say—but I don't argue with them. They are fascinating people, and I love them without reservation.

On my early trips to Aboriginal Australia, out of the love and respect I have for the Blackfellas, and having gotten some idea of how important the land is to them, I would always seek out a place to visit that was special to them and then respectfully ask for permission to go there. It seemed important for me to honor them in this way, especially given that they have been so beaten down and disrespected by the Whites who currently occupy and control most of the continent.

I was surprised once when I received a response to one such request from Tranby Aboriginal College in Sydney (one of only two Aboriginal colleges in Australia). The letter read: "Yes, you can visit our country. We all come from the same mother. We all come from Africa." This acceptance of African roots was the exception, not the rule. The African/Aboriginal Australian connection should be deeply explored. That investigation might start with a tragedy, however, beginning with the murder of one of greatest eighteenth-century Aboriginal Australian resistance leaders—Pemulwy—by an African. It would also include historian Tony Martin's assertion that Marcus Garvey established a branch of the United Negro Improvement Association and African Communities League (UNIA-ACL) in Sydney, Australia during the 1920s. More recently, in 1975, a branch of the Aboriginal Australian Black Panther Party was established in Brisbane, and an Aboriginal Australian delegation attended FESTAC (the Festival of African Arts and Culture) in West Africa in 1977. Aboriginal Australians were also present at the Durban Conference on Racism in South Africa in 2001, and an Aboriginal Australian woman was invited to participate in a forum on the ancient African Diaspora at the third World Conference of Black Arts and Culture Conference (FESMAN), which I also attended, in Dakar, Senegal, in 2010.

One of my favorite John Henrik Clarke stories puts the need for the African/Aboriginal Australian connection in clear perspective. In 1996, I was invited to Aboriginal Australia to be a keynote speaker at the first World's Indigenous People's Conference, which was being held there. It was my first invitation to that part of the world. I was honored and excited. I had always wanted to interact with Aboriginal Australian sisters and brothers, and had never visited that continent. Plus, I had been invited by Gracelyn Smallwood, one of my all-time favorite people and a woman I have long regarded as the "Queen of Aboriginal Australia." To my dismay, I had signed a contract to go to Egypt at the same time as the Australian conference to lecture to an African American tour group there. The Egyptian group sponsoring my visit would not let me out of the contract. I was so distraught.

When Gracelyn found that I could not come to Australia, she asked me to pick someone to go in my place. After much deliberation, I selected my best friend and research associate, Dr. James E. Brunson III, to attend in my stead. When we both had returned to the United States, I called James and asked him how his Australian experience had gone. He told me that the conference was okay but that his presentation had not been terribly well received. When I asked him why, he said that the Aboriginal people at the conference seemed to have no appreciation for the idea of their ancestors having come from Africa.

I was, of course, crushed. I want all Black people—no matter where they are, no matter how long they have been away from Mother Africa—to embrace their African roots enthusiastically. That is what I live for. Brother James's report was a definite setback.

So I called my guru. I called John Henrik Clarke.

When Dr. Clarke answered the phone, he could tell that I was upset. He asked, "What's wrong, man?" I told him, "Dr. Clarke, a friend of mine went to Australia and met with Aboriginal Australians and they said that they weren't from Africa. What do you think?"

Dr. Clarke was surprisingly calm in his response. "Runoko," he said, "don't worry about it! I can take you down to 125th Street in Harlem and show you the blackest person in New York City, who will also tell you that he is not African."

My Global Journeys in Search of the African Presence

"Wait until Africa is strong again," he said reassuringly, "Then, even you will be surprised at who says they are African!"

That story, one of many involving Dr. Clarke, has served me quite well over the years.

Years ago, after returning to the States from one of my numerous lecture tours to Hawaii, I gave an early morning interview on Stevie Wonder's Los Angeles-based radio station KJLH. While discussing the Black presence in the Pacific with the show's host, a Native Hawaiian man called in to inform us that, when he was a little boy, his grandmother used to tell him about how when King Kamehameha the Great was attempting to unify the Hawaiian Islands in the early nineteenth century, he ran into trouble and had to "send back to Africa for reinforcements." The caller informed us that this was a well-known bit of Hawaiian folklore. I found his comment especially intriguing because I had long been searching for, and finding, historical verification of a real and abiding connection between the islands of the Pacific and Africa. Indeed, the Pacific islands are some of most fertile and relatively untapped areas of research regarding the African Diaspora and the Global African Presence.

Among the few works on this subject are Yosef ben-Jochannan's telling of his visit to Papua New Guinea, recorded in his long out-of-print work, They All Look Alike! All of them?: From Egypt to Papua New Guinea with ben-Jochannan. And then there are the article about the 1970s explorations to the South Pacific of the late Roosevelt Browne of Bermuda, documented in Black World magazine; the interview with the foreign minister of West Papua New Guinea, published in Black Books Bulletin in 1975; the travel writing and research on the South Pacific island of Vanuatu by Arthur Lewis, M.D.; and newspaper articles on the late Stan Simmons' guided tours to Papua New Guinea.

I am proud to add to this list of excellent resources my own recent research conducted during my travels to Hawaii, Fiji, Papua New Guinea, Micronesia, and New Zealand; and my writings about my interactions with Chief Benny Wenda of the majority Dani people of West Papua, New Guinea. This latter work came about as the result at Chief Wenda's acceptance of my invitation for him to participate in the third World Black Arts and Culture Festival in Dakar, Senegal, in December 2010.

These writings are all very exciting because they confirm that many Pacific Islanders happily, even arrogantly, embrace their African roots. (I have found this personally to be the case in Fiji, in the Buka and Bougainville Islands of the North Solomons, and in Papua New Guinea.) But there is much more work to be done—a tremendous void must be filled as we expand our vision of Pan-Africanism and the Global African Presence. That being said, my reflections on my travels in the Pacific Islands offer a small peek into the thrilling possibilities that await us in that area of the world.

Runoko Rashidi

With my bodyguard (top) and Humelo
and Samora Biko in Toowoomba, Australia

In front of Uluru in Central Australia

My Global Journeys in Search of the African Presence

An Aboriginal Australian woman on Palm Island

With Gracelyn Smallwood and the indigenous mayor of Yarrabah, Australia

Runoko Rashidi

With Indigenous elders in Townsville, Australia

The Indigenous mayor of Palm Island, Australia

My Global Journeys in Search of the African Presence

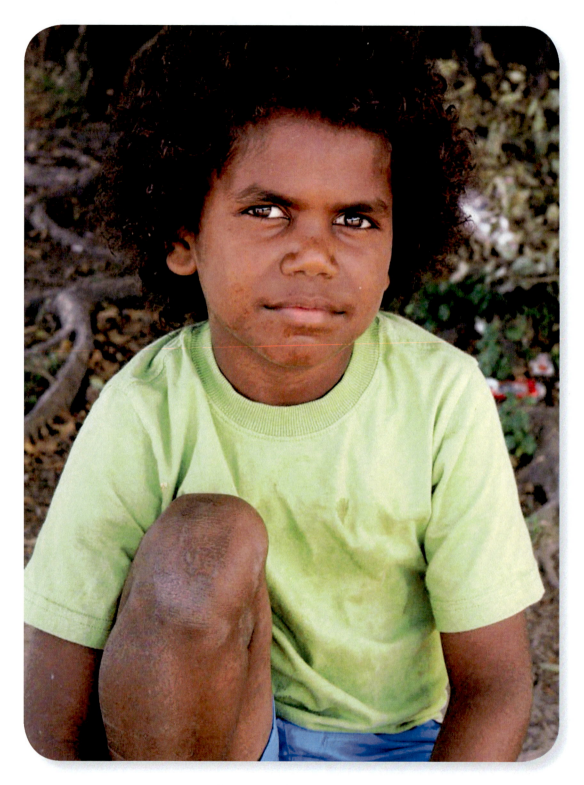

A young boy on Palm Island, Australia

Indigenous youth on Palm Island, Australia

My Global Journeys in Search of the African Presence

A young Indigenous woman
on Palm Island, Australia

A sign at Oyster Cove, Tasmania, Australia

Runoko Rashidi

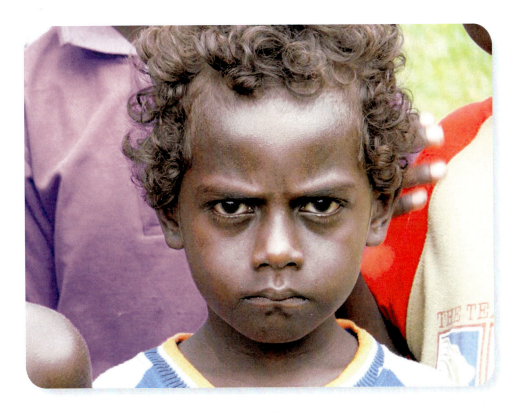

Children in Bougainville, Papua New Guinea

My Global Journeys in Search of the African Presence

A Black man on Buka Island, Papua New Guinea

Runoko Rashidi

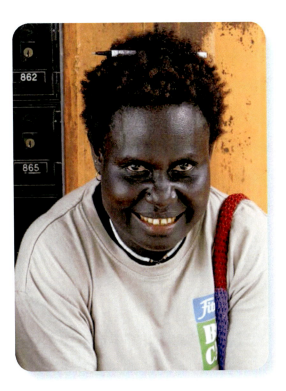

Black women on Buka Island, Papua New Guinea

My Global Journeys in Search of the African Presence

 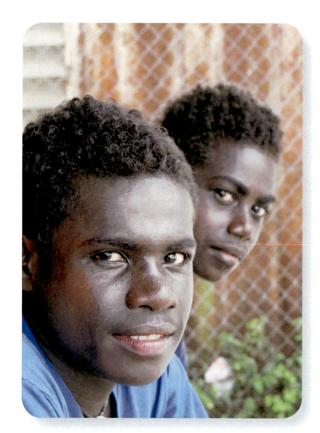

A young girl and two young boys on Buka Island, Papua New Guinea

Runoko Rashidi

A young man on Buka Island, Papua New Guinea

My Global Journeys in Search of the African Presence

With the airport staff on
Buka Island, Papua New Guinea

A young woman in East New
Britain, Papua New Guinea

A young boy in East New Britain, Papua New Guinea

Runoko Rashidi

An elder in East New Britain, Papua New Guinea

My Global Journeys in Search of the African Presence

A youth in East New Britain, Papua New Guinea

Young girls in East New Britain, Papua New Guinea

Runoko Rashidi

School teachers in East New Britain, Papua New Guinea

A Buka man and a Tolui woman in East New Britain, Papua New Guinea

My Global Journeys in Search of the African Presence

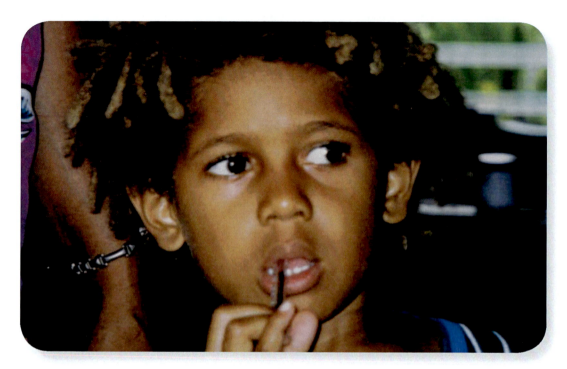

A young boy in Fiji

With an elder in Fiji

With an elder in Fiji

A young blond child in Fiji

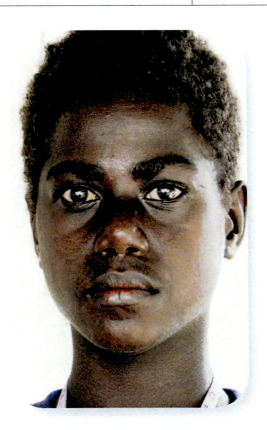

A young man on Buka Island, Papua New Guinea

My Global Journeys in Search of the African Presence

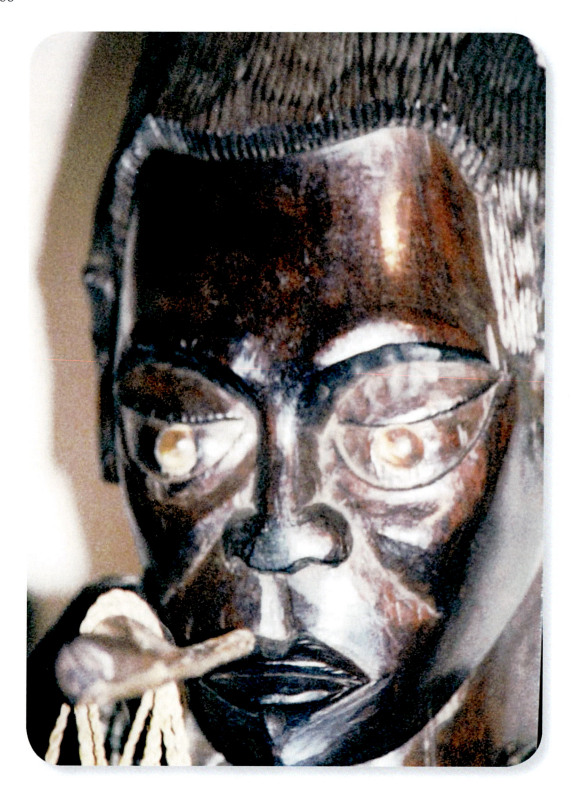

A wooden mask Palau, Micronesia

Runoko Rashidi

A statue of Kamehameha the Great in Honolulu, Hawaii

My Global Journeys in Search of the African Presence

HANGING WITH THE "BLACKFELLAS" DOWN UNDER[1]

On November 19, 1998, I boarded a Qantas Airlines plane for the fourteen-hour flight from Los Angeles to Sydney, Australia. It was my first trip to Australia. Thirty minutes after going through customs in Sydney, I boarded a connecting flight to the city of Darwin located at the so-called "top end" of Australia's Northern Territory. Darwin was the start of the initial leg of my Australian travel adventure. Named after Charles Darwin and with a tropical climate, it is a city of 70,000 people, about a fourth of whom are Black.

On Saturday afternoon, November 21, 1998, after a long series of flights, I landed in Darwin. It was there that I met Aboriginal people in Australia for the first time. Indeed, the first Black people I saw were sitting in several groups on the floor of the airport's lower level. They were very dark with straight to wavy black hair, and they paid me not the slightest bit of attention. I was told later not to take their seeming indifference personally, and that it was "a "cultural thing."

I was met at the airport by two Aboriginal women, Jacqui Katona and Christine Christophoson, whose job, they told me, was "to take care of all my needs" The two sisters were also hard-core activists who more or less introduced me to Black Australia. They checked me into a local hotel, got me something to eat, and later took me to their homes to meet their families.

The next morning, after a relatively uneventful night, Christine drove me to Jabiru in Kakadu National Park. Kakadu is located on Aboriginal land. It is magnificent country and quite rightly regarded by many Australians, Aboriginal and White, as a national treasure. It was there that I learned how much Aboriginal people regard themselves as the custodians of the land. It is also where I became acquainted, for the first time, with the legacy of the "Stolen Generations."

The term Stolen Generations refers to those Aboriginal people who, as children, were abducted from their families and raised largely as slaves in White foster homes, reformatories, and industrial schools. White Christian missionaries began the practice of abducting Aboriginal children, particularly the lighter-skinned children of mixed White-Aboriginal heritage (the so-called "half-castes"), in the mid-nineteenth century. By 1911, virtually all Australian states had enacted legislation that called for the removal of Aboriginal children from their families and the institutionalization of those youth. Tasmania was the exception, for it denied that it even had an indigenous population.

An estimated 40,000 Aboriginal children were removed from their families under such legislation. Government officials, acting under the authority of the Chief Protector of Aborigines or the relevant welfare board, had absolute power over the fate of Aboriginal children and could simply order the removal of any Aboriginal child from his or her family without recourse, on the basis of race alone.

Once removed, the children were forbidden any contact with their families or they were told that their families had died or abandoned them. They were not allowed to learn anything about their

---

1   Dedicated to Sister Gracelyn Smallwood. My inaugural visit to Aboriginal Australia was such a phenomenal experience that it was virtually impossible for me to write much about what I was seeing, hearing, or feeling while I was actually there. I was still very much floating on something of a cloud when I completed this travel note in December 1998, after my return to the United States, but I was determined to record at least some aspects of the trip down for posterity.

Runoko Rashidi

origins or their Aboriginal heritage. They were forbidden to speak their indigenous languages. Any violations of these rules were met with severe punishment, including floggings.

The dominant ethos behind the removal laws was that there was nothing of value in Aboriginal culture and that all value lay in European culture. The children's names were changed to European names. They were forced to wear European clothes and adopt European diets. They were even forced to wear dog tags for purposes of identification.

Until the 1970s, when Australia's Aboriginal child-removal laws were repealed, Aboriginal families lived in constant fear for the children who might be taken away, and constant grief for those already gone. There is today not a single Aboriginal family in Australia that has not been affected by the legacy of the Stolen Generations. In Kakadu National Park, I met many of the victims of this cruel government policy and heard their stories firsthand. Unfortunately, I learned, reminders of this extremely cruel process live on, even now.

A Visit to Alice Springs

At noon on my second day in Aboriginal Australia, I left Darwin and flew to Alice Springs, a relatively small town in the very center of the continent. That part of Australia is sometimes called "the red center," because the soil there has a dull, orange-reddish hue. Vegetation in the region is sparse and there are several strange rock formations.

The two sisters, Jacqui and Christine, took me on a tour of the city of Alice Springs, visiting every institution and facility directly affiliated with or run by the Blackfellas. I met with representatives of the Central Land Council there, an extremely polite group who they seemed a little uncertain about how to act toward me–but then, very few of the Aboriginal people that I met on my trip to Australia had much experience with Black folk from America, and they knew almost nothing of me personally. They only knew that an African professor from the United States was coming to Australia and wanted to visit them. But this African professor will be eternally grateful to them because every Aboriginal brother and sister that I met in Australia sure looked after me. And once they knew something about me, they became very anxious to talk with me.

Perhaps the highlight of my visit to Alice Springs was my tour of a women's center there. The center was for Aboriginal women, many of whom had been the victims of domestic abuse, which is a major problem in Aboriginal communities in Australia. Much of this violence apparently stems from the massive alcohol and drug abuse problems rampant among the Aboriginal people. Such is the degree of despair and hopelessness among them that many seemed determined to drink and drug themselves daily into a state of complete oblivion.

At the women's center, I was introduced to a number of sisters, including two women about fifty years old, although they looked much older. Life had not been very kind to them. Through a translator, I asked them many questions, like where they were born, their life stories, their goals, and so forth. At first, they patiently answered my questions, but then, all at once, they began to ask me questions! They wanted to know who I was, what I was, what I wanted, and why. It soon became extremely obvious to me that these sisters, who probably spoke for most of the Black people in Australia, knew almost nothing of their brethren in America.

So I told them our story. I talked to them at length about the mighty African empires and how Africans came to America. I told them of our enslavement and about the "door of no return." I told them how our families were separated and our names changed, and how we were forbidden to speak our own languages.

It was a very emotional experience. The more I talked, the more agitated the sisters became. They told me that they had never before heard any of what I was telling them.

Then I told them of the African American struggle for justice and about some of our great leaders. When I spoke in some detail about the lynchings in America, they started to become visibly disturbed. It was at that time that one of them stopped my narrative and questioned me in a sad and plaintive way. She asked, "Do you want us to help you?" It was then my turn to wipe away the tears.

Uluru National Park

The next day, I flew Quantas Airlines from Alice Springs to Uluru, or as the White folks in Australia commonly call it: "Ayers Rock." Uluru, which is 273 miles from Alice Springs, was not on my original itinerary, but I had hoped to travel there from the very beginning, so I was prepared for it. I was the last person to board the plane, and naturally, I was the only Black man on the flight. But that was the norm for this trip.

After a very short flight, I departed the plane with the hope that someone would be at the airport to meet me. After about an hour, Sister Joann Wilmot, accompanied by another lady, swooped me up. It didn't take me long to realize that the brothers and sisters in Australia, apparently like brothers and sisters everywhere, had their own sense of time!

But once again, I was in the company of two Black women, and being that I am a brother who happens to adore African females, I was quite content and felt in good company. Because I had no idea where I would be lodging, Sister Joann, who was a kind of Aboriginal director for Uluru and the person designated to escort me around, asked me if I had a problem with the idea of staying "with a Blackfella." That idea sounded good to me.

Aboriginal people, I learned, attach great spiritual significance to Uluru. It is one of the world's largest monoliths and rises more than eleven-hundred feet from the flatness of the surrounding plain. More impressive than its size, however, is its color: a brown-to-bright, glowing red that changes throughout the day. About forty miles from Uluru is another fascinating rock formation, Kata Tjuta, which some view as even more spectacular than Uluru.

Uluru, however, is viewed, at least by many Aboriginal people, as the "navel of the world" and the center of creation. Although many visitors climb to the top of Uluru, I was forbidden to even touch it. Joann drove me around Uluru and told me "dreamtime stories" from the Aboriginal culture about the beginning of the world.

Runoko Rashidi

Sister Joann also drove me to an Aboriginal community located about a couple hundred yards from Uluru. The community, she told me, was forbidden to non-Aboriginal people. Indeed, signs warning trespassers to "stay out" were posted nearly everywhere. Well, I didn't see myself as a tourist so, quite naturally, I felt that it was just the place where I most wanted to go. Sister Joann was only too happy to take me there. I soon realized that this Aboriginal community wasn't the most pleasant place to be. Squalor, disease, and poverty were the rule. Seeing Black children running around dirty and naked with mucous running down their faces was not an endearing sight.

Dinner, Aboriginal Style

After touring the community, Sister Joann invited me to dinner. She asked me if I had any preferences, and because I felt lucky to even be in Aboriginal Australia, naturally I said, "Well, sister, anything that you cook will be just fine with me." But when she told me that she would be cooking kangaroo tail, a whole host of second thoughts ran through my mind! She was determined to treat me to what she viewed as a real delicacy, however, and all the polite excuses from me about her not going to any trouble were fruitless.

As a result, she drove me to the company store, where she purchased three large, frozen kangaroo tails (which she called "whippers" and which, I could see, still had the animals' hair on them!). She even shut down her office a little early, just for me, before heading off to pick up her "skin mother" (a concept that I never really understood) and granddaughter. We were going to have a feast!

Immediately upon our arrival at her home, Sister Joann began accumulating quite a bit of dry wood, which she used to start a fire in an outdoor pit. As the fire began to blaze, she tossed the frozen whippers on top of the iron grill. As the fire began to thaw them out, the hair began burning off. The smell was nauseating. My protests that I didn't want to be the source of so much fuss again got me nowhere. After about fifteen minutes, she took the whippers off the fire and scraped the remaining hair off with a knife. Then she dug a hole where the fire had been, placed the whippers in the hole, and put the burning wood on top of the hole. An hour later, dinner was ready and the feast was consumed.

The Second World Indigenous Pathways Conference

Besides my lifelong interest in the Black people of Australia, the major reason for my 1998 travel to that continent was to attend the second World Indigenous Pathways Conference. This historic event was sponsored by the Kumbari/Ngurpai Lag Higher Education Center at the University of Southern Queensland, Toowoomba, Australia, from November 28 to December 4, 1998. My invitation to participate in it came after I met Dr. Gracelyn Smallwood, a wonderful woman whom I now call a good friend and the absolute "queen" of Aboriginal Australia. Sister Gracelyn is perhaps the most dedicated and dynamic of all of the indigenous Australians I have ever met. She lives in Queensland and was certainly the driving force behind the 1998 conference.

The 1998 World Indigenous Pathways Conference was designed to present the opportunity for indigenous and non-indigenous people from around the world to engage in discourse about issues such as identity, culture, reconciliation, multiculturalism, and social activism. I had been invited to the first conference, held in 1996, but could not attend because of a major scheduling conflict. Like the second conference, the first gathering drew together a cross-section of high-profile participants from Australia's indigenous peoples and oppressed groups from around the world.

The theme of the 1998 conference was "Pathways: Journeys of Discovery Within Diversity." The program was dedicated to the following topics: what it means to be Australian, civil rights and social activism in the struggle for a socially just society, indigenous universities, ancient cultures, the identification of oppressed groups, reconciliation, youth perceptions of the struggle for justice, and recognition of the wisdom and knowledge of our elders. Rather than issuing a call for papers, the conference organizers decided simply to invite speakers to address the topics indicated and to organize discussion panels based on those presentations. For reasons that I never quite fully understood, I was invited to speak on the US civil rights movement. For me, however, it really didn't matter what topic they wanted me to address, I was just so glad to finally get an invitation to go to Australia. All I knew was that a wish of a lifetime was about to be fulfilled.

The second World Indigenous Pathways Conference was definitely an international event. There were contingents from southern Sudan, Hawaii, New Zealand, Canada, and Barbados, among others nations. Four African Americans presented, including the great Dr. Tony Martin, from Wellesley College in Massachusetts, and me. The high-powered delegation from South Africa included Reverend Makhenkesi Stofile, the premier of Eastern Cape Province; and the two youngest sons of Steven Biko: Samora and Hlumelo. I found all the attendees to be interesting, engaging, and a great pleasure to be around. Most interesting of all, however, were the Blackfellas themselves. I was particularly impressed with a brother named Murandoo Yanner, a dedicated young activist from northern Queensland. Others who impressed me included Charles Perkins, a pioneering Black Australian civil rights activist (now an Ancestor); Gary Foley, a Koori activist in Victoria; Errol West, a Black Tasmanian and noted poet; and, of course, Dr. Smallwood herself.

The 1998 conference as a whole was an experience never to be forgotten. The most poignant part of it for me was the stories told of and by actual survivors of the Stolen Generations. Accounts of the racism of the White supremacist government of Australia and of the police brutality and resulting Black deaths in police custody aroused great anger and fierce indignation in me and the other participants. The life stories of the Stolen Generations survivors, on the other hand, were heartrending. Other distressing narratives told of Aboriginal children being torn from their parents and never united with them again. There was hardly a dry eye in the auditorium when those stories were recited. Those tales haunt me still.

Runoko Rashidi

Sydney and Canberra

Following the Second World Indigenous Pathways Conference, I left Queensland and journeyed south to the cities of Sydney and Canberra in Australian province of New South Wales. My Sydney visit was highlighted by multiple visits to Redfern, the downtrodden but heroic Black community that is sometimes called the "Harlem of Australia."

I will never forget a conversation I had with several sisters and brothers in Redfern, who regarded me as a real curiosity and a bona fide celebrity and treated me with great respect and courtesy during my visit. When I asked them what they knew of Black folk outside of Australia, particularly about African Americans, they told me that most of their knowledge of Blacks in the US was derived from television. Few had ever interacted with an African American close-up or intimately. At one point, I halted the conversation and told them that I did not believe that Africans in America had been captured, enslaved, and taken away from their homeland for no reason. Instead, I maintained, the Africans in America have a special mission and purpose: to help return African people to global power. I then paused and looked around the room and asked the group collectively, "Do you believe that you and your people a have a mission and purpose in life?" Their responses were unilateral: "Yes," they told me, "to have one last dust-up with the White man to get our land back!"

I couldn't help but let go a broad smile of great satisfaction. These, indeed, were truly my sisters and brothers. We all learned a lot from the interaction and enjoyed the opportunity.

In Canberra, I visited the Aboriginal Embassy and paid more respects to the traditional owners of the land. In both cities, I was guided and accompanied by another impressive woman: Sister Isabel Coe. Sister Isabel, like Dr. Smallwood and several of the Aboriginal women I met in Australia, is a wonderful and dedicated activist. Being in the presence of these women was a great honor. I shall never forget their warmth, dedication, commitment, and hospitality.

Well, suffice it to say I gave a very good speech at the Queensland conference. It was about forty minutes in length and, for once, I did not use any visual aids. Before I began, I judged the audience and decided what I thought they most needed to hear. As a result, the majority of my talk touched on civil rights in only a peripheral manner. Instead, I began by talking about the origins of humanity (Black people) and the spread of those early Black people around the world (including Australia). I then went on to discuss the rise of classical African civilizations, the coming of the White man, and the international subjugation and forced dispersal of Black people. Only then did I talk about the US civil rights and Black Power movements. My presentation was extremely well received. I was satisfied with it too, and I believe you would have been proud of me as well.

I left Australia in 1998 with the distinct impression that the Blackfellas were a very special people indeed, highly spiritual and real "survivors of the storm." Despite all the setbacks they have suffered at the hands of Europeans, they refuse to accept the concept of defeat. Instead, most Aboriginal Australians believe that they have been fighting an unrelenting war of survival for more than two centuries against the White invaders of the Land Down Under.

MY SECOND TRIP TO ABORIGINAL AUSTRALIA

Where in Perth is the History of Aboriginal Australia? (August 2004)

A couple of days ago, I was in the Australian city of Perth, located on the Indian Ocean side of that continent in the state of Western Australia. While there, I wanted to go visit the statue of the great leader of the Aboriginal resistance movement, Yagan. I also wanted to do some research at the Noongar Cultural and Language Center in East Perth. Once again, I learned that life doesn't always follow a simple path, does it? When I asked several people about the best way to find Yagan's statue, which I understood to be located on Heirison Island on the Swan River, no one could (or would) tell me how to find it. Now this statue is mentioned in both the country's official tour guides—both of them, mind you—but most folks said that they had never heard of it! Others told me that they had heard of it, but did not know how to get there.

Still I persisted. Finally, someone in the neighborhood told me that he knew where the statue was, but that it was far away. To get there, he told me, I would have to go a long way, first to find a ferry that would take me to another boat, and from there to find another ferry and then a captain who would allow me to charter his boat and take me there. Then he gave me a condescending smile as if I was crazy to want to go there in the first place and suggested that I visit another "really nice tourist island" instead.

So, that was that. Undaunted, I set out to find, walking this time, the Noongar Cultural and Language Center. I had been told before my trip that it was located right in the heart of East Perth, and this time I had the name, address, and phone number of the place in advance. But when I called there, no one answered. Then I found that the address did not exist, even though it too was listed in the state's official tourist guide. Only a few people in the area had heard of the place but, once again, no one could tell me exactly where it was.

I found this state of affairs very depressing, and I recalled the epigraph from Chancellor Williams's marvelous book, The Destruction of Black Civilization, in which he writes: "What became of the Black people of Sumer?" the traveler asked the old man, "for the records say that the people of Sumer were Black." Ah, the old man sighed, "They lost their history, so they died." And I was moved to the point of tears. I wondered if this was the future of the Aboriginal people of Australia, of Africans generally. Will future generations say that there once lived a great and mighty people, an African people, who lost their history and died? Indeed, travel abroad gives one a lot to ponder over.

A Visit to the Kulin Nation (Victoria, Australia)

This is my second day in the Kulin Nation (the Aboriginal Australian name for what the Western world knows as the state of Victoria) in southeastern Australia. I am right in the middle of the Victorian capital, in the busy and hectic city of Melbourne. Melbourne is Australia's second largest city after Sydney. It is a very beguiling city that reminds me of London, Manhattan, Paris, and Beijing, all rolled into one. I am staying in a very nice and pretty expensive hotel in the heart of the city center, right next to China Town. There are shops and restaurants and trams everywhere, but no Aboriginals to be seen. So I guess I have to get up, leave my hotel room, and go seek them out.

The sisters and brothers here in the Melbourne area are known as Koori. Most people seem to think that this term can be applied to the entire Aboriginal population of Australia, but it actually applies only to those Aboriginals from Victoria and its bordering state of New South Wales (the capital of which is Sydney). In that regard, one should never forget that Australia, in addition to being a big, modern country, is also a continent onto itself. That is, the sisters and brothers in various parts of Australia are as different as a Nigerian is to a Kenyan or an Ethiopian to a South African or a Senegalese to a Somali. Yes, they are all Africans, but their distinct differences must also be considered. Such is the case with the Aboriginal Australians. There are so many differences among the various groups, and I don't mean that in a negative way.

Anyway, after penning my first note to you about my misadventures in Perth, I went to the Koorie Heritage Trust in Melbourne where I was actually able to meet with some Koorie and Maori sisters. And what an education I got! They were very friendly and seemed as interested in connecting with me as I was with them. The spirit of Pan-Africanism is vibrant and strong in Melbourne, and don't let anyone tell you different! I was so excited that I even left the staff there with one of my cherished original copies of the Garvey Voice newspaper.

Did you know that Marcus Garvey established a branch of the UNIA & ACL in Brisbane, Australia, way back in the movement's early days? I can't wait to talk with Tony Martin about this when I travel to Ghana next month. I hope that I see him.

I later went to the Melbourne Museum to check out its Aboriginal exhibits, and there I saw, once again, how brutalized our sisters and brothers here have been. People roasted alive. People buried up to their necks in the sand and their heads clubbed off. Women kidnapped, assaulted, and murdered. Black men's scrotums used for tobacco pouches. These were some kinds of despicable creatures, the early White men in Australia-- thieves and criminals, rapists and murderers. Even now, some of their descendents deny that Black people even live on this continent! And yet the spirit of our people here is still, in many cases, extremely strong, as I am living and learning on this journey. One minute, I am angry as hell; another minute, I am ready to cry; and the next minute, I am laughing. I feel a very strange set of emotions here, and I am running the gamut of all of them. And I haven't even gotten to Tasmania yet, where the worst of the atrocities were perpetrated.

Despite all that I have learned on this trip about the injustices and brutality perpetrated against the Blackfellas, the Koori, the Tasmanians, and the other indigenous groups here in Australia, I have to tell you this: I am very much in love, not just with the Aboriginal Australians, but with life itself. I have never felt more blessed to be able to travel to the far corners of the African world—that is, the entire planet—and to have the experiences that I am having here. Meeting the people I am meeting and learning all that I can about them and the land and their reverence for it, I feel as if the Ancestors have given me a super-special mission. And I, for one, do not intend to flunk it!

When I return to the US early next month (September 2004), I hope to be able to spend some quality time addressing some of the many questions and concerns about Aboriginal Australia that you, my readers, have been sending in my direction. In the meantime, my search continues "Down Under" for remnants of Africa in Aboriginal life, history, and culture.

August 20, 2004: A Brief, but Overwhelming Trip to the "Ghostlands" of Tasmania

What an experience I am having! When you last heard from me I was in a Chinese Internet cafe in Melbourne. Feeling a little congested, I decided to leave the city and check out some nature. This led me to embark on an all-day trip along the Great Ocean Road, one of the world's great coastal drives. I have rarely, if ever, seen such an abundance of natural beauty. Ultimately, I ended up at Port Campbell National Park, where I visited these huge limestone rock formations jutting out of the Southern Ocean. The rock stacks are called the Twelve Apostles, even though there really are only nine of them.

From there, I took a good dip in the ocean at a place called Loch Ard Gorge. Utterly breathtaking! It's a good thing I took a lot of photos because I words simply cannot adequately describe the things I've seen on this trip.

I have been on the island of Tasmania these last two days. Yes, there really is such a place! I even met and talked to and laughed and cried with the indigenous people here—yes, some of them did survive the European invasion. They call themselves Palawa, meaning "the original men." I have seen many photos of these sisters and brothers, even traced some of their genealogies.

Today, I went where the last full-blooded Tasmanians were kept, in virtual captivity, until they all finally just died off. I also visited the island where the last full-blooded Tasmanian, Queen Truganinni, was born. Yesterday, I went to the Tasmanian Museum and Art Gallery, where her bones were kept on display until 1947.

I have been to many, many places, but I can honestly say that I have never had an experience quite like this! Tasmania—or, as I call it, the "ghostlands"—is a hauntingly beautiful place. I feel as though I am communing with the spirits of our Ancestors here. I wish I could write more, but I am very full of emotions right now.

I wish you were here with me!

THIRD TIME'S A CHARM, MATE!: REFLECTIONS ON MY RETURN TO ABORIGINAL AUSTRALIA

January 29, 2008

I've been to Aboriginal Australia four times now. I've even taken two groups there, and have visited every state of that nation. But in all my global travels, I have never come across a more interesting group of people than the Blackfellas there. Some people still criticize me, however, for including Aboriginal Australians within the African community. Indeed, it is not uncommon for Aboriginal Australians themselves to take issue with the assertion of their African identity. But they are indeed

Runoko Rashidi

Black people, and all humanity did come from Africa, and Marcus Garvey did have a branch of the UNIA & ACL on the Australian continent, and there was a branch of the Black Panther Party in the Australian city of Brisbane, and they did have freedom rides and sit-ins there. And then again, Aboriginal Australians did attend FESTAC (the Festival of African Art and Culture in 1977) and the reparations conference (the first World Conference Against Racism) in Durban, South Africa, in 2001. All of this says a great deal.

I am so drawn to the plight of our Aboriginal sisters and brothers in Australia. They are some of the most fascinating of all the members of the Global African Family. I was reading an article in the paper this morning about how the government of Australia is going to apologize to the indigenous people of that land for the past wrongs of their European Ancestors, and that got me started thinking. It reminded me of an article I read a couple of months ago that recalled the time in recent history when the Blacks in Australia were not even considered humans by the Australian government. Many of you may recall the excellent movie called Rabbit-Proof Fence, about how Aboriginal children for many years were forcibly removed from their natural mothers and fathers, and shipped off to boarding schools—concentration camps, I call them—way out in the hinterlands, where they were stripped of their cultural memory, practices, and history. It really seems incredible to me that the Whites were finally realizing, after hundreds of years, the awful truth about their past!

In any event, before 2008 is over I hope to return to Australia and use it as a base for deep explorations of the South Pacific.

IN THE FOOTSTEPS OF THE FORERUNNERS: FIJI'S AFRICAN ROOTS [2]

> *"We, the Black people in Fiji, came here a long time ago to our present homes in Fiji from Tanganyika, in East Africa. We don't know exactly when we came to Fiji, but we know that we came from Africa." (Fijian Tradition)*

March 20, 2000

During February 2000, in honor of African History Month, I gave major presentations in ten states and the District of Columbia, traveling to most of the geographic regions in the United States. The tour was a wonderful travel experience, but it was also extremely demanding. By the end of that month, I was really, as they say, "fried."

I was so tired, I could barely talk! I even had some difficulty sitting down and standing up. My resistance was vastly depleted, and I had somehow managed to catch a rare but bad head cold. I needed a break, big time, and believed that I had justly earned one. So, on the first day of March, I got on yet another plane and flew from Los Angeles to Hawaii. The trip was not entirely recreational or recuperative. My plan was to give a slide-lecture presentation at the University of Hawaii at

---

[2] Dedicated to Joel Augustus (J. A.) Rogers and John Henrik Clarke.

Manoa, and then to embark from Honolulu on a combined, and very much needed, nine-day vacation-holiday–study-tour to Viti Levu, Fiji.

Now, Hawaii is a wonderful place, extremely beautiful, and always a pleasure to visit. It just doesn't have enough Black folk to satisfy my needs. Fiji, however, promised to be different.

I had been to Hawaii numerous times and once to Australia, but I had never actually been to the South Pacific, so my trip to Fiji was really something of a fantasy realized or a dream come true. I was really excited about the prospects, and ready for something even more special.

By the time I got to Hawaii, however, all I had was a plane ticket, a little money, a credit card, and loads of good intentions. Because I was traveling alone, it wasn't hard to get hotel accommodations. My lecture topic was focused on the Dalits or Black Untouchables of India, indeed some of the most oppressed people on earth, bar none. It seemed an especially appropriate lecture, given my plans to visit Fiji, because almost half the population of that island nation is of Indian origin. The next day, with great excitement but still encumbered with fatigue, I was finally on my way, via a six-hour flight on Air Pacific, to the South Pacific!

Fiji is only the twentieth country that I've visited so far. For many, I know that this is no big deal, but I intend to do better. As I've stated before, J. A. Rogers, one of my idols, traveled to sixty countries during his lifetime; and Sister Sibyl Williams-Clarke, the widow of the great John Henrik Clarke, told me that Dr. Clarke had traveled to every country in Africa except South Africa as well as to Asia, Europe, Central America, South America, and the Caribbean. With all due respect and with the blessings of these illustrious Ancestors, two of the greatest Africans of the twentieth century, my goal is to travel to at least sixty-five countries and extend and build upon their contributions.

Fiji is an island nation located deep in the South Pacific. The Fijian isles, of which there are more than three hundred, are situated at a kind of ocean crossroads between the mighty island chains of Polynesia and Melanesia. The island of Viti Levu (which means "Great Fiji") is the largest and most populous of these, with an approximate area of 10,400 kilometers. Seventy-five percent of the total Fijian population lives on Viti Levu.

I found Fiji to be a tropical paradise indeed, and the Fijians turned out to be some of the most beautiful Black people I have ever encountered. Much to my delight, the brothers and sisters in Fiji, most of whom are dark-skinned, Black people who wore big, Afro-type hairstyles, didn't merely identify themselves as Black—they said flat out that they came from Africa! And, to my delight, they said it with great pride! What a refreshing revelation!

Of course, Fiji was not completely utopian. In fact, it is with some sadness that I must report that, just like in Trinidad and Guyana (where I visited last year) and even in the United States to some extent, the relationship between the African people and the Indian settlers in Fiji (even between them and the blackest Indians) is generally a very uneasy, almost antagonistic one. The Indians of Fiji tend to demonstrate a strong "Indian-first" mentality; however, on a more positive note, although the Indians control the government, the Fijians control the army, the police force, and over eighty percent of the land.

Runoko Rashidi

Needless to say, I felt right at home in Fiji. These Black folk were just my kind of people, and they seemed just as interested in me as I was in them. As often as possible, I traveled to the native Fijian villages, many of them deep in the interior of Viti Levu. There, I was always designated as a distinguished visitor, and the Fijians told me that they were honored by my presence. They always referred to me as "brother" and singled me out for special treatment. We drank kava (a calming local brew) together—an extremely important Fijian tradition—and really bonded.

Plus, I met people in Fiji who looked just like so many other Black folk I have met and known around the world. One Fijian village chief that I met, for example, could have been Dr. John Henrik Clarke's twin brother! And when I mentioned this resemblance to him, he seemed to be extremely pleased and insisted that I come and sit next to him.

Of course, if there is one thing that I excel in, it is in asking questions. And I asked the Fijian brothers and sisters all kinds of questions. like, exactly what part of Africa did they come from? When did they come to Fiji? How did they get there? What is the nature of their oral traditions, myths, and religious, male-female relationships, diet, and health beliefs? What was their relationship to other Pacific islanders and to the recently arrived Indian population? What are their present living conditions like? What did they think the future holds for them? How did they feel about White people? What did they know about African Americans?

Oh yes, I asked just about everything I could possibly think of, and surprisingly, they never got tired of answering my questions. Among their responses they told me that the two most well known African Americans in Fiji were the Reverend Martin Luther King, Jr., and Muhammad Ali. Of course, they knew all about Michael Jordan and Magic Johnson and most of the major African American sports figures too.

One Fijian brother, a businessman I met in the lobby of a luxury hotel, told me how proud he was of the brothers and sisters in America and how much African Americans had advanced the causes of Black people around the world. Yet, when I asked several Fijians how often they encountered Black people from the United States, they typically replied that African Americans frequently came to Fiji for holiday vacations, but that I was different. When I asked why, they said it was because I spent a lot of time with them and seemed to want to get to know all about them. Of course, these responses thrilled and delighted me to no end.

ON TO MICRONESIA

August 16/17, 2005

I regret to inform you that over the last few days we lost at least two giants that I am aware of: Nana Ekow Butweiku I and Dr. Mary Hoover. I first met Nana about ten years ago and enjoyed a very good relationship with him. I actually stayed with him and his wife, Sister Mut (who became an Ancestor about a year ago), at their residence in the Bronx on more than a couple of occasions. Nana was a world traveler, an African patriot, philanthropist, active lecturer, and prolific author. He even allowed me to write an introduction to one of his books. He was humble and serious, a great man, and a very decent person. He will be sorely missed.

Dr. Mary Hoover was a noble educator who spent the last several years of her life in the Washington, DC, area. She was a really good human being and a very sweet and caring woman. she invited me to participate in an education conference at Howard University a couple of years ago, along with Cain Hope Felder of Howard's School of Divinity. That was the last time I saw Dr. Hoover.

I also want to point out that that the recent plane crash in Venezuela was almost certainly full of Africans from the Caribbean island of Martinique. So our prayers must go out to all of those families as well.

On a lighter note, depending upon what calendar you use, I had the good fortune of turning fifty-one years of age either yesterday or today. That is, I crossed the International Dateline yesterday, heading west, so where I am today it is now August 16 all over again. I guess the advantage of this is that I get to celebrate my birthday twice! But as far as birthdays go, I am in grand company. August 12 marks the birthday of the late, great Edward Wilmot Blyden; August 14 is the birthday of one of our finest contemporary educators and my cousin, Dr. Joyce Elaine King; and, of course, August 17 is the birthday of Marcus Mosiah Garvey. So there should indeed be a lot of celebrating going on this month!

I am writing to you from my hotel room on the island of Kosrae, Federated States of Micronesia. This is country number fifty-seven for me. Kosrae is a beautiful island with a population of less than eight-thousand people. Here is the description of the island you will find in the tour books:

> *"Kosrae is a casual, unpretentious backwater, where people consistently return a smile. It is one of the least spoiled and least developed areas in Micronesia, an unhurried place that retains a certain air of innocence....Kosrae is rich in natural beauty. It has an interior of uncharted rain forests, a pristine fringing reef and a coast that is a mix of sandy beaches and mangrove swamps."*

Me, I'm not exactly sure how to characterize the people here. What I mean is, I'm not certain where to place them regarding their ethnicity. They are copper- complexioned, but even I am not sure if I can characterize them as African. But they sure are warm and friendly people, and most of them are darker than a lot of African Americans I know, so, of course, I'm glad that I'm here.

Today I went to the small, one-room Kosrae Museum, where I managed to find, to my utter delight, a single image of a man who looked as African as (then-UN Secretary General) Kofi Annan. Unfortunately, no one in the museum could tell me much about the man in the picture; the local tourist office could not tell me much, either. Indeed, when I asked a number of people on the island where the people of Kosrae came from, I always got the same vague response: "Somewhere in South Asia."

The other highlight of my day was my trip to the Lelu Ruins. The Lelu Ruins are the remains of a six-hundred-year-old basalt-stone city. It is a large site, and I am not sure if I have ever seen anything quite like it. Except for an abundance of lizards, the city is completely abandoned, but it is surely an interesting place, lizards and all. If it had not been so steamy hot outside today, I would probably have explored the site a lot longer. In any event, I hope the pictures I took come out well.

And if Kosrae is a new name for you, don't feel too lonely because I had not heard of it myself until a few months ago. So you might say that we are all in this together! And, for once in my life, I brought along my laptop computer, so with the aid of a not-too-expensive phone card, here I am communicating with you while I gaze out at the Pacific Ocean, listen to CDs of Wes Montgomery and Earl Klugh, and order lunch.

Life is not too bad. I am working on a new book that I figure is going to be my best so far. I am dedicating it to J. A. Rogers, Chancellor Williams, and John G. Jackson. Dr. Asa Hilliard has agreed to write the introduction; Legrand Clegg is preparing the foreword; and Horen Tudu, one of my students of Bangladeshi ancestry, is contributing a piece on Pan-Africanism in South Asia. How can I miss?

Tomorrow I travel to Chuuk, farther west and deep in the heart of Micronesia. I decided to go there because not only is it described as a beautiful island paradise but also because the only person that I've ever met from there so far looked like a dead ringer for Miles Davis, so it should be a most exquisite journey! And I promise to do my best to keep you updated as I continue to search out the African presence in Micronesia. In the meantime, do enjoy Marcus Garvey's birthday, as he represents the best in all of us!

FROM CHUUK TO PALAU

August 23, 2005

It is raining and overcast here in Chuuk (actually, just the way I like it!), and what better time for yet another letter from Brother Runoko in Micronesia? I have been in Chuuk now for five full days and will be leaving soon, but I will be going with some reluctance as the people here seem to have just started to open up to me. At first, the locals looked at me with curiosity. I tried to talk to a lot of them with not a whole lot of success. Finally, yesterday afternoon, I decided to take a different and more direct approach. Now, they keep asking me why I have to go so soon and everyone tells me that they wish I could stay.

Now Chuuk, I have learned, is a beautiful place with beautiful people, but, alas, I fear that I shall probably never return. There are just so many places to see and not nearly enough time (or money) to see everything and everybody. So, as I prepare to leave, I find myself having some emotional conflicts. Oh well, such is life!

Before I head to the airport and get on the plane, however, let me share with you some of the life experiences and information I've come up with thus far. Let me share too some of the lessons I have learned since you last heard from me.

Just after I arrived at the hotel here last week, I saw a large, young, dark sister giving me a friendly eye. Well, being a really shy brother I didn't make much of it. But with my time running short and considering that she worked in the hotel, and realizing that she spoke very clear English and had been very helpful to me so far, I asked her if I could treat her to dinner in the hotel restaurant. Her eyes lit up in response to my request, and she responded with, "Well, I'll have to ask my mom."

Well, it turns out that her mom had been listening all the while and quickly appeared from an adjoining office. Mom was a beautiful, middle-aged, brown-skinned woman who just happened to be the hotel's general manager. With a smile that could have lit up an entire city, she replied to her daughter, "It is up to you." And with that, the deal was sealed, and the young lady and I set a dinner date for 7:00 pm.

Sisters and brothers, I was both excited and content at the prospect of this meeting. Finally, I thought, I am going to get some real information! I spent the time leading up to dinner working on a chapter for my forthcoming book and thinking about all the questions I was going to ask this sister. I decided to conduct a structured interview. After all, I had been an anthropology major for a while in college, and I thought that I might as well use some of the skills I had paid for.

First, however, I wanted to make sure that both mother and daughter clearly knew that I was not trying to "hit on" the sister. Nothing could have been farther from my mind, and so, to prove it, I rummaged through my suitcase and found the single copy of my latest travel book, which I had brought along for just such an occasion. (That book's jacket cover featured my new favorite photo of me looking, I believe, very much like an anthropologist.) Then I went downstairs to the hotel's front desk about thirty minutes before dinner, where I found the young woman's mom waiting for me. I showed her my book. Mom seemed duly impressed with me and, after a brief discussion, she told me that her daughter was in the restaurant waiting for me.

Well, sister and brothers, the dinner turned out to be something of a disappointment. Over a meal of soup, seafood pasta, and ice tea, I began by asking the younger woman some very basic, personal questions, like her name, age, and background. She told me that her name was Mary Christian Walter; that she was twenty-four years old; and that she was born in Weno, Chuuk. She also told me that the hotel in which we were dining was owned by her grandparents and that she had been working there since 1998. Respect for one's elders, she added, was the most important element in Chuukese society.

Eager to get to the heart of my inquiry, after Mary had answered those basic questions, I pressed her, and perhaps pressed her too hard, for more information. I wanted to know what she thought about Chuuk's educational and health care systems, about the presence of HIV/AIDS on the island, and about Chuukese views on family matters (including whether Chuuk society was matriarchal or patriarchal and the degree of domestic violence there). I also wanted to know about island's employment statistics, the prevalence of drugs there, and whether the people of Chuuk were optimistic or pessimistic about the future. Last and most importantly, I want to know what she and the people of Chuuk thought about other Pacific Islanders, about African Americans, and about African people overall.

Well, I guess I must have overwhelmed the young lady because the conversation quickly "went downhill," as they say. She did tell me that the dropout rate in the local schools was very high, , but that young Chuukese were aware of the value of a good education. She lamented that she had not learned a whole lot about the history of the Chuukese in school, except that during World War II the Japanese has used the Chuukese as slaves. She maintained, however, that relations between the Chuukese and the numerous Japanese tourists who visited there annually were generally very good.

Mary told me that generally Americans were viewed very favorably in Chuuk and, much to my satisfaction, when I asked her how she viewed people from the continent of Africa, she smiled her biggest smile of the evening and told me that she really identified with the Africans. She really liked them, she said, and stated that the Chuukese and Africans had a lot in common.

The turning point in the interview came when I asked Mary what she and the Chuukese people thought of African Americans. You should have seen her squirm! It was as if I asked her about the most personal aspects of her life. I never did get a comprehensible answer. The closest I could figure was that she thought some African Americans were okay and others were not; that she viewed us as sisters and brothers but really did not feel comfortable being called "Black." The Chuukese, she claimed, believed that they came originally from Melanesia and identified themselves not as Black people per se but as Pacific Islanders.

She did say that hip-hop and reggae were taking the island by storm, but when I tried to press her for more or clearer answers about her racial views, she squirmed even more, so I decided not to push it any further, and that was that. She smiled as though she had been let off the hook, and I let her enjoy the last of her meal in peace.

So that was my dinner interview in Micronesia. It did not go as I would have liked it to, and the whole experience left me a bit unsettled. After Mary left the restaurant, I ordered another drink, engaged in some quiet reflection, and returned to my room, where, I must admit, I had a hard time going to sleep.

This morning I woke up in a quandary. I was worried that maybe I had inadvertently offended Mary with all my questioning and probing during last night's dinner. Maybe, it was better to listen more than speak. Maybe building trust and confidence takes more time than I have been allowing. Maybe it is unhealthy to get too disappointed when I don't get the kind of answers that I want to hear. And maybe, just maybe, I was making a mistake by attempting to impose what I perceived as an "African-centered" (or African American-centered?) worldview on other Black folks.

But what a difference a day makes! When I went to the front desk this morning to confirm my flight out of Chuuk later today, Mary was there to greet me—with a big smile on her face! I immediately felt better. She seemed cool with me, and I let it go at that.

During breakfast, I was chatting with my waitress, who was a really beautiful woman, and asking her about her family and other matters, when an older Chuukese man sitting at an adjoining table jumped right into our conversation. How quickly the world turns! The man was having breakfast with his wife and he seemed to have wanted nothing more than a good conversation. With a big smile on his face, he told me that he liked African Americans above all other people in the world, and that Miami center Shaquille O'Neal was his favorite athlete! He even said that African Americans were the favored tourists on Chuuk, and that some of them even married the local Chuukese women!

To my delight (and relief!), this conversation went on and on. The man told me that Chuuk was a male-dominated society and that this, in his view, was a very good thing! He also noted, however, that HIV/AIDS was a growing problem, and that the overall health of the Chuukese people was deteriorating with the spread of western diets, especially soft drinks. Alcohol and drugs were also becoming greater and greater problems. As a result, he claimed, many of the young people were leaving Chuuk for Guam, Hawaii, and the United States mainland for education, employment opportunities, and better health care; but the remaining local people were friendly and warm and did not discriminate against anyone.

The man told me over and over again how he wished that we had met earlier and how he would have introduced me to so many people who would have given me so much more information than I had obtained thus far during my brief visit! And then, when his wife signaled that it was time to go, this "male-dominant" brother quickly jumped up, excused himself, and rushed off to follow behind her!

So here we are, and here I am, about to check out and head to the airport for my next Micronesian experience. I feel relaxed, well rested, and confident, glad that I came to Chuuk. My visit here was not a waste of time at all.

By the way, in case you are wondering, I never found the Miles Davis lookalike I told you about. I asked a lot of people on the island if they knew or had seen anybody who looked like him and they simply smiled and told me that maybe he lived here or maybe he lived there, but that probably he lived on one of the outer (and very hard to get to) islands. So, the Pacific Islander Brother Miles, perhaps like the actual Miles Davis of American jazz fame, may simply be a more elusive character than I thought, but I am certain I will find him. Perhaps at my next stop, perhaps on the next island, but whatever the case, I will be sure to keep you informed!

THE REPUBLIC OF PALAU

August 26, 2005

It is late Friday afternoon, and I have been in the state of Koror in the Republic of Palau for three-and-a-half days now. This makes country number fifty-eight for me as I count down to sixty, sixty-five–who knows? God willing, eventually perhaps, I'll get to seventy-five or eighty countries on this global African travel odyssey that I am so deeply in the midst of undertaking.

First, though, and before I write any further, let me see if I can give you a brief geography lesson. The island nation of Palau (called Belau by the indigenous people) is located in the northwest portion of the Pacific Ocean. Geographically, it is a few hundred miles north of the island of New Guinea, about five hundred miles southeast of the southern tip of the Philippines, about a thousand miles south of Japan, and (I would imagine) close to six thousand miles west of California. Palau is part of Micronesia, the so-called "small islands" of the northern Pacific, and it marks, up to this point, the farthest western point of the journey that I began in Los Angeles two weeks ago.

Runoko Rashidi

I've really covered a lot of miles on this trip after having spent the summer so far in France, Italy, and Egypt, and traversing from one end of the United States to the other. I've covered a lot of ocean, too. Just to review for you: on August 14, I flew from Los Angeles to Honolulu, where I stayed overnight. Early the next morning, I flew westward from Honolulu to Kosrae, Federated States of Micronesia. On the way to Kosrae, I touched down in Majuro, Marshall Islands, where the people looked good and brown, and Kwajalein, where I did not get off the plane. Don't worry if you have never heard of these places. Until quite recently, I had not heard of them, either!

On the way to Kosrae, I crossed the International Date Line and enjoyed my fifty-first birthday on August 16 twice. (It's not too late to get me a present, by the way! Hint: I have always thought that books make great gifts.)

Anyway, I enjoyed my two days in Kosrae immensely and found the people there very shy but very warm. From Kosrae, I journeyed west to Chuuk by way of Pohnpei, the capital of the Federated States of Micronesia. I did not stop in Pohnpei, but I found out later that it is home to a very ancient culture. I wish that I had added some time there to my travel plans because I'm sure I could have learned a lot there. But that's just sour grapes now—moving on!

Palau is a wonderful place, so wonderful that it's hard to find a more appropriate description for the island, its people, and my total experience here. Indeed, of all the trips I have taken and the scores of places I have been blessed to visit, I cannot recall a time or a place when or where I have felt so much as one with the local people. There is no question that I felt a great emotional bond with and a strong sense of family connectedness to the Dalits and Tribals on my three visits to India, with the Aboriginal people of Australia on my four journeys "down under," and with the sisters and brothers of Fiji on my two sojourns to Melanesia. Likewise, I have shared a kind of mystical and magical bond with the people of Ghana on my two visits there and with the many, many other groups of Black people I have met and interacted with during the course of my travels. I would not trade those experiences for anything, but right about now, I'm thinking that Palau might top them all!

It is as though I have been here many, many times before. Have you ever felt that way about a place? I mean, I am feeling kind of emotionally overwhelmed right now, and I know that when I have to leave Palau for Yap early Saturday morning, I am going to be really distraught.

Maybe something will happen to make me feel otherwise. Maybe something will occur to dampen my feelings of joy about and satisfaction with this trip, but who can say? Who can predict the future? For now, I am feeling really, really comfortable here.

First of all, the people of Palau are the most consistently dark-complexioned group that I have seen in Micronesia so far. And if you love Black people as much as I do, that is a very, very good thing. I know that we as a people range in complexion, as it has been said, "from snow to crow and bright to night," and I love us, whatever the complexion. But there is something about the beauty of blackness that is just oh-so-special. And we should never apologize about it! As far as I am concerned, if you don't love blackness, you might as well get out of town—or off the island, as it were!

So, to begin, I've found a whole bunch of Black folks here in Palau who seem real comfortable in their own skins and with themselves generally. For me, this got things off to a superb start from the *git-go*. Point number two: Palau itself is a physically gorgeous, and I mean gorgeous, place. It features hundreds and hundreds of large and small, lush, green islands, including a special group of islands called the Rock Islands. These are about three-hundred fairly small limestone islands covered with vegetation that rise majestically out of the sea. They mostly resemble enormous green mushrooms jutting out of the ocean.

The waters around the Rock Islands range in color from dark to pale blue to aquamarine to light green to crystal clear and are home to millions and millions of brilliantly colored fish of many varieties. I spent all day yesterday boating through the Rock Islands and I have never seen anything quite like it. Perhaps the closest thing to it is Halong Bay in North Vietnam.

Yesterday, I was, of course, the only African on a sightseeing boat full of Japanese tourists, and I'll admit that I did feel a bit awkward. But about a third of the Japanese were friendly, and the others pretty much ignored me, so it all worked out okay. The best part about the trip was that the boat driver and one of the guides were Palauan, and they made it a point to look after me. I had a wonderful time, and I can honestly tell you that the Rock Islands are some of the world's great natural wonders.

There are two excellent museums in Palau. The first is the National Museum of Belau, which features a great collection of small wooden replicas of Palauan villages, assorted wood carvings, and story boards. As far as I could tell, story boards are brightly painted wooden boards about the size of automobile license plates that tell that story of the people.

The second museum is the new and privately owned Etpison Museum. Etpison is a powerful Palauan politician and philanthropist. His museum contains a marvelous collection of black-and-white photos of indigenous Micronesians, both ancient and modern. One lesson that emerges from these pictures is that the most Africoid-looking people in Micronesia live on the region's outer islands. That explains why I had so much difficulty finding my Miles Davis lookalike in Chuuk. You have to go to the outer islands, and those islands are so isolated and so far removed from the main population centers that they are almost impossible for the casual traveler to get to.

Palau has a matriarchal social structure, and the Palauan women are highly respected. They are the ones who determine who the chiefs are. It is also interesting to note that Palauan women inherit their mothers' property, and Palauan men inherit their fathers' property. On my first day here, Roman, my first taxi driver, pointed out to me, with a marked degree of reverence, a Black woman whom he referred to in hushed tones as "the queen of Palau."

The food in Palau is delicious, and the island hosts a number of different excellent restaurants. So far, I have enjoyed Indian, Jamaican, and Palauan cuisine. I've had Indian butter chicken and naan, Caribbean jerk beef and curry chicken, and Micronesian parrot and napoleon fish. Steamed rice comes with everything. At a restaurant featuring Palaun cuisine, someone suggested that I try the fruit bat, a Palauan delicacy. They claimed that "it looks really ugly, but it sure does taste good!" When I passed on that one, the other diners in the restaurant all laughed, but I just couldn't go there.

African Americans and Palauans seem to have a special relationship. At one restaurant, as a waitress approached me, I almost forgot where I was—she looked as if she came straight out of Brooklyn, New York! To top it off, she told me, with a wide, wide smile, that one of her parents was African

American and the other Palauan. My favorite taxi driver on the island, a brother named Leo, had a story that was pretty much the same as the waitress's. His father, he told me, was African American and his mother Palauan.

In terms of character and personality, the Palaun people are remarkable and refreshing, and they really know how to look after you. Let me give you probably the best example so far: the morning after I arrived here, as I was exiting an Internet café, I noticed an African-looking police officer in a squad car parked just across the street from me. Now, my experience in America has told me that, as a Black man, when police officers are giving you the eye, be they Black or White, generally that means trouble. So, much to my dismay, this brother seemed to be seriously checking me out. As I walked down the street, he started his vehicle and began following me.

Damn! I thought, what now? Now, sisters and brothers, I grew up in the 1960s and early 1970s in urban Los Angeles in the United States, and I learned well the bitter lesson that when a cop starts to follow you, it is time to worry. Anyway, the officer pulls up to me and asks me, a bit demandingly, I thought, "Where are you from?" "From the US," I told him. He then asked me, "What are you doing here?" "Just vacationing," I responded, with a slight smile designed to disarm him. He then asked me, "Where are you going?" Now, by this time, I confess, I was feeling really nervous and wondering if US justice and racial profiling had found a home here in farthest Micronesia.

Anyway, to make a long story short, the officer, a Black man, next beckoned me to his car and told me to get in! At that point, I was thinking that I should show him my passport and assure him that I am one of "the good guys," but it never came to that.

To my great surprise and relief, the next words out of the officer's mouth, which had turned upward into a beautiful, miraculous smile, were that it was "much too hot for me to be out walking." He then offered to take me anywhere I wanted to go on the island. I was in shock! I almost could not believe my eyes and ears!

The Palauan police officer's demeanor had changed instantaneously. He even got out of his squad car, vigorously shook my hand, and introduced himself to me on a first-name basis. He asked me what hotel I was staying in and then inquired about whether I wanted to go "hang out" with him that evening. And that, sisters and brothers, is how my trip to Palau really got started!

The next morning, when I asked my driver Leo what he liked most about Palau, his answer was "that everybody cares about everybody here." I asked Leo a lot of other questions about life in Palau. When I pressed him about crime on the island, he told me that drug dealers were "quickly put behind the bars." A rape occurs in Palau about every ten years or so, he said. He also said that there had not been a murder here in more than ten years.

Brother Leo also reaffirmed for me some of the most deeply rooted Micronesian values, including respect for elders. He then went on and on, at considerable length, about how "all Palauans believe that our children are our greatest asset." All I could do in response to these comments was smile in agreement, let go a deep sigh of satisfaction, and glow with pride.

The Republic of Palau is a very special place indeed. Every Palauan I have encountered so far treats me like family. It all seems so genuine and easy and real, I get extremely emotional every time I think of it.

So that's what's happening with Brother Runoko here in Palau. I only wish that you were here to share some of this experience with me.

IN YAP PROPER

August 31, 2005

It is early on a Wednesday morning, and the clock on my travels in Micronesia is quickly winding down. I have really and truly enjoyed myself here. I've learned a whole lot too, but it is time to move on.

I am now in Yap, Federated States of Micronesia. Yes, there is such a place and, yes, we are indeed today experiencing my favorite kind of weather: cloudy, overcast, and rainy. So, as a kind of wrap-up to my Pacific island adventures, the following is perhaps my last letter from Micronesia for this time around.

My last two days in Palau were definitely highly successful ones. I spent time with the locals, went back to the museums, relaxed at the national aquarium, and generally enjoyed myself immensely. I just loved the place!

Just after midnight on August 28, I took a late-night flight from Palau to Yap, and I was fortunate to ride first class. Tonight, I will begin my long journey back to the United States, first by catching another first-class flight from Yap to Guam, and then by flying out tomorrow morning from Guam to Hawaii. After a delay of about four hours, I will then catch a connecting flight from Hawaii to California. I'll be sure to have a good book to read along the way and some food to eat.

I guess I am as ready to go as I am going to be. I have seen a lot of things and spent a lot of money, but new horizons beckon me. Beginning this week, and in the course of the next three-and-a-half months, I am scheduled to lecture in California, Washington, Illinois, and Ohio before I venture back to France. From France I will return to southwest Turkey, where I will visit more of the African communities there. From Turkey, I will venture for the first time to Syria, where I will visit Damascus and the ancient and enduring archaeological site of Palymra, among other places. Then I will return briefly to France and the United States.

All of this should be extremely exciting, but it gets better. Beginning November 11, I will escort an African American tour group to Brazil and then take a much-needed personal vacation in the US Virgin Islands, before returning again to France to promote my French-language book on the African presence in Asia. So I guess you could say that I have a very full travel plate ahead of me and that life for Brother Runoko, who loves to travel, will be good indeed.

Runoko Rashidi

Each of my stops in Micronesia has had its own unique character and feel. The islands are similar in many ways but at the same time quite different. Kosrae, for instance, was extremely quiet. Chuuk is a little rough-edged. Palau was the best of the best. Yap, however, is a world apart.

Located 515 miles southwest of Guam, Yap proper consists of the four, tightly clustered islands of Yap, Tamil-Gagil, Map, and Rumung. Rumung is forbidden to outsiders, but the other three islands are open and connected by bridges, and so far, I have visited them all. There are also scores of outer islands, but they too are very isolated and difficult to get to. The majority of the people here live in Yap proper.

Like the other parts of Micronesia that I have visited, Yap proper is lush and humid. It is compact and seemingly more self-contained, and it doesn't have the mountainous terrain characteristic of the rest of Micronesia. The people are friendly, but not as friendly as those in the other places I have visited in this region. They seem more reserved. Then again, there aren't that many people on this island to begin with. There are only about twelve thousand Yapese, about three-hundred guest workers, and less than a hundred foreign tourists.

Yap, the indigenous name of which is Wa'ab, is believed to have been settled about eighteen hundred years ago. It is the most traditional of all the places I have visited in Micronesia. By that I mean that although foreign missionaries have been here for generations and outsiders (most notably the Spanish, Japanese, and Americans) have had an impact, the traditional values of the Yapese remain strongly intact.

Just across the street from the hotel that I am staying in, for example, in front of a Chinese-owned market so reminiscent of the liquor stores that I see in the urban centers of the United States, sit elderly, bare-breasted Black women. On the island's country roads, elderly Black men walk around with only a loincloth around their waists. The traditional money takes the form (most prominently) of large circular stones with small holes in the middle that resemble nothing so much as skinny automobile tires and of clam shells that are found throughout Yap. This stone money, known as rai, is displayed prominently at the entrance to every village, and such displays are referred to as "money banks."

The power and influence of the local chiefs is unchallenged. A traditional caste system, which divides Yapese society into three distinct divisions, remains strong. Virtually all of Yap is private property and there are strong traditional laws about passing from one village to another or even walking down the road. Essentially, you must seek permission to go anywhere!

And everybody here chews betel nut—men, women, and children! Betel nuts grow on trees and look kind of like green acorns. To eat them, you split them in half and cover them with dry coral lime. You then spread about half a cigarette on the nuts and then wrap that mixture in pepper leaves or some other natural wrapper. When you chew these, you get a mild high for about ten minutes. Chewing betel nut causes you to salivate excessively and something in saliva turns the betel juice a bright red color. And so, you'll see all these people on the island with their jaws bulging with betel nuts and spitting all over the place. Everywhere you go, there are red betel-nut stains!

Yesterday, I passed by an elementary school during lunch time and even the little kids were chewing betel nuts! My driver for the past two days told me that he goes through about twenty per day. He carries a special little black bag for his betel nuts, lime, cigarettes, and pepper leaves. He asked me if I wanted to try it, but I declined. I tried it in India several years ago but did not like it. Apparently, it is an acquired taste.

The Yapese caste system makes me wonder if East Indians came to Yap a long time ago. Indeed, the Indian colonization of Yap is a Yapese tradition, and there is a section of Yap called Tamil, which suggests a Dravidian influence. I drove through a low-caste village yesterday and took a few photos of the local inhabitants of that area.

The position of women in Yap is a subservient one, which also reminds me of India. Unlike Palau, Yap is a male-dominated society, and domestic violence directed at women is common.

So, there you have it. I only have a few hours left here, and I am going to get out of my hotel room to see what else there is to see and do here in my last Micronesian stop, at least this time around. The more that I think about it, however, the more I think that I might try some of that betel nut after all. Perhaps I am "going native"! So don't be surprised if the next time you see me, I just might have a bulging jaw!

THIS MUST BE PARADISE?: PORT MORESBY, PAPUA NEW GUINEA

October 19, 2008

Today I am in Port Moresby, the capital of Papua New Guinea, sitting in the beautiful lobby of my hotel, which is super nice and ultra comfortable. I don't know how much time I will have on the Internet, as my connection is slow and expensive, so I will try to write fast.

This is my first time in Papua New Guinea, or Papua Niugini, as the local folks say in their pidgin language. I have only been here for a couple of hours, but from the time that I arrived at the airport I have felt like I was in a place that I always wanted to be. The only reason I put a question mark after the word "paradise" in my title is because I am afraid it is almost too good to be true. I mean, if the hotel and the capital are this nice, my goodness, what must the rest of the country be like?

First of all, Papua New Guinea is a Black nation. Perhaps as many as ten million Black people live here. The weather is hot and humid, tropical. Sometimes it is hard to tell if you are in Africa or the Caribbean. And the people here are lovely, with a wide diversity of physical types, and the women are gorgeous. They give off an aura of being kind and gentle, humble, and a little shy. And (did I mention this?) they are Black!

Now I love the sisters and brothers in Australia, but, at the risk of being offensive, they have been so dispossessed of so much that they seem almost to be like fringe dwellers in their own country. But the difference in the energy levels between the people in these two places, Australia and Niugini, is like night and day. In Australia, White supremacy is clearly dominant, so being here in this vibrant island nation full of peaceful and proud Black people is like a breath of fresh air. I love it!

I mean, the people here are really wonderful, and they act like they actually care about you! On the one hand, many of them look just like people I have known all my life. Others look like no Black folks I have ever seen before. Does any of this make sense, or do I sound like the crazy man that I oftentimes think that I am?

Like I said, I am in a very nice hotel with an Internet connection. It is an expensive hotel, but from what I gather, all of the tourist hotels are expensive here, so I just have to deal with it. Besides, I am only here for two nights before I fly off to the island of New Britain and perhaps New Ireland.

Oh, and while I was sitting in the lobby admiring the view, I asked one of the sisters at the front desk one of the questions that you asked me to ask. I asked her: Where do the people here say that they come from? Her answer was short and direct. She said that they come from Africa! And she said it boldly and with an expression of pride on her face!

The vibe in northern Queensland, Australia, which is where I just came from, was vastly different. There, I asked a prominent brother how he felt about his people's origins. When I told him that I placed the Aboriginal people of Australia within the family of African people, he just smiled and nodded his head. When I later got the courage up to ask him how he would feel if I simply called the Australian Aboriginals "Africans," he told me that he would be deeply offended.

Now I don't believe that the sisters and brothers in Australia dislike Africa, but, as the brother told me, the tradition handed down from generation to generation of Aboriginals is simply that the Aboriginal people have always been in Australia, and that is that. Well, he was pretty firm about it, so there didn't seem like much I could say after that.

Anyway, I will spend more time on that matter in another note because the topic is nothing to be glossed over. I also want to share a conversation that I had two days ago with a Ugandan brother about the similarities between sisters and brothers in Australia and those in Africa. So at least I am talking with different folks about this, and I am asking a lot of questions.

But I am happy in Papua New Guinea, and in love with the world all over again. This nation occupies the eastern half of the large island of New Guinea, located about fifteen-hundred miles by air from Australia. In fact, New Guinea was once a territory of Australia. he western half of the island is called West Papua New Guinea. It has been occupied for some time by Indonesia, which seems to be waging a genocidal campaign against the Black inhabitants.

The word papua is a Malay word that means something like fuzzy hair Some people translate the word to mean slave. The Portuguese settlers, and later the Spanish, called the entire island New Guinea after their experience in Africa.

So far, being here is like my wonderful trips to and experiences in Fiji and Palau, only bigger and better. I guess there is something about the South Pacific that I have found nowhere else on earth. I will write more when I can, but at least you know that, at least for the present, Brother Runoko is safe and sound and most content.

MORE FROM PAPUA NEW GUINEA

October 20, 2008

I finished early today and these are probably my last or next to last notes from Port Moresby (but don't count on it!). It is now going on three o'clock in the afternoon, and it is hot and humid outside. It has to be about ninety degrees Fahrenheit outdoors. So I am back in my hotel room, pondering and wondering and writing and relaxing.

Today has been an easy day, and I spent quite a bit of time chatting with several members of the hotel staff. They are a most friendly and easy-going group, and it seemed like they were as interested in answering my questions as I was in asking them.

I just got to Port Moresby yesterday, but it seems like I have been here for a long time. African Americans are pretty rare here, I've been told. I know that I am the only one in my hotel. For all I know, I may be the only one—in the entire town, even! People are curious about me, but not intrusive, and I seem to fit right in, given my color and the fact that English is widely spoken here. I think the people that I have encountered tend to take me for a local—that is, until they hear my accent.

The literature that I read about Port Moresby says clearly that it is dangerous for tourists to walk about alone, and that one must be very careful where one goes. But hey, I grew up in South Central Los Angeles! As long as I can understand the language, I don't get frightened or rattled very easily. With a little common sense, I believe I can go just about anywhere here without fear of being bothered.

I went to the national museum today. A sign on the door said that the museum was officially closed until further notice and the door was locked, but the brother in charge had few qualms about me, as he put it, "taking a quick look around." He seemed really shocked but quite pleased when I gave him five dollars for his trouble, and when I left he bade me a fond farewell.

After a quick pass by the parliament building, I went to a supermarket to get my lunch. Shopping and going to the market here, like shopping just about anywhere else, is an education in itself. The coin of the realm here is the kina (pronounced keena) and I have spent quite a lot of them. I am, as Barack Obama might say, "spreading the wealth." (Nobody begs here, but I give very good tips.) By the way, everybody that I have talked to here is pulling for Brother Barack and hoping that he gets elected president. I have been asked my opinion about him quite a lot, and they are all happy when I tell them that I am a big Barack Obama supporter. For better or worse, I have found that Barack Obama represents the hopes and dreams, not just of the sisters and brothers in the United States, but of the entire African world. At least, that is my impression.

Like I said, the population on Papua New Guinea is very diverse. About five million live here, with the greatest concentration in the Central Highlands. The country is made up of nineteen provinces, and they all seem interesting. I wish that I had the time and money to visit all of them. I could stay here for a very long time.

Runoko Rashidi

You might hear from me later since I am scheduled to meet with a local anthropologist early tomorrow morning before my flight to Rabaul, the former capital of the Papua New Guinea island province of East New Britain. Rabaul was destroyed by falling ash from a volcanic eruption in 1994. From there, I will try to go, maybe by ferry, to the island of New Ireland, if only for a day. Then I will head to Buka Island and, hopefully, to the semi-autonomous province of Bougainville before returning to Aboriginal Australia and then to the United States late next week.

Despite how gentle the people of Papua New Guinea may seem today, from what I have read, head hunting and cannibalism were once common practices here, and apparently even a number of European missionaries were eaten on these islands until relatively recently—as little as about thirty years ago. My driver, who is a Christian, showed me the graves of some Christian missionaries whom he said were eaten about 110 years ago. He and I both thought it was all very funny, so I guess I am right in my own element! I should have some interesting stories to tell as long as I keep my head! So far, so good!

EAST NEW BRITAIN

October 23, 2008

Today I am in the small town of Kokopo in the eastern portion of East New Britain. I believe this area is part of the Bismarck Archipelago. To my southeast is the Solomon Sea, and northeast of me is the Bismarck Sea, all of which is part of the South Pacific Ocean. On a clear day, looking due north, you can see the island province of New Ireland. Tomorrow, I will fly to Buka Island in the province of North Solomons. (Does all of this sound very foreign to you? Well, imagine how it is for me?)

Everybody here but a few Australian and East Asian tourists is Black, and they are more friendly than the people of probably anywhere else I have ever been. Many of them have bright-blond kinky hair; several sport large, orange-reddish naturals or Afros. Most of the people are of medium stature with medium-brown skin complexion. Some of the people I've talked with here believe that their ancestors came originally to this island from Africa by way of New Ireland.

Most know next to nothing about contemporary America but have a favorable opinion of it because of the US involvement in the South Pacific during World War II. Hardly no one has ever met an African American before me, so I am a real novelty. A lot of people have told me that they think I am South African. I think most of the folks here think that I am just one of the locals. And the people here speak at least three languages, one of which typically is English, and some speak it better than I do.

Malaria is rampant here, and Papua New Guinea has the highest incidence of HIV in the Pacific. And almost everything on this island is very expensive because almost everything, from gasoline to food, is imported from Australia. I have eaten a lot of mangoes, but no real Melanesian food. And I have chewed no betel nut!

But it is very peaceful here too. I am staying in a pleasant bungalow in a garden on the beach. The ocean is about fifty yards from my balcony, and I have a wonderful view. You can also see from my balcony, maybe about thirty miles away, a smoking volcano that exploded about four years ago and which could blow again anytime. That is where I am!

Yesterday morning, I took a long walk along the beach. The people seemed very curious about me, but nobody bothered me. Instead, they looked at me and smiled and, if given a chance, they would strike up a conversation.

And, like in Yap, almost everybody here, even the children, chews betel nut. The only restrictions against chewing it are on planes and in my hotel!

Yesterday I ventured out into the countryside and ended up doing a short presentation at the St. Augustine middle school. The students, the teachers, and I each asked each other a lot of questions. Surprisingly, they didn't know much about African Americans, but that's OK, I told them. African Americans don't know a lot about them. nobody had ever heard of Barack Obama, Venus Williams, Michael Jordan, Oprah Winfrey, or Martin Luther King, Jr.. What I am strongly suggesting to Diasporan Africans in the Western Hemisphere is that there is an almost entirely unknown world of Black people here. I have had many incredible travel experiences, sisters and brothers, but this one, along with my visit with the Black Untouchables of India, may top them all.

I have now been to ninety-three different sovereign nations, along with a couple of colonies, and a couple of overseas territories. On one hand I feel terribly isolated, but I feel tremendously connected at the same time. The strangest thing is, though, that I rarely feel nervous. I don't know a soul here. I have no contacts. I did not organize this trip through a travel agency, and if anything happened to me, you would be the last one to know about it. Every now and then, this reality all dawns on me and that is when I get a little unsettled. But I am basically doing what I want to do, and my only complaint is the shortage of time and money to see more.

As someone once said, "We have nothing to fear but fear itself."

A couple of nights ago, when I was in one of those rare nervous moods, I had a dream in which my dear mother and my late friend Asa Hilliard appeared. I lost both of them last year. I did not clearly see my mother, but I could sense that she was there. And I never quite saw Asa, but I heard his wonderful laugh; and when I woke up, my confidence had been restored! It was as if they were telling me not to worry, that I should go on about my business, and that they were watching over me. It was all very reassuring.

And tomorrow I am going where the most jet-black people on earth dwell, so I guess the best is yet to come!

Runoko Rashidi

OF BLACKNESS AND BLONDNESS: POST-JOURNEY REFLECTIONS ON NUIGINI

November 1, 2008

Well, I have been back in the US for a few days now, and I am still excited about my recent journeys to Aboriginal Australia and Papua New Guinea, or Niugini, as the locals call it. Specifically, I visited northern Queensland, Australia; the Niugini capital of Port Moresby; the areas around Rabaul and Kokopo on East New Britain; and the islands of Buka and Bougainville in the North Solomons, a semi-autonomous province farthest away from the Niugini mainland. It was a fascinating odyssey.

The dominant group in East New Britain and in the neighboring province of New Ireland is the Tolai. My driver for the three days that I was in East New Britain was Tolai. Among other places, he took me to his village, where I met his children, his wife, his sister, his mother, and a lot of his neighbors.

The Tolai tend to be Black people with medium builds and medium brown skin. Many of them have naturally orange-colored and blondish hair, and in many cases, their hair is actually bright blond. I saw some of this in Fiji, but in East New Britain it was common. Several times I met the parents and grandparents of young blond children, and most of them were brown-skinned. I tried hard to get a good explanation for such incredibly contrasting hair and skin color combinations. I confess that I was fascinated by it because, for me, it demonstrated most clearly the vast range of Africoid phenotypes.

I was told that sometimes a person's hair color would grow darker with age, and sometimes it would not. I was assured over and over again, however, that it was all completely natural, and that it had nothing to do with the water or with chemicals or with bleach. It was the real deal.

I just found the whole thing intriguing. I took a lot of photos in East New Britain and would have taken a lot more but my natural shy disposition limited me from systematically sticking my camera in everybody's face. But it sure was tempting!

I had a lot of problems booking hotels in Niugini. Mostly, the hotel websites did not work, so you had to call the hotel directly, either from the United States or once you landed, to make reservations. On one of the islands that I wanted to visit, New Ireland, absolutely no hotel accommodations were available during the time that I wanted to go there, so I opted to stay instead on Buka Island. But even the Buka Island hotel was officially booked solid. I pleaded my case, however, and the hotel staff somehow found a room for me.

Now, there are only two hotels on the whole of Buka Island, and I stayed at the smallest of them. It was Black-owned, a little shabby, and badly in need of a paint job. There were no comfortable places to sit outside, and there were only one or two television channels available for viewing inside. What the hotel did feature were lots of flying insects and scores of tiny, little crawling ones (it is, after all, the tropics!). The hot water in my room never got very hot, and once or twice I thought that I saw something small and dark and furry scurry across the floor.

Still, all things considered, especially given the lack of room availability, it was not that bad. The airport transfer fees were cheap, the owners are really cool people, everybody was really nice to me, and everybody is Black. So if you ever visit Buka Island, I can recommend Hani's Inn.

A couple of other big factors to consider if you're interested in going to Buka Island are the intense heat and humidity and the lack of effective transportation. I must have walked about three or four blocks every day just to get to some concrete steps in front of the local post office. That was my spot on the island, and by the time I got there I would be soaking wet with perspiration. But it was a great place to sit and watch people, and usually a small crowd would gather there. The people would look at me with some curiosity but rarely would any of them say anything to me. I could tell that they were curious, but just too polite to do anything about it.

I was polite too, and, I thought, unpretentious. If anybody was sitting on the steps when I got there, I would always say "good morning" or "good afternoon" and ask if I could join them and pass the time of day. That would always break the ice. Typically, they would start asking me questions, always beginning with "where do you come from?" And I always told them that I was a historian of African origin living in the United States and visiting Niugini for the first time. Most folks were incredibly friendly and welcoming toward me, and I took some of my best photos ever.

ONE LAST LOOK BACK: NEW ZEALAND, BRIEFLY

April 14, 2011

Why I never wrote any essays on my travels to New Zealand I cannot recall. Maybe I didn't have my laptop then—that was before I started carrying my computer around with me all the time—or perhaps the Internet connection was poor. Or maybe it was because there are no major museums there, and the weather was cold and rainy. The whole trip was quite dull. Plus, I didn't see any Black people during my first stop there, in the city of Christ Church, which is modeled after an old English town.

In any event, I'll try to catch up with my reflections here. I do recall that the train ride from Christ Church to Wellington, my last stop in New Zealand, was rather nice. Wellington itself was a far more bustling city than Christ Church. It also has a good museum, but I could not take any photos there. Instead, I found a good book with several late nineteenth-century photos of the indigenous people of New Zealand, the Maori.

A few of the Maoris I encountered in Wellington clearly looked like Black people. I also met a woman, a Maori tour guide, who made it a point to tell me that New Zealanders were Polynesians who had nothing to do with Aboriginal Australia. I did not argue with her.

And so it goes, and so I went. On to the Caribbean, the Americas, and other parts of the Global African Diaspora!

Runoko Rashidi

PART V

IN SEARCH OF THE AFRICAN PRESENCE
IN THE CARIBBEAN ISLANDS
AND
IN CENTRAL, SOUTH, AND NORTH AMERICA

With an elder in the Chota Valley, Ecuador

Like most people, I looked forward to traveling to the Caribbean. To me, that part of the world represented the ultimate combination: beautiful islands and lots of beautiful Black people. Who could resist? Surely not Runoko Rashidi!

Although the Caribbean did not have the same appeal, in my view, that other regions with monuments and antiquities have, I knew that it was only a matter of time before I visited there for myself. After all, some of the great personalities and towering figures of the Pan-African experience have emerged from those islands. We all know their names: Nanny, Boukman, Toussaint, Dessalines, Luis Delgres, Paul Bogle, Arturo Schomburg, Marcus Garvey, Aimé Césaire, Frantz Fanon, Eric Williams, George G. M. James, Walter Rodney, Bob Marley, Peter Tosh, and Ivan Van Sertima—just to name a few. Yes, I had to go to the Caribbean!

My travels to Central America began with my first trips to Belize in 1994 and Costa Rica in 1996. And for that, I must thank Nzingha Barkley-Waite in Belize and Ligia Baldi and Arzinia and Barbara Richardson in Costa Rica for opening up the doors to Central America for me. In Panama, the mere mention of the name Claral Richards, sometimes called the "Nelson Mandela of Panama," cleared many a hurdle before me. In Honduras, Jose Angel Manaiza saw to all my needs. To these all, and their various networks of dedicated and committed Africans, I owe a great deal. I like both the people of Central America and the region, and have always felt at home there among them. The feelings must be mutual because I have been invited back a total of eight times now. And I intend to keep coming back!

Some of my greatest travel adventures in the Americas have been in South America. Brazil was my first South American destination. There, I found a vast and fascinating Black presence and experience. Indeed, Brazil has the largest African population in the Western Hemisphere, although most of us see little of it beyond the Black presence there in soccer, music, and carnival. The African people of Brazil have produced one of our greatest and most admired heros—Zumbi, the African freedom fighter of Palmares, the so-called African republic of colonial Brazil.

Although Brazil was the first South American country I visited, I probably had my first "early glory" in South America in Venezuela at the International Reunion of the African Family in Latin America. Now that was a conference! It was the first time that I met so many different groups of Black people. It was wonderful! Plus, I gave some of my finest presentations ever at that conference. It was truly a shining moment for me.

But possibly my most fascinating journeys to South America have been to the Andean countries of Peru, Ecuador, and Bolivia. These are places where Black people are still fighting for the simple acknowledgment from their wider societies that they are human beings; indeed, for recognition that they exist. In the Andean countries of South America, African people, like African people in so many other places, are impoverished and downtrodden. Yet, the Black communities there are vibrant and full of life. For me, they have been wonderful travel destinations filled with beautiful people.

In North America, I have traveled to Mexico, Canada, the United States, and Bermuda in the North Atlantic. Mexico has always held for me the irresistible allure of Antiquity—the Olmec, Maya, and Aztec being the Big Three in that region—and I have found an African connection to and presence in each. More recently, I have uncovered an extremely fascinating presence of Africans in contemporary Mexico, including the descendants of African people who were brought to Mexico as the result of enslavement. To me, because they probably number well into the millions and are discussed so little, these Africans represent one of the most interesting groups of Black people in the Western Hemisphere.

The Black presence in Canada has also had great appeal to me. In Canada, you will find a mix of the descendants of Black people such as those in Halifax, who have been living in that region for generations. They are complemented by African immigrants to Canada from the English Caribbean who live in the bigger cities of Ottawa and Toronto. They are augmented by Africans from the Continent, including a growing Somali community, who have migrated to Canada. In Montreal, for example, I met many Africans from Cameroon and Haiti. Vancouver, in southwestern Canada, also has its own mix of Africans. And then there are the not-at-all-uncommon sprinklings of Africans from the United States who live in various parts of Canada. Altogether, the blend of Black folk who live in the "True White North," as Canada is sometimes called, is truly lovely!

As for me, I live in the United States of America and, as we all know, the USA is a big country with many large and historic Black communities. I have included in this book my reflections on three of them: Philadelphia, the so-called "City of Brotherly Love," which is considered to have one of the highest homicide rates in the world for Black youth today; Beaumont, Texas—deep in the "heart" of Texas, a state in the American Southwest with its own unique Black history; and finally Jackson, Mississippi, a city with a racist past and defiant legacy.

We finish with my reflections on my travels to and in Bermuda, that jewel of an island located just nearby, in the North Atlantic. With its rich history, Caribbean-like climate, and inviting beaches, Bermuda is a place that has special significance for me. Find out why as you read ahead!

SEA-ING THE CARIBBEAN THROUGH AFRICAN EYES
JOURNEYS IN JAMAICA

Jamaica is a Caribbean island nation that I have visited three times now. Neither of my trips there was uneventful. Each provided me with more than a little bit of excitement and stress.

Beginning in 1998, having moved from Los Angeles to San Antonio, I decided that I would take an international research trip every year during the month of March. That first year then, I went to India. In 1999, I went to Thailand. I honestly don't recall where I went in 2000 and 2001, but in 2002, I went to Jamaica for the first time.

The September 11, 2001, attacks on the Twin Towers in New York City and the Pentagon building in Washington, DC, changed international travel dramatically. Increased security measures, fewer flights, modified check-in procedures, and numerous other additional hassles made international travel more stressful than ever. The fear that such attacks might happen again was also real, and I if they did, I did not want to find myself stuck somewhere far, far away with no way to get back to the US.

Nonetheless, I decided that I would still take my March trip the following year, but that I would visit an English-speaking country not too far from the States and not too terribly expensive. Jamaica seemed like a good choice and when a young Jamaican brother named Yekengale, with whom I had been interacting via the Internet for several months asked me if he could facilitate my trip to his home island, I agreed to go.

I had always wanted to go to Jamaica and always figured that I would go one day, especially given that I am African American and live in the United States and because the Caribbean is so close. I figured that it was only a matter of time before I got there. I consider all of the Caribbean islands to be important but three of them in particular, stood out early in my mind: Cuba, Jamaica, and Haiti. As it turned out, of these "Big Three," Jamaica was the first that I visited.

Why Jamaica? First, it has the largest, or certainly one of the largest, populations in the Caribbean. It also has a prominent history of insurrection and is the birthplace of one of the men that I honor the most—namely, Marcus Mosiah Garvey. How could I resist?

Jamaica: On the One

In March 2002, I flew into Kingston. Brother Yekengale, a Rastafarian and musician by trade, met me at the airport. First, he treated me to a sumptuous dinner at a local restaurant and then he drove me to his picturesque hillside residence in the Blue Mountains.

My first reaction to being in the Blue Mountains was that it stood in such stark contrast to the city of Kingston below. The city and the mountainous countryside were like two different planets. On one hand, Kingston was all grit and intensity, hustle and bustle. On the other, the Blue Mountains were cool and tranquil and serene. I loved the Blue Mountains. If only I had had good access to the Internet at Yekengale's house, I would have thought I was in an absolute paradise!

With Yekengale's assistance, I was able to see a lot of Jamaica in a short time. He arranged for me to be the guest of honor at a number of events on the island. He escorted me to the poor, hard-core, tough community of Trench Town and to the Maroon community of Nanny Town. He even arranged lecture dates for me in Port Antonio and Mandeville (one such talk, at the Seventh Day Adventist University in Mandeville, went particularly well).

Indeed, I was having an amazingly pleasant sojourn in Jamaica. Then events took a sudden turn for the worse. Unexpectedly, Brother Yekengale was offered a job and, rightfully so, he accepted it—after all, at the end of the day one still has to pay one's bills, right? So we had to make a choice: should he drastically limit his time with me or should I simply return to the US sooner than I had anticipated? I did not want to be a burden and was prepared to leave early, but Yekengale argued for me to stay. He claimed that historians like me did not get to Jamaican very often and he really needed me to stay and offer moral support to the other Pan-Africanist sisters and brothers on the island.

How could I resist? Yekengale had been so nice to me that it was hard to say no. He had hosted me and even paid for a good portion of my trip on his own. Another compelling reason for me to stay was that I had not yet visited the town of St. Ann's Bay, the birthplace of Marcus Garvey. I decided to stick with my original travel plans and continue my visit.

The question from that point on, however, was what would I do with myself? Brother Yekengale had to begin preparing immediately for his job, and I did not want to be in his way. So this is what we decided: Yekengale would drive me to Ocho Rios, where he would leave me, and where I would be interviewed by Rasta legend Mutabaruka on his Irie-FM radio program. Apparently, Yekengale told me, Brother Mutabaruka (Muta) not only knew of my work, but admired it and was (and remains) something of a fan of mine. After a few days, Yekengale and I agreed, I would journey back to Kingston.

Okay, I thought, this sounded like a plan. I would get to see another part of Jamaica and spend a minute or two with Muta. It would also give my good brother Yekengale some peace and quiet. So that was it.

The radio interview went well. Muta was satisfied and I was honored, either just before or just after the interview (I don't remember, I was in such awe), to visit not only Garvey's home town of St. Ann's Bay. I actually went to the house that Garvey was raised in. I loved it! I mean, I was in Marcus Garvey's childhood home! To me, it was like visiting the birthplace and residence of a saint!

After that, everything went sour. Yekengale left me in the hands of what we thought was a reputable tour company that was supposed to arrange for me to travel into the Cockpit Country of Jamaica. There, I was to visit the descendants of the Maroons of eastern Jamaica before heading back to Kingston. That turned out to be a disaster of a decision.

Now just briefly before I go on with this awful tale, let me tell you about the Maroons of Jamaica. In the early days of slavery in the Western Hemisphere, Maroon was the name given to those Africans who, like their counterparts throughout the Americas, refused to accept enslavement and who ran away into the hills or other isolated areas to establish their own hidden, separate communities. For many, myself included, the very name, Maroon, conjures up images of great African freedom fighters, but on my first visit to Jamaica's Maroon country, it meant another thing entirely.

To say that the so-called tour operators Yekengale left me with were dishonest and utterly without scruples is a tremendous abortion of reality and a gross understatement of the truth. They were scum! Once they got me to Maroon Town, which is way up in the mountains and miles from any city, they decided to kidnap me! That's right, they chained me to the front porch of a house and held me hostage while they phoned Yekengale to make ransom demands for my release!

Can you believe it?! Well, it is all true! I think they were just a gang of crackheads who somehow came to believe that I was some well-to-do historian from the United States that they could scare and rip off. And, by the way, apparently I increased in value during the course of the day because their demands jumped from three to ten to thirty-thousand dollars while they held me captive! I don't remember if this was in US or Jamaican currency, these deranged crooks were obviously out of their minds and out of their league.

Runoko Rashidi

When Yekengale learned of their demands, his answer was clear and firm: he told them that he would pay nothing! He ordered them to release me on the spot or he would have every police agency in Jamaica after them. Well, this standoff and hostage situation lasted for the better part a day before the crooks suddenly released me and fled. Wow!

Fortunately, I somehow managed to hold on to my most precious possessions—mainly, my nerve—but also my passport, my wallet, and my camera. I also managed, thank God, to keep my head! Shaken and lost, I made my way back to the roadway, found a taxi, and paid the cabbie an exorbitant fee to drive me all the way back to Kingston, where I checked into a room in the finest hotel in the city.

What an adventure it had all turned out to be! In Kingston, I found out that I had been the subject of an intense manhunt involving the tourist police of Jamaica and other police agencies. Apparently, Brother Yekengale—whose mother, it turned out, was the CEO of a Jamaican bauxite company and whose father was a Harvard University professor–had used his family's clout to launch a thorough search for me.

I was given one apology after the other by all the local authorities. A representative of the Jamaican tourist bureau came to the hotel personally to explain that what had happened to me was very rare and that, normally, tourists are perfectly safe in Jamaica. She even gave me a very nice gift and agreed to pay my hotel bill and provide me with a government driver for a personal tour around the region. Before she left, she assured me that the crooks who had held me hostage would soon be apprehended and brought to justice. She also admonished me to use only officially sanctioned tour companies in the future.

And that, again, was that. So much for my first trip to Jamaica!

Jamaica Redux

Now, the average person might imagine that I would have had enough of Jamaica, that I would have licked my wounds and returned to the US emotionally bruised and battered, vowing never again to set foot on Jamaican soil. But, I guess, that simply is not my style! I went back to the States—definitely scarred but basically unbowed. And when Brother Yekengale invited me to come back to Jamaica the following year to lecture, I quickly agreed.

My second trip to Jamaica was purely as a lecturer. I had made a vow and meant to keep it: there would be no great adventures this time! I gave two presentations at a university in Kingston and left right afterward.

Still, my first lecture turned out to be a challenge. It was to a group of about fifteen hundred schoolchildren who had been transported to the university from many parts of Jamaica just for the occasion. It was not one of my better talks. I wasn't in very good form, and I don't even remember what I talked about.

What I do remember, however, was how well disciplined and polite the children were. I had never seen anything quite like it. I didn't have to tell anyone to be quiet, to sit up, to pay attention, or to stop talking. The children's exemplary behavior left a lasting impression on me. It was wonderful!

I gave my second presentation that evening. The lecture took place in a big auditorium, but the audience was sparse. I don't believe I gave what could be called an electrifying presentation that evening, either; but the question-and-answer period and the aftermath were memorable.

A reporter in attendance at that session asked me two questions: First, what did I think about Robert Mugabe and the government seizure of White-owned farms in Zimbabwe? And what did I think about the recent Pan-African conference in Barbados, where all the White delegates were asked to leave by the majority of the Black delegates? In response to the first question, I told him that I had recently been in Zimbabwe and that I had visited some of the farms there and talked to the Africans who were now living on the confiscated land again. I told him that I supported the seizure move, but cautioned that proper and constant management was key to its success. Regarding the Barbados question, I informed the reporter that I did not attend the conference and that I understood the sentiment behind the Black delegates' request, but asking the Whites to leave, in my view, might have been a tactical error and an embarrassment to the conference hosts and the government of Barbados.

The next day, the Jamaica Gleaner newspaper reported that noted historian Runoko Rashidi, who was visiting Jamaica, had been in Barbados and had demanded that all White people leave the Pan-African conference there. It also claimed, falsely, that I had acted as an advocate for Robert Mugabe! When I contacted the paper and pointed out the inaccuracies in the story, the paper's editors printed a short, two-sentence retraction in the next day's edition that hardly anybody noticed but me.

And that was my second trip to Jamaica! Well, at least you cannot say that my trips there were dull and without incident!

TRAVELS IN THE SAN ANDRES ARCHIPELAGO[1]

December 2003

San Andres Island is part of a three-island archipelago located in the southwest Caribbean that also includes the sparsely populated Providence and Catalina islands. The people of the three islands are primarily English-speaking Africans who consider themselves "the Natives." They sometimes are called Raizals, a Spanish word, and believe that they are closely related to the Black populations on the Atlantic periphery of Nicaragua, Costa Rica, Panama, and Honduras. The balance of residents are mostly Spanish-speaking Colombians from the South American mainland, many of whom are also Black people. Officially, San Andres Island is a possession of Colombia, and the Natives think of Colombia as an occupying power.

---

1   Dedicated to Dr. John Henrik Clarke, a great Pan-Africanist.

The official population of San Andres is about 60,000; unofficially, however, the population numbers well over 100,000. These figures border on the incredible given that just fifty years ago the total population of this tiny island of only ten square miles was only about 5,000 people.

Here's what happened. Originally, the Natives, who today constitute about forty percent of the archipelago's entire population, were brought to San Andres by English Puritans early in the seventeenth century. The Whites were either absorbed into the dominant population or abandoned the archipelago altogether, and the Blacks were left to themselves. So, for the next two hundred years, the people of San Andres led an existence described as close to idyllic.

What was San Andres like before the 1950s? Just imagine a beautiful Caribbean island surrounded by crystal blue waters, swept by soft summer breezes, dominated by perpetually warm weather, somewhat isolated, with only a few thousand people engaged in fishing and agriculture. Everybody knew everybody, crime was almost nonexistent, the family unit was strong, good health abounded, there was no drug culture, and the living was easy. All of this changed dramatically beginning in 1953, when the island became the focus of attention for mainland Colombia and tens of thousands of Colombians, many of them poor and Black, flooded the island, looking for a better way of life and jobs associated with the rising tourist industry on the island.

Life on San Andres is surely not idyllic now. With the rise of tourism, an entire way of life has been disrupted. Shops and hotels are everywhere, but the Natives are all but shut out of the tourism industry. The unemployment rate among them is about fifty-five percent. The official language, including the language in the island's public schools, is now Spanish, though the Natives speak English, Spanish, and Creole. Even so, the literacy rate among the Natives is pretty nearly one hundred percent.

The population density is intense; even space to bury the dead is limited. Garbage is piling up, slums are cropping up, drug trafficking is thriving, urban violence is real, prostitution is prevalent, and AIDS is on the rise. The agricultural and fishing economy that dominated San Andres for scores of years has been relegated to a thing of the past.

Despite their high unemployment rates, I have never been around a group of people more hardworking and determined than the Natives of San Andres. They were warm, friendly, caring, and hospitable toward me, and I felt right at home among them. All seem to take immense pride in their island and are clinging desperately to their land. A few run small restaurants around the island. Many drive taxis, and some still confine themselves to farming and fishing. There is even a university on the island: Christian University, run by Dr. George May, a very distinguished Native clergyman.

The purpose of my visit to San Andres was to keynote the first Indigenous Native Congress, which took place from December 9 to December 12, 2002. The theme of the Congress was "Building a Firm Foundation for the Destiny of the Native People." I had met several of the principal organizers of the Congress, including Harry McNish and Juan Ramirez-Dawkins in Barlovento, Venezuela, at the Reunion of the African Family in Latin America, held in the Maroon communities there in the summer of 1999.

I made three big presentations in Barlovento. The San Andres Africans were duly impressed and invited me to come visit their island. They asked if I would come down and do some talks and help with their efforts to elevate the Native's self-esteem. I gladly accepted their invitation. I didn't know anyone who had been to San Andres before, yet on Monday afternoon, December 9—only six days after completing the historic "Looking at Southeast Asia Through African Eyes" educational and cultural tour, and only two days after speaking at the Association for the Study of Classical African Civilization's Western Regional Conference in Oakland, California—I touched down on beautiful San Andres Island. It took weeks of dealing with logistical issues and exchanging emails with the principal Congress coordinator, Dr. Juvencio Gallardo, to coordinate my trip, but I finally arrived.

To be honest with you, the first thing I noticed after arriving on San Andres were the gorgeous Black women there. I don't mind telling you that the sisters were fine! I mean, Black women are beautiful everywhere, but so many of these sisters were just stunning. Some of them looked remarkably similar to the images of the beautiful Black women of antiquity that I show in my slide presentations, particularly the images of the sisters of ancient Egypt. So, needless to say, things got off to a good start, and I was happy to be there.

And all of the Natives seemed like they were really pleased to see me. Folks made it clear that my comfort and pleasure were top priorities for them. This made a big difference because my trip to San Andres was not an easy one. I was already tired to begin with, and I had to catch a long midnight flight from Los Angeles to San Jose, Costa Rica. When I got to Costa Rica, I had to wait for several hours at the airport before catching a short flight from there to San Andres.

On Monday evening, December 9, the Congress convened at the landmark Native First Baptist Church. The church was built in 1834, and it has a lot of historical significance for the Native population. The first thing that I observed upon entering it was a large painting over the pulpit depicting an image of a White Jesus. Of course, when I began my talk that evening, that was the first thing I took aim at. That talk set the tone for the entire week—that this was going to be a take-no-prisoners affair, and that little quarter was going to be asked or given.

Well, things went pretty well that first night. The first full day of the Congress began the following morning, December 10, at the Sunrise Beach Hotel, which is the finest hotel in the city and located in the downtown area. This choice of venue, however, angered a lot of the Natives, who felt that the Congress should have been held in the heart of the Black community. Another point of contention was the translation of the English-speaking portions of the Congress into Spanish. There is such a general resentment on the part of the Natives toward the Spanish-speaking Colombians that many of them actually objected to a Spanish translation of the Congress proceedings.

One thing that became painfully apparent to me very early in my visit to San Andres was the great divide between the English-speaking Natives and the Spanish-speaking Africans from Colombia. As a strong believer in Pan-Africanism, this was very discouraging to me. I observed that there seemed to be very little empathy between the two groups. I also noted that the Colombian Africans seemed to have been, on the whole, a lot more mixed than the Natives. Or maybe it was just that the lighter-skinned Colombian Africans were the most visible and the ones that the Colombian government and the reigning elites prefer to employ in the hotels and restaurants. The Black San Andres residents from Colombia that I saw and met during my travels around the island looked more like unmixed Africans.

Runoko Rashidi

As for the Africans in mainland Colombia, I learned that they number about ten million people and make up about thirty-six percent of the total population. Concentrated in the Columbian regions of El Choco, Cali, and Cartagena, they are severely oppressed and caught between the paramilitary forces, the guerillas, and the government. So Colombia, much to no one's surprise, has another one of the world's struggling African populations and much work has to be done there.

The Congress opened with a prayer, followed by comments from coordinators Juvencio Gallardo and Juan Ramirez-Dawkins. Then, there were two panel discussions, entitled "Territoriality, Environment and Biodiversity" and "Alternative Economic Development." That evening I gave my first slide presentation and really lit the audience up with one of my finest talks.

It was obvious that much of the information I shared that evening was new to the people there, and they responded most enthusiastically. I took them around the world with me, showing them images of Africans as the "parent people" of humanity and of Africans as the mothers and fathers of civilization. I traced the widespread movements of African people around the world and added dimension to the global African community. Most of the people in the audience had never seen anything like that before, and the information was a big hit.

Probably the most controversial photo that I showed was an undated image of Jesus Christ painted by Coptic Christians in Egypt. I took the photo at the Coptic Museum in Cairo in 2001. I figured that if anybody had a right to claim that they knew what Jesus looked like, it was the Copts. The image reveals a particularly dark-complexioned Christ with a large Afro hairstyle. In other words, I said, the man is portrayed as "fair (meaning "black-")-skinned" with "good (meaning "woolly") hair," and he is surrounded by his equally Africoid disciples.

The photo is stunning, and I show it as often as possible in an effort to counteract the images of White Christs that bombard Black communities the world over. And it is so detailed, you can even see blood dripping from the palms of Christ's hands where he is nailed to the cross. I firmly believe that until we Africans begin to worship God in our own image, we will never make real progress as a people. If White people want to worship God as a White man, I told my audience, then by all means let them do so. But Black people worshipping White gods is a clear indication of where we stand in the world. The photo caused such a ruckus that I was actually asked by the island's Minister of Culture, a rather confused but hopefully well meaning young woman from Colombia who became extremely agitated by the photo, to provide documentation for my assertions.

Overall, however, my presentation went so well that I was immediately invited to come back to lecture in San Andres. The Secretary of Education, Dr. Ricardo Gordon May, turned out to be one of my biggest supporters. I was so excited afterward that I did not sleep a wink the entire evening.

On Wednesday, December 11, the Congress was dominated by two panel discussions, "Ethnic Education" and "Self-Determination and Human Rights." That afternoon, I did another very good slide presentation on the history and majesty of African women around the world. It went well, but I was so upset about my confrontation with the Minister of Culture that my attitude was not the best. That evening, at another large Black church, the Congress attendees celebrated San Andres Island's Christian University with a brilliant keynote address by Dr. Shelby Lewis, the only other African American to attend the Congress.

Thursday, December 12, marked the last day of the Congress. That day, about 150 Congress participants branched off into individual commissions and drafted proposals and solutions that were later read aloud to the entire body. The purpose of their efforts was to produce a manifesto that would serve as the basis for future such activities. Thursday was also the day on which attendees were feted by more of the island's performing artists. One of the bands that day played one of my favorite songs, "No Matter Where You Come From, You Are an African," by Peter Tosh.

After the reading of the commission reports and the band, I made my final presentation to the Congress, and it too was one of my best. As a matter of fact, I think it was one of the best presentations I have ever given—anywhere. I was emotional, the audience was primed, the images were excellent, and the Ancestors seemed to be very much with us. I showed that same image of the Black Christ from Coptic Egypt and some other ones to boot, and once again took the audience around the world as living witnesses to the greatness of African people. I do think that you would have been proud of me, and I do believe that the Ancestors who guided the Congress attendees and who watched over our actions were satisfied. It is indeed inspiring to provide positive historical information to people hungry and thirsty for knowledge of themselves.

My presentation that evening was followed by an outstanding address by Jonathan Adams of Barbados on the color of God and why it is important. His presentation was nothing short of awesome, and it closed out the Congress on a fitting note. We had come full circle, and we were duly moved. Afterward, it was time to reflect on what we had done, celebrate our achievements, rejoice with the family, and party a little bit.

Indeed, the Congress was a great success, and I have already placed it among my list of the greatest programs that I have ever participated in, but it was soon time for me to pack my bags and go. The next day, Friday, December 13, I was on the move again. I had a hearty breakfast at a beach resort in Colombia, an excellent lunch with some close friends on a hillside in Costa Rica, and a late night dinner and conversation with my family in Los Angeles. What a life!

I've since been invited back to San Andres Island, its archipelago neighbor Providence Island, and mainland Colombia. , but in closing, I must tell you that I have been thinking about John Henrik Clarke a lot lately. Indeed, on December 14, the evening after I returned from San Andres to Los Angeles, I was given the first annual John Henrik Clarke Afrikan Achievement Award and granted an honorary doctoral degree from the Amen-Ra Theological Seminary. It seemed like a more than appropriate way to cap off the week.

Now I place Dr. Clarke, Chancellor Williams, J. A. Rogers, John G. Jackson, and a few others in a special pantheon of pioneer African scholars that have paved the way for the reconstruction of our global African family. Dr. Clarke, as you know, was an ardent Pan-Africanist and a real role model. I miss him a great deal, and even though he is now an Ancestor, he remains a real inspiration for me. I do believe that he is watching over me and checking things out for me. I would like to believe that he is saying right about now, "Well done, Brother Runoko. You completed your San Andres assignment and got high marks. Now try and get a little rest. We have a lot more work for you."

Runoko Rashidi

SUNRISES AND SUNSETS IN ST. CROIX, UNITED STATES VIRGIN ISLANDS

November 25, 2005

It is just before sunset, and right now I am at my computer looking out onto the broad expanse of the Atlantic Ocean, which is right outside my hotel window, only about seventy feet away. I have been swimming in the ocean twice today, and the water is incredibly warm. St. Croix, along with St. Thomas and St. John, constitute the United States Virgin Islands. There are about 57,000 inhabitants here, the majority of them African. It is a rocky island and there is a large oil refinery here, but I picked St. Croix to visit because I understood it to be the least visited of the three islands, and that fits me just fine.

For once, I wanted largely just to get away for a few days, rest up, and do some writing, and I have four more nights and three more days here to do just that. I hope to see at least some of the place, however. I want to get on a sailboat, talk to some local folks, and find me some good Caribbean food. And if it does not cost too much, I may even try to get over to St. Thomas, birthplace of the great nineteenth-century scholar and activist Dr. Edward Wilmot Blyden. Dr. Blyden, along with Martin Robison Delany, Alexander Sergeivich Pushkin, and a few others, is one of my strongest "patron saints" as I travel throughout the globe in search of our African past and present.

Anyway, I was thinking that I would make St. Croix my sixtieth international travel destination, but I must have been really tired when I planned this trip because it did not dawn on me until I got on the plane that St. Croix is part of the United States Virgin Islands, so I'm really not leaving the country to visit there! What could I have been thinking? Oh, well, but the reason nation number sixty means so much to me is because the great African Jamaican journalist and historian, J. A. Rogers, visited sixty nations in his lifetime, and Rogers is the Ancestor that I am most often compared to in terms of my world travels. He was truly a great historian, photojournalist, and world traveler. To my ears, duplicating his achievements is flattery of the highest order.

For those of you not familiar with Rogers, you should know that he wrote such works as Nature Knows No Color Line, Sex and Race, World's Great Men of Color, 100 Amazing Facts About the Negro, The Real Facts About Ethiopia, and a number of other classics. Check him out! Rogers is imminently readable, and his works tend to have a lot of photographs to spice things up. Rogers' articles were carried by a number of African American newspapers, including the Pittsburgh Courier as well as the Chicago Defender, the Norfolk New Journal and Guide, and the New York Amsterdam News. So get hold of some of his published works and add them to your library. You will not regret it.

I am staying at a seaside resort, and there are a lot of White people here. Matter of fact, it seems that almost all of the Africans that I see are working here rather than staying here. They are pretty friendly, though.

As I said earlier, I came here to work on a new book, which I plan to title, All Sides of Earth: Essays on the Global African Presence. I expect that it is going to be a good one, and the great Dr. Asa Grant Hilliard III (also known as Nana Baffour Amankwatia II) has agreed to write the introduction, so how can I go wrong? Dr. Hilliard is one of our greatest living scholars, and it is just a delight to interact with him.

I now have the basis for fourteen chapters, and I hope to have the entire manuscript ready for the publishers of the book late next spring. I am going to include some photographs in that book that will pop your eyes out! To top that off, my publisher in France recently sent me a draft copy of the cover of the French edition of a book I wrote on the African presence in Asia. That book features a photo I took of the Bayon temple in Cambodia. It will be out soon and, as the young people say, it is "da bomb"! I am really pleased that both my publisher in France and my publisher in the United States are Africans! I like that a lot.

Okay, sisters and brothers, I better get back to work now. But first, I am going to watch the sun set over the beautiful island of St. Croix and count more of my many, many blessings.

MUSINGS ON ST. MAARTEN

July 2, 2007

My visit to St. Maarten was, I think, my eighth trip to the Caribbean and one of my better experiences. To be certain, my travels to this part of the world have been a mixture of sunshine and shadow—that is, I have had some great times and some terrible times in the Caribbean. I have given some of my best speeches there, including some outstanding talks in Georgetown, Guyana, San Andres Island, Colombia, and Trinidad. I've also had mostly positive and memorable experiences in Barbados, St. Vincent, St. Croix, and Puerto Rico. On the other hand, I also met a sister in Curacao who turned out to be a stalker, and I was once held hostage for a day in Jamaica's Cockpit Country.

Still, there are a number of Caribbean islands that I have yet to visit and long to see before too long. For one, I'd like to visit Cuba before Fidel Castro passes. I'd also like to get to Haiti because it has such a rich history, but apparently, conditions there are rather unstable just now. Then there are the islands of Dominica, the Dominican Republic, Granada, Tobago, Nevis and St. Kitts, St. Thomas, Guadeloupe, Martinique, and all the rest. They remain on my "go-to" list, but all things in time, I suppose.

St. Maarten, like most of the Caribbean, is a beautiful place. It is about forty square miles and divided into Dutch and French sides. The Dutch side is part of the Netherlands Antilles, and the French side is officially a part of France. Most of my time on this island was spent on the Dutch side. Officially, the population of St. Maarten totals about 40,000 people, most of whom are Africans, but a lot of White folks and Asians (Chinese, Arab, Indonesian, and Indian shopkeepers) live there also.

My invitation to visit St. Maarten came from Hondo Rami, one of the hardest-working, most industrious, and most modest Africans that I have ever had the pleasure to interact with. Brother Hondo is the director of the Imhotep Foundation. That organization was started in the 1990s and is named after the great African scribe, scientist, sage, architect, and all-around genius: of Egypt's Third Dynasty. Indeed, this African was so accomplished that, more than two thousand years after his death, it was popular for people around the world to pose the question, "Could there ever be another like Imhotep?" I wonder what future generations will say about you and me?

The Imhotep Foundation first distinguished itself by hosting the great Dr. Yosef A. A. ben-Jochannan on three occasions, twice in the 1990s and the last time in 2003. From what folks there told me, Dr. Ben was, not surprisingly, a big hit. So I had some large footprints to stand in, but the Imhotep Foundation had confidence in me and I tried not to disappoint.

I almost did not make it to St. Maarten. I left from Texas amidst a series of fierce and violent thunderstorms. Rarely had I seen so much rain before. Almost all the flights out of the airport had either been cancelled or were running late. My flight left on time, but it also left my luggage behind. Of course, I did not realize this until after I arrived. So when I arrived in St. Maarten late on a Friday night—even though the Imhotep Foundation had flown me there first-class—I was tired, grumpy, and without luggage.

It was raining when I arrived in St. Maarten, but the clouds soon cleared and revealed a beautiful full moon. I was met at the airport by Brother Hondo himself and, true to form, he was patient and accommodating. But I suppose that I really did not have much to complain about anyway. The Imhotep Foundation treated me like a celebrity. They gave me the finest room in one of the better hotels on the island, and soon I was dining on fresh seafood and drinking piña coladas. After a bit of rest, though, it was time to go to work.

Early Saturday morning, my hosts took me out for breakfast and a sightseeing tour of the French side of the island. The highlight was the African marketplace. After that, it was on to the local television station, where I recorded a two-part show covering a broad range of topics focusing on the quest for African liberation. The television program, called "Speaking About Everything," was later broadcast and turned out to be excellent.

Saturday evening I gave my lecture, which was in commemoration of Emancipation Day, celebrating the abolition of slavery in the Caribbean. The official starting time for the program was seven o'clock, but we did not begin until nearly eight. The locals called this "island time," and even though a lot of people came late, nobody left early.

I thought my lecture, which highlighted the African presence in Asia, was pretty good, but it was hard to tell because the audience of about fifty people seemed so quiet and subdued. I showed most of my best photos on the subject, starting with the African presence in the Arabian Peninsula and finishing with a flourish with the African presence in China and Japan. To my surprise, an animated question-and-answer period followed the presentation.

Afterward, the organizers told me that the reason the audience was so quiet was because hardly anybody in St. Maarten had ever heard anything about the African presence in Asia before. They seemed pleased with the results, however, and so I felt victorious. A few of us went out for food and drinks at an African-owned restaurant later that evening. Of course, I always feel good when we recycle African dollars, but the food was great, and I enjoyed the company and conversation.

Sunday morning, however, I woke up feeling a little depressed. I had been dreaming that I was running through an airport trying to catch a plane. Then I found out that the hotel at which I was staying was Indonesian-owned rather than African-owned. I thought to myself, do Africans control their own economies anywhere in the world?

But, I rarely stay depressed for very long, and my mood soon lifted. That afternoon, I was interviewed for an hour on the Conscious Lyrics radio show. The show was all about African emancipation, liberation, and reparations. Naturally, I had an opinion about just about everything, but I reminded myself to speak in generalities and I refrained from spelling out a specific program for the sisters and brothers in St. Maarten. I've always believed that the ultimate form of arrogance is to come from thousands of miles away from a place and attempt to tell the Africans there what they should be doing locally. Still, this did not stop me from generalizing about the African past, present, and future. After all, what is the role of the African historian anyway?

The rest of my Sunday afternoon in St. Maarten was spent dining, wining, strategizing, and sightseeing with members of the Imhotep Foundation staff. Indeed, things went so well from then on that we had already figured out a program for my return visit before I left the island. I intend to be accompanied by two other scholars on my next visit. I think St. Maarten, thanks largely to the Imhotep Foundation, will be more than ready for that.

Remember that I noted that I had been feeling, just for a short time, a little depressed about where Africans are as a people? And that my fits of depression, although they do come from time to time, seldom last very long? Well, I think the reason my bouts of depression fade away so quickly is because wherever I go, and this includes eight-two countries now, there are Africans just like you and me who are thinking the same thoughts and doing the same things to help set the stage for a new day for Africa and Africans.

In St. Maarten, this work is being carried out by the Imhotep Foundation. In Uganda, the Marcus Garvey Pan Afrikan Institute is leading the way. In Southern Sudan, that coalition is centered around the work of my tireless brother, Bankie F. Bankie. In Ghana, the African Study Center, headed by Maulana Hamid, is doing this. In the United States, we need only check out the work of the Pan-African Organizing Committee-USA, the Sankofa African Study Group, the UNIA & ACL, the d'Zert Club, the Karast Unity Center of Afrikan Spirituality, and so many others to find reason to be hopeful. In France, Consciousness Noir and all of the wonderful scholars and activists who are a part of that group are at the forefront of our efforts, and I have been blessed to interact with them there. Really, in every place that I have visited around the globe, some more than others—be it South Africa or Rwanda or Australia or Austria or the Netherlands or Germany or Canada, Honduras, Costa Rica, Trinidad, Panama, England, India, Brazil, Barbados, or St. Vincent—my experience has been the same: everywhere, there are always Africans working to free Africans. Everywhere within our hands, sisters and brothers, are the keys to a great victory. Or, as the great Marcus Mosiah Garvey expressed it, "Up you mighty race! You can accomplish what you will!"

So what is there to be depressed about?

Runoko Rashidi

STEPPIN' OUT IN SANTO DOMINGO AND MARCHING IN MARTINIQUE

May 26, 2008

Tomorrow night I begin my long journey to Peru and, from there, to Bolivia. Last week, I was in Martinique after a too-brief stay in the Dominican Republic. But before the memories of my visit to the Caribbean recede ever deeper into the recesses in the back of my mind, I just wanted to share a few observations with you. Don't worry, I won't be very long-winded about it. For some reason, I'm not feeling terribly inspired this morning, but I feel as if I just must write!

A Quick Shout-Out About Santo Domingo

I was only in the Dominican Republic for a total of about ten hours; the first time during a layover while en route to Martinique, and the second time upon returning from that island on my way back to the US. On the return trip, I didn't even leave the airport. On the first stop, however, I left the airport. The weather was warm and humid, so I caught a taxi, and asked the cabbie to drive me along the coast near the Caribbean Sea and from there to the downtown area of Santo Domingo. Downtown, I hung out in the lobby of one of the luxury hotels and tried to visit a local museum, which turned out to be closed. Then, it was back to the airport for the final leg of my flight to Martinique.

From what I saw in those few hours, I regretted that I did not have more time to spend there. It seemed as if at least sixty percent of the people in Santo Domingo were Black (Hamara Holt, who has been spending a great deal of time in the Dominican Republic lately, tells me that eighty percent of the population there is African). Generally, the people seemed very friendly, and they spoke just enough English for me to get by.

One thing that I noticed right off the bat was that so many of the younger women that I saw in Santo Domingo were dressed in such an incredibly sexy and provocative manner. I had never seen anything quite like it. The one person that I was able to talk with extensively about that explained to me that women who dressed like that were seeking attention, but that their doing so was just a normal part of modern Dominican society.

The woman also told me that racial distinctions in the Dominican Republic were very blurred. She claimed that she herself had somewhat diminished her own standing within her biological family by marrying an African American. Her family was not angry with her because her husband was African American, however; rather, they were upset because he was not Dominican.

Sainte-Anne, Martinique

From Santo Domingo, I flew to Martinique, which, along with Guadeloupe, is a former French colony in the Caribbean. In the mid-1940s (I think), led by Aimé Césaire, Martinique became a

French department—that is, it officially became a part of France. About 400,000 people, the vast majority of whom are African, live there now under French law. There is, however, a sizable segment of the population in Martinique that wants reparations and sovereignty.

My destination on the island was the city of Sainte-Anne, where a reservation had been made for me and for one of my good friends from the United States, Dr. David Horne, who was traveling with me, to stay at a somewhat isolated resort not far from the sea. Sainte-Anne stands out from the rest of the island because, taking their cue from the mayor, the people there insist on flying large red, black, and green flags everywhere. Indeed, I had been invited to Sainte-Anne to give two lecture presentations during the week commemorating the French abolition of slavery. The sponsoring organization, a reparations advocacy group known as MIR (I'm not quite sure what that translates to in English), was led by the mayor.

I gave two slide presentations in Sainte-Anne, both of which I thought were very good; and I engaged in two extensive question-and-answer forums with the audiences after both. Before the first lecture, I did a very animated radio interview. The radio show was hosted by this beautiful young African sister, who spoke both French and English. She translated all of my answers to her questions into French for her local listeners. She also seemed extremely grateful and very enthusiastic to have me as her guest, asking me over and over again about the importance of Africa, the issue of reparations, and my work on the African presence in Asia. I met her husband two days later, and he seemed like a really good person too.

After the radio interview, it was on to give my first presentation on the African presence in Asia, then to do two more interviews with a newspaper and a television station. Again, I had great translators at each event, and everything that morning went exceptionally well.

I will always remember my third night in Martinique as the Night of the Great March! Apparently, part of MIR's strategy for raising consciousness about reparations involves nightly marches with flags and banners, drums and torches. Now, marching, in and of itself, is not something that I look forward to, but my hosts made it quite clear to me that they expected me and Dr. Horne to show up and march. I tried to explain to them that I was only an historian, but they were not buying it! They put big pressure me and David to march with them, and so, march we did!

Well, we must have marched at least ten miles that night. We were joined by about a thousand other, mostly African, people. And I mean fast marching too, not slow steppin'! The pace was often tremendous. Indeed, I marched as fast as my feet could carry me, but it seemed like I was almost always at the back of the crowd! A few times, it felt like a death march. The humidity levels were high, and even though it was well past sunset, I was soon soaked with perspiration. Finally, when I was on what I thought were my last legs, the marchers gathered in a crowd by the sea and, in an emotional ceremony, raised a large red, black, and green flag. This was followed by speeches and music, dancing and food. We did not get back to the hotel until after three in the morning!

The next day, I gave my last presentation, this time on the subject of identity, which seemed to be a major issue in Martinique. During the question-and-answer period, a couple of sisters became very engrossed with the issue of African as opposed to non-African hairstyles. One of the sisters, who had served as one of my translators for a short while, turned out to be a relative (specifically, a grand niece) of the great Frantz Fanon. (Why I did not think to take a photograph with her, I do not know!)

I gave this last talk inside the ruins of what seemed to be an old stone slave dungeon. It turned out to be a most appropriate setting. Afterward, I was invited to dinner at the mayor's home, a beautiful house with a great view. I had some of the best rum there that I've ever tasted. I also tasted and ate sea urchin for the first time in my life, and it wasn't at all bad.

So here I am, back in Los Angeles, getting ready to head to Peru on a journey that could turn out to be historic. Sisters and brothers, a couple of weeks ago, a good friend of mine from Trinidad expressed concern to me via email about what he perceived as my "punishing schedule." Let me tell you, I get quite a few emails like that from people who seem genuinely concerned about me, about all my travel and whether I get enough rest, what I have to eat and drink, and so forth. But despite all the flying and hotels, and the different foods, time zones, and climate changes, I am holding up pretty good. To be sure, after the march in Martinique, I feel like I can handle just about anything. In fact, I feel like a man on a mission, marching into history! So let's get on with it, okay?

LOOKING BACK AT HAITI: TRIUMPHS AND TEARS

My visit to Haiti was one of richest cultural experiences I have had anywhere. Indeed, I considered it an honor to set foot on that island's hallowed soil. Who has not heard of the Haitian Revolution and the role and influence of Haiti on African liberation struggles throughout the Americas?

In November 2009, I landed at the airport in Port-au-Prince, capital of Haiti. This time, I told myself then, I would do things differently. I would not stay in a hotel; instead, I would stay with a family in a working-class district not far from the center of town. Well, in the house where I stayed, located in a hilly neighborhood, there was no electricity most of the time. There was never any running water, much less hot water. But my hosts were exceedingly nice and very knowledgeable about the history and culture of Haiti, so I had no complaints. And, as if to compensate for the lack of conveniences, the husband of the woman who initiated my visit made me some fruit juices that were just delicious.

Port-au-Prince is a crowded, densely populated, and congested city with a lot of slum areas, awful traffic, and major problems with trash disposal. Images of White Jesuses abounded. Still, I enjoyed myself. I liked the people, and I liked the energy of the city. I asked a lot of questions and listened carefully to the answers. I saw a lot and took a lot of pictures. I visited the National Museum and learned more about Toussaint L'ouverture and Jean-Jacques Dessalines and Henry Christophe—the great national heroes of Haiti.

I gave four presentations in Haiti. The first two were at art galleries with distinguished audiences. They were followed by interesting discussions. One Sunday afternoon, I was the guest of honor at a sumptuous banquet at the beautiful home of Max Beauvoir—regarded by many as Haiti's leading authority on vodoun or voodoo. Toward the latter part of the trip, I was driven to the Haitian district of Benet, where I climbed something between a steep hill and a small mountain. I also spent the night in a Maroon community there, where everyone was a practitioner of vodoun. A Rara (the popular Haitian music) band was there to greet and play for me, and scores of big-eyed children gathered around me in awe of my digital camera and the instant images it produced.

And, to make things even more exciting, I found a large tarantula crawling across the center of my bed that night. I tell you, between that climb, the band, the members of the Maroon community, their children, and the tarantula, I had a night that I will never forget!

On my last full day in Haiti, I did some early morning shopping. I purchased some attractive Haitian artifacts and keepsakes at very good prices before having a nice Haitian lunch. That afternoon, I gave the third of my four presentations. It was at the university in Port-au-Prince and was well attended by the students there. Believe me, the questions they asked at the end of my lecture were, well, brilliant. One student asked me if I was familiar with the nineteenth-century Haitian scholar Antonio Firmin. When I told him that I had heard of the man but was not really knowledgeable about his work, the student told me that he that I should be, for Firmin was "the Cheikh Anta Diop of the nineteenth century." I thanked the young man for sharing that information with me, and you can bet that I made a note to myself to look up what I could about Firmin once I got back to my hotel room.

A lot of people don't realize it, but I am a very shy, bashful, socially awkward person who borders on being, quite literally, almost antisocial. So when the students told me that they had organized a small reception for me after my lecture, my first inclination was try to get out of it. I soon realized that they had gone to so much effort that I decided to go along, but something happened there that I will never forget.

During the reception, two young male students came in. I am not sure if they were at the lecture itself. They were polite and sat down next to me. They asked me if I was an historian, and I replied that I was an historian and an anthropologist. They asked if they could talk to me. I told them yes, that they could talk to me about anything and ask me any question they liked. But the question they asked me, I must confess, dismayed, stunned, and thrilled me.

They asked: "Do you think that it was a mistake for us to break with the French and fight for our freedom?" I was shattered! Did they really doubt that all the sacrifices the African Haitians had made, all the deprivations that they had suffered in the name of freedom and liberation, had been worth it? The question caught me completely off-guard.

I mumbled some sort of muddled response, assuring them that the Haitian people's fight was our fight, and that they should be proud that they were in the vanguard of the struggle for Black liberation. But the two young men seemed unconvinced. It was one of the most poignant experiences in all of my global travels.

I did my last presentation in Haiti later that evening in a small, dilapidated room next to a cyber café in the same neighborhood where I was staying. The audience was a group of mostly poor Haitian teenagers and young adults. Afterward, several of them told me that they were trying to be role models in their communities and trying to make a difference. I was so proud of them, and talked with them well into the night.

Runoko Rashidi

I wonder now what has become of them all. About a month after I left Haiti, the island was struck by a massive earthquake and whole sections of communities around Port-au-Prince were simply swallowed up into the earth. I was told that the university where I spoke was turned into rubble, and that the neighborhood where I stayed, indeed the house in which I lived, were badly damaged. Such is the tragedy of Haiti!

CARIBBEAN SNAPSHOTS

If you include Guyana and San Andres Island, Colombia, I think that I have been to more than a dozen destinations in the Caribbean. I have written about most of these, but there are several others that I have not mentioned that merit description, if only briefly, to give a more complete picture of my time spent in this fascinating part of the African world. The following are just a few retrospective comments about those locations.

Trinidad

Trinidad was the first Caribbean island that I visited, in either 1999 or 2000. I did two lecture tours there. Both were organized by the Emancipation Support Committee and, on both occasions, I stayed in the home of two of the committee's members: Jean and Tracy Wilson.

I was so naïve about world traveling then—maybe "stupid" is a better word. I thought Trinidad was so small that I could literally walk around the entire island in a couple of hours or so, or at least in a day! Was I ever wrong—ask my aching feet!

Trinidad: the birthplace of Kwame Ture, one my great heroes! When I first encountered him in the early 1970s, I was a college freshman and he still went by the name Stokely Carmichael. Anyway, he gave a speech that so mesmerized me, it helped put me on the path to becoming an historian. Trinidad is also the birthplace of one of our greatest scholars: the great Garveyite, Tony Martin. In fact, Tony, for whom I have the ultimate respect, attended a presentation that I gave on my second Trinidad lecture tour, a couple of years after the first. After that presentation, he invited me and several other participants to his home for more discussion and interaction. He proved an excellent host.

Of course, one cannot ignore the divisions evident between the Africans and East Indians in Trinidad. It is not as bad as in Guyana, but it is still pretty bad. The East Indians in both Trinidad and Guyana are the descendants of laborers imported by England more than a century ago to work in the local sugarcane fields. There is a sharp and generally ugly division in both countries between them and the descendants of enslaved Africans. In both countries, however, the Indians have a distinct stranglehold on the local economies, and the resulting resentment towards them on the part of the Africans is deep.

Guyana

I have been to Guyana, like Trinidad, twice, both times at the behest of Rudy and Penda Guyan, two dedicated Pan-Africanists based at the time in Los Angeles. Given my travels and experiences in India, Rudy and Penda thought that it was important for me to go to Guyana, and they arranged for the African Development Cultural Association to sponsor my trips there.

Guyana, as you know, is actually on the mainland of South America, but culturally, it is very Caribbean. It is a large country with a small population, the greatest concentration of which is in the capital city of Georgetown. The division between Africans and East Indians there is very ugly. The Indians dominate the retail economies and the government. The Africans run the army and civil service.

Guyana is also the site of the earliest known African revolts in the Americas—namely, the Berbice Rebellion in the eighteenth century, led by a great leader named Kofi. It has also produced some of our greatest scholars, intellectuals, and activists, including George G. M. James, author of the classic work, Stolen Legacy; Ras Makonnen, author of the book, Pan-Africanism from Within; and Jan Carew and his protégé Ivan Van Sertima.

I love Jan Carew. He is one of the greatest men I have met. He is more than a scholar, he is a great human being—and, believe me, the two don't always go hand and hand. Among his books are Ghosts in the Blood and Fulcrums of Change. And Ivan Van Sertima, as a scholar, was probably my greatest mentor and teacher. I worked with him for more than twenty years. He was the author of They Came Before Columbus: The African Presence in Ancient America and the editor of the Journal of African Civilizations. He co-edited with me the book, The African Presence in Early Asia.

Guyana also produced Walter Rodney—the highly respected author of How Europe Underdeveloped Africa. One of Dr. Rodney's colleagues—the political activist Eusi Kwayana—also hails from Guyana.

Yes, Guyana has produced a number of African men of distinction. All praises!

Barbados

I have done two lecture tours in Barbados, an island nation that I have found to be one of more developed and the most touristy of my Caribbean destinations. Matter of fact, I was struck by all the evidence of White privilege that I have seen in Barbados. A few times, it even seemed as if I was in Florida, rather than the Caribbean.

Barbados is the birthplace of the African socialist activist Richard Benjamin Moore (1893-1978), who wrote the booklet, The Name "Negro": Its Origins and Evil Use. It is also the birthplace, considerably earlier, of Charles C. Seifort, a powerful African historian who was active in the Garvey movement. It also seems to me that I quietly celebrated a birthday on my first trip to Barbados.

Curaçao

Curaçao is a part of a group of islands called the Netherlands Antilles. A lot of cruise ships stop there; and there is a pretty good museum in Willemstad, the capital, which is a fairly attractive little city. My single trip to Curaçao was in 2003, I think. I gave three or four talks there over a three- or four-day period.

Generally, the people of Curaçao were pleasant to me, but, as a result of that trip and its aftermath, I have concluded—and I know that this is probably going to sound awful—that this little island is home to some of the most confused Black people I have ever encountered! There must be something odd in the water they drink. I say this because, on my visit to Curaçao, I was asked by a Black organization to give a talk to a Black audience on the theme, "Can Black Women Raise Black Boys?" Now just why the organizers thought that I was any more qualified than anyone else to address this question, I never figured out. But I was asked to talk about it, I had nothing better to do, and the organizers were willing to pay a nominal fee. So I agreed.

I addressed the theme, gave a presentation that I thought was pretty good, and felt rather pleased with myself afterward. However, for some people, it seems as if speaking about Black people with pride somehow translates into hating all White people. I say that because during the question-and-answer period, a light-complexioned Black woman in beautiful traditional African attire angrily denounced me, accusing me of forcing her to choose between her Black father and her White mother! I have never quite figured out her logic.

Curaçao is also the only place where I have ever missed a flight because the plane took off early. I have had a lot of flights leave late and some that never even took off at all, but in Curaçao the airline agents told me, after the fact, that it was more convenient for the flight to leave "somewhat early." They also told me, after apprising me that I would not be able to fly out for two more days, that it was "unfortunate" that I had "missed" my flight. Can you believe that?!

And, oh yes, Curaçao is also the place where I encountered my first and only stalker. I won't even go into that!! So, for all those reasons and more, Curaçao is, for me, a place that is better left alone. Goodbye!

St. Vincent

St. Vincent, which belongs to the Lesser Antilles chain of islands in the Caribbean Sea, is a pretty place that I found less touristy than some of my other Caribbean destinations. I only gave one presentation and stayed just one night, and that was at a nice, Black-owned, bed-and-breakfast hotel. But met several Black Caribs there, members of that bold, historic group of sisters and brothers who have a legacy of heroic resistance to enslavement.

Similar to my lectures in Jamaica and Curaçao, the question-and-answer period following my presentation in St. Vincent was more memorable than the presentation itself. On that occasion, a very attractive young Black couple came up to me and asked, "Have you forgiven White people for all the terrible, mean things that they have done to us?" My response was simply, "Most of them have not asked for forgiveness," to which the couple responded with yet another question: "Is it necessary for them to ask for forgiveness in order for us to forgive them?" I was too taken aback to even comment. Quietly, however, I thought, "These Black people have lost their minds!"

I have yet to be invited back to St. Vincent. My one regret is that my camera was broken while I was there.

MAKING CONNECTIONS IN AND TO CENTRAL AMERICA PASSAGE THROUGH PANAMA: FROM THE CANAL TO COLYN CITY[2]

Between the spring and summer of 2003, I had the good fortune of visiting Central America on four occasions. During that period, I went to Belize (twice), Guatemala, Honduras, Costa Rica (for the fifth time), and Panama. All of these countries have African communities. Most are generally depressed, however, and most often they are found along the Atlantic coastal periphery.

The indigenous name for Panama means abundance of fish, and I went to this land of abundance, located at the southern end of Central America (or the northern end of South America), for the first time at the end of August 2003. The Republic of Panama was my forty-first country, and I traveled there from Costa Rica, which I had already visited numerous times before. I had made up my mind on that last trip, however, that the next time I was invited to Costa Rica, I would visit one of the neighboring countries as well. And that meant either Nicaragua or Panama.

I had only a few days to spend in either place, but I was determined to take advantage of the opportunity and to make the best of it. I'm not sure what my thinking was at the time, but Panama soon became the desired country of destination. In making that decision, I surely must have been influenced by the knowledge that African people have a long history in Panama—a history that, by the way, begins well before the massive enslavement and deportation of Africans to the Americas.

According to Dr. Ivan Van Sertima, in his comprehensive and seminal work, Early America Revisited: "Vasco Nunez de Balboa, 25 September 1513, coming down the slopes of Quarequa, which is near Darien (now called Panama) saw two tall black men who had been captured by the Native Americans." Further, in his classic work They Came Before Columbus, Ivan Van Sertima cites Peter Martyr, who writes that, "Negroes had been shipwrecked in that area and had taken refuge in the mountains." Martyr refers to those refugees as "Ethiopian pirates."

Lopez de Gomara, according to Van Sertima, describes the Blacks that the Europeans sighted for the first time in Panama in this way: "These people are identical with the Negroes we have seen in Guinea." Van Sertima also cites De Bourbourg, who reported that there were two peoples indigenous to Panama: "the Mandinga (black skin) and the Tule (red skin)."

This knowledge was very important to me because I have long argued, along with many others, that the history and presence of African people, even in the Western Hemisphere, should not and cannot be traced solely to enslavement and its aftermath, and that assessments of the enslavement

---

2   Dedicated to Claral Richards.

period need to be revised as a result. It should come as no surprise that the great J. A. Rogers has done an excellent job of this and that he provides us with a sense of historical continuity as well. Allow me to quote at length from the second volume of his classic work, Sex and Race, to drive home this point:

> "Negroes, thirty of them, not only were with Balboa at his discovery of Panama and the Pacific Ocean in 1513, one of their number being a black nobleman, Nuflo de Olano, but there is the clearest possible evidence that they had been living in that region before Columbus, and were strong enough to make successful war on the Indians.
>
> Later, the Spaniards brought in slaves in such great numbers, and they throve so well in the hot climate that Panama has remained chiefly a Negro country to this day, though modified somewhat by white immigration since the building of the Canal began in 1878. Under the Spaniards, the white strain was quickly absorbed by the Negroes, who were often rebellious, and joined the pirates. There is the romantic story of King Bayano, an escaped slave, as told by Pedro de Aguado, a sixteenth century historian. Taking to the mountains with a number of other slaves, Bayano set up a kingdom of his own, from where he descended on the pack-trains of the Spaniards, capturing a great quantity of gold, silver, and precious stones. It was only with the greatest difficulty that the Spanish commander, Pedro de Orsua, succeeded in defeating him and his valiant band. Finally captured, Bayano was taken before the Spanish viceroy, who not only received him with honors for his bravery and resourcefulness but sent him a free man to Spain where he lived in luxury from the loot he had captured."

Given this historical background, coupled with the knowledge that English is widely spoken in Panama, I more or less made up my mind that Panama was the place to go. My decision was buttressed by the role played by my initial Panamanian contacts, who were absolutely instrumental to my success there. The most important of these contacts were Sonia Ford, who facilitated my hotel arrangements and opened the first door for me there; and Brother Claral Richards, described by many of his fellow Panamanians as the "Nelson Mandela of Panama." Through these two Africans, a whole other world of contacts opened up, most notably with Ricardo Richards and Arturo Branch. Between these men and women, I had a profound traveling and learning experience, I never really got lonely, and I always felt connected. It makes a huge difference to your peace of mind while you are traveling to know that somebody at your destination is looking out for you.

In all my conversations with these brothers, I was assured that Panama was at least sixty percent African but that only about fifteen percent of the Blacks there embraced their African identity. They told me that a typical brother or sister from Panama might say something like, "Well, my grandmother was Black, but I am just Brown." Or they might say, "Well, although my Ancestors came from Africa, I am now just a Panamanian." This level of argument and denial sounded so very, very familiar to me, and it reminded me how deeply African people all over the world are taught to hate themselves.

Claral, Ricardo, and Arturo also gave me some inkling of understanding about the division between the Spanish- and English-speaking Africans in Panama. Of the two communities, they

A Mochica figure in Peru

Runoko Rashidi

An Africoid mask in Western Canada, date unknown

A bronze statue of Toussaint L'Ouverture in Port-au-Prince, Haiti

My Global Journeys in Search of the African Presence

Machu Picchu, Peru

Runoko Rashidi

A sacred lake near Cuzco, Peru

At an archaeological site near Cuzco, Peru

My Global Journeys in Search of the African Presence

Brazilian historian Abdias do Nascimento

With an elder in
the Yungas, Bolivia

With the Maroons
in Haiti

With a businesswoman
in El Carmen, Peru

My Global Journeys in Search of the African Presence

Children in El Carmen, Peru

A young Garifuna girl in Sambo Creek, Honduras

Children in Costa Chica, Mexico

My Global Journeys in Search of the African Presence

Schoolchildren in Hamilton, Bermuda

Runoko Rashidi

informed me, the English-speaking Africans, many of whom are the descendants of the builders of the Panama Canal, seem to have it a little easier than their Spanish–speaking peers. It should not surprise you to know that there is a pronounced degree of friction between the two groups, much of it rooted in class distinctions. Will we never learn?

To my delight, however, I found that Africans were much more visible on the streets of Panama City than in Costa Rica's capital of San Jose. In San Jose, I saw only a smattering of African faces, but in Panama City, Black people seemed to be in the majority, and it was rather exhilarating just to see them there—and especially (of course!) to see all the beautiful African women! Unfortunately, there seemed to be very few Africans working in the banks, restaurants, museums (even the African museum!), airport, and office buildings in Panama.

On another level, for those of you into sports, especially American baseball, Panama has produced such greats as Rod Carew, Roberto Kelly, and the current New York Yankee sensation, Mariano Rivera. My Panamanian brothers told me that Rivera, to his credit, does a lot for the downtrodden community that produced him. They also told me about efforts underway to name the national stadium after baseball Hall of Famer Rod Carew, but it seems that Carew is just, they claimed, "a little too Black" for the deal to be sealed. Beyond the world of sports, they informed me that the noted African scholar, Dr. Kenneth Clark, is also Panamanian.

April 4, 2004

Uncovering the African-Panamanian Connection

On my first full day in Panama, Ricardo drove me around a great deal. Even before going to the Panama Canal, which Panamanians generally regard with great pride, he took me to the Afro-Antillean Museum, which chronicles the lives of the African builders of the Panama Canal, who were mostly Africans from the English-speaking islands of the Caribbean. Following our museum tour, Ricardo and I traveled across town to attend two meetings of local African activists. We also visited portions of the Pacific side of the canal.

The first real highlight of that first day in Panama was a journey to the town of Portebelo, which gave me a chance to really savor my excursion from Panama's Pacific side through the rain forest and Maroon country and on to the magnificent life-sized image of the Black Christ in the church in Portebelo. The Christ figure is actually what I call a "deep biscuit brown" in complexion. He wears a crown of thorns and a purple robe, and is carrying a cross. The church is large and regularly visited by devout pilgrims journeying from all over Panama.

One of the additional attractions of Portebelo for me was because it located in Maroon country, the Maroons being those Africans who, like Bayano, refused to accept enslavement and established their own independent communities. And as if their ethnic identity needed any additional clarity, let me point out from the git-go that these sisters and brothers proudly call themselves "Congos"!

From Portebelo, we journeyed to Colón (also called Colón City), a largely African city, located on Panama's Atlantic coast on the shores of the Caribbean Sea. Colón is rather crowded with automobiles and densely populated. Most of the people there are Spanish-speaking. All of the travel books that I read on Panama depicted Colón in a deplorable light and essentially advised visitors to stay away from the place, if at all possible. Here is what one travel guide said about it:

> *"Children run about in rags, and the city's largely black population lives in rotten buildings. With the exception of one seaside residential neighborhood where some fine houses are tucked away behind high walls and security systems, the city is a slum. If you walk its streets, even in the middle of the day, expect to get mugged. It really is that bad. Walking in this city is very dangerous. A white tourist leaving a bank here will likely be mugged. If you have something to mail, send it from another city."*

I really resented this kind of biased writing, but after reading it and realizing that Colón was a major African population center, I determined early on that it was someplace that I would have to visit or my trip to Panama would not be complete. It also seemed special to me that I could begin my day on the Pacific and spend the late afternoon and early evening on the Atlantic.

Back in Panama City, Ricardo and I capped off the day in an African-owned restaurant, feasting on some of the tastiest fish I have ever had. I'm glad that I went to Colón City. I found it to be a vibrant and pulsing and fascinating place, full of Black people and rich in culture, and I walked its streets unafraid. It is true that there is a rampant material poverty in Colón, but strangely enough, the most downtrodden and foreboding-looking section of the city is referred to locally as "the Vatican." I do not have the words to fully describe Colón City, however. I suppose that you will just have to see it for yourself, but my first day in the Republic of Panama is a day that I will always remember.

The next day, at Claral Richards' request, a brother named Arturo Branch took time out of his busy schedule to provide me with a personalized tour of Panama City. Like Ricardo Richards the day before, Brother Arturo introduced me to a great many of the local residents and social activists, including a number of aspiring politicians and businesspeople. I say "aspiring" politicians because I was told by several people that although Panama is sixty percent African, it had no Black elected officials. I found this shocking and very hard to believe, but that was what I was told. Elections were coming up soon, however, and two or three Africans were on the ballot. The major question was whether or not the local sisters and brothers would come out and vote. No one seemed to be very confident about the election outcomes, but the potential was great.

With Brother Arturo, I traveled through several of Panama City's African neighborhoods, many of them real slum areas mired in great poverty. One area was so bad that it was referred to as the "Pig House," and Arturo told me that many of the residents there literally dreaded venturing outside their doors for fear of being the victims of violent acts. The Pig House area in Panama City and the Vatican in Colón City were about the most depressed communities that I have ever seen in the Western Hemisphere. They made me wonder what some of the African communities of Brazil, Columbia, and Haiti must be like.

The neighborhoods that Brother Arturo escorted me through were populated by both English-speaking Africans and Spanish speaking African-Panamanians as well as African-Colombians and African-Dominicans—with each group being tucked away in their own semi-separate enclaves. I found the whole separation thing utterly fascinating, and began to view the entire day as akin to an anthropological field study, including the part of it that I spent later that day in the section of Panama City that had been most devastated during the 1989 US invasion.

My Last Day in Panama

I began my last full day in Panama with a visit to the Pre-Columbian Museum and, just as I suspected (and just as I had noticed in the National Museum of Costa Rica), there was little to be found in the way of Africoid images, statues, and figurines there. Nevertheless, I made it a point to visit this museum in hopes of discovering an African treasure trove. At least, I am happy to say, my tour guide in the museum was a sister, but whether she actually saw herself as one is a very different matter.

Thanks to Ricardo and Arturo, I was able to give a slide presentation on the global African presence on my last evening in Panama City, making Panama the twenty-eighth country in which I have lectured thus far. Although the presentation was organized on very short notice, it went very well. The gathering was held at a local school, and a broad cross-section of Africans attended, ranging from university professors to business people to Rastafarians, elders, and young people. The audience seemed very impressed by my overview, and I was able to gather even more information from the attendees in a wide-ranging discussion after my presentation. Several of the attendees took it upon themselves in those conversations to fill me in more completely about African life in Panama from health care to the impact of Marcus Garvey.

Overall, I really enjoyed Panama. I liked the people, learned a lot, had some fun, did some educating, and built some bonds. I also felt a bit melancholy as I left the place. My great regret is that I was only there for such a short time. I trust that my next visit will be of considerably longer duration. Perhaps we can go together!

YOU GOTTA BELIZE!

August 27, 2006

My travels to Belize were among my important early journeys. They began in late spring 1994, when I gave a series of lectures there with the great African Jamaican poet, Mutabaruka, on Africa Day. I have been to Belize about five times now, and every one of those visits has been a good one. Now, a good visit to me often has its basis in the people that I meet "on the ground"—that is, in the country that I choose to hang out in. And since we are talking about Belize, I have to begin by mentioning the Queen of Belize: Nzingha Barkley-Waite.

I worked with Nzingha during my lecture tour on my first visit to Belize in the early 1990s, and she has organized programs for me there on all my subsequent visits. The last such program, however, was really historic. It centered around a big conference at which Molefi Asante and I were the keynote speakers.

That conference, which I guess you could call "African-centered" in nature, took place over the course of a weekend at a hotel in Belize City. Its proceedings were broadcast throughout the entire country too, I believe. Anyway, each of the presenters was in top form and gave everyone an earful of information.

The conference was well attended by everyone from politicians and judges to university professors, Rastafarians, and community activists. Sister Nzingha seemed to know at least half the people in Belize. She is a hard-working political and community activist and, more often than not, if she makes a promise to do something, it is pretty much a guarantee.

Belize is a small country, I think the smallest country in Central America. It used to be known as British Honduras. They speak English in Belize but also, increasingly, more and more Spanish. This should not come as a surprise. There is a huge influx of folks coming into Belize from neighboring countries like Guatemala and Honduras, and Mexico is her big neighbor to the north. The economy is not the best, however, and many Belizeans have left their homeland for the United States.

On the east, Belize is bordered by the Caribbean Sea, and a strong English Caribbean cultural influence permeates the island. The one really big city, comparatively speaking, in Belize is Belize City, but the official capital is the smaller and, for me at least, much duller city of Belmopan.

Besides its African population, which may be a small majority, Belize has a substantial Mayan population. Indeed, one of the nicest parts about travel to Belize is the opportunity to travel to some of the Mayan archaeological sites. Both the Africans and Mayans have a long and relatively unexplored history.

Over the past few years, I have managed to photograph Mayan artifacts from Mexico, Honduras, Guatemala, and Belize that reflect the African presence in the pre-Columbian Americas of the Maya. I took one such photo in the National Museum in Belize City of a beautifully painted Mayan bowl about 1,500 years old. On the outer surface of the bowl are painted several vivid depictions of Black men in leopard or jaguar skins going into battle. For any African-centered visit to Belize, the National Museum is an essential stop.

The Honorable Marcus Mosiah Garvey used to be big in Belize. There were Universal Negro Improvement Association and African Communities Leagues chapters there, and I believe that a building that used to be one of the UNIA & ACL's historic Liberty Halls is still standing.

There seem to be at least two distinct African populations in Belize: the Creoles and the Garinagu (singular: Garifuna). The Creole population is the larger of the two. Those sisters and brothers are the descendants of Africans who were enslaved by the English, and they live largely on the Atlantic coastal periphery of the country. The other, smaller group of African people in Belize is the Garinagu, although some suggest that Garifuna is actually the language members of that group speak rather than their name. In Belize, they are concentrated in the coastal towns of Dangriga, Hopkins, and Punta Gorda. There is at least one Garinagu community in Guatemala, but the bulk of them reside in (Spanish) Honduras. In addition to their own language, the Garinagu have their own religion, their own cuisine, and their own music. Indeed, they are a fascinating group of people who deserve a lot more study.

Runoko Rashidi

One thing that struck me about Belize, and something that strikes me everywhere I go, is that the retail economy of the African community is almost never controlled by Africans. There seems to be few exceptions to this rule, even in Africa itself. Everybody, it seems, takes our money but us! Or should I say, we give everybody our money! In Belize, it seems to be the Chinese and East Indians who dominate economically.

But overall, I like Belize. It is a relaxed and easy-going place with a beautiful coastline and a rugged interior. It is a small and relatively poor country, but one with a rich African history and culture. And a lot of good people are doing some good things in Belize, trying to make a difference. In addition to Sister Nzingha, there is an excellent African-centered activist newspaper coming of out Belize called Amandla. And there is a brother named Bert Tucker who is coordinating a wonderful project with mahogany trees. And some of the members of the Garifuna community in Belize are engaged in some really progressive projects.

CENTRAL AMERICAN SNAPSHOTS

Costa Rica

To this day, I am not sure why I have not written more about my travels to Costa Rica. It could have been that I was just having too much fun. I like Costa Rica, and I've always enjoyed myself there.

On my first trip to Costa Rica, I was invited to speak at a conference in the capital of San Jose. Among the other speakers there was my "elder brother" and now Ancestor, the great Dr. Asa Hilliard III. As always, Asa's presentation was superb. He had such tremendous wisdom and love for African people. He also had such a winning smile and a great, big laugh. I miss him a lot.

The African American journalist Nate Clay also spoke at the conference, on the very important topic of anti-Black racism in the Arab world. As for me, I can't even recall what topic I addressed or even whether my presentation was any good. What I do remember is that I got a chance to spend quality time with none other than John Henrik Clarke—the most noteworthy of all the conference participants.

Dr. Clarke and I walked and talked together for hours, and I helped to look after him since he was, by then, blind and in failing health. The conference was, after all, only about two years before his death. I regard the time I spent with him in Costa Rica as one of the great highlights of my life. I loved John Henrik Clarke, and I still do.

Imagine being in Costa Rica with two of your greatest heroes and icons. In my case, it was Asa Hilliard and John Henrik Clarke, and I was in an historian's heaven! Apparently, I must have done something right because a year or so later, both Asa and I were invited back to Costa Rica to speak on the occasion of what is called Black Day in that nation, in honor of Costa Rica's magnificent and enduring African presence and culture.

On a couple of occasions during that second trip, I was driven to the Atlantic coastal city of Limón. That area, which is largely impoverished now, was once home to a big following of Garveyites. It was there that I met Sister Harmara Holt, a wonderful woman from New York City, who has been instrumental in a number of my travel and lecturing successes since. I also had the good fortune on that trip, during a tour organized by the African Puerto Rican scholar Dr. Georgiana Falu, to review early efforts to translate and publish, in cheap Spanish-language editions, the late great George G. M. James' book Stolen Legacy and (I think) two works by Yosef ben-Jochannan. It was all very encouraging.

No wonder I have returned to Limón and its environs now on three occasions—to lecture and just have fun!

Guatemala

In April 2003, I took a motor coach from Belize City, Belize, to Flores, Guatemala, along with my good friend and colleague Nzingha Barkley-Waite. Flores is only about an hour's drive from the ancient Mayan city of Tikal. Right after we got off the bus, we found an inexpensive and fairly decent hotel, and I began preparing for the next day's early-morning journey deep into the jungles of Guatemala.

One cannot help but admire the industry of the Maya. I had already visited the Mayan ruins of Altun Ha in Belize and Chichen Itza in Mexico, but I was very excited about going to Tikal. Tikal, I had been told, had a unique character all its own, and everyone assured me that it would be worth all of the effort to get there. Sad to say, I could find nothing overtly African about Tikal. The pyramids were nice, however, and I would not mind returning one day. And when I do, another part of Guatemala that I would like to visit is the city of Esquipulas, to see the statue of the Black Christ that is so important to the Indigenous Americans of the region.

Honduras

After that first trip to Guatemala, I visited Honduras, where, through an African American woman named Diedre Fair, I was introduced to the brother who would be my host in Honduras: Jose Angel Manaiza. Mr. Manaiza was a businessman and activist in the local Garinagu community. Garinagu is the plural form of Garifuna, which is the name given to a person of African, Arawak, and Carib ancestry in Central America's Atlantic Coastal periphery. Also known as Black Caribs, the Garinagu are 250,000 strong in Honduras. I had previously visited other Garinagu communities like Dangriga, Stann Creek, and Punta Gorda in Belize, but the purpose of my visit to Honduras was to journey to the Garinagu heartland.

The Garinagu are Black people of mysterious origins who have never quite blended into the Central American countries in which they reside—namely, Belize, Guatemala, and Honduras. Some of them, or so they believe, came to America before Columbus. They have their own distinctive language (Garifuna), cuisine, and religion. If they were enslaved at all by the European invaders in their land, it was only for a short time.

Mr. Manaiza coordinated his entire schedule around mine during my stay, and he personally drove me all the way to Copan Ruinas to visit that historic Mayan city. (By the way, I think Copan Ruinas is the most overhyped archaeological site that I have ever visited. I didn't see anything that really impressed me.) He also arranged for me to tour a number of Garinagu communities and to lecture in a Garinagu town called Sambo Creek. There, I spoke before a Garinagu women's group. The lecture was translated into Garifuna, and the audience must have liked what I said because they did a special dance for me after the lecture that made me feel as if I had been transported straight to Africa.

For my part, however, I thought that my talk was one of the worst presentations that I have ever given. I don't know, perhaps it was all the beer that I had consumed that day, but the audience had drunk a lot of beer that day too. In any event, they seemed to think that my oratorical skills were exceptionally impressive. I even got a couple of marriage proposals!

AMERICA DEL SUR: IN SEARCH OF AFRICA IN SOUTH AMERICA SHINING HOURS IN VENEZUELA: THE INTERNATIONAL REUNION OF THE AFRICAN FAMILY IN LATIN AMERICA

Before 1999, I had never been to Venezuela, and I didn't think I would ever go there, either. I had heard that a rising leader there, Hugo Chavez, the current president of Venezuela, was a man of African descent and that there were other Africans there. And an organization based in Washington, DC, called the Organization of Africans in the Americas was putting together a conference with an impressive title, "The International Reunion of the African Family in Latin America," that was to be held in Venezuela. That sounded pretty good to me. Plus, that organization had invited me to be the major keynote speaker.

So off I went!

Now the conference was held in the city of San José de Barlovento, located right on the coast in the Venezuelan state of Miranda. San José de Barlovento is about a hundred miles east of the capital city of Caracas, and it is indeed a beautiful town. I saw some of the most exquisite sunsets there that I've ever seen. It just seemed like the sky merged with the ocean in a series of shades of blue. It was magnificent!

But the major reason the conference was held there was because it is an area where the Venezuelan Africans known as Maroons had established themselves. And the Maroons, as you know, never accepted enslavement.

The theme of the Reunion was "People with an Ancient Past Working in the Present for a Glorious Future." Scholars and non-scholars alike attended. Some were educators, some were community and political activists, some were religious leaders, and others were artists and musicians. The conference brought together African people from as far away as Ethiopia, but the vast majority of the attendees were Africans from the Western Hemisphere. From North America came African people from

Canada, the United States, Mexico, and the Caribbean. From Central America came Africans from Belize, Guatemala, Honduras, Nicaragua, and Panama. And from South America emerged the Black family from Peru, Bolivia, Ecuador, Brazil, Argentina, Uruguay, Paraguay, Columbia, and the host nation of Venezuela.

The Reunion was both one of the greatest events I have ever participated in and the site of one of my finest hours. All of the forums were wonderful and, during the height of the conference, I gave keynote presentations on three consecutive nights. The first was titled the "African Presence in America Before Columbus," the second was "Ancient African Empires," and the third and biggest of them all was "Unexpected Faces in Unexpected Places: The Global African Presence." The latter presentation, however, was one of my best ever. But how can you go wrong when you are animated and lucid and have three hundred enthusiastic people looking at you, and your every word is being translated simultaneously into English, Spanish, and Portuguese, and everybody's eyes are open wide, and they are seeing, in some cases for the first time, rare and positive images of African people in places where Black people are seldom identified?

On that one night, at least, everything seemed to work to perfection. I scored a knockout blow with the audience. Indeed, I will never forget how the members of the various national delegations lined up afterward to shake my hand and have their photographs taken with me. And how the oldest person in attendance at the conference—a petite, elegant Black woman from Jamaica—pushed all the other delegates aside, walked squarely up to me, and, with great dignity, embraced me and told me how proud my "mother"—meaning Mother Africa, I surmised—was of me.

I was so touched. Her gesture, in front of so many people, was the icing on the cake. My cup overflowed. She and I were both so overcome with emotion and gratitude to the Ancestors, the audience, and our hosts afterward that, I confess, I shed tears for a long time that evening back in my hotel room.

But even the food at the conference was special. Every day, a different African group from a different country would make their cuisine available to the delegates. It was divine! One day, we would be eating African Venezuelan food, the next day the food would be prepared by the Black people of Ecuador, followed by food from African Colombians, then by mouthwatering dishes from African Peruvians. And this went on for a solid week!

To top that off, every evening, after dinner, the delegates danced and played drums. One night, the drums were played with so much vigor, so loud and so long, that one musician quite literally beat a hole in his drum!

But perhaps the most remarkable thing about the Reunion was the revelation that many of the delegates, almost all of whom were Black, seemed largely unaware that African people lived in the countries neighboring them. The Black people from Bolivia, for example, indicated to me that they were not aware that there were Black people in Peru, and the ones from Peru didn't know that there were Black people in Ecuador!

Another electrifying moment came about during a panel discussion on African-Latino relationships that I had the good fortune of moderating. In the midst of the discussion a Black man from Ecuador—a big, masculine-looking, dark-complexioned Black man about forty years old, who looked like he could play professional football on a United States team—came up to the microphone and told all those in the attendance the following: "I don't have a question," he said, "but I just wanted to say 'thank you' to everybody for making me feel proud to be Black for the first time in my life." Then he broke down and cried like a baby!

And that's the way the conference went. The International Reunion of the African Family in Latin America—it was a treasure house of memories

SEEING PERU THROUGH AFRICAN EYES[3]

Unlike some travelers and scholars, I would contend that, with the exception of Brazil, the African presence in Latin America is largely invisible. It simply has not been sufficiently explored and documented. And, believe it or not, sisters and brothers, there is an African presence in Peru!

I first remember becoming aware of the African presence in Peru about twenty years ago. I was watching a weightlifting competition during the Olympic Games when I noticed a Black man on the Peruvian team. My first reaction was, "Wow! We really are everywhere!"

Reflections on the Ancient African Presence in Peru

For ten days in June 2001, I toured Peru and found it to be a fascinating place. I had already been to Brazil, Venezuela, and Guyana, but I was hungry for more, so Peru became my first destination on South America's western side.

To begin with, the museums in Peru are excellent, and I was astounded by the Africoid features of many of the Moche portrait vases I saw there. The churches and cathedrals weren't bad, either, and there were a lot of them. I was especially impressed with the Church and Monastery of Santo Domingo, with its life-sized statue of the St. Martin de Porres, a Black man. And who could ever forget the sacred Urubamba Valley and the mysterious city of Machu Picchu? Equally impressive, and perhaps even more so than the other sites, were the ceremonial centers of Sacsayhuaman and the ancient urban complex of Ollantaytambo.

Contrary to popular belief, the first Africans to come to Peru did not come as captives—that is, as enslaved people. Rather, the country that is now called Peru in all likelihood became home to many of the first waves of Blacks who crossed into the Western Hemisphere tens of thousands of years ago. The bones of these ancient Blacks have been found in Bolivia, Ecuador, and Brazil, so why would Peru be an exception? Peru is probably the most archaeologically rich country in South America, and one of the most important phases of its history is the Moche period.

The Moche (or Mochica), a militaristic people little known to all but a few, erected their empire along the northern Peruvian coast around 100 C.E. They built their capital in the middle of the desert around what is now the Peruvian city of Trujillo. It featured the enormous pyramid temples

---

3   Dedicated to the immortal spirit of Francisco Congo. Though I initially traveled to Peru in June 2001, this note was not penned until three years later, in May 2004.

of the Huaca del Sol and Huaca de la Luna (the temples of the Sun and the Moon). The Temple of the Sun, one of the most impressive adobe structures ever built in the Western Hemisphere, was composed of over a hundred million mud bricks. Moche roads and a system of way stations are believed to have been an early inspiration and prototype for the sophisticated Incan network of highways. The Moche also built extensive irrigation projects and carried out skillful engineering efforts such as the La Cumbre Canal, still in use today, and the Ascope aqueduct, both on the Chicama River. The Moche civilization was not eclipsed for seven hundred years.

Perhaps the greatest achievement of the Moche was their art, especially their amazingly lifelike portrait vases. I managed to view a number of these Moche pieces in the museums in Lima, Peru's capital. Many of them were so Africoid that I thought that they could easily have been manufactured in the Congo. I am talking here about vase after vase after vase! Indeed, based on the artistic evidence alone, one could say that the Moche are among ancient America's best-kept secrets.

Africans in Colonial Peru

Although some Africans came to Peru with the Spanish invaders as soldiers and translators, beginning in the sixteenth century significant numbers of enslaved Africans were taken to Peru. During the 1550s, an estimated three thousand enslaved Africans were in Peru, about half of them residing in Lima. But wherever there are enslaved people, there is also slave resistance, and colonial Peru was no exception. The one name that seems to most personify that resistance is Francisco Congo. Indeed, he must have been extraordinary man, and I have been trying diligently to find whatever information I can on him since my first visit to Peru.

Because of its geography and the fact that Peru was not on the direct path of the trans-Atlantic slave trade routes, the majority of Africans in Peru were not brought over directly from Africa. Instead, they were bought from British, Dutch, and Portuguese slave traders and transported to Peru after they had already been in other parts of the Americas. Even under the yoke of enslavement and poverty, however, some of these Africans achieved great distinction. One such person was Martin de Porres, the son of a Spanish nobleman and a freed African slave mother, who eventually became St. Martin de Porres

De Porres was born December 9, 1579, in Lima, Peru. At age eleven, he became a servant in the Dominican religious order. As he grew, Martin begged for money from the rich every week to support the poor and sick of Lima. He was later placed in charge of the Dominican order's infirmary, where he became famous for his "tender care of the sick and for his spectacular cures." He also established both an orphanage and a children's hospital for Lima's poor and, interestingly enough, set up a shelter for stray dogs and cats, where he nursed the animals back to health.

Martin de Porres lived in self-imposed austerity, never ate meat, fasted regularly, and spent much time in meditation and prayer. Because of him, the Dominicans dropped the stipulation that "no black person may be received to the holy habit or profession of our order," and Martin took his vows as a Dominican brother. In 1639, he died of fever, but he has been venerated since the day of his death. He was beatified in 1873 and canonized on May 16, 1962. He is, to my knowledge, the first African American saint.

Africans in Contemporary Peru

The African presence in Peru today numbers about two million people out of a total population of about twenty-three million. During my visit, however, I saw only a handful of these sisters and brothers. I did manage, with some expenditure of effort, to find one African Peruvian taxi driver, a brother named Enrique. Unfortunately, the only words of English that brother Enrique knew to utter were "Black power," but that was enough for me to hire him!

Beyond that, I saw no Africans working in the airport, in the markets, in the museums, in the banks, in the hotels, or on TV. Therefore, the reports of pervasive and rampant anti-African racism in Peru did not come as much of a surprise to me. According to one account, that racism is "systematic and permanent." Moreover, it goes "from patronizing attitudes to outright discrimination: blacks are dirty, thieves, all the stereotypes."

New York Times correspondent Calvin Sims documented some of the racial bias directed against Africans in Peru in an August 1996 article, in which he pointed out the following:

> *"Although nightclubs feature Afro-Peruvian musical groups and a third of Peruvian soccer players are black, the number of black professionals is estimated at fewer than 400, and there are no black executives of Peruvian companies, no blacks in the diplomatic corps, judiciary, or the high ranks of the clergy or military. The country's even smaller Japanese community has produced the current President, but no black politician has risen even as far as Congress.*
>
> *While incidents of open discrimination are far less common in Peru than in the United States and Brazil, which has the largest black population in Latin America, Peruvian blacks say they encounter racism daily.*
>
> *In public, they say, they are frequently called derogatory names like 'son of coal' or 'smokeball.' At job interviews, they say, they are often told that their experience and references are excellent but that the owners are looking to hire people with 'good presence'—a euphemism for someone who is white."*

Such is the difficult life of Black men and women in Peru!

AN EXCURSION TO ECUADOR

October 2, 2007

It is early morning, and I am busy packing my bags, for I today I'm on my way to Ecuador. I would like to say that I am excited, but I have taken so many trips now that my excitement has become somewhat subdued. I guess you could say that I am possessed of a quiet anticipation instead. Thanks in large measure to our dear sister Hamara Holt, I have lots of contacts in Ecuador and should gain an abundance of information about the African presence in this fascinating part of the world. Of course, I will also visit as many of the relevant museums as humanly possible, and I plan to take a lot of pictures.

Just two days ago, I picked up a travel book on Bolivia, another poor Andean nation. That book indicated that Bolivia has a small African population in an area called the Yungas. I can already begin to see myself there. Argentina, in the region referred to as the Southern Cone, is also calling me, and I have a strong desire to visit mainland Colombia. My only concern with the latter country is whether or not it is physically safe to travel there. I am also anxious to visit the African communities in Nicaragua. And I shouldn't leave Surinam, in the Dutch colonial sphere, off of my go-to list, either. Surinam is. another South American country with a rich African history.

Did you know that it was in Argentina that African people invented the popular dance known as the tango? Did you know that there are large and much-oppressed African communities in Colombia? Well both statements are true. It is also true that I love Africans all over the place, but for whatever reasons the Africans in the Spanish-speaking countries in the Americas seem to be calling to me loud and clear.

So, soon I'll be on my way to South America. I have visited twenty-one countries this year already—making my grand total eighty-two countries in the last eight years—and next year promises to be just as big. I know that my dear mother, Dr. Hilliard, Dr. Clarke, Alexander Pushkin, J. A. Rogers, Chancellor Williams, and all of the esteemed Ancestors will continue to watch over me.

Highs and Lows in Quito

It is now just after five o'clock in the morning. I can't sleep, so I figured that I might as well write. I am staying in a very nice hotel located not far from two dormant, snow-capped volcanoes. I arrived here just before midnight three days ago. The flight from Houston was uneventful and collecting my luggage and clearing customs wasn't so bad. Then the confusion began, but more on that later.

Today I am in Quito, the beautiful capital city of Ecuador, high in the Andes Mountains. The other two major cities that I plan to visit on this trip are Esmeraldas (I will also explore Esmeraldas Province) and Guayaquil. I have lectures and meetings scheduled in all three areas. Quito is high in the Andes and currently rather cold and rainy. Esmeraldas, which has deep historical significance and has long contained settlements of African people, is on the north coast near Colombia and semitropical. Guayaquil, the largest city in Ecuador, is on the south coast near the border with Peru, and it should be warm and dry there. As a result, I had to prepare for three climatic zones for this trip.

Located high in the Andes, Quito, Ecuador's second largest city, is laid out on hills set in a valley in the midst of the Andes Mountains. Ecuador is the smallest of the three Andean countries of Ecuador, Peru, and Bolivia. (I visited Peru a few years ago and hope to go to Bolivia in a few months.) The currency here is the US dollar, the electrical system is the same as that in the US, and a few people speak English. The majority population is Indigenous ("Indians"), with a large percentage of Mestizos" (mixed Indian and White). Officially, African people make up about ten percent of the total population, although it seems like more to me.

Quito does not seem to be terribly congested. Public transportation is made up largely of old buses. Small yellow taxis are everywhere. The people are fairly friendly, but I have been told by more than a few folks here that the city is infested with crime and that I should not walk around outside at night.

Ecuador is a relatively poor country. Fishing and tourism, I am told, dominate the economy with agriculture playing an important part. Tomatoes, beans, and maize are very popular crops here. I've already tasted a lot of different foods. Some of it tastes pretty good, although I confess that I have no idea what a lot of it is. Indeed, some of the meals that I have eaten I have prudently avoided asking about the ingredients.

Overall, I guess I'm glad that I came to Ecuador. In some ways, this trip has already surpassed my expectations; in others, it has been a disappointment. For the most part, the African people here are almost completely lacking in power. Unemployment among them is sky high, and even those Africans with university degrees often find themselves working as domestics and security guards. In that regard, the situation resembles what I saw in Peru. So far, I have seen only one Black man working in my hotel and only one African taxi driver. Worse still, institutionalized racism is the norm and is thoroughly entrenched, although things seem to be changing ever so slowly.

I have already encountered one incident that seemed to be clearly racist in nature. That incident occurred when I was about to enter the national museum. A White man looked in my direction and called out to me, in a rather loud and condescending voice: "Black man!" Now, I love to be called Black, but I got the distinct impression that this guy meant it as an insult. My first inclination was to break my camera over his head, but he quickly walked away. I had been informed in advance that Ecuadorian jails are not nice places, so I let it go, but the incident did not leave me with a good feeling.

If this were not depressing enough, I have some more bad news to tell you. From what I have witnessed, at least in Quito, a lot of the sisters and brothers in Ecuador don't seem to like each other very much. Indeed, if you really want to get a Black Ecuadorian riled up, just mention another African! Do that, and a person who might have seemed so calm and pleasant a moment ago all of a sudden becomes a mountain of anger and resentment. I hate stuff like that, and it seems I am caught right in the middle of it. Indeed, two sets of Africans here seem to be fighting over me and struggling over who is going to control my schedule. I just hate it! I experienced something very nearly like it in India in 1998, and I haven't gotten over it yet.

But here's what happened, and what I alluded to at the beginning of this note as the major catastrophe of this trip. To begin, I started planning this trip a couple of months ago. For whatever reason, Ecuador just seemed to have been calling out to me, so I purchased my flight ticket first and started the serious planning second. After I bought my plane ticket, I started seeking out good African Ecuadorian contacts. The response was slow at first, but largely with the help of Hamara Holt, it started to pick up. Soon various individuals and organizations in the various cities I wanted to visit in the three distinct parts of the country started to express interest in my visit, and eventually I had a full schedule.

One African Ecuadorian sister, who got on board with my planning late in the game, asked if I needed a lift from the airport once I arrived in Quito. Considering that I was scheduled to arrive in the middle of the night in a strange city that I had never visited and with only a smattering of Spanish in my vocabulary, I jumped at the offer. Little did I know that this would infuriate someone whom I can only call one of her rivals. And to cap it off, the sister who picked me up at the airport came completely surrounded by her Mestizo entourage! That was not a good start!

To make matters worse, the sister seemed to love non-Africans, and I soon found out she had plans to keep me all to herself! Normally, this would not have been a terrible idea if that was what it took for me to see Quito. But when I inquired about her specific arrangements, I learned that she had engaged a car and a Mestizo driver for me at the rather expensive price of $120.00 per day! This meant that, in addition to paying for my own ticket, my own hotel (and a rather expensive one, at that), and my own meals, I would have been socked with an extra $120.00 per day that I had not anticipated. Of course, I was not happy about that, but I went along with the program.

The next day, I took advantage of the car and driver and visited two archaeological museums, neither of which was very impressive. I was determined to find evidence of Africans in Ecuador before Columbus and before slavery, but all I found was one small pre-Columbian figurine of an African woman in childbirth. I found nothing similar in the larger, national museum; however, it did possess an exquisite set of wooden figurines of the three magi, one of which was Black. Each of the figurines was on horseback and beautifully attired. Of all the figures that I have seen of the three wise men, this one was by far the best.

That day, I also visited the equator at La Mitad Del Mundo ("The Middle of the World"), a big tourist attraction here, where I stood with one foot in the northern hemisphere and another in the south. A rather nice ethnographic museum was attached to the site.

That evening, I was encouraged by Blain Watson, a really excellent brother who teaches at one of the local universities in Quito, to meet with the organization that was to facilitate my first lecture. It was only then that I found out about the rancor existing between the Black folk in Ecuador.

The irony of the situation is that I like both groups. Indeed, the sister from the lecture-organizing group, who has been touring around Ecuador with me for the last couple of days, was confirmed to the Ecuadorian National Assembly just a couple of days ago, and there are only four African members out of a total of 130 in that august body. Plus, her organization is a cultural one, and I like that a lot.

Some of the division between the two groups, it seems, is based on class. The Assemblywoman, for instance, was born in poverty. Yesterday, we visited her hometown, which was near the Chota Valley, and I saw firsthand how tough things are for African people here. (I will write more about this experience, probably in my next note.) The sister who picked me up from the airport, and who runs the other organization, has also had a rough time of it, but she is a university graduate. It reminded me of the struggle between Booker T. Washington and W. E. B. Du Bois in the United States more than a hundred years ago—that is, of the Talented Tenth and the dispossessed ninety percent.

Runoko Rashidi

So that's part one of my Ecuadorian story. And here I am, wide awake at five o'clock in the morning again, listening to an Aretha Franklin CD, and feeling a little angry, a bit depressed, and somewhat let down. I am supposed to present my lecture tonight at six, but I confess that I just am not feeling it. Indeed, I am actually questioning whether I am insane for being here in the first place.

This travel bug, for me, has become something of a fever, and I am wondering if it is becoming unhealthy. It certainly is costing me a lot of money! I am also wondering if I haven't let my ego just run away from me. It's as though I have an obsession with time and believe that I must do as much as possible every available minute of it because I fear tomorrow might not come.

I wish I had Dr. Hilliard to counsel me and assure me that I'm doing the right thing. I miss him so much! But I suppose I'll get by. I always have. Anyway, tomorrow, I leave for the great African Ecuadorian province of Esmeraldas, where I hope to find more positive things to write to you about.

Well, I almost did not do it—twice!—but tonight I finally delivered my lecture at the university in Quito. So now I've lectured in forty-five countries! I had to call on the Ancestors to give me guidance and wisdom on this one, though, and they came through.

Originally, three or four speakers were supposed to be presenting tonight for a kind of mini-conference, but, for whatever reasons, I was the whole show. It actually turned out very, very good. My lecture was translated from English to Spanish as I spoke. I did not do a slide presentation, but there was an excellent question-and-answer session afterward. And we had a nice audience turn out. In addition to the Ecuadorians in the audience, who reflected the whole spectrum of Ecuador's ethnic groups, there were Africans from Nigeria, Colombia, the United States, and, I believe, Venezuela. And I was the star! The organizers seemed very happy, and I was happy that they were happy!

After the lecture, I joined a number of the organizers in a visit to an African cultural center in Quito, where we spent a couple of hours talking about the state of the race. We later shared African Ecuadorian food, nice beverages, good vibrations, and some excellent live African Ecuadorian music.

So now I am back in love with African Ecuador all over again, and I am delighted to be here! Indeed, it is turning out to be a sensational trip! Tomorrow morning, I leave Quito for Esmeraldas, where, I am told, my visit is eagerly anticipated. It seems the people there are waiting excitedly for me and that I am guaranteed to have a good time and a great learning experience. I can't wait! I think I'm going to sleep very good tonight! Thanks Baba Asa!

Guayaquil and Esmeraldas

It is early Thursday morning here in the city of Guayaquil on the southern coast of Ecuador. I am up listening to some real hot salsa music on a CD I picked up in Esmeraldas province. The music is dynamite, and it sounds like it's straight out of Africa. Believe me when I tell you I'm having a hard time sitting still enough to write, but I'm going to try.

The sun came up a little while ago, and I have just now looked outside my hotel window for the first time. There is a big, beautiful, white church located right across the street from me, and I've made up my mind that is will be the first place that I'll visit this morning. I also plan to visit three or four museums and, after that, I hope to visit some of the Black communities here. Then, I have a lecture planned—I think. And after that, I'll have to check out of my hotel, get to the airport, board my plane, and say goodbye to Ecuador… for now.

So much has happened on this trip, and most of it has been good. Let me see if I can give you a recap because it seems like I have been here for a long, long time. I arrived in Ecuador last week, and began my Ecuador journey in Quito. I already told you some things about that, so I guess it's safe to fast forward.

One of the early highlights of this trip was my journey to the Chota Valley and the adjourning mountain areas. I was accompanied by a Black woman named Olga Mendez, who was just recently elected to the National Assembly that will write the new Ecuadorian constitution. First, Olga took me to her hometown, the community of Santa Ana, which is made up largely of unmixed Africans who were brought to the region hundreds of years ago to work as slave labor. Santa Ana is a very poor area, although much more prosperous than some of the other areas predominated by Blacks that I've seen around the world. We also visited a sugar mill and one of the old haciendas from which the mill bosses ruled like a feudal monarchy.

Probably the single most interesting experience of that day was our visit to the House of Oshun, which is a refuge center for African Ecuadorian women who have been victimized by domestic violence. I was given a guided tour of the center, where I met the oldest resident in the community: a tiny, very black, eighty-four-year-old woman full of energy! She was a real delight, and we took a bunch of photos together. (Of course, she charged me a fee!)

From the House of Oshun, we went to a small and humble African house for a traditional African Ecuadorian meal before heading off to the Chota Valley, site of the major African concentration center in the Ecuadorian Andes. There, I was able to visit an art center run by African Ecuadorian women. I have found a great prominence of African women in Ecuador so far, and I am most comfortable with that.

Later, I was taken to meet the mayor of the town of Mir, where I was cordially welcomed to the region. Then we began the long ride back to Quito.

In an earlier email, I told you about my lecture at the university in Quito and how pleased everybody was with the results. What I did not tell you about was my translator, Blain Watson. Blain is a young African who was born in the United States and who teaches at one of the universities in Quito. He really looked after me while I was in that city, and he was instrumental in the success of the early part of the trip. I owe him a great deal.

No doubt the most memorable part of my visit to Ecuador so far has been the time I spent in Esmeraldas. Someone told me some years ago that there were pockets of Africans in the Americas. Esmeraldas Province, especially the northern part, is one of those pockets. Southern Colombia, parts of Panama, and (definitely) Bahia in Brazil are certainly others. There are probably plenty of others in the Caribbean, including parts of Haiti, Jamaica, and Cuba.

Runoko Rashidi

I knew that Esmeraldas was special, however, the moment I stepped off the plane. The energy was entirely different than in Quito. There were Black people everywhere! I immediately felt the tropical climate upon my arrival, and, after a short delay, I was met by three women. The first of these was Ruth Diaz, a short, sweet, good-humored Black woman and university professor. Ruth, I soon learned, moves back and forth between Quito and Esmeraldas City. She facilitated everything associated with my visit to Esmeraldas.

Ruth was accompanied by another short, sweet sister, who drove the car that picked me up at the airport. Unfortunately, I never saw her again after that first afternoon. My translator that first day and for most of my stay in Esmeraldas was Ana Maria Rodriguez. Ana Maria was a young woman—European, but very sympathetic to African issues.

I came to regard both Ruth and Ana Maria as angels. I mean, they really looked after me every step of the way, and I never had to worry for anything during my stay in Esmeraldas. They treated me like I was some sort of dignitary and, were simply wonderful.

I also have to mention and give thanks to my other translator, Professor Radnitz Oko. Oko, who hails from Nigeria, also teaches at one of the local universities, and he shared with me some of his own distinctive local insights into the Esmeraldas scene.

Esmeraldas City, the major population center in Esmeraldas Province, is a very poor, mostly African city on the north coast of Ecuador. It kind of reminded me of Colón City in Panama. I stayed in one of the better hotels there, one with a great view of the Pacific Ocean. I soon found out that people eat a lot of seafood in Esmeraldas, and I had my share of fish and shrimp during my visit. Plus, to tell you the truth, I was just glad to be around so many African people.

On my second day in Esmeraldas, I met with a group of African community leaders. They had a lot of needs, and I committed myself (and you, too!) to getting some Spanish-language, African-oriented books to them, as they have next to nothing and that is what they requested. They also expressed a need for some equipment to help them record their meetings. I intend to step up to the plate on that one, also.

That afternoon, I met with some of the "regular" people in this hard-pressed African city at a local high school. These were really poor people, a lot of them young students, and they have really suffered. I heard their stories about police brutality and racial discrimination in Ecuador and told them about similar circumstances in the United States, separated only by degree. I also asked them a lot of questions, including whether or not they were proud of being Black. To my delight, in response to that latter question, they all jumped up and shouted, "Yes!"

On the next day, I headed north to the city of San Lorenzo accompanied, thanks to Ruth Diaz, by two translators. San Lorenzo is located near the border with Colombia. I saw some of the worst poverty I had seen so far in that locale, and I am talking about poor, relatively unmixed African people. Through my interpreters, many of them told me their sad and pathetic stories. Unemployment, they claimed, hovered around ninety-nine percent. Virtually no jobs were available anywhere in the city or in the tiny little villages that dot the area, the local schools were terrible, and health care was nearly nonexistent. And yet, the people were so incredibly sweet to me. It was a day of both joy and sadness, and a time that I will never forget.

On the way back to Esmeraldas City, this time thanks to Ana Maria, we stopped at the Church of Loretto, which is named after a church in Italy. I was able to photograph the statue of the Black Madonna that the local people adore.

The following day, I guess it was a Tuesday, I lectured in the Esmeraldas City Hall. Actually, I only did a slide presentation, with a lengthy question-and-answer session thereafter. My audience was comprised mostly of high school-aged children, almost all of whom were Black, and some local dignitaries. The event was hosted by the office of the mayor's of Esmeraldas City. The mayor, who was a Black man (and a very progressive one, I was told), was away in Chile at the time, trying to raise some money for another municipal project. But the vice-mayor, a very kind African woman, was in the audience, along with a kind of deputy minister of culture and a bunch of other important folks. The press was there too, of course, and I got a fairly big write-up in the regional newspaper the next day. It didn't even bother me that both my first and last names were horribly misspelled! I picked up several copies of the paper to bring home.

The purpose of my lecture was to show that African people had a history before enslavement and that African people live all over the world. Apparently, this was a totally new concept in Ecuador. I must say, however, that I did an excellent job. You would have been proud.

It seemed as if nearly everybody got in on the long, long question-and-answer period afterward. Indeed, I was touched (brought to tears, actually) when I young Black girl stood up and thanked me profusely for coming to Esmeraldas. As she told me and everyone in the audience, for the first time in her life she was proud to be Black! It was a very emotional moment. Actually, it brought the house down, and the girl received a standing ovation. That one moment made all the sacrifices that I had made to come to Ecuador seem worthwhile.

Later that day, I visited the community of St. Martin de Porres, named after the African saint of the poor and downtrodden. I also visited another arts center, this one focusing on African women's crafts, and traveled south along the coast to the communities of Atacames and Sua. I tell you, it was a quite a day!

On my last morning in Esmeraldas, I went to the local museum and saw what seemed to be conclusive archaeological evidence of the African presence in pre-Colombian Ecuador. It was an excellent way to cap off my visit.

Last Thoughts on Ecuador

Well, I am now back in Guayaquil. I got here last night, and after a brief overnight stay downtown in the elegant Unipark Hotel, I am ready to begin my last day in Ecuador. I have learned from this visit that Ecuador is, by all standards, a poor country; and that the Africans here, like Africans in most places, remain terribly oppressed. But, like their African counterparts around the globe, they are not standing still. They are organizing and struggling and standing up. I am happy to be a small part in this process.

It is late in the evening, and I am sitting in the hotel lobby just passing the time away for a few hours, listening to salsa music, and sipping a cubra libre until I leave for the airport for my flight back to the USA. With all this extra time on my hands, I thought that I'd send you one last, long, rambling note.

I have had the best of times here in Ecuador. I've had some not-so-good times too. But all in all, it has been another really interesting trip. Indeed, I'd rank this trip not far behind my earlier incredible journeys in India, Aboriginal Australia, Fiji, Cambodia, Venezuela, Uganda, Malawi, Myanmar, and Turkey. Those were all experiences of a lifetime, but there have been others as well, including my travels in Ghana, Egypt, Ethiopia, Namibia, Zimbabwe, Jordan, Syria, Lebanon, Italy, Spain, Nova Scotia, Palau, Lesotho, Swaziland, and Morocco. Russia, China, Honduras, Panama, Costa Rica, Belize, Thailand, Vietnam, San Andres Island, Peru, Guyana, Brazil, Jamaica. Tunisia, Scotland, Benin, Rwanda, Southern Sudan, Belgium, Germany, the Netherlands, and a lot of others have been memorable journeys also. Then, I spend so much time in France and I have been to England so many times that I almost take those places for granted. All these places, like Ecuador, present both the fascinating and the annoying. But, despite a few bumps in the road, I am really glad that I came here.

This morning, I visited a big Catholic church across the street from my hotel. It was majestic on the outside but nothing much on the inside. Whenever I go to places like that, I always hope that I will find those Black icons that thrill me so much. Nothing like that today, though.

Then I went to the first of three museums on my list today and again, it was a big waste of time. I toured it with two local brothers and a translator, a young Black woman from Milwaukee. The two brothers assured me that there was nothing at all African in the other two museums, and, like a weak-willed idiot, I said okay. I did not want to annoy my hosts, but I will always wonder what I missed, and I could kick myself for not going anyway.

Instead, accompanied on our odyssey by Ibsen Hernandez—a real heroic figure in these parts—we all squeezed into a taxi and went to visit some of the Black communities in the area that the locals call barrios. These are fascinating places. I think that we visited four of them, and each one was different than the others.

In the barrios live some of the most downtrodden and poverty-stricken people I have ever seen in the Western Hemisphere. Of course, the poverty I've witnessed in Ethiopia, and especially India, was much worse, but a couple of these communities were just awful. One community was strewn with trash. Its roads were unpaved and its schools were shoddy. The houses there were elevated on rickety stilts above the stream of dirty water that flowed beneath them It was horrible, but I made the best of it, and the residents were hospitable. I took a lot of photos.

One of the places within the barrios that we visited was the public school where Ibsen teaches. I enjoyed meeting, talking, and laughing with his students, and took quite a few pictures of them, too. But something happened there that really did a number on me. First, I noticed that the physical appearance of the students at the school ranged from really dark-complexioned kids to those who seemed a little mixed. The really dark kids, all of whom were girls, were, I thought, extremely beautiful. When I asked a couple of them if I could take their pictures, they adamantly refused. When I asked why they did not want me to photograph them, they told me it was because they were "too ugly"! What they clearly meant was that they were too Black.

My Global Journeys in Search of the African Presence

I was really hurt. Indeed, I was devastated! They were deadly serious. They walked away from me as if they were insulted that I would even consider photographing them.. I am just so fed up with this obsession that many of us have with light skin and long, straight hair! I hated to leave Ecuador with anger in my heart, but that really upset me, and it carried over into my last lecture, which I was to present right before leaving for my flight.

Apparently, the program at which I was to lecture was put together very hastily, and it showed. It was poorly planned poorly attended, and poorly translated. Plus, I gave one of my poorest talks in living memory. I think I was still reeling from my visit to the barrios, or maybe it was just one of those afternoons, but afterward, I was more than ready to get out of there. I guess that you can't win 'em all!

And, with that, I said goodbye to Ecuador. I loved Esmeraldas, just loved it—with all of its poverty and warts—and I look forward to returning there again someday. Quito and the Chota Valley were also fascinating, but I hope never to visit Guayaquil again. Oh well, such is life! I've been to twenty-two countries this year alone—the most ever for me in one calendar year. And I still have England and Spain on my calendar, in addition to France and Morocco, where I have already been three times each this year.

And what horizons await me in the coming year? In addition to the group tours I am planning next year to Egypt and Morocco, Uganda and Rwanda, and Ghana and Mali, I hope also to visit the Persian Gulf, Libya, Tunisia, Nigeria, Cameroon, Congo Brazzaville, Aboriginal Australia, Papua New Guinea, and the Solomon Islands. I am also planning a long overdue visit to Cape Verde and a return lecture engagement in St. Maarten. Sounds like a full plate, doesn't it? Well, it is, and I just love it!

Just one last thing before I go, however: I want to say that I cannot express enough gratitude and love to Sister Hamara Holt. Sister Hamara, who worked so hard to put together the big book project she and I conceived at the Sunrise Academy in Ghana, is also very fluent in Spanish. She worked nonstop to make my trip to Ecuador a success, making calls and emailing and translating without fail—and she never asked for anything except that the trip go well.

Sister Hamara, I owe you more than I can ever repay, and I will remain eternally grateful to you. Thank you ever so much. You have been an angel!

THE AFRICAN PRESENCE IN BOLIVIA

June 7, 2008

Today finds me in an airport lounge in Lima, Peru. My flight to the US does not leave for almost ten hours, and for the first time in a few days, I have access to the Internet. So with the music of Pharaoh Sanders, Patti LaBelle, Gladys Knight, and Phyllis Hyman pumping into my brain via my CD player and headset, I was thinking that I would spend some time telling you all about my adventures in the Bolivian Yungas in search of the African presence.

Runoko Rashidi

Hanging Out with "Royalty" in the Yungas

When last you heard from me, I believe, it was early Thursday morning and I was excitedly about to depart for the area in Bolivia called the Yungas—a transitional area at the gateway to the Amazonian rain forest and the Andes Mountains. It also is where the great majority of the Africans in Bolivia reside. From what I could gather, there are a little over fifty thousand African people in Bolivia, but it was hard to get an exact accounting, as nobody seems to know for sure. Not even the African Bolivians themselves!

I first heard of the Yungas two or three years ago, in an email sent to me from Dr. Willie Thompson, a brother who has traveled extensively in South America. His description of the region seemed so very mysterious and exciting, but it also sounded like a place that I would never get to visit. But here I was am, and strange as it may sound coming from me, this trip has been facilitated, to a large extent, by the United States Agency for International Development (USAID), thanks to the intervention of my good friend Hamara Holt. I guess that you could say that, for once, the US government and I had mutual desires.

Indeed, the American government, which does not have the best relations with the present government of Bolivia (led by Evo Morales), is down in the Yungas right now, trying to suppress the spread and proliferation of coca, the bushy plant whose leaves are the source of what we in the West call cocaine. The Yungas is one of most prolific areas of coca production in the world. I saw probably hundreds of coca fields during my stay. In order to combat coca production, the US government is spending tons of money developing relationships with the local people.

Some of those people, it turns out, are African, and apparently, they have been imploring US agencies to send them African American experts to come and talk to them about their African origins and the struggles of African people in the United States. So when word got out that Runoko Rashidi would be visiting Bolivia, they practically begged me to go to the Yungas and fulfill those requests. They even provided me with a car, a driver, a translator, and two facilitators. They also made all of the contacts I would need and got a top-notch journalist and photographer from one of the leading national newspapers in Bolivia to accompany me and cover what everybody thought was going to be an historic event.

Although I was fairly suspicious of and skeptical about all the US government involvement in one of my travels, I must say that I probably would not have been able to visit the Yungas without it. The whole crew turned out to be most pleasant and helpful. My Indian driver was superb. The journalist and I actually struck up a pretty good relationship; we even found out that we had a great deal in common. Truthfully speaking, before the trip was over, I thought of them all as friends.

The Africans in the Yungas live in a series of small and isolated towns and mountain villages. Apparently, they were brought to the region from a vast area in West Central Africa ranging from Senegal to Angola. Indeed, the surname "Angola" is very common among them. They live alongside the Aymara Indians but have never really lost their African identity. Like the Africans in Peru, they were introduced to South America through the gateways of Panama, Colombia, and Argentina.

They first worked in the silver mines of Potosí in Bolivia's Central Highlands, where they died in astronomical numbers. Those who survived that ordeal were relocated to the Yungas.

The Yungas is divided into northern and southern regions. I went first to the north and found the countryside there to be stunning. After checking into my hotel, which was perched on the side of a mountain, I ventured to the town of Coroico. From there I traveled to the even smaller town of Mururata where, with some effort and searching, I was taken to the home of the king and queen of the Afro-Bolivianos, which is what the people call themselves. This latter visit, by itself, was enough to make the trip a big success, as far as I was concerned.

This fascinating couple, who spoke no English but who were extremely pleasant, entertained my questions through an interpreter for some time. I took a lot of photographs of and with them. They told me that there had been a king and queen of the Afro-Bolivianos since at least 1834, even before the end of slavery in Bolivia. I was, however, the first African American they had ever met. (I would hear this comment often over the two days of my Yungas travels.) When I asked them if they would be interested in meeting more sisters and brothers from the United States, they said that they would be delighted.

The king and queen also told me that life for the people in their community—both the Blacks and the Indians—was very hard. They confided that they did not want to grow coca, but it was their only real source of income. They were such nice people and so very poor that, naturally, before I left I put a nice amount of money in their hands. It seemed that I had so much more in terms of material wealth than they, and it made me feel extraordinarily good to be able to share.

Like so many others I have met, I believe that if you give freely and from the heart, you will be blessed many times over in great abundance. I carry this philosophy with me wherever I go. Perhaps that is one of the reasons I have been so fortunate in my travels.

From king and queen's house, I was driven to the town of Tocana, which was real highlight of my stay in Bolivia. Thirty or forty African families live there. Rarely have I ever felt so much at ease and so much at home anywhere else in the world.

At first, I was surrounded there by children who were apparently having a lot of fun at my expense. They called me the "African Yankee," and they laughed hysterically both at the way I talked and the way I walked! I took a lot of photos of and with them, regardless.

Then it was time for me to talk with the elder men of the community at the Tocana community center. It seemed that just the mere presence of an African American historian lifted their spirits, big-time. That night, I talked about Africa. I talked about Africa as the birthplace of humanity and the cradle of civilization. When I told those brothers that we Africans had a history before enslavement, the smiles of satisfaction that crossed their faces were a joy to behold. It all got to be very, very emotional. They asked me a lot of questions about history and identity and my love of all things African. Then they danced and beat the drums for me. A stranger witnessing the scene would have been hard-pressed to determine if we were in Africa or the Americas. It was a truly powerful evening, and I slept that night like a newborn babe.

Runoko Rashidi

The next morning, I woke up with the sunrise to the sounds of the jungle. I gazed with wonder and appreciation at the snow-capped Andes Mountains. I guess to appreciate it fully, you just would have had to have been there.

My final day in the Yungas was a long and demanding one. We stopped in the community of Chulumani in the South Yungas, where I toured a big church that held images of a Black Christ. I engaged in a final round of lecture/discussions in the Afro-Bolivian town of Chicaloma, where I was particularly drawn to an elderly sister who seemed to exude a strong spiritual aura. A crowd gathered around me, and I gave out photographs of a Black Christ figure I had photographed years ago in the Coptic Museum in Cairo, Egypt. That was a really big hit!

And then it was back through the high and steep mountain passes for a late-night drive to La Paz. On the way back to La Paz, my interpreters told me ghost stories about the enslaved Africans who are still believed to walk the mines of Potosi. They said that even now people regularly report seeing the footprints of those poor Africans in the mines.

And that, sisters and brothers, was that, as least as far as my experience in the Yungas of Bolivia in search of the African presence was concerned. It was an adventure that I will never forget!

BONDING WITH BLACK BRAZIL

November 21, 2008

The first Africans to come to Brazil probably arrived there as early as 32,000 years ago. They likely sailed across the Atlantic, or perhaps they were part of the migratory waves of Africans who traveled by land from the Motherland, crossed the Straits of Gibraltar into Europe, passed through Asia, and traversed the Bering Strait into the Americas, tens of thousands of years ago. I once saw a newspaper account which mentioned that an ancient human skull with African features was housed in the National Museum in Rio de Janeiro, formerly the capital of Brazil (the capital is now Brasilia). Unfortunately, my efforts to find and view that prized artifact were not fruitful.

Despite evidence of a very ancient African presence in Brazil, the huge African population that is in Brazil today is there mainly as the result of the transatlantic slave trade. Africans were enslaved and transported to Brazil by the Portuguese for centuries from a broad area ranging from Angola to Nigeria until slavery was abolished in Brazil in 1888.

I have long argued that Brazil has the third largest national concentration of Black people in the world. The largest is in India, followed by Nigeria, and then Brazil. Most people are surprised that I put India first on this list, but given that country's enormous Dravidian, Tribal, and Dalit (Black Untouchable) populations, there are easily more Black folks in India than in any other place on earth. Nigeria has the largest concentration of Africans on the continent of Africa, but Brazil has the most of any country in the Western Hemisphere. Indeed, the African population in Brazil will soon reach one hundred million people.

Life is very hard for Black people in Brazil. That nation's large African population suffers from huge inequalities in health care, police brutality, lack of educational and employment opportunities, and incarceration rates. They further experience low self-esteem and scant representation in government, among other symptoms of social inequity that African people seem to suffer from, to one degree or another, the world over.

In the Favelas

On this, my third trip to Brazil, I was able to do something that I had never done before: I visited a favela. Favela is a Portuguese term for what many of us might refer to as a slum or shanty town. In Rio, I was told, there were over 350 favelas. I also concluded that these are places that the government of Brazil does not want visitors to see, for in the favelas, I believe, reside the greatest concentrations of Africans in Brazil.

My visit to a favela was made possible by some students I met at the State University of Rio de Janeiro. After delivering a lecture at the university one evening, I expressed a strong interest in making such a visit to a cadre of law students who had gathered around me to ask questions and continue the lecture discussion. No sooner than I had asked, they began making the arrangements for me to do so.

So on my last morning in Rio de Janeiro, two very beautiful and highly intelligent young African women law students picked me up at my hotel and escorted me to my desired destination. But first, they told me that it was their great honor to accompany me into "the real Rio."

The favela they took me to was a large one and, unlike most of the other favelas in Rio, it was not built on a hillside. It was instead on a mostly flat expanse of land. It was also a very densely populated, largely African, and decidedly poor urban community. True to form, all of the businesses that I saw in the favela were owned and staffed by non-Africans—mainly Mestizos (mixed-race persons) and Blancos (Whites). I saw no hospitals or doctor's offices. The sisters told me that there were only two schools in the community but there were a bunch of churches. The police, they claimed, refused to come into the favelas so the real law in areas such as the one we visited was the druglords.

Most of the walkways and streets of the favela were poorly lit, if at all, and seemed far too narrow for vehicles to negotiate. The whole thing seemed rather haphazardly thrown together. Electrical wires were strewn everywhere and the whole place stank of open sewage. It also seemed, to my great dismay, that the further we got from the entrance to the favela, the greater the poverty became.

The sisters told me that right next to the favela we were in was another far more impoverished one named after Nelson Mandela. They asked me if I wanted to go there, and I declined. It was hot and humid, and I felt a little nauseous. I was also beginning to feel as if my presence in the favela was becoming intrusive, even though I had not bothered to bring my camera. I hadn't wanted to be thought of as a tourist, come to peer into the lives of oppressed people. You know what I mean?

One of my student escorts made a big deal out of wanting to bring me to her house so she could introduce me to her family and fiancé and treat me to some "real" Brazilian food. To refuse such an offer would have been really rude, I thought. And with me being the shy and bashful guy that I am, even though my stomach was still a little upset, I reluctantly agreed and we stopped for lunch.

That afternoon I ate lunch with four generations of Africans from the same favela and I heard how much things had changed over their lifetimes and how they much they had remained the same. Everyone seemed genuinely cheerful, although I was a bit depressed by it all. But the food was plentiful and good, so it wasn't a bad day after all.

My Introduction to Color Categories and Labels in Brazil

At the beginning of the Pan-African conference that brought me to Brazil for this trip, I listened intently as the great scholar, Professor Abdias Nascimento, referred to Brazil—the land of his birth—as "an African country." Proudly noting the recent election of Barack Obama, Nascimento further predicted that Brazil would one day have its own Black president. For my part, I sat there wondering just how is it that all the sisters and brothers in Brazil could have been held down so comprehensively, so solidly, and for so long? Everywhere I looked in Brazil, White people seemed to be in charge.

It then dawned on me. One thing stood out distinctly: African people in Brazil have been thoroughly and historically divided. And, to put it rather crudely, their divisions have been made on the basis of the amount of so-called "white blood" that runs through their veins! The students at the State University of Rio de Janeiro that I mentioned earlier referred to their homeland as a "pigmentocracy." To me, this all boiled down to the "racial" or ethnic divisions that had been imposed upon the "race," ultimately by White exploiters. Indeed, I recalled hearing any number of terms referring to people of African descent in Brazil: Pardo, Mulatto, Morena, Moreno, Negro, and Black. Each of these categories served to further separate one group of African people from the other, weakening and dividing their political power, pitting them against one another for who knows how long into the future.

All things considered, however, and all trepidations about present and future Black presidents aside, I had a good trip to Brazil. I was a big hit at the Pan-African conference, and I made a lot of useful contacts. I saw and spoke with Professor Nascimento for the first time. I went to the National Museum and capped off my visit with a journey to "the real Rio."

Plus, this was my third big visit to South America in just over twelve months. I visited African communities in Ecuador last October and Peru and Bolivia in May and June of this year. It was exciting to be able to compare notes on the past and present of African people in these four fascinating countries. So, all in all, I was glad that I came to Brazil and grateful to the conference organizers for inviting me.

Still, I left Rio in much the same frame of mind that I left Papua New Guinea just a couple of weeks earlier. That is, I left feeling that I had barely scratched the surface of such a culturally and historically rich part of the African world. I learned so much but I still feel as if there is so much left to know. Perhaps I'll never stop feeling that way. The only way to know is to keep on going!

EL NORTE: MEXICO, CANADA, AND THE UNITED STATES

MEXICO: FROM THE OLMEC TO COSTA CHICA[4]

I have enjoyed three significant trips to Mexico. Actually, my family drove from Los Angeles across the border into the Mexican city of Tijuana more than once when I was a young boy. Those early trips were actually my first international travel excursions. My first really big trip to Mexico as an adult was in the late 1970s, and it had big consequences.

In 1978, I flew with a friend from Los Angeles to Mexico City on my first grown-up, international trip. I carried with me a good book: John G. Jackson's Introduction to African Civilizations, the first book after Chancellor Williams' Destruction of Black Civilization that encouraged me to trace the wanderings of those great and mighty Africans who left Africa long before slavery. I was traveling to Mexico in search of the African presence among the Olmec—the first great civilization in the Americas—and I found what I went looking for right away.

On my first day in Mexico City, I ventured to the National Museum of Anthropology, where I found at least two of the massive stone heads from the Olmec civilization that show clear African features. I could have said "mission accomplished" right then, but then I traveled to Vera Cruz. I don't recall finding anything of an African or cultural nature there, but I did have a lot of fun, ate some great food, and enjoyed a terrific walk along the beach.

After that, I went back to Mexico City, where I got a bad case of upset stomach and spent the rest of my time in Mexico in bed or running to the toilet or reading John Jackson's book (often on the toilet!). I also ran out of money, but despite the way my trip ended, it really instilled in me, more than anything else up to that point, the desire to travel and see the world first-hand. I still have that desire!

On my second trip to Mexico, I think it was in 1985, I was accompanied by my first wife. This time, we flew from Los Angeles to the tourist resort of Cancun, which is a very lovely tourist destination. That first day, something happened that I will never allow to happen again. Late that afternoon, I fell asleep in a deck chair on the beach. When I woke up it was completely dark, but my backpack, camera, and all personal possessions were still at my feet, completely untouched. To my relief, nobody had bothered me or disturbed anything, but I can't imagine ever being so careless or nonchalant about my well-being and personal safety again.

The other interesting thing about that trip was a day journey that my wife and I took to Chichen Itza, a major Mayan archaeological site in the Yucatan Peninsula. I explored the site thoroughly, especially the ancient pyramids, ball field, and astronomical observatory. We climbed to the top of the great pyramid and caught a tremendous view of the whole region.

My third trip to Mexico was far different from the first two. That time, I went with a group and did not visit the Olmec relics. It was April 2009, and I was invited to Mexico as a guest lecturer by a distinguished contingent from the Nation of Islam led by none other than Mother Tynetta

---

4   Dedicated to Mother Tynetta Muhammad.

Muhammad, widow of the Honorable Elijah Muhammad himself. For some reason I have never quite understood, Mother thought of me as a great scholar. Anyway, I was not about to turn her invitation down!

Again, Los Angeles was my departure city, and I transited in Houston for Mexico City. On the first stage of the tour, however, the participants did not seem particularly impressed with me. I got the distinct impression that because I was not a member of the Nation, I was not seen as having a whole lot of value to them. Basically, they viewed me as just another outsider. Well, so be it, I thought.

We traveled by bus from Mexico City to Acapulco, a place that I had never been before. We stayed at a small, isolated, and rustic tourist resort that was not unpleasant. We visited a nice museum there during our stay, and I took a couple of good photos with Mother Tynetta. Acapulco was not bad, either, but I must confess that the humidity there was monstrous and I was not sad to leave.

Still, the major reason that we were in Mexico was to see Black people, so our ultimate destination was a region south of Acapulco on the Pacific Coast called Costa Chica, which means, I think, "small coast." In that area, there are two hundred small, largely African communities, and the sisters and brothers of the region were hosting a large community gathering to coincide with our visit.

To call Costa Chica a backwater area is to put it very mildly. On the scale of one to five stars, the hotel at which we stayed was probably a 0.5. I mean, it was really basic! Luckily, we were traveling as a group and that, for me, meant we had security in numbers and could handle anything that came our way. If I had been there alone and on my own, I would have felt more than a little nervous.

As it was, Costa Chica turned out to be delightful. Indeed, Mother Tynetta was delightful: very polite, gracious, charming, and humble. She was simply a joy to be around. And, much to my additional delight, a couple of the Africans in Costa Chica, two of the major organizers of the big gathering to be held there, knew me and were familiar with my work. Apparently, I had met them in Barlovento, Venezuela, at a major conference ten years earlier, and I had made a lasting impression on them. They were so happy to see me again, and I them.

I had never been around such a large number of Black people from Mexico before. Unfortunately, what stood out to me the most about them was the feeling that they really suffered from low self-esteem. Overwhelmingly, they seemed to think of themselves as very unattractive—ugly, actually—and they seemed overly suspicious of our group's motives. It took some big-time convincing on our parts to assure them that we were there to assist them in raising their standards of living and boosting their sense of ethnic identity and pride. And one of the major ways in which we hoped to accomplish this was via a presentation by your humble servant, Runoko Rashidi.

It took some effort to secure a suitable facility for my lecture-slide show, but finally, on a Saturday afternoon, a classroom at a local school was made available for that occasion. The place was packed, I guess about seventy-five folks came, including members of our tour group and local people. I don't know how many people stood outside, looking and listening, but there were quite a few.

My presentation was on the Global African Presence. I scored a hit immediately with the members of the Nation of Islam by dedicating the presentation to Mother Tynetta and early on showing a photo of her late husband, the Honorable Elijah Muhammad. The rest of my talk was a passionate overview of the lives of African people in ancient and modern times and our myriad contributions to humanity and civilization.

Oh, I was on a roll that day! I was so good that several members of the audience became emotional to the point that they were moved to tears. I had generated similar reactions in Venezuela and Ecuador when I gave my presentations on similar topics. It is a profound thing to witness the reactions of Black people when they realize that they have a history beyond slavery. Indeed, it is as though you are witness to a kind of personal metamorphoses.

I remember one very large, masculine, middle-aged Black man, wearing what we in the United States would call a cowboy hat, who came up to me afterward with tears streaming down his face. He thanked me profusely for telling him that Black people have a history that is second to none. There are few experiences that are more rewarding in life than sharing a pronounced feeling of validation. And that was both the goal and the achievement of my presentation in Costa Chica.

After the lecture, a lot of people wanted to take pictures of and with me. By that time, I was a minor celebrity. I think I may have even gotten a marriage proposal or two! But what I remember most is a conversation I had with an attractive and shy nineteen-year-old African Mexican teenager. I am always, of course, very complementary of Black women and I told her, in my very limited Spanish, how pretty she was. I meant no harm, and I certainly was not trying to be fresh. I just think that, as Black men, it is important for us to express to our sisters, with no hidden agendas, how beautiful they are. And this girl was beautiful, still she argued and argued with me, insisting that she was very ugly. That, for me, reinforced right then and there how much work we as a people have ahead of us.

Well, sisters and brothers, in closing out this note on Mexico, allow me to say that I have tried very hard to bring another tour group of my own to Mexico, but to no avail. One year I thought I had it all together, and then the H1NI influenza epidemic erupted. Currently, with the all the violence and negative press associated with the Mexican government's war against the drug cartels, it is virtually impossible to talk people into going to this fascinating part of the world with so much African history within its borders. What a shame, but hope springs eternal!

THE AFRICAN EXPERIENCE IN CANADA: TRAVELS IN THE "TRUE BLACK NORTH"

I have been to Canada—that vast expanse of land atop the US and dubbed the "true white north" by some—oh, any number of times. My first trip there was to Ottawa (or maybe it was to Toronto) in or about 2002. I have also been to Toronto quite a few times, by far more so than to any other city in Canada. And I've been to Halifax, Vancouver, and Montreal. So, I guess you could say I've experienced quite a bit of that country.

Now, if you're a US citizen, going to Canada is a pretty easy trip. If you travel by air, you simply land in the city of your choice, show your passport at customs, collect your luggage, and off you go. US currency is used widely and, in all of the places in Canada that I have ever been (with the exception of Montreal), English is widely spoken. Plus, the Canadian culture is not fundamentally different from that in the United States.

The purpose of each of my visits to Canada has always been to give presentations. I usually speak on the Global African Presence, but several times I have presented talks and slide shows before Canadian audiences on the African presence in Asia or a related topic. And I don't mind saying, after all these years, that I am pretty good at what I do. In fact, on the topic of identifying the Black presence internationally, especially visually through photographs and other images, I am probably the best in the world. Maybe the best ever.

But hey, does that sound arrogant to you? Well, at least you can't say that I lack confidence. I work hard on my presentations—gathering, documenting, and reviewing all of my source materials; shooting or assembling the hundreds of images I use in my slide shows; perfecting and practicing my lectures over and over—and I am passionate, very passionate, about the overall quality of my work.

But I digress. Most of my earlier trips to Canada have been during the winter time, often during the February celebrations of Black History Month. So, when I visited Ottawa for the first time, in the mid 1990s, I thought that I had landed in the coldest place on the planet! There are a lot of Black people from the Caribbean who live in Canada, and honestly, I just don't see how they make the adjustment to the cold!

A Tough Talk in Toronto

Most of the talks that I have done in Canada have been in Toronto. An organization called the GOD Collective (Growth/Order/Development), along with Rad Dockery and Winston LaRose, have been my hosts on at least four occasions. And, believe me, they have worked the heck out of me every time. Mr. LaRose coordinated my February 2011 Toronto lectures, and I worked so hard that I was actually angry (and exhausted) by the time I left!

Anyway, Toronto, like all the cities I have been to in Canada, is generally a pretty city. I have not seen the gritty poverty there that characterizes some of the inner cities in the US. A lot of Asians live in Toronto, especially East Indians. Indeed, they seem to be the great majority of airport staff. They are also present everywhere as the owners and managers of hotels and retail business establishments throughout the city. They seem to be a very exclusive group, however, and generally keep to themselves, at least as far as I have seen. But perhaps I am biased, given my experiences around the world wherever African people tend to be and where I have seen Asians generally taking control of the retail and service markets.

Of the Black people in Toronto, the majority seem to be from the English-speaking Caribbean nations. And of these West Indians, a great percentage come from Jamaica. Barbados, Trinidad, and Guyana are also well represented; and I've seen a number of Black people from Bermuda and West Africa in Toronto too. A lot of the taxi drivers I encountered there were from Ghana; and you can't leave out the Nigerians or the Black folks from the Horn of Africa–the Ethiopians, Eritreans, and Somalis! And, of course, there are a number of African Americans in Canada.

I wish I could tell you that this mix of African people in the "true white north" is a harmonious one, but the truth is that that would be more wishful thinking than actual fact. It is not that that the Pan-African relationships in Canada are antagonistic. There is just not the interaction and cooperation that I—Runoko Rashidi—would like to see!

All in all, however, I am usually a big success in Toronto, but not all of the time. On my last trip there, for instance, I accepted an invitation to do a short visual presentation at a local Christian minister's house. I was excited by the possibility of winning over some more converts to the cause of African redemption, and the minister seemed so happy and enthusiastic that I just knew everything would go well.

Well, just the opposite happened! I gave my presentation, entitled "African Contributions to the World," before a group of African Christians from the Caribbean. To my dismay, they really did not seem to be very interested in what I had to say, but I went through the motions anyway. It was during the question-and-answer period that all hell broke loose.

One young man insisted (and I have no idea what he was smoking!) that the Jews built the pyramids. When I asked him to present his evidence for such a claim, he said simply: "The Bible." To that, I said, "But the Bible is not a history book," to which he responded, "That doesn't matter. You can't refute the Bible."

This back and forth went on for a long time and both he and I grew increasingly heated. I was ready to lose my temper when one lady tipped me over the edge with her comment that, "If it is not about Jesus, it doesn't matter!" For that, I had no response and figured that it would not make a difference anyway. I was done, and I walked away from the podium in thinly veiled disgust.

Now what really annoyed me about this encounter is that the previously friendly and enthusiastic minister never came to my defense—and I was giving the presentation at his house! He just let this angry back-and-forth go on and on until finally he said: "Let us pray." Oh, I was really hot by then! I just collected my equipment, put on my heavy coat and hat, and walked out into the cold and snow to catch a cab back to my hotel. I didn't even stay to join in the prayer.

I know that was rude of me, but by then I just did not care about appearances. I get so upset at people who are so dogmatic that they are unable to go beyond blind faith to accept the facts of history. I later prayed that Jesus would not be too mad at me about that.

To kind-of balance that experience, I gave one of my best presentations ever in Toronto, or anywhere else, just a couple of days later. It was at the Toronto Africentric School to a standing-room-only crowd. To my relief, I was in the best possible form, and the images that I used showed brilliantly. Now that was a night to remember!

In Halifax and Vancouver

One of the most interesting Canadian experiences I've had occurred in Halifax, in the far northeast of Canada. Fortunately, it was not during the winter months. I spoke at a conference at Dalhousie University at the invitation of Dr. Esmeralda Thornhill. Dr. Thornhill is a great and gifted scholar, absolutely brilliant. I met her on a trip to Russia in 1999 and apparently she liked what I had to say. In Halifax, I visited some of the older Black communities in the region, some of which had been established in the late eighteenth and nineteenth centuries. It was a fascinating experience.

At the beginning of February 2011, I visited Vancouver for the first time. I had a free day from a conference I was attending in Seattle and took the train there for an overnight stay. I found Vancouver, set as it is on the Pacific Coast, to be a beautiful city. It is frightfully expensive, however, with a tiny Black population. In the company of my colleague Marilyn Clement, who also gave me a tour of the city, I was able to visit the anthropology museum there and give an impromptu presentation to a local gathering of African-Canadians artists and activists. I must have done something right because I was told that I would be invited back.

En Montréal

Now, Montreal was different than all of the other Canadian cities that I have been to, not just because it is French-speaking, but because it seemed so much more compact and cosmopolitan. I was hosted there in March 2011 by the African Student's Association of Quebec. That organization has been responsible for an annual African education conference for the past three or four years now, and that year I was to be the keynote presenter.

Most of the conference organizers were Cameroonian men who were novices to conference planning and who, though they were young and made several mistakes, generally meant well. I took an immediate liking to many of them, and they, in turn, liked me and what I had to say at the conference. I guess they saw me as a kind of elder brother, a baba (Kiswahili for "father"), and I did not discourage them in that. I believe that young people in the African liberation movement need mentors; and I find myself, more and more, playing a mentorship role. Indeed, it is a relationship that I am consciously trying to foster and maintain. Time will tell.

In the meantime, I look forward to my next visit to Canada. Just puh-leeze let it not be in winter!

FULL-CIRCLE 'ROUND: TRAVEL NOTES FROM THE USA

Building Bridges of Understanding From Liberia to Philadelphia (February 21, 2006)[5]

Sad to say, but this month is winding down too, too quickly. It seems especially so since, here in the United States, February is the month that we devote to trying to tell the greatest story that has barely been told. Why can't it we celebrate Black History Month all year long?

For the better part of the past three weeks, I have been in the Philadelphia area doing my "historian thing,." I have also given big presentations at Lafayette College in Easton, Pennsylvania;

---

5   Dedicated to the late, great Dr. Asa G. Hilliard III (Nana Baffour Amankwatia II), my dear friend and mentor.

St. Augustine Church in Youngstown, Ohio; and the University of Missouri at Kansas City. But mostly I have been toiling right here in the Philadelphia public schools, doing a few other talks here and there on the side. I think I have given presentations at about a dozen schools now, with about eight more to go before I depart for California later this week.

Things started off in February on a very positive note and, for the most part, my presentations have been very well done and positively received by students, teachers, administrators, and especially my hosts: the Praxis Institute Rites of Passage organization. Typically, I give two or three talks a day, going from one school to the next. Last Saturday, I delivered my best talk this month at a community forum held at University City High School. I was in fine form that day.

The major problem I have encountered in all these presentations, however, is the frequent lack of discipline I have seen demonstrated by many of the students. A lot of these kids are incredibly silly, I have found, and they seem to have no concept of the noble history and heritage of African people. I guess we can blame the White man for that generally, but I often want to crack some of these kids over the head with the microphone they give me to speak to them with!

Today, for example, something very, very interesting happened. First, I presented at two more elementary schools. I know that I reached a bunch of those children, although I had to spend a lot of my time getting some of the young rowdies in the bunch to be quiet and listen—and that is not always an easy task. I mean, it is one thing to talk to kids who don't know, but quite another to talk to kids who know that they don't know and who could care less! That is probably the hardest part of this job.

Anyway, after speaking at those two schools, I gave a presentation at an after-school program in southwest Philadelphia, an area regarded by some as one of Philly's toughest inner-city neighborhoods. The program was organized by David Barnes, host of an excellent, African-centered, weekly radio show in Philadelphia. Now, for the most part so far this month, I have been dealing with African American students, but what made this afternoon's program so interesting was that almost all of the students I would be speaking to were Liberians. Apparently, there is a growing Liberian community here in Philadelphia. Most of the young people in my audience, David told me, were recently arrived from Africa and, in large measure, were victims of the recent civil war in Liberia. The purpose of the after-school program in which they were enrolled was to bridge the gap between Africans who were actually born in Africa and those of us born in America.

Well, I thought, I have been to a lot of places, but I had not yet set foot in Liberia, so I was very excited by the prospect of my upcoming presentation. I was especially excited after the two tough sessions I'd just had with the hard-headed African American kids that I had dealt with earlier in the day!

Based on my earlier lecture experiences at the Sunrise Academy in Accra, Ghana, and before groups of Black students in Jamaica, Ethiopia, and London, I figured that my presentation would be nice and easy. Those students had been really disciplined, attentive, and, in general, hungry for education, so I started off by sharing with them some of the comments that I have heard African Americans make about continental Africa. Then I asked them, "What do you think of when you think of African Americans?"

Runoko Rashidi

What I wanted to do, more than anything else, was to open up a discussion. Boy, did I open up a can of worms instead! The first student to respond told me that when he thought of African Americans, he thought of slavery. Another young Liberian child said that poverty came immediately to his mind in that regard. I gently reminded the first child that many Liberians were themselves the descendants of Africans who had been enslaved, brought to the United States, and later repatriated back to Africa. I told the second child that many African Americans associated Africa with poverty, just as he associated them with the same. Many other Liberian students told me that their experiences with African Americans so far had been very negative. Some said that they had been beaten up by African American schoolkids, and that it was common for the Liberian kids to be called "African booty scratchers" by their Black American counterparts.

Although I appreciated the Liberian students being forthright and honest about their experiences, I must confess that I was really wounded by what they told me. I also felt their hurt, and I apologized profusely for all the indignities that they had suffered at the hands of Africans born in the United States. Then I told them about my work in the classrooms of Philadelphia. I told them that it was my job to make Africans in America proud of their African roots and to convince them that we are all members of the same family. Then I began my formal presentation.

First, I showed them a photograph of an African scientist holding the bones of Denknesh, one of our earliest Ancestors. Then I took them on a tour of dynastic Egypt, only to find that they were as ignorant of that phase of African history as just about everybody else. I then showed them some images of Africans, ancient and modern, from various parts of the Continent. Much to my surprise, they began to laugh at these various African people! A few even commented about how "ugly" some of the Africans were! I stared at them in disbelief and expressed my shock and dismay out loud. Then it dawned on me, as if for the first time after the more than thirty years I have struggled in this field, that Africans on the Continent have been just as mentally damaged as we here in the hells of North America have been! And here I had naively believed that only African Americans were so ignorant of the glorious African past, that only we in the United States suffered from such low self-esteem and general lack of knowledge of self. What a lesson this experience turned out to be!

I guess you could say that I swallowed a bitter pill today, but the Liberian students seemed to appreciate my candor and sincerity, and I was extremely pleased that we were able to talk to each other. There are few things more valuable than communication, no matter how eye-opening. Nonetheless, I will always be a steadfast soldier in the army of African redemption. And though I will remain ever full of resolve, I must say that I received a real dose of reality in Philadelphia today.

Well, like you, dear sisters and brothers, I know that we still have a lot of work to do. African people did not get into this situation overnight, and we are not going to achieve total victory from it by tomorrow. But I am convinced that we are well on our way to liberation, for African people are nothing if not resilient. I am also convinced, as never before, that we are going to win! As the great African patriot Marcus Garvey once said, "Up, you mighty race! You can accomplish what you will!" And I, for one, believe that no force on this earth can stop us!

An African Triumph in the Heart Of Texas (November 5, 2006)

Well, howdy, sisters and brothers! Today I am in Beaumont, a sleepy little Texas town about sixty miles west of the border with Louisiana. It's early Sunday morning, and within a few hours I will be driven to the Houston International Airport for my one-hour return flight to San Antonio. I am scheduled to be in that city for four nights, and I am rather looking forward to it. Sometimes it's nice to be able to sit still for a little while!

Beaumont, home to Lamar University, is an interesting city of about 140,000 people, most of whom are African Americans, with a very rich history. Hurricanes struck the town hard last year, destroying its only African bookstore and you can still see a lot of damage here and there. Last night, I was the keynote speaker for a big program in Beaumont. It was my first presentation in North America in more than a month, and I was in what I thought to be the best of form. About eight-hundred people showed up, although only about half of them remained to hear me speak—still, that's a pretty big crowd. The program, which was part of a conference, was sponsored by an African-owned business called Compro Tax, and, believe me, that firm is nothing less than wonderful. I really like the sisters and brothers involved in it.

The theme of the conference was "Truths About African Americans that White Americans Need to Know...and Black Americans, Too." Several other speakers participated besides me, the most notable of whom was my esteemed friend, Dr. Kwa David Whitaker. Also included were sociologist Dr. James W. Loewen and journalist Dr. Anne Farrow (both White Americans); and Paula McCoy-Pinderhughes, an African American woman who focused on the need for Black businesses. Dr. Evelyn Bethune, granddaughter of the noted African American educator, Dr. Mary Mcleod Bethune, was also featured, but I was the keynoter.

Just why I was picked to deliver the keynote address, I am not sure. Perhaps it was because the principal organizers of the conference went with me on the 20/20 Club's August 2006 tour of Egypt and Ghana. I spoke several times before that group, and the Texas conference organizers must have been pretty impressed. They even changed the original dates of the conference to accommodate my schedule!

The title of my presentation was "The Global African Presence, and What Does it Mean to Us?" and I indicated from the onset that although I was honored to speak on the history of African people, I did not care one bit about the universal fellowship of man and was only concerned about African power for African people. I also made clear my views that, one, the salvation of African people lies with the unification of all Africa and the utilization of Africa's vast mineral wealth for the benefit of the African masses; and two, that only Africans can free Africans.

I then went on to explain that we Africans have a heritage second to none, taking my audience on a three-and-a-half million-year history of African people at home and abroad.

Well, I hope that I did not embarrass the conference organizers too much because I was, true to form, pretty uncompromising in my statements, and I gave the audience everything that I had. The equipment worked to perfection, and I'm not sure if I have ever spoken so passionately before. It was as if the spirit of our great African Ancestors came over me, and I embraced that spirit fully.

Runoko Rashidi

The largely African audience seemed delighted with my presentation and, to tell you the truth, with all due modesty, so was I. And I must have been really on point because one of the White women in the audience was so overcome with guilt that after my presentation she came up to me and apologized profusely. " I know that you must hate me," she said, "because my grandfather was in the Ku Klux Klan." She also told me that she had seen a Black man lynched when she was a little girl. I really wanted to laugh at her, but we ended up getting into a contentious discussion as I tried to convince her that, rather than hate White people, I tend to ignore them and largely just have contempt for them. But she would not let it go. Finally, I just walked away.

After the program, about a dozen of the conference organizers, speakers, and I discussed the future of Africa over dinner, and we all came away convinced that we as African people are on the road to victory. So, sisters and brothers, believe me when I say that it was quite a night here in Beaumont, Texas—a night that I will not soon forget.

It is indeed good to have such a triumph, at least occasionally, in the midst of so many defeats. Yes, sisters and brothers, I believe that we are going to win this fight. So keep the faith, and don't be discouraged!

Musings in Mississippi (April 3, 2009)

Today I am in Jackson, Mississippi, of all places, watching television coverage of Barack and Michelle Obama, who are visiting in France right now. And I'm thinking about three things. First, France is probably where I should be too, with my wife and child. Second, I am still very much in love with the Obamas. I know that makes some of my friends mad, but I could care less. They would probably be mad even if Garvey or Malcolm or King were president!

But I just love the pure symbolism of the Obamas and what they mean for our people: a highly intelligent and articulate Black couple, very much in love, presiding confidently on the world stage. Just them being there and being who they are—it does so much for our global self-esteem. That's the big picture. I love the Obamas!

But the third thought that has been tearing at my consciousness here in Mississippi is one that has long preoccupied me. And it is this: Many of us say that we are all for African liberation (or Black liberation, if you prefer). But when we say "African liberation," what exactly do we mean? Now I know this might sound like a stupid or rhetorical question, but I don't mean it to be. It's simply a matter of going back to basics.

I mean, we say we love our people and that we want to save Africa, but as I wander about the world—from Amsterdam to Accra, Honduras to Haiti, Paris to Panama, and Jamaica to Jackson—I am constantly taking a close, hard look at the status of our people, and often I am discouraged by what I see. And it strikes me, at the risk of sounding very arrogant, that here I am, giving my life to make a difference for our future and yet most of the Africans that I see, whether they be in Europe, Africa, America, or wherever—well, I can't help but wonder if we are all on the same page.

I don't know about you, but most of the sisters and brothers that I encounter in my world travels seem to be more interested in hair styles and fashions than in improving life in the Congo or Darfur.

And this is bound to sound cold, but sometimes I have serious doubts when, for example, I see so many of our young sisters from the Continent whose primary focus seems to be largely on getting a long, blond weave. What's really going on with that? Or am I totally missing the point when a brother in Mississippi corners me after one of my presentations on the Global African Presence (which I just gave in Jackson last night) and his sole question for me is whether I have accepted Jesus Christ as my lord and personal savior. And I think: am I just spinning my wheels here?

Really, is it just me? Am I being elitist? Do I really believe that I have a better idea of what is best for Africans than do Africans themselves? Do I have the right to impose my own set of values on people who do not seem the least bit interested? Do those of us who say we are part of the African liberation movement know more about what is better for our people than do the masses of our people?

I admit that I am experiencing a bit of confusion here, if only temporary, in my Mississippi musings. But sometimes I wonder: Am I any more right than they are?

What about you? What do you think?

LAST CALL? NOT HARDLY! COUNTRY NUMBER 100: BERMUDA

Upon setting foot on the British Overseas Territory of Bermuda in March 2011, I reached another great personal milestone in my career: I had visited a total of one hundred countries, colonies, and/or overseas territories! And, to magnify that achievement, I had done so in just a twelve-year period, from March 1999 to March 2011. Yes, I am now in the triple digits and perhaps the most traveled historian of my era!

Bermuda, the capital of which is the city of Hamilton, is a wealthy set of islands of about 65,000 people located in the North Atlantic Ocean, directly east of the Carolinas. It is often mistakenly called a Caribbean island, but it is actually hundreds of miles north of the Caribbean Sea.

Although Black people are in the majority in Bermuda, I still regard it as a bastion of White privilege. Even so, the organization that hosted my trip was a group called Citizens Uprooting Racism in Bermuda (or CURB). CURB is a very diverse group, with members from several different ethnic backgrounds and very dynamic leadership.

The staff at CURB assured me that my visit would be a positive and productive one. They put me in perhaps the nicest hotel on the island—the venerable Hamilton Princess—and coordinated all four of my scheduled lecture-presentations to a tee. I must especially thank Nicole Stovell, a young, beautiful, and well-connected Black businesswoman on the island, who did so much to make my stay in Bermuda comfortable and rewarding. She even had her father, a local authority on Bermudan history, take me to see the magnificent bronze statue of Sally Bassett that had recently been erected on the grounds of the Bermudan Cabinet building. Her father explained to me that Sally Bassett was an enslaved Black woman who was burnt at the stake in the 1700s, supposedly for supplying poison meant to kill a number of White slave owners. She is now widely acclaimed by African Bermudans in many circles as a freedom fighter and resistance leader.

Runoko Rashidi

My first presentation, the best attended of them all, was held in an Anglican church in Hamilton, the territorial capital of Bermuda. About two hundred people showed up. Given that the audience was a racially diverse one, I took a more measured, and perhaps more moderate, stance than usual in my remarks. That is, I was not apologetic for, nor was I any less factual about, my research and travel findings. Yet, I tried, as I typically do, to make everyone in the audience feel comfortable. (I realize, of course, that I am not always successful in this regard, but I do try!) I also made (again as I usually do) every effort not to deliberately offend anyone's ethnicity, gender, sexual orientation or religion. Maybe that is the politician in me, or maybe it is just common decency.

Yes, I want to be liked. Yes, I want to be approved of. And yes, I want to be popular. But no need to worry, I will always be honest and true to my Ancestors and to myself. Even though I might have been a little more restrained that night than if I was speaking to an all-African audience in a big city setting in the United States or the UK, I did not fundamentally alter my message or compromise the content of the presentation. I simply adapted my message to the audience and the setting.

By virtually all accounts, the presentation went well. To my great surprise, however, some of the Black people in the church attendance that night felt that I had let them down. Some even claimed that I had been "too soft" on White people! Go figure!

My next presentation was at a local school, the Berkeley Institute in Pembroke West, outside of Hamilton. It too went well. The students in attendance were overwhelmingly Black and averaged about fourteen years of age. That morning lecture was followed in the afternoon by my most comprehensive presentation in Bermuda, which was held at Westgate Prison. The fact that the presentation took place in such somber surroundings was not lost on anybody, but I must say that the inmates there—all of whom were Black—seemed really grateful that I had shared my time and research with them. I felt as if all of the men were giving me a great, big hug.

On my last night in Bermuda, I gave an encore presentation at a local Black establishment called the Leopard's Club. The focus of my talk was African women on the continent of Africa, past and present. I was really fired up that night and, still stinging from the criticisms from my first lecture, I was deliberately more forceful and strident than usual. I fired up my audience as well.

POSTSCRIPT

EVERYWHERE WE ARE: REFLECTIONS AND A LOOK AHEAD

When I returned to the United States from Bermuda, I took a moment to reflect back on my trip and bask in a bit of glory. I was, to begin with, so glad that I had finally visited Bermuda. It was a great learning and travel experience, and I believe that I had an impact. Will I ever go back? I don't know, but it sure feels good to have a hundred countries, colonies, and overseas territories "in the bag," as they say. I did it! Whew! That was a lot of work, and full of challenges!

But during the course of my travels I rarely doubted myself. And even when I did doubt and question myself, when I was afraid and lonely and uncertain and full of anxiety, I always felt that the Ancestors had my back, that they were on my side, watching over me, guiding me, protecting me. Such faith sustained me, and was the rock of my existence.

It is also gratifying to think that, as an historian, I am not only recording and disseminating history—I am a part of history. I have done something that, to my knowledge, not a single living African scholar has done, and probably few have ever done in the long annals of human history. I am in rarefied air. I am blessed. And I am proud of it.

I must also say that in my journeys I have benefitted enormously from the knowledge, wisdom, and insights of so many who opened the door for me, who walked in my footsteps even before I did. Immortal trailblazing pioneers like Joel Augustus Rogers, Langston Hughes, Chancellor James Williams, John Henrik Clarke, Asa G. Hilliard III, and Ivan Van Sertima—now Ancestors all—to name but a few, along with Yosef A. A. ben-Jochannan, Jan Carew, and Tynetta Muhammad—great men and women we are blessed to have with us still.

It is also humbling to reflect back on all the many wonderful and wise and exciting and generous and selfless people I have met in the course of my travels. These include people all over the world who shared their time, their experiences, their struggles, and their lessons with me over the years. I am truly grateful to have been taken into their lives and confidences, to have evolved, in the eyes of so many, from stranger and visiting scholar to brother and friend.

And so, where to now? I'm definitely not finished yet, nor am I tired. Where now, then, for Runoko Rashidi, historian and anthropologist for the Race? What next? Where will the next road take me? What path will I travel? Where will I go?

There is an African proverb that says, "If you don't know where you are going, any road will take you there." I would add to this proverb the following: "To know where you are going, you must know where you have been." It could be that the Ancestors have a plan for me all their own, but I know at least one thing for certain, and that is that whatever I do and wherever I go, wherever my journey takes me, it will surely be in search of African people.

And so it is. I'm ready. My bag is packed. Let's go!

Runoko Rashidi